GENEALOGICAL RECORDS
MANUSCRIPT ENTRIES OF BIRTHS, DEATHS AND MARRIAGES
TAKEN FROM FAMILY BIBLES
1581–1917

Title-page of the Bible of Colonel Jacob Glen, 1686

THE COLONIAL DAMES OF THE
STATE OF NEW YORK

GENEALOGICAL RECORDS

MANUSCRIPT ENTRIES OF BIRTHS, DEATHS
AND MARRIAGES, TAKEN FROM FAMILY BIBLES
1581 – 1917

EDITED BY
JEANNIE F-J. ROBISON
AND
HENRIETTA C. BARTLETT

NEW YORK
MCMXVII

Notice

In many older books, foxing (or discoloration) occurs and, in some instances, print lightens with wear and age. Reprinted books, such as this, often duplicate these flaws, notwithstanding efforts to reduce or eliminate them. The pages of this reprint have been digitally enhanced and, where possible, the flaws eliminated in order to provide clarity of content and a pleasant reading experience.

Copyright © The Colonial Dames of the
State of New York, 1917

Originally published:
New York: 1917

Reprinted:
Janaway Publishing, Inc.
2011

Janaway Publishing, Inc.
732 Kelsey Ct.
Santa Maria, California 93454
(805) 925-1038
www.janawaygenealogy.com

ISBN: 978-1-59641-218-7

Made in the United States of America

CONTENTS

	PAGE
THOMAS ALEXANDER	3
ANDREW BARCLAY BACHE	4
PETER BEDLOW	8
GERARD BEEKMAN, JR.	11
JOHN BEEKMAN	24
JAN JANSE BLEECKER	27
SEVERYN BRUYN	30
JOHN BURTON	33
COL. GEORGE CARRINGTON	35
CHARLES CHAUNCEY	37
JOHN CHURCH	39
COL. AUGUSTINE CLAIBORNE	40
FEMMITJE CLARK	43
WILLIAM COATS	45
WILLIAM CORWIN	49
WILLIAM COVENTRY	52
ISAAC COVERT	59
HENRY CRUGER	62
ABRAHAM DELAMETER	65
EDWARD DUDLEY	70
WILLIAM DYCKMAN	74
CORNELIUS ELMENDORF	76
PETRUS EDMUNDUS ELMENDORF	79
REBECCA PALMER FISH	81
RICHARD FLOYD	83
RICHARD FLOYD, JR.	85
JACOB FROST	88
JAMES GILLILAND	89
COL. JACOB SANDERS GLEN	90
BEEKMAN VERPLANCK HOFFMAN	102
JEREMIAH HOUGHTALING	103
ADAM HUDE	104

	PAGE
AUGUSTE JAY	106
PETER AUGUSTUS JAY	110
CATTRIN JOHNSON	118
SAMUEL JONES	119
COL. JOHANNES KNICKERBACKER	125
JOHANNES HERMENSEN KNICKERBACKER	127
FRANCIS LEWIS	130
PHILIP PHILIP LIVINGSTON	132
ROBERT LIVINGSTON	134
GOVERT LOOCKERMANS	143
WILLIAM MACEY	145
ISAAC MAZŸCK	146
JOHN MILLER	149
JUDGE LEWIS MORRIS	150
CHIEF JUSTICE RICHARD MORRIS	154
RICHARD VALENTINE MORRIS	156
THOMAS MORRISON	160
GEN. WILLIAM NORTH	164
MOSES OGDEN	167
HENDERICK ONDERDONCK	169
JOHN PARKER	171
JOSEPH PETTES	177
BENJAMIN RHOADES	180
CHRISTOPHER ROBERT	182
HENDRICK RUTGERS	184
GEORGE RYERSON	188
JOHN SCHUYLER	190
CHARLES SHELDON	193
LAWRENCE SMYTH	195
SAMUEL STIMSON	198
JUDGE SELAH STRONG	202
SAMUEL SWAN	206
JOHANNES TEN EYCK	212

	PAGE
HARMANUS TEN EYCK	214
HERMAN TEN EYCK	217
GEORGE TOWNSEND, II.	219
JAMES TOWNSEND	225
WILLIAM TOWNSEND	227
DANIEL TOWNSEND	230
MARY TOWNSEND	234
ADAM TREADWELL	236
DANIEL UNDERHILL	239
MARIA VAN BEVERHOUDT	247
JANE BEEKMAN VAN CORTLANDT	249
KILIAEN VAN RENSSELAER	250
STEPHEN VAN RENSSELAER	255
PETER VAN SCHAACK	258
ANTHONY VAN SCHAYCK, JR.	261
GUERT VAN SCHOONHOVEN	267
DIRCK TUENISEN VAN VECHTEN	268
REV. NICHOLAS VAN VRANKEN	273
PHILIP VER PLANCK	275
JOHN CHRISTOPHER VOUGHT	278
JOHN WEEKES	280
THOMAS WRIGHT	281
CORNELIUS WYNKOOP	284
CHRISTIANNA VOUGHT YOUNG	287
DANIEL YOUNGS	288

LIST OF ILLUSTRATIONS

Title-page of the Bible of Col. Jacob Glen, 1686 . . . . *Frontispiece*

                                                                   FACING PAGE

John N. Bleecker, born 1739 27

Margaret Van Dusen, wife of John N. Bleecker . . 28

Charles Chauncey, President of Harvard College, 1654–1672 37

Henry Cruger, Sr., born 1707 62

Dyckman House, New York City. Presented to New York City in 1916 by Mrs. Dean and Mrs. Welch . 74

Elmendorf House, Hurley, New York 79

Brick House built by Major Thomas Jones in 1696 . 83

Fort Neck House, Massapequa, Long Island (originally Tryon Hall). Built by Judge David Jones for his son Judge Thomas Jones in 1770 . . . 85

First page of the Glen Record 90

Title-page of the Bible of Auguste Jay, 1707 . . . 106

First page of the Auguste Jay Record 109

Old Knickerbacker Homestead, Schaghticoke, New York. Built by John Knickerbacker, Jr., about 1770, to replace the original house 125

Colophon and records in the Bible of John Miller, 1578 149

Lewis Morris, II, 1698–1762 150

Trintje Staats, wife of Lewis Morris, II 151

FACING
PAGE

Ross Hall, Raritan, New Jersey. The home of Mrs. Edward Antill, who was Ann Morris, sister of Lewis Morris, II 153

Hendrick Onderdonck, 1724–1809 169

Schuyler House, Belleville, New Jersey. Erected about 1710 190

Harmanus Ten Eyck, 1749–1828 214

First page of the Van Vechten Record, 1634 . . . 268

Dutch Church, Fishkill, New York 273

PREFACE

"Without genealogy the study of history is lifeless."
                                        JOHN FISKE.

THE publication of this book represents ninety genealogical records found in old family Bibles. Such Bibles are fast disappearing and with them are lost the missing links eagerly sought for by genealogists.

The keynote of our efforts in transcribing these records has been accuracy—accuracy in all the details of the written words found upon the pages of the Bibles.

Where interpolations have been necessary—as in the translations of the Dutch records—the matter added has been enclosed in brackets. Some one has stated: "A compiler is not responsible for the original correctness of the statements he transcribes. He should, however, be held to a strict account if the information he furnishes be not *true to record.*"

The Bibles are entered under the names of the original owners when known; otherwise, under the names of the first entries as given by descendants. A few late records were accepted where they supplemented earlier ones, as the Committee realized their value to genealogists, but in each case there had to be an entry in the Bible prior to 1800.

The editors have compared the transcribed copies with the original Bibles, or with photostatic reproductions, where possible; the few exceptions are accompanied by explanatory notes, stating the conditions which rendered comparison impossible.

Perhaps some follower in this field of industry, able to ignore the cost, will secure the temperamental atmosphere, as it were, of these old family Bibles by reproducing the various handwritings of all the entries and by entering them upon the printed page in their original form. Needless to say this will prove of inestimable value and interest.

Inspired by the faint hope of touching the spirit of the past, several of the Dutch and French records have been left untranslated and a few reproductions are given of original title-pages and records.

In 1913 Mrs. Wilmot Townsend Cox, for many years the able and efficient Chairman of the Committee on History and Tradition, conceived, planned, and began collecting old Bible records for publication.

In 1915, owing to ill health, Mrs. Cox resigned, and Mrs. Benjamin Franklin became the Chairman with a new Committee. A few months of assiduous labour were followed by the sudden death of Mrs. Franklin. To the present Committee, therefore, in the spring of 1916 was given the opportunity for continued sowing, reaping, and garnering where others had ploughed. Profoundly sensible of the work accomplished by these Committees under their two gifted Chairmen, the present Committee deems it not only fitting, but eminently proper that this book, the fulfilment of visions, and in part the result of their labours, should testify to the honour due their memories. It had been Mrs. Franklin's express desire that Miss Bartlett, expert bibliographer and author of "The Census of Shakespeare's Plays," should be frequently consulted. Therefore in the autumn of 1916 Miss Bartlett's services were engaged for the editorial work in collaboration with the Chairman.

To Mr. Kent of the Metropolitan Museum, and through him to Mr. Dow of the Essex Institute, we are greatly indebted for many valuable suggestions. The Committee likewise desires to extend its hearty thanks to the New York Public Library, the American Bible Society, and to all others who loaned Bibles, copied records, and assisted in various ways in rendering possible the completion of the book. To those friends whose records have not been included in this publication we desire to express our sincere regret at the necessity for taking such action. Many of these records, while of great interest, had been previously published; others were of too late a date, and others again bore no proof that they were Bible transcripts.

We put the query: Is the family Bible to be a thing of the past? In many homes we found it necessary to use "Aladdin's Wonderful Lamp," as it were, to have the portals unlocked and secure access to this sacred family treasure. Again, we learned by advertisement of its sale at public auction; while another proof of its lack of interest to the present generation lies in the fact that rarely are the records carried down to the present day.

In the past no book was held in greater reverence than the Bible; and with its own marvellous genealogies, what more natural than for families who possessed Bibles to enter therein the important records of their lives?

We learn from William Stowell Mills' little gem of a book entitled "Foundations of Genealogy" and published in 1899, that "Among the earliest Bible records now to be found in this country is that in the family Bible of Richard Bartlett, who came to America from England before 1640 and settled at Newbury, Mass. . . . It is one of the famous 'Breeches' Bibles and contains the Book of Common Prayer and the Sternhold and Hopkins Metrical Version of the Psalms, with the music. On a page at the end of the Prayer Book is the entry, in writing, that Richard Bartlett bought the book in 1612. Then follows the records of his family, the dates ranging from 1611 to 1625. . . . The family record was written on a blank page."

Mills also urged that family Bible records be copied and deposited in public libraries.

Time, effort, and money have been cheerfully expended upon this book, with the belief that we are rendering service to the historian, lightening the labours of genealogists, and voicing a call for similar publications.

JEANNIE F-J. ROBISON,
Chairman.

GENEALOGICAL RECORDS

THOMAS ALEXANDER.
(Born, 1740.)

Holy Bible in English; apparently the first edition of the Bishops' Bible, London, 1568.

Contains the entries of the brothers and sisters of Thomas Alexander. The Bible is now the property of the American Bible Society.

William Alexander June 16th 1798 / Saturday Afternoon ½ 5 O'Clock.

Thomas Alexander / was born ye 17 of May 1740

Mary Alexander was born June 14 1742

Elizabeth Alexander / was born ye 9 of October 1744.

Ann Alexander was born / the 2d of May 1747

Margret Alexander was born / the 22d of August 1749

William Henry Alexander was born / the 27th of May 1751.

Marthor Alexander born / the 3th of November 1753.

ANDREW BARCLAY BACHE.
(Married, 1798.)

Holy Bible in English, Boston, S. Walker, no date.

It contains the records of Andrew B. Bache and his wife Charlotte Phillips Bache of New York. It descended through their daughter Sarah Bleecker Bache Nevius to her daughter Charlotte Gesima Duckwitz Dudley, and is now the property of Miss Charlotte Elizabeth Dudley, of Brooklyn, N. Y., a great-granddaughter of the original owner.

Family Bible of Andrew & Charlotte Bache

MARRIAGES

In St. Mary's Church, Islington, England by the Rev. Mr. Williams, April 21st 1798, Andrew Bache of New York to Charlotte Phillips of Islington, England.

At St. Paul's Church Feb. 14th 1821, by the Rev^d Wm. Berrian Francis B. Lynch to Charlotte daughter of Andrew & Charlotte Bache.

Andrew Theobald married on the 5th July 1820 to Caroline McVoy by the Rev. Dr Lyle of Christ Church N. Y.

At Trinity Church April 25th 1832 by the Rev^d Wm. Berrian George Frederick Duckwitz of Bremen, Germany, to Eliza Barclay, 2nd daughter of Andrew and Charlotte Bache.

At 35 Broadway Septr 11th 1832 by the Rev. Wm. Berrian, John Daniel Kleudgen of Hamburg, Germany, to Sarah Bleecker, 3rd daughter of Andrew & Charlotte Bache.

At Rahway, New Jersey, by the Rev^d Mr. Janeway, on the 22nd Feby 1833—Ja^s T. Bache to Rosabella Trueman of this City.

At Trinity Church by the Rev^d Wm. Berrian Jany 13th 1834 George Perry Bache to Eliza Horne both of this City, d. of Dr. T. Horne.

Married in Calvary Church April 29th 1852 by the Right Revd Bishop Wainwright—William W. Jones, M. D. to Helen, fourth daughter of Andrew and Charlotte Bache.

Married in Calvary Church by the Revd Francis L. Hawks rector, Oct. 7th 1852, Jacob R. Nevius, merchant to Sarah B. Kleudgen, 3rd daughter of Andrew & Charlotte Bache.

Married in Calvary Church April 28th 1857—by the Revd Francis L. Hawks, D.D. Rector—Revd William Rudder (native Barbadoes) to Catherine Satterthwaite, fifth and youngest daughter of the late Andrew and Charlotte Bache.

BIRTHS.

Andrew Theobalds son of Andrew & Charlotte Bache, born May 4th 1799 & at 4 o'clock in the Morning Christened in St. Mary's Church, Islington.

James Theophylact son of Andrew & Charlotte, born the 8th day of December 1800 at 7 o'clock in the Morning. Christened do — do. —

Anna Maria daughter of do. — do — born the 16th day of October 1802, at 2 o'clock in the afternoon.

Charlotte daughter of Do — Do — born 31st day of May 1804 at 4 o'clock in the afternoon.

Theo. son of D° — D° born 7th day Septr 1806 at 12 o'clock in the morning.

George Perry, son of D° — D° — born 4 o'clock in the morning the 8th day of March 1809.

Eliza Barclay, daughter of D° — D° — born at 4 o'clock in the morning the 28th day of October 1811.

Sarah Bleecker, daughter of Andrew & Charlotte Bache, born at 7 o'clock in the morning the 28th day of May, 1815.

William Satterthwaite, son, of D° — D° — born at 4 o'clock in the morning the 3rd day of November, 1817.

Richard T. son of D° — D° born at 7½ in the Evening the 28th day of December 1819.

DEATHS

Anna Maria, daughter of Charlotte & Andrew Bache departed this life the 4th day of August aged 2 yrs. 10 months, & was buried in St. Paul's Church yard.

Theo. son of D° — D° — died 15th November 1808 aged 2 years 2 months, buried in St. John burying ground Greenwich.

Richard T. Son of D° — D° — died . . . 1809 and buried in the family vault in Trinity Church yard.

Charlotte daughter of D° — D° — wife of F. B. Lynch died at 11 o'clock in the morning the 23rd day May 1830 aged 25 years, 11 months, 23 days and was buried in St. Thomas Church & removed to the family vault in Trinity Church Yard 11th Jany 1843.

Charlotte wife of Andrew Bache died at ¼ before 2 o'clock on Saturday Morning, October 1st, 1842 aged 60 years 8 months and Twenty-four days buried in the family vault Trinity Yard.

And^w Barclay Bache died at ¼ before 2 o'clock P. M. Friday Augst 13th 1847 aged 77 years and 12 days and buried in the family Vault Trinity Church yard.

At Morristown, New Jersey, November the 12th 1855 at 9 P. M. Andrew Theobalds, eldest Son of Andrew & Charlotte Bache, in his 57 year buried in St. Peters Church yard, N. J.

At 61 East 31st Street Augst 9th — 1862 James Theophylact second son of And^w & Charlotte Bache—buried in family vault Trinity Ch. Yard.

Died May 24th 1866 at 7 West 19th Street—7¼ A. M. Catherine Satterthwaite youngest child of And^w & Charlotte Bache and wife of the Revd Wm Rudder, D.D. buried in the family Vault Trinity Ch. yard.

Died Monday at 2.25 A.M. Dec^b 23rd 1867, Jacob R. Nevius in 59 year of his age. Buried in Nevius family vault at Greenwood.

Died—October 18th 1875, at 51 West 28th Street at ¼ past 4 P. M. Helen, wife Wm W. Jones, M.D. & daughter of And^w & Charlotte Bache—buried in the Herring Vault — Greenwood, N. Y.

Eliza Barclay, widow of G. F. Duckwitz, daughter of Andrew & Charlotte Bache, Died 8^{15} p. m. 1887 at Bellport, L. I. buried in Duckwitz family Plot, Greenwood.

Died on Saturday at Whitehouse, New Jersey on the 9th of March 1889, George Perry Bache—Buried in Family vault Trinity Ch.—yard.

Died in his home 51 West 28th Street on the July 11th 1891 at 7 A. M. William W. Jones M.D. in his 78th year was buried in his family Vault by the side of his wife in Greenwood.

Died on Tuesday Feby 21st 1893 at 4 P. M. William Satterthwaite Bache in his 76th year. Buried in the Family Vault, Trinity Church yard, N. Y. City.

BIRTHS

Helen daughter of Andrew & Charlotte Bache born the 28th day of Feby 1822 at 10 o'clock at night.

Catherine Satterthwaite daughter of D° — D° born the 12th day of October 1824 at 7 o'clock in the morning.

Andrew Bache Son of Theophylact and Dorothy Bache born in Flatbush 1770.

Charlotte Phillips daughter of John & Mary Phillips born 7th Jany 1782 in Hertfordshire, England.

(MEMORANDUMS—)

Charlotte Lynch, George Perry Bache and Eliza Barclay children of Charlotte & Andrew Bache Confirmed in St. Ann Church Brooklyn by the Right Revd Bishop Hobart.

Sarah Kleudgen, Helen Bache & Catherine Ann Children of Charlotte & Andrew Bache Confirmed in Old Trinity by Right Revd Bishop Onderdonck.

Sarah Bleecker Bache Nevius, the last of her generation, departed this life, January fifth 1903, in New York. "Blessed are the dead that die in the Lord."

PETER BEDLOW.
(Married, 1713.)

Holy Bible in English; London, Thomas Baskett, 1759.

Contains the records of Peter Bedlow and Mary Nazereth his wife with their descendants. Inherited by their great-great-grandson, the late William Bedlow Beekman, Esq., and is now owned by Mrs. Beekman.

April the 25th 1713 Mary Nazereth Daughter of Eleoner & William Nazereth, was married to Peter Bedlow by the Reverend Mr. Freeman on Long Island.

July the 12:1716 was born Mary the Daughter of the above Peter & Mary Bedlow.

May the 22:1718 was born Cornelius the son of Peter & Mary Bedlow.

Nov. the 19:1719 Departed this life, Mary the Daughter of Peter & Mary Bedlow.

Dec. the 6th 1722 was born William the son of Peter & Mary Bedlow.

Feb'y the 10th 1737 was born Elizebeth the Daughter of Peter & Mary Bedlow & departed this Life the 2nd March following.

Clinton House on the 11th October 1781 Catharine Daughter of William & Catharine Bedlow, was married to Ebenezer Crosby by the Reverend John Moffat, at New Windsor Ulster County.— Witnesses present—William Bedlow & Catharine his wife, Doc't Stephen McCrea, Henry Rutgers, Henry Bedlow, Maria Rutgers, Mary E. G. Bedlow, Andrew Dunscomb, Catharine Clinton Daughter of Governor Clinton, William Bedlow.

August the 12th—1749 William Bedlow Son of Peter Bedlow & Mary Nazereth was married to Catharina Rutgers, Daughter of Hendrick Rutgers and Catharina Depeyster By the Reverend Mr. Boel. May the Lord vouchsafe his Blessing to us.

August the 24th—1751 Was born our Son Peter and was Baptised in the New Dutch Church, My father Peter Bedlow and My Mother Mary Bedlow Sponsors.

Dec. the 26th—1751 Departed this Life in hopes of a glorious Immortality our son Peter. His remains being deposited in Mr. Rutgers' Family Vault.

Nov. the 9th 1756 Was born our Third son William on Tuesday at seven in the Morning, and was baptised in the House by the Reverend Mr. John Ogilvie the 16th following. Mr. Hendrick Rutgers & his wife Catherina Depeyster Sponsors.

May the 15th—1757 Departed this life our son William and was entered into the Family Vault. The Lord I hope has received his soul.

May the 19th—1758 Was born our daughter Catharina and was Baptised on the 28th the same Month at St. Georges Chaple by the Reverend Mr. Barcley. Catharina Rutgers, Anna Bancker & Wm. Bancker Sponsors. May the Almighty, Grant her to live, and grow up a child of his.

Jan'y the 3—1767 Was Born our fourth son Henry, and was Baptised in the House by the Reverend Mr. John Ogilvie on the 12th of the same month. Mr. Henry Rutgers Jr. Mr. Gerardus Depeyster and Mary Rutgers, Sponsors. God Grant him to Live and Grow up in Knowledge, & True Holyness.

Feb'y the 19th 1768 Was born our fifth son William and was Baptised the 18th March Following in the House by the Reverend Mr. John Ogilvie whome with Mr. William Anderson and Mrs. Elisabeth Goade were Sponsors.

March the 16th 1768 Departed this life our fifth son William, his Remains were Deposited in the Family Vault, the Lord I hope has received him into Glory.

Aug. the 1st—1771 Was Born our Third daughter Mary Elizth Goad and was Baptised, the 11th of the same month in the House by the Reverend Mr. John Ogilvie. Mrs. Mary Chevet, Mrs. Elizabeth Goad, and Robert R. Livingston Jr. Sponsors. May the Lord Bless and Preserve her a Child of his

July the 7th 1786 Was Born William, Son of Henry Bedlow and Catherine Van Horn, he was Baptised in the House by the Reverend Samuel Provoost, William Bedlow Senr. Henry Bedlow &

Mary Eliz^bth Goad Bedlow Sponsors. Catherine Van Horn, wife of Henry Bedlow Dyed in Labor of this child.

Catherine Bedlow his wife   William Bedlow Crosby Son. Ebenezer Crosby & Catherine his wife   this Life Doc't Ebenezer Crosby

19th was entered in Mr. H. Rutgers in the New Dutch Churchyard.

Departed this life My daughter Catharine and was on the 22d entered in the Family in the New Dutch Church Yard.

June the 11th was born Henry Rutgers Crosby son of Dr. Ebenezer Crosby & Catherine his wife

1788 May the 22 Departed this life Henry Rutgers Crosby and on the 24th was entered in the Family Vault.

1756 was born Flora, a Black

1779 was born Nan Daughter of the above

1781 was born Mosanah   Ditto

1789 was born Flora   Ditto

GERARD BEEKMAN, Jr.[1]
(1693–1742.)

Holy Bible in Dutch; Dordrecht, Jacob en Pieter Keur, 1714.

Contains the family record of Gerard Beekman, Jr., and his descendants through his daughter Effie who married Philip Ver Planck in 1761. Some earlier Ver Planck records torn from an earlier Bible are pasted in. The Bible is now owned by William Gordon Ver Planck of New York City who is the great-great-great-grandson of Gerard Beekman. Part of the records are in Dutch and have been translated by Dr. L. Bendikson.

Annoq Domini 1693 Op den 10 June Is gebooren Gerard Beekman Junr. Soon Van Gerard Beekman die gedoopt is te Midwout door Domini Varick Voor getuygen Syn oom Hendrickus Beekman En Syn Ed Huysvrouw woonende Tot Kingston Esopus.

Annoq: Domini 1696 Op den 2 December Is gebooren Anna Maria van Hoorn Doghter Van Gerrit Van Hoorn die gedoopt is Tot NieuwYork door Domini Salyn voor getuygen haer Groot moeder Provoost En oom Sanford

In den Yaare Anno: Dom: 1718 den 12 Oct. Syn de Twe Bovengemelde persoonen Gerard Beekman Jr. met Anne Maria van Hoorn t'samen In den Houwlijk . . . Staet Bevestight door D: Hoogh geleerde [God] Salige Hendrickus Boel Predicant Tot New York

Anno Dom: 1719 En op dingsdag den 21 Van July Tussen Elf En Twaelf uuren overdag is myn huysvrouw verlost Van een son die op den 29 van de selve maendt is gedoopt Door Domini Gualtherus Du Bois Predicant Tot NewYork voor Syn getuygen Vader Gerrit van Hoorn En Syn Ed huysvrouw. Is genaamt Gerardus

Anno Domini 1720 En op Vrydag den negende Van December Ontrent . . . uuren des naghts is myn huysvrouw Verlost van

---

[1 The Dutch character ÿ is not cut for fonts of English type. Therefore the letter y has been used in the Dutch records where ÿ is meant.]

een Doghter die op den 14 van de Selve Maandt is gedoopt door Domini Gualth: Du Bois predicant tot NewYork voor getuygen Vader En Moeder Beekman. Is genaemt Elizabeth

Anno Domini 1722 En op den Sevenden dag December Vrydag naghts ontrent een uur in de morgen is myn housvrouw verlost van Een Soon die op den . . . [torn] den dag van de selfde maant is gedoopt door Domini Boel Predicant Tot NewYork voor getuygen Broder Cornelius Van Hoorn En Syn huysvrouw. Is genaemt Cornelius

Annoq: Domini 1724 En op Sondagh Den 13 dag van September Ontrent five uuren in den morgen is myn huysvrouw verlost van een Soon die doodt ter Werelt Quaam

Annoq: Domini 1725 En op Saterdag den 21 Augustus Ontrent te negen uuren in de morgen is myn huysvrouw verlost Van een Doghter die op den 27 Van de Selve maandt is gedoopt door Domini Gualtherus De Bois Predicant Tot NewYork voor Getuygen Broeder William Beekman En Syn huysvrouw genaamt Magdalena. Is Genaamt Magdalena

Annoq: Domini 1725 En op Septemb: den 6e Synde Maendag ontrent te negen uuren in de Morgen is myn Waarde En Seer Lieve huysvrouw in den Heere gerust Synde oudt negen En twintig yaer Min Drie Maanden

Anno: 1704 op den 8e October is gebooren Catharina Provoost Doghter van Willem Provoost die gedoopt Tot NewYork door Domini Du Bois voor getuygen Cornelius Van Exveen En huys vrouw van Gerrit Van Horne

Anno: 1727 op Saterdag den 10 Juny Syn ik Gerard Beekman in den Houwelycken Staat bevestight met de bovegenaamde Catharina Provoost door de geleerde [God] Zalige Rynhert Erickson Predicant op Hackinsack

Anno 1728 op Vrydag den 29 maart ontrent Middag is myn bovengenoemde huysvrouw verlost van een Soon die op den derde Aprill is gedoopt door Domini Boel Predicant Tot N. York En is genaamt William voor getuygen Vader Provoost Grootmoeder Byvank

Anno Domini 1729 op Sondagh den 16 Maart ontrent te Middernagt is myn Doghter Magdalena na een langhdurende Siekte in den Heere ontslaapen oudt Synde drie Yaar En Seven Maanden Min 5 dagen.

Anno 1730 op Woensdag den 25ᵉ maart ontrent five uuren in de Morgen is myn huysvrouw verlost van een Dogter die op den 9 Aprill is gedoopt door Domini Du Bois Predikant Tot NewYork En is genaamt Magdalena voor getuygen Broeder David Provoost En Syn huysvrouw.

Anno Domini 1731 op Dinsdags den 7ᵉ Septembr Ontrent te Elf uuren in de nagt is myn tweede Dogter genaamt Magdalena in den Heeren ontslaapen Synde out ontrent Seventien Maanden

Anno 1732/3 op Dingsdag den 8ᵉ January ontrent te drie uuren in de Morgen is Myn Housvrouw verlost Van een Soon die op den 16ᵉ Van de Selve maant is gedoopt door Domini Boel Predikant tot NewYork En is genaamt David voor getuygen Broeder David Provoost En Syn huysvrouw.

Anno 1735 op Maendag den 10ᵉ maart ontrent agt des avonts is myn huysvrouw verlost Van een Dogter die op Woensdag den 19ᵉ des Selfs maant is gedoopt door Domini Du Bois predikant tot NewYork met de naem van Magdalena Voor getuyge Broeder William Beekman En Syn huysvrouw. deceased ye 20 Septr 1783 and buried at Fishkill. Magdalen maried Abm. Lynsen of the City of New York Mercht.

Anno 1736/7 op Woensdag den 16 Febry. ontrent tien uuren des nagts is myn huysvrouw verlost van een dogter die op Frydag den 25ᵉ des Selfs maant is gedoopt door Domini Du Bois predikant tot NewYork met de naem Effie voor getuyge Broed La Roux En Syn huysvrouw.

Anno 1738/9 op Fryday den 16 maart ontrent te drie uuren na de middag is myn housvrouw verlost van een dogter die op Woensdag den 21 des Selfs maant is gedoopt door Dom. Henrickus Boel Predikant Tot NewYork met de naem Van Catharina voor getuyge Broed Edickson En Syn huysvrouw.

Anno 1740/1 op Sondag den 18ᵉ January Ontrent tien uuren des avondts is myn huysvrouw verlost van Een Soon die op

Woensdag den 21ᵉ des Selfs maant is gedoopt door Dom Du Bois predikant tot NewYork En genaamt Jacobus voor getuyge Broeder Hendrickus En Suster van Dam

[TRANSLATION]

[Anno Domini 1693, June 10ᵗʰ: Born Gerard Beekman Junʳ, son of Gerard Beekman, baptized at Midwout by Domine Varick; as sponsors his uncle Hendrickus Beekman and his honourable housewife, living at Kingston Esopus.

[Anno Domini 1696, December 2ⁿᵈ: Born Anna Maria van Hoorn, daughter of Gerrit Van Hoorn, baptized at New York by Domine Salyn; as sponsors her grandmother Provoost and uncle Sanford.

[In the year Anno Domini 1718, October 12ᵗʰ both the above mentioned parties Gerard Beekman Jr. and Anne Maria van Hoorn are united in matrimony by the very learned and reverend Hendrickus Boel, minister at New York.

[Anno Domini 1719, on Tuesday, July the 21ˢᵗ, between 11 and 12 o'clock in the day-time, my wife was brought to bed with a son, who on the 29ᵗʰ of the same month is baptized by Domine Gualtherus Du Bois, minister at New York; as sponsors Father Gerrit van Hoorn and his honourable housewife. Christened Gerardus.

[Anno Domini 1720, on Friday, December the 9ᵗʰ about . . . o'clock at night my housewife was brought to bed with a daughter, who on the 14ᵗʰ of the same month is baptized by Domine Gualth. Du Bois, minister at New York; as sponsors father and mother Beekman. Christened Elizabeth.

[Anno Domini 1722, on Friday, December the 7ᵗʰ about 1 o'clock in the morning, my housewife was brought to bed with a son, who on the . . . of the same month is baptized by Domine Boel, minister at New York; as sponsors brother Cornelius Van Hoorn and his housewife. Christened Cornelius.

[Anno Domini 1724, on Sunday, September the 13ᵗʰ about 5 o'clock in the morning, my housewife was brought to bed with a still-born son.

[Anno Domini 1725, on Saturday August the 21st, about 9 o'clock in the morning my housewife was brought to bed with a daughter, who on the 27th of the same month is baptized by Domine Gualtherus De Bois minister at New York; as sponsors brother William Beekman and his housewife Magdalena. Christened Magdalena.

[Anno Domini 1725, on Monday September the 6th about 9 o'clock in the morning, my dear and beloved housewife died in the Lord, in the age of twenty-nine years, less three months.

[Anno 1704, October the 8th, born Catharina Provoost, daughter of William Provoost, baptized at New York by Domine Du Bois; as sponsors Cornelius Van Exveen and Gerrit van Horne's housewife.

[Anno 1727, on Saturday, June the 10th I, Gerard Beekman, am united in matrimony with the above mentioned, Catharina Provoost by the learned and reverend Rynhert Erickson, minister at Hackensack.

[Anno 1728, on Friday, March the 29th about noon, my housewife, above mentioned, was brought to bed with a son, baptized on the 3rd of April by Domine Boel, minister at New York and christened William; as sponsors father Provoost, and grandmother Byvanck.

[Anno Domini 1729, on Sunday, March the 16th, about midnight my daughter Magdalene died in the Lord, after a lingering malady, in the age of three years and seven months, less five days.

[Anno 1730, on Wednesday, March the 25th, about 5 o'clock in the morning, my housewife was brought to bed with a daughter, baptized on the 9th of April by Domine Du Bois, minister at New York, and christened Magdalena; as sponsors brother David Provoost and his housewife.

[Anno Domini 1731, on Tuesday, September 7, about 11 o'clock at night, died in the Lord my second daughter, called Magdalena, about 17 months old.

[Anno Domini 1732/3, on Tuesday, January the 8th, about 3 o'clock in the morning my housewife was brought to bed with a son, baptized on the 16th of the same month by Domine Boel, minister at New York, and christened David; as sponsors brother David Provoost and his housewife.

[Anno 1735, on Monday, March the 10th about 8 o'clock in the evening my housewife was brought to bed with a daughter, baptized on Wednesday the 19th of the same month by Domine Du Bois minister at New York, and christened Magdalena; as sponsors brother William Beekman and his housewife. [In the margin:] "Magdalen married Abm. Lynsen of the City of New York, Merch[an]t." "Deceased ye 20 Septr 1783 and buried at Fishkill."

[Anno 1736/7, on Wednesday, February the 16th, about 10 o'clock at night, my housewife was brought to bed with a daughter, baptized on Friday, the 25th of the same month, by Domine Du Bois, minister at New York, and christened Effie; as sponsors brother La Roux and his housewife.

[Anno 1738/9 on Friday, March the 16th, about 3 o'clock in the afternoon, my housewife was brought to bed with a daughter, baptized on Wednesday the 21st of the same month by Domine Henrickus Boel, minister at New York and christened Catharina; as sponsors brother Erickson and his housewife.

[Anno 1740/1 on Sunday, January the 18th, about 10 o'clock in the evening my housewife was brought to bed with a son, baptized on Wednesday the 21th of the same month by Domine Du Bois, minister at New York; and christened Jacobus; as sponsors brother Hendrickus and sister van Dam.]

Anno Dominie 1742 on the Sunday ye 24th Octbr. between 2 & Three a Clock in the morning my mother was delivered of a boy Whome Died 4 days after he was born on thursday between one & two a Clock afternoon being the 28 day of Same month.

Annoq Domminiee 1742 On Thursday being 23rd day November about half hour after Eleven at night my Father Gerard Beekman Departed his life aged forty nine years 5 months & 13 days.

Annoq Domini 1746/7 on Wednesday Morng being the 28th January about Six a Clock our Sister Cathrine Departed this Life & was Intered in the Old Dutch Church ye 30th Inst. G. GB.

Annoq Domini 1746/7 on Sunday morning being the 8th day of February about Ten a Clock Our Brother James Departed this Life & was Intered in the Old Dutch Church ye 10th Instant. G. GB.

Anno 1757 Satterday 26 Febry my Daughter Magdalen was Married to Mr. Abm Lynsen Junr son to Mr. Abm Lynsen Merchant.

Anno 1758 Tuesday 15 August my Daughter Magdalen was Deliv'd of a Dauger & Named her Catharine her god Mother Cathr Beekman & Cathr Lynsen & her god Father Abm Lynsen Crismed in the Old English Church by . . . Barcly Crismed 15 days after it was born on a Wednesday.

Anno 1761 Satterday the 7th of Aprill Philip Verplanck Jun Son of Philip Verplanck Esq was married to Miss Effe Beekman Doughter of Mr. Gerard Beekman of New York.

Anno Dom 1765 on Monday the 21 day of Aprill my Wife Effie was delivered of a Doughter and was Crisend by Domney Rubell att the Manor of Cortlandt and was Crisend Cathren Philip Verplanck Es^r & Gertrud Verplanck Stands God Father and God Mother. November 4 1786 She married Herman Hoffman Esq of Red Hook

Anno Dom: 1766 on Tusday the 26 of Augs my Wife Effie was Delivered of a Doughter and was Crisend by Domeny Isaac Rysdick at Fish Kills and was Crisend Gertruy. James Verplanck Esq God Father and sister Gertruy Verplanck as God Mother. March 8 178/9 married Anthony A. Hoffman Esq of Poughkeepsie

Anno: Dom: 1766 my Mother Gertruy Verplanck wife of Philip Verplanck Esq Departed her life the 20: Sep. 66

Anno: Dom: 1767 My sister Margret Verplanck Dep^t Her Life in Novr. Intered at the Manor Cortlandt.

Anno: Dom: 1768 the 8 Day of July my son Philip was born on Monday Morning at 3 oclock & was Crismed by Domeny Ruble of Longisland at the Manor of Cortlandt His God Fathers my Father Philip Verplanck Esq & Corn^l Philip Schuyler of Albany My Sister Ana Mariay Verplanck as God mother. 17 Sepr. 1796 Married Sally Arden of New York.

[17]

Ano Domeny 1770 the 2ᵈ day of March at 5 oclock in the morning my son Wm. B. Verplanck was born and Crisened by Domeny Isaac Rysdyk at Fish Kills & was Crisened Wm. Beekman Verplanck. Wm. Beekman in Liverpool as Godfather and Catren Verplanck as Godmother. July ye 12ᵉ 1798 Married to Melinda daughter of the Honorable James Gordon of Balltown

Anno: Dom: 1772 The 7 Day of Sep. My Doughter Margret was Born 11 oclock at Night Was Cresened by Domeny Rise Dyck of Fish Kills and was Crisend In my one House God Mother Anna Mary Verplank & Johanes Verplank God Father June 15 1799 Married Peter Mesier Junr son of Peter Mesier of Fishkill Town.

Anno Dom 1771 Departed this Life Octob 13th day Philip Verplanck Esq of the Manor of Cortlandt and was Entered at the same place Aged Seventy-seven years and Three Months & fifteen Days.

Anno Dom 1763 Departed the Life in April 20 our Mother Catharine Beekman & was bur'd in the Old Duch Churuch aged fifty nine years 5 months & 18 days.

Anno: Dom 1773 On Tusday the 19ᵗʰ of Oct. my Doughtor Anna Mariah was borne and Crisned by Domeny Rysdyk at Fish Kills David Beekman & Sarah Beekman his wife Stand as God Father and God Mother. April ye 22 1797 Married Andrew Deveaux of So. Carolina.

Anno Dom 1774 On Monday ye 14 Feb. Brother John Verplanck Departed this Life, of the Manor of Cortlandt and Enterd at the same place. the 17ᵗʰ day Ageid — years.

Anno Domini 1774 on ye 30 December departed this Life James Verplanck Esq & was interred in the Manor of Cortlandt, N. B. James & John Verplanck dyed without Issue.

Anno Domini 1777 at half past twelve at night of Friday the 20 June departed this Life Philip Verplanck & was buried in the Dutch Church Yard at Fish Kills in Rumbouts precinct—near his deceased wife Effie Verplanck who departed this life on the 15 November one thousand seven hundred & seventy five aged thirty nine years.

Anno Domini 1779 on Wednesday the 20th October departed this life Anna Maria Verplanck Eldest surviving daughter of Philip Verplanck Esq of the Manor of Cortland aged 50 & was buried in the Dutch Church Yard at Fishkill in Rumbout Precinct.

"Translation of a Dutch Record taken from a Dutch Bible "which formerly belonged to Gulian Verplanck the elder of the "City of New York, Merchant, and which now is the property "of George Brinkerhoff of Hopewell Rumbouts Precinct, Dutch-"ess County, State of New York, late of Newtown on Long "Island."

"Anno 1668 10–20 June at New York in America, I, Gulian "Verplanck aged Thirty-one years the first of January Married "Henrica Wessells aged twenty three years in September last. "The Ceremony was performed by the Reverend Samuel "Driesyas.

"Anno 1669 About four O'Clock P.M. of Thursday the 16–26 "December, our first child being a Son was born, and the Sun-"day following the 19th of December Christened by the Rever^d "Mr. Driesyes his Name Samuel. His Sponsors were Nicholas "Rackers, Johannis Van Bruggen and my Mother Mary Ver-"planck.

"Anno 1698 on the 20th November Samuel Verplanck dyed at "sea on a voyage from Coracoa to Jamaica and is buried in the "Island of Jamaica.

"Anno 1671 on Friday Morning about nine o'clock of the first "day of December, my second Son was born, his name James "his sponsors my father Abraham Verplanck and Anna Eliza-"beth Wessells."

"Anno 1699 on the 30th October James Verplanck deceased and "is buried in the Church.

"Anno 1674 in New Orange—I. E. Albany at one O'clock in the "Morning of Saturday the 3–13 Jany. was born our third child "and christened on the 24th of the same month his Name "Abraham Sponsors Stephanus Van Cortlandt Francis Rum-"bouts and my wife's sister Joanna Edsalls.

"Anno 1695 on the 7th of June Abraham Verplanck sailed on "the Brothers Adventure as mate for Newfoundland. He went "from thence on the 18th of July but has since never been "heard of.

"Anno 1675/6 about 10 O'clock at Night of Thursday the 23rd of "March our fourth Son was born and baptised on Sunday the "26th being Easter his sponsors Sam'l Edsall, Warner Wessels "and Samuel Edsall's daughter, Anna Edsall.

"Anno 1676 about 11 O'clock in the forenoon of Friday the 14th "July our fourth Son Named John dyed and on Sunday the "16th after Sermon was buried

"Anno 1677/8 March the 17th Old Stile being Sunday our fifth "child was born and Wednesday following the 20th of the "Month Christened Benjamin his sponsors Garret Roos Abraham "DeLanoy and Judith Edsall wife of Benjamin Bleg."

"In New York
"Anno 1678 on Sunday the fourth of August old Stile about Six "O'clock in the afternoon our son Benjamin deceased and was "buried on the 6th of the same Month.

"Anno 1679 on Monday the 20th July Old Stile at four o'clock "in the Morning our sixth Son was born on the 27th he was "christened his name Benjamin. His sponsors, my wife's "brother Warner Wessells and Peter Jacob's son Mauris as also "Elizabeth wife of Warner Wessells.

"Anno 1680 on the 21st of July Benjamin deceased and was "buried on the 23rd.

"Anno 1680 on 2nd September old Stile Thursday at one o'clock "in the morning my daughter was born and on Sunday the 5th "of September Christened her name Anna her sponsors David "Schuyler, Peter Dila Noye and Gertrude Schuyler wife of "Stephanus Van Cortlandt.

"Anno 1684 on the 23rd of April my father deceased of a fever "and Imposthume in the Ear and was buried on the 26th of the "same Month.

"Anno 1684 on Monday the 22nd June was born our eighth child
"Named Gulina her sponsors, Peter Jacobson's Mauris, Hartman
"Wessells and Elizabeth Bedlow."

"Anno 1701 on the 30 November Gulina Verplanck deceased and
"on the 4th of December was buried in the Church.

"The foregoing was copied and translated on the 7th of June
"One thousand seven hundred and Eighty-six as Witness my
"hand. Sam'l Verplanck"

"N. B. By the testimony of Mary Brockhurst daughter of
"Saml Verplanck the Elder her aunt Anna Verplanck deceased
"in the year 1702 having married Teller. Sam'l Verplanck."

"Anno 1691 on the 8th Sept. O. S. I Jacobus Verplanck was mar-
"ried to Margarita Schuyler of New Albany by the Rev'd Good-
"wirkies Delius Minister of New Albany.

"Anno 1693 the 28th March my son Guilliaum was born Ste-
"phanus Van Cortlandt and my brother Brandt Schuyler God-
"fathers my mother Kipp Godmother and dyed in Dutchess
"County the 6th June 1745.

"Anno 1695 the 28th of June my son Philip was born Coll:
"Peter Schuyler and Coll: Jno Schuyler Godfathers Mrs. Ger-
"trude Cortland Godmother departed this life the 13 day of Oct
"1771 Aged 76 years 3 months 15 ds.

"N. B. The above is taken from the family Bible of Philip
"Verplanck, Esq., of the Manor of Cortland. Witness my hand
"this 3rd of Aug. 1786 Sam'l Verplanck."

Aprill 10th, 1718, I. Philip Verplanck was marryed to Mrs. Gertruydt Van Cortlandt only Daughter of Johannis Van Cortlandt, Deceased, by Barnardus Freeman Minister at fflatbush on Long Island.

May 21st, 1719, My Daughter Anna Marya was born, her Godfather was Coll. Peter Schuyler and her Godmothers were Madm. Gertruydt Van Cortlandt and Mother Collins—Dyed Augt. 23rd, 1726.

January 4th, 1720/1. My Son Jacobus Verplanck was born—John Collins and Gulian Ver Planck Godffathers and Mary Van Renselaer Godmother.

ffebry. 18, 1723/4. My Son Johannis Verplanck was born—Coll. John Schuyler Godffather and Mm. Cornelia Van Cortlandt Godmother—Dyed March 7th, 1724.

January 18th, 1725/6. My Daughter Margaret was born—Robert Livingston, Esqr. Godffather and Madm. Gerretie Drawyer, Godmother.

June 29th, 1727. My Son Johanns. Verplanck was born—Edward Collins, Godffather and Mother Collins Godmother.

June 23rd, 1729. My Daughter Anna Marya was born—Uncle Barnard ffreeman Godffather and Margaret ffreeman Godmother.

Novembr. 9th 1731 My daughter Gertruy was born—Uncle Philip Van Cortlandt, Esqr. Godffather and Aunt Gertruydt Beekman, Godmother. Deceased the 24th June 1794 Interred at Fish Kills.

June 20th 1734 My Daughter Catharin was born—Unckle Samuel Bayard Godffather and Margaret Bayard Godmother. Deceased Septr. 1804 Interred at Fish Kill.

1736 August 30th My Son Philip was born—Couzn. Gulian Verplanck Godffather and Cousn. Anna Verplanck Godmother.

1768 July 18 day at 3 o'clock in the morning my Grandson Philip was born—My selfe God Father and my Daughter Anna Maria Verplanck Godmother.

Anno Domini 1798 July 12 William Beekman Verplanck was married to Melinda Gordon the only daughter of the Honl. James Gordon of Ball Town in Saratoga County.

Anno Domini 1799 July 22 My Daughter Mary Ann Catharine was born and christened by Nicholas Van Vranken, minister of the Dutch Churches in Fish Kill Town. W. B. V. P.

Anno Domini 1801 October 12th My son William Gordon was born and christened by the Revd. Nicholas Van Vranken. W. B. V. P.

Anno Domini 1804 Jany. 22nd Our son Philip Alexander was born and christened by the Revd. —— Bartello. M. Verplanck.

Anno Domini 1804 July 19 departed this life Mary Ann C. Verplanck and was buried in the Dutch Church Yard at Fish Kill. M. V.

Anno Domini 1804 Decr. 30 departed this life Willm. B. Verplanck and was interred in same grave with his daughter Mary Ann Catharine in the Dutch Church Yard at Fish Kill. Melinda Verplanck.

JOHN BEEKMAN.
(1765–1843.)

Holy Bible in English; lacking title, date not known.

Contains the records of John Beekman and Mary Elizabeth Goad Bedlow, his wife, with their descendants. The later entries giving the descent to the present day have been omitted at the request of the family. The Bible is now in possession of Mrs. William Bedlow Beekman of New York, whose husband was a descendant of John Beekman.

MARRIAGES.

1792 Nov. 3: On Saturday evening was married by the bishop Samuel Provoost, John Beekman, son of James Beekman and Jane Keteltas to Mary Elisabeth Goad Bedlow, daughter of William Bedlow and Catherine Rutgers all of New York.

1819 Jan. 5th was married by Rev. Philip Milledolar, Catharine Bedlow daughter of John Beekman & Mary E. G. Bedlow to Abraham K. Fish son of John Fish & Sarah Keteltas, all of New York.

1822 Oct. 18 was married by Rev. Dr. McMurray, Mary, daughter of John Beekman & Mary E. G. Bedlow to Wm. A. de Peyster, son of Abraham de Peyster & Catherine Augusta Livingston, all of New York.

1833 Nov. 6th was married by the Rev. F. L. Hawkes, Jane daughter of Jno Beekman & M. E. G. Bedlow to Jacob Hallet Borrowe, son of Samuel Borrowe & Sarah Hallett, all of this city.

1832 Jan. 12th was married, by Rev. Dr. Brownley, Lydia, daughter of Jno. Beekman & Mary E. G. Bedlow to Joseph Foulke, son of Joseph Foulke & Charlotte Brion, all of New York.

1841 June 1st was married Wm Fenwick son of Jno Beekman and Mary E. G. Bedlow to Catharine Alexander, daughter of Wm Neilson & Hannah Coles by the Rev. F. L. Hawks, all of this city.

BIRTHS.

Saturday 1794 Feb 1st This Morning at ½ past 9 o'clock was born our first son & On the 21st Inst. he was Baptised in the house by the name of William, by the Rev. Dr. Wm. Linn, God-father, uncle Wm Beekman, with myself & wife, sponsors.

1796 May 8th, on Sunday afternoon ½ past 4 o'clock was born our second, & on Sunday afternoon 29th, inst he was baptised in the house, by the name of James by the Rev. Dr. John H. Livingston, after my father, my wife & self sponsors.

1798. Sept 11th on Tuesday afternoon ¼ after 1 oclock was born our first daughter on Sunday Nov. 4th she was baptised in the New Dutch Church, by the name of Catherine Bedlow by the Rev. Dr. Wm Linn. After her Grandma Bedlow, my wife & self sponsors.

1800 Sept. 15th On Monday afternoon at ½ past 3 o'clock was born our second daughter & on Sunday Oct. 26th was baptised in the New Dutch Church, by the name of Mary by the Rev. Jno. Abeel, my wife & self sponsors.

1802 Sept 21st On Tuesday afternoon ½ after 5 oclock was born our third son & on Wednesday Nov. 4th was baptised, in the house, by the name of John Crosby, by the Rev. Jno. Abeel, my wife & self sponsors.

1805 Feb'y 10th On Sunday morning at ½ after 4 o'clock was born our third daughter, & on Saturday March 9th was baptised in the house, by the name of Jane, after her Grandmother Beekman, my wife & self Sponsors. (by Rev. Jno. Abeel.)

1807 June 28th On Sunday afternoon at 1.06 oclock was born our 4th daughter & on Sunday July 26th 1807 was baptised in the Presbyterian church on Henry Rutgers estate, by the Rev. Philip Milledoler, by the name of Sarah Ralston (after our cousin wife of Robert Ralston of Philadelphia my wife & self sponsors.

1809 Aug. 4th, On Friday afternoon at 20 min. after 2 oclock was born our fourth son & on Sunday Sept. 3rd, 1809 was baptised in the Presbyterian Church in Rutgers st, by the Rev. Philip Milledolar, by the name of William Fenwick, myself & wife sponsors.

1811 July 12th On Friday evening at 10 minutes after 10 o'clock, was born our fifth daughter & on Sunday August 18th 1811 was baptised in the Presbyterian Church Rutgers St. by the Rev. Philip Milledolar, by the name of Lydia, (after her aunt Lydia wife of James Beekman wife & myself sponsors.

1814 Jan'y 12th on Wednesday morning at 10 minutes after 7 o'clock was born our 5th son & on Sunday 22nd of May 1814 was baptised in the Dutch Church at Bloomingdale by the name of James, by the Rev. Alexander Gunn, my wife & self sponsors.

DEATHS.

1797. Aug. 21st On Monday evening at 6 o'clock died our son James aged 15 months & 13 days, and was interred in our family vault in the new dutch church graveyard.

1805 Oct. 24th on Thursday morning at the Wallabout (Long Island), died our eldest son Wm aged 11 years 8 months & 23 days, after a severe illness of three days & was interred in the new burying ground of the dutch church.

1816 May 12th On Sunday afternoon at ½ past seven o'clock died our fifth son James aged 2 yrs & 4 months with dropsy of the brain & was interred in our family vault in the new Dutch churchyard.

1832 Aug. 16th, on Thursday morning died our fourth daughter Sarah Ralston aged 25 years & 1 month of consumption & was interred in the tomb of her brother William, in the new burying ground of the Dutch Church.

1843 Dec. 8th on Friday afternoon a quarter before 5 o'clock died John Beekman, aged 76 years & 8 months, & was buried in the family vault in the New Dutch churchyard in Nassau Street.

1848 April 5th on Wednesday afternoon about 6 oclock died Mary E. G. Beekman, aged 76 yrs, 8 mons. & 3 days & was buried in St. Thomas churchyard corner of Broadway and Houston St. New York.

John N. Bleecker, born 1739

JAN JANSE BLEECKER.[1]

(Came to America in 1656, married at Albany in 1667.)

Holy Bible in Dutch, Dordrecht, Pieter en Jacob Keur, 1736.

It contains the records of the Bleecker family to John N. Bleecker, 1776. It has descended in the direct line to Robert Fanshawe Bloodgood, of New York City, the great-great-great-grandson of the original owner.

1689 den 29 July Is ons Een Soon gebooren en hebben Syn Naam Genoemt Hendryck

1692 den 19 Aprill is ons Een Soon gebooren en hebben Syn Naam genoemt Johannis.

1694 den 26 aprill is ons Een Soon gebooren en hebben Syn Naam genoemt Johannis

1697 den 16 february Is ons Een Soon Geboren en hebben Syn Naam genoemt Gerrit

1700 Den 22 January Is ons Een Dogter Gebooren en Hebben haar naam Genoemt Elisabeth

1702 den 27 december Is ons Een dogter Gebooren en hebben haar naam genoemt Geertruy

1706 den 19 Aprill Is ons twe dogters Gebooren en hebben haar Naamen genoemt Margrieta en Anna.

Being anxious to know when or at what time my Great Grand Father left his native Country, from which of the Seven United Provinces, the City or Town he came from &ca, &ca, for this purpose, I applied to my kinsman, John R. Bleecker, who informed me, that it appeared from entries amongst the papers of his late Grand Father John R. Bleecker, our ancestor Jan Janse Bleecker, had arrived in this country Unmarried in the year 1656, that he came from the Province of Overyfsel and Town of Meppel. And I have been informed by near relations, that he married shortly after his arrival, either in the now Dutches or Ulster Counties, in the Family of the Rutzies, now nearly extinct, that he died at

[1 The Dutch character ÿ is not cut for fonts of English type. Therefore the letter y has been used in the Dutch records where ÿ is meant.]

the age of about ninety or ninety two years, that he left four sons and four daughters, namely Johannis my Grand Father, Rutger, Nicholas and Henderick, the two last died unmarried, Jannitie Married to Johannis Glen, Catherine married to Abraham Cuyler, Margaret married to Henderick Ten Eyck, And Rachael died unmarried in an advanced age. from the above it is to be seen, that all those who at present bear the name of Bleecker in this place, New York &c. are the descendents of my Great Grand Father, from the branches of his two sons Johannis and Rutger. Albany 16th August 1809   John N. Bleecker.

For the information of my Children, it appears proper to mention, That I was born on the 22nd of August, 1739, which is to be seen in my late Parents Family Bible in pofsefsion of my late Brother Henry's Widow; but as an Act Pafsed in May 1751 for regulating the commencement of the year, by which the old Style was abolished and the new Style established, this was done by sinking eleven Days in September 1752, hence my Age, instead of the 22nd August is to 2nd Septr. Albany 16th August 1809. N.B. It appears from entries made by my Great Grand Father . . . Jan Janse Bleecker which I have seen since the above was wrote, that instead of his Marriage in Dutches or Ulster Counties, he was married on the 2nd Jany. 1667 to Margarrieta Rathze at Albany.   17th September 1812.

Dese Bybel belanght Aen Nicolaes Bleecker
Dewelke hem is Aengekomen by Erfenifs van Johs Rofeboom Overleden August 15th 1765. John N. Bleecker's Property August 1776.

I John N. Bleecker was married on Wednesday the 21st day of June 1775 to Margaret van Duessen of New Brunswick in the Province of New Jersey, at Sowerland, at the parsonage House by the Reverend Johannis Martinus Van Hurlingen

Tuesday 30th day of April 1776 my Spouse was safely delivered of a daughter at ten oClock in the forenoon, who was Baptized on Sunday the 5th may by the name of Margaret. Godfather Henry Bleecker & my mother Margaret Godmother

Tuesday 10th January 1778 My Spouse was delivered of a Son at Six oclock in the morning, who was Baptized on Sunday the

Margaret Van Dusen, wife of John N. Bleecker

15th Feby. by the name of Henry. Godfather William Van Duessen and his wife Anna Godmother.

Saturday the 1st day of April 1780 my Wife was delivered of a Daughter at Seven oClock in the morning who was Baptized on Sunday the 9th following and named Arriantje Godfather Johannis Martinus Van Hurlingen & his Wife Elizabeth Godmother

Mondy 26th day of Novr. 1781 my Spouse was delivered of a Daughter at four oclock in the morning who was Baptized on Thursday the 13th Decr. and named Giertje Godfather Nicholas Bleecker & his mother Catlence Bleecker Godmother

Friday the 12th March 1784 My Wife was delivered of a Daughter at Twelve Oclock at noon who was Baptized on Sunday the 21st Instant by the Reverend Elardus Westerlo and named Elizabeth—no God Father nor Godmother

Sunday the 2nd day of April 1786 My Wife was Delivered of a Daughter at three oClock in the Morning who was Baptized on Sunday the 9th Instant By the Reverend Eliardus Westerlo and named Annatie—no God Father nor Godmother

Tuesday the 18th Day of April 1786 my Daughter Baptized by the name of Gerritze but Called & known by the name of Gitty, died at Eight Oclock in the morning, aged Four years, four months & Twenty three Days.

Wednesday the 16th day of January 1788 My Wife was delivered of her Seventh Child being a Son at three Oclock in the Morning who was Baptized on Sunday the 3rd Day of February by the Reverend John Bafset one of the Ministers of the Gofpel of the Reformed Low Dutch Church at this place *Albany,* and the Child was Named Nicholas no God Father nor Godmother

Saturday the 15th day of August 1789 My son Baptized by the name of Nicholas died at Six Oclock in the morning, aged 19 months.

Thursday the 12th day of November 1789 my Wife was delivered of her Eighth Child being a son at two oClock in the afternoon who was Baptized on Sunday the 22d. Instant By the Reverend Doctor Westerlo and named Nicholas. No God Father nor Godmother.

SEVERYN BRUYN.
(1726–1759.)

Holy Bible in Dutch, Dordrecht, Jacob en Hendrick Keur, 1741.

It contains the records of Severyn Bruyn and his descendants and has come down in direct descent through Jacobus S. Bruyn, Severyn Bruyn, and Mary Bruyn Forsyth to the present owners, the Misses Katherine Bruyn Forsyth and Petronella Bruyn Forsyth of Kingston, N. Y.

[From Severyn Bruyn, the original owner, the book passed to his son Jacobus Severyn, then to *his* son Severyn, and from him to his children, Augustus Hasbrouck Bruyn and Mary Bruyn Forsyth, my mother. Katherine Bruyn Forsyth.]

Severyn Bruyn is born the 25" May (Old Stile) in the year of our Lord Christ seventeen hundred and twenty six and has to Godfather and mother (To Witt) Cadwalader Colden Esqr and his wife.

Catharine Ten Broek, who is now my present wife, was born the 8th day of June (old Stile) In the Year of our Lord Christ one thousand Seven hundred and Twenty Seven, and has to her Godfather Cornelis Vernay and godmother Mary Delametter, wife of Johannes Delametter Esqr. In the year of our Lord Christ one thousand Seven hundred and Forty-nine and fifty, on the thirteenth day of January (old Stile) In the 24" year of my age, and Catharine Ten Broek in the 23rd year of her age, was bound in bonds of Holy Matrimony by Parson Mancius.

My eldest Child Jacobus was born in the year of our Lord Christ One thousand Seven hundred and fifty one. On Sunday morning about five of the Clock of the 27th day of October (Old Stile) and was Baptized the same day in Kingston by Parsons Petrus Vass and has to Godfather and mother Abraham Hasbrouck and his wife Catharine.

My second Child Rachel was born in the year of our Lord Christ One thousand seven hundred and fifty four on fryday about half an hour past four of the Clock, in the Morning of the 24th day of May (New stile) and was Baptized the Sunday following, by Parson Petrus Vass, has to God-father and Godmother, Johannes Ten Broek and Geertry Ten Broek.

My third Child Johannis was born in the year of our Lord Christ One thousand seven hundred and fifty six, On Saturday Morning about five of the Clock of the 29th day of May (New Stile) and Baptized the next day by Parson Whilhelmus Georgius Mancius, has to God father and Godmother Coenrad Ten Broeck and his wife Margariet.

My daughter Rachel dyed in the Lord the 15th November 1756 after a Severe illness of Nine Days. She dyed about Eleven of the Clock of the said day it being on a Monday and was Intered in the Church yard in Kingston near the Church opposite the North corner, the Wednesday following.

Severyn Bruyn departed this Life the 19th Day of August, 1759 Newstile. It being on Sunday Morning fifteen Minutes after 12 o'clock In the Morning Aged 33 years 2 Months and fourteen Days, And was Buryed on Munday following Upon the Church Yard at Kingston, and Rests in the Lord untill his Coming to Judge both the Quick and the Dead. He was about six feet high, well proportioned. Light blue eyes, Light brown Straight hair, he was very Active in the Vigour of his Life. Was Endowed with a Share of good Sense and Agreeable Companion. He dyed of what they Doctors called The Long Fever, after an Illness of 15 Days. He was The Latter part of his Sickness very Delerious.

And his Son Johannis Departed This Life The 21st of August 1759 About 12 of the Clock of the Day and Buryed near his Father. And Rests in the Lord until his Coming.

Kingston January 8th (New Stile) 1760 is my daughter Catharine born And Christened by Domine Whilhelmus Georgius Mancius, and has for Godfather and Mother Petrus Ten Broeck and Catharine his wife.

Catharine Bruyn died in the year one thousand seven hundred and Seventy six on the night of the . . .

Jacobus S. Bruyn was married to Blandina Elmendorph Daughter of Petrus Edmundus Elmendorph on Monday the eighteenth day of March in the Year of our Lord one thousand seven hundred and eighty two by Parson Doll.

My Eldest son Edmund was born on the 4th of April, one thousand seven hundred and eighty three in the same year when Peace was Restored to America and was baptized by Parson Doll, and has for Godfather and Godmother Petrus Edmundus Elmendorph and Mary and Elizabeth Elmendorph.

My Second son Severyn was born on good Fryday the 25th of March in the year of our Lord one thousand seven hundred and eighty five, was baptized by Parson Doll and has for Godfather and Godmother Lucas Elmendorph and Sally Elmendorph.

My mother Catharine (who was married after my father's death to Jonathan Elmendorph) departed this life on the first day of November in the Year of our Lord one thousand seven hundred and two aged seventy five years.

Col Jacobus S. Bruyn died 12th July 1825 N.S.

Blandina Bruyn, relict of Jacobus S. Bruyn died 25th January 1832 aged seventy eight years, five months and seventeen days.

Edmund Bruyn died 5th March 1847 after suffering for more than two years from an affection of the throat, which terminated in a cancer, aged sixty three years, eleven months, and one day.

Severyn Bruyn died October 27th 1856, aged 71 years seven months and two days. After a sickness of about a fortnight he calmly and quietly departed this life in the faith and hope of the gospel and in the full enjoyment of that peace of God which passeth all understanding.

JOHN BURTON.

Holy Bible in English; London, Robert Barker and John Bill, 1620.

It contains records of the Burton and Rigden families in England. The Bible descended collaterally to the late William Bedlow Beekman, Esq., and is now the property of Mrs. Beekman, New York City. It has the heraldic book-plate of William Bedlow on the front cover.

Edmun: Rigden was baptised The 7th day of August in the eight yeare of the Reigne of our soferint lord king Charles: 1632

The sun of Jon Burton was borne in [b]ushipborne The — 22 daye of may 1653 and battised The — 31 daye of may — 1653 — in bushipborne by the name of Richard Burton

The sun of John burton was borne one this 25 daye of aprell 1655 and battised one The 9 daye of maye by the name of John burton in bushipborne

Edmond Rigden was baptised the 6 august

John Burton the sun of Richard burton was Baptised the 19th of April 1620 in littelborne

Elisabeth Burton wos maried one the fortene daye of desember 1648 vnto steven Atkines at hotfelle dafter of Richard burton The Elder living at Bushipborne Then

thomas the sun of John burton was baptiesed the sixtenth daye of october 1659 in bushborne and borne the ninth of october

William burton sun of John Burton was borne one The seventene daye of January 1660 and Battised one the Therty and won daye of that same mont

John Burton was maried to Elisabeth denn the first daye of october 1674.

Thomas burton sun of John Burton 1658 beried

Abraham[?] burton sun of John burton beried 1661

August 2. 1692 John burton was maried to mary mos

Elisabeth wife of Richard Burton The Elder was beried one The tente daye of August in bushipborne Church 1661—in age The foure score and to yere ould

Elizabeth . . . daughter of Richard Rigden[?] was baptised in the church of Eastrie March the 16 1598 as appeareth in the Regester booke of Eustrie

[Tho]mas [Rigden?] was baptized the 29th of July 1581 in the [pa]rish of . . . hards and borne in Petham.

COLONEL GEORGE CARRINGTON.
(1711–1785.)

Holy Bible in English; London, John Baskett, 1718.

Col. Carrington was born in Barbadoes, West Indies, and emigrated to Virginia in 1723, where he married Anne Mayo in 1732. They lived at "Boston Hill," Cumberland County, Virginia. He occupied many positions of public trust and was a vestryman and warden in the Episcopal Church from early manhood until his death. The Bible is supposed to have come over from Barbadoes with Col. Carrington and contains records of his family and of that of his son, Mayo Carrington. It is now preserved in the Virginia State Library.

Hic Liber Pertinet ad Georgius Carington.

Paul Carrington the Son of George & Anne Carrington, born ye fifth day of March 1733. between 2 & 3 a Clock, tuesday morning

William Carrington the Son of George & Anne Carrington born the seventeenth day of November 1735 about one a clock Monday in the morning. Obit Sepr. 14 1739

George Carrington the Son of George & Anne Carrington w born the 15th of March 1737 in the night Obit 9th Nov. 1784 At. 47.

William Carrington the Son of George & Anne Carrington was born the 22d. day of December 1739 between 7 & 8 Saturday Night Died 20 April 1757 At. 18

Joseph Carrington the Son of George & Annie Carrington was born the Sixth day of February in the morning Saturday 1741. died April 4th 1802 aged 61 yrs.

Nathaniel Carrington Son of George & Ann was born the Twenty Eigth Day of February 1743, between 7 & 8 in the evening.

Henningham born 4 Decr. 1746 between 4 & 5 in ye morning on thursday. Intermarried with Jno. Bernard 1767.

Edward Carrington born the 11th of February 1748/9 about 11 oClock Saturday Night.

Hannah Carrington born the 28th March 1751 about 12 oClock Thursday. Married Nah⁸ Cabell 1772

Mayo Carrington born the first Day of April 1753 in the Night.

Mary Carrington born the 9th January 1759 in the Night intermarried with Jos. Watkins 1783.

[The above records are all apparently in the handwriting of George Carrington. Those that follow were written by his son, Mayo.]

George Carrington father of the foregoing persons departed this life on the 7th day Febr. 1785 aged 74 yr.

Ann Carrington mother of the same departed this life on the 15th day of the same month aged 78.

Mayo Carrington was Married to Ann daughter of Richard Adams Esqr. on Wednesday the 30th day of September 1784 7 oClock in the evening.

Their issue.

Eliza Griffin Carrington a daughter born on friday the 1st October 1790 at 3 oClock in the evening

George Mayo Carrington a son born on Thursday the 9th of April 1792 3 oClock in the morning.

Richard Adams Carrington a son born on Sunday the 29th of September 1793 at 5 oClock in the morning.

John Carrington a son born on Wednesday the fourth of January 1797 at four oClock in morning.

Charles Chauncey, President of Harvard College, 1654–1672

CHARLES CHAUNCEY.
(1747–1823.)

Holy Bible in English; London, Charles Eyre and William Strahan, 1772.

It contains the records of Charles Chauncey (the grandson of Charles Chauncey, 1592–1672, second President of Harvard College, 1654–1672) and of Abigail Darling, his wife. It is now the property of Mrs. Seth Low Pierrepont, New York City, the great-granddaughter of the original owner.

Charles Chauncey, son of Elihu and Mary Chauncey, was born the 30th day of May, A.D., 1747 O.S. 3 o'clock P.M.

Abigail Chauncey, daughter of Thomas and Abigail Darling was born 9th day of Novr A.D., 1746 O.S. Married 2d Feby A.D. 1775.

Charles Chauncey, the son of Charles & Abigail Chauncey was born the 17th day of August N.S. about 11 o'clock A.M. A.D. 1777,—Sabbath Day.

Elihu Chauncey, second son of Charles & Abigail Chauncey was born 15th day of Jany A.D. 1779, about half an hour after 4 o'clock P.M. Friday.

Sarah Chauncey, daughter of Charles & Abigail Chauncey was born the 2nd of Decemr A.D. 1780 about half an hour after 4 o'Clock P.M. Saturday.

Abigail Chauncey, second daughter of Charles & Abigail Chauncey was born the 29th day of June A.D. 1785 about seven o'clock A.M. Wednesday.

Nathaniel Chauncey, third son of Charles & Abigail Chauncey was born the 27th day of Feby A.D., 1789 at ¾ after 10 o'clock A.M.,—Friday.

Abigail Chauncey, daughter of Thomas and Abigail Darling and the wife of Charles Chauncey died the 24th day of December A.D. 1818, 20 Minutes after 9 o'clock A.M.

Abigail Chauncey, second daughter of Charles and Abigail Chauncey died the 14th day of June A.D. 1819 at 12 Minutes after eight o'clock P.M.

Charles Chauncey, son of Elihu and Mary Chauncey, died the 28th day of April A.D., 1823, at four o'clock A.M.

Elihu Chauncey, second son of Charles and Abigail Chauncey, died at Philadelphia on Thursday the eighth day of April, A.D. 1847 leaving two daughters, Henrietta Chauncey and Sarah C. Savage surviving him. His remains were removed to Burlington, N. J. on the 13th of April 1847.

Charles Chauncey, eldest son of Charles and Abigail Chauncey, died at Burlington, N. J., on Thursday the 30th of August 1847, leaving two daughters Elizabeth C. and Hannah Chauncey His remains were removed to Philadelphia, Tuesday the 4th of September 1847.

Sarah Chauncey Woolsey, eldest daughter of Charles and Abigail Chauncey, died at Philadelphia, on Friday the 8th of February 1856.

Nathaniel Chauncey, youngest son of Charles and Abigail Chauncey, died at Philadelphia on Thursday, February 9th, 1865.

JOHN CHURCH.
(Born 1748.)

Holy Bible in English; London, Christopher Barker, 1577.

The records cover the births of all the children of Richard and Elizabeth Church. John Church came to this country and married Angelica Schuyler, daughter of Philip Schuyler; the Bible descended to her great-great-grandson, Philip Schuyler Church of Geneva, New York, the present owner, who has deposited it for safe keeping in the Library of Hobart College, Geneva.

Mattilda ye Daughter of Rich^d & Eliz. Church was born at Lowestoft, on monday ye Ninth of Augst. 1736 at twelve o Clock at noon answered for by ye Revt. Wm. Tanner & wife & Mrs. Jane Barker Senr. of Lowest.

Sam: Church ye Son of ye Sd. Richd. & Eliz^a Church was born at Great yarmouth on Friday ye Seventeenth of Sept. 1737 at eleven o Clock in ye morning.

John: Church the Son of Rich^d & Eliz. Church was born on Wensday ye 28th of Mar. at 9 o clock in ye morning in ye year of our Lord 1739

Jane Church the Daughter of Rich^d and Eliz^a Church was born at Great yarmth on Saturday the 15th of March at half an hour after five o Clock in ye afternoon 1740 answered for by Mr. Frd. Porter of yarmt & and Mis. Eliza Paulsom & Mrs. Jenny Barker.

Elizabeth Church the daughter of Rich. & Eliz^a was born on Munday the 22^d of Novr. 1742: at 9 o Clock at night answered for by Mr. Sam: Barker and Mrs. Margt. Barker and Mrs. Sarah Barker, of Lowestoft.

Elizabeth Church the daughter of Rich^d and Eliz^a Church was born on Saturday the 12th of April 1746: at 2 o Clock in the Morning, and answerd for by Capt. Jno. Barker Mrs. Ann Kitteridge, and Mrs. Hannah Rymer.

Jno Barker Church the Son of ye Sd. Rich^d & Eliz^a Church was born on Sunday ye 30th Octr at 9 o Clock in ye morn, 1748, answerd for by Mr Jno Barker of London & Mr. Robt. Barker, Lowes^t & Mrs. Jane Barker Junr.

COLONEL AUGUSTINE CLAIBORNE.
(1721–1787.)

Holy Bible in English; Birmingham, John Baskerville, 1772.

> Contains the records of Col. Augustine Claiborne and his wife Mary Herbert, of "Windsor," Sussex County, Virginia. It belonged to his son Herbert and has descended to the present owner, Herbert Augustine Claiborne, who is fifth in descent from Col. Claiborne.

I William Burnet Browne (farther of Mary B Claiborne) was born at Salem in New England October 7th 1738 and departed this life May 6th 1784 at his Seat in King William Virginia he married Judith the Daughter of Charles Carter of Clive in Virginia—And left three daughters Viz^e Mary Burnet Elizabeth Carter & Judith Walker

Augustine Claiborne (farther of Herbert Claiborne) was born in King Wm County at Sweet Hall — He married Mary Herbert daughter of Butler Herbert of Puddledock Near Petersburg — And departed this life on the 3^d day of May 1787. At his Seat Windsor in Sussex County — And had by his Wife Mary, thirteen Children — Eight Sons, and five Daughters—Viz^e $\overset{1}{\text{Mary}}$ — $\overset{2}{\text{Herbert}}$ — $\overset{3}{\text{Augustine}}$ — $\overset{4}{\text{Ann}}$ — $\overset{5}{\text{Suckey}}$ — $\overset{6}{\text{William}}$ — $\overset{7}{\text{Butler}}$ — $\overset{8}{\text{Elizabeth}}$ — $\overset{6}{\text{Lucy Herbert}}$ — $\overset{10}{\text{John Herbert}}$ — $\overset{11}{\text{Thomas}}$ — $\overset{12}{\text{Richard}}$ Cook and $\overset{13}{\text{Bathurst}}$. Mrs Mary Claiborne Mother to Herbert Claiborne depart this life at Windsor on . . . day of

I Mrs Judith Browne (Mother to Mary B Claiborne) departed this Life at Elsing Green the 2^d day of December 1801

Betty C. B. Claiborne daughter of H. and Mary Claiborne, departed this life August 23, 1845. in the 46th year of her age

Milly Ann Watson [some words erased] Third daughter of Wm F. and M. A. Watson was born on the 21st day of November A.D. eighteen hundred and forty two. 1842 in the city of Richmond V^a and baptized by the Rev Wm Norwood of the Episcopal Church on the day of her mothers death, and the tenth from her birth.

L. B Claiborne Jan 10 1850

I give this Family Bible to my nephew Howard Claiborne M. C. B. Bramhorn June 18th /59

Herbert Claiborne Eldest Son of (Augustine & Mary Claiborne of Windsor) was born on Monday the 7th of April 1746

Mary Burnett Browne (Eldest Daughter of William Burnett & Judith Browne of Elsing Green) was born the 7th of August 1765

The above Herbert & Mary Burnet was Married the 17th Feby 1781 — By the Revd Henry Shyring

1 William Burnet Browne the first Son of Herbert & Mary Burnett was born the 19th day of December 1782 — at Elsing Green. 12 Oclock at Night Baptised at Chestnut Grove by Henry Shyring.

2 Herbert Augustine Claiborne the Second Son of Herbert & Mary Burnet was born the 5 day of March 1784 — at Chestnut Grove — 10 Oclock in the Morning Baptised by Mr Shyring.

3 Mary Carter Burnet the first Daughter of Herbert & Mary was born the 20th day of August 1786 — at 3 Oclock in the morning. Newkent Court House — Baptised by the Revd James Sample. Obit. August 2″. 1864

4 William third Son of Herbert & Mary was born the 31st day of March 1787 at half after 4 Oclock in Morning at Newkent Court House — Baptised by the Revd James Sample.

5 Judith Browne Claiborne Second daughter of Herbert & Mary was born the 7th of March 1789 at half after 3 Oclock in the Morning at Newkent Court House — Baptisd at St Peters Church in Newkent by the Revd Benjamin Blackgrove

6 Lavinia Herbert the third daughter of Herbert & Mary was born the 23d of August 1790 — at 2 Oclock in the morning. at Wm Armsteads in Newkent Baptised by the Revd Price Davis. She departed this life on the 30th day of March 1792. and buried at Elsing Green near her Grand father

7 Harriot Herbert the fourth Daughter of Herbert & Mary was born the 16th of January 1793 at Eight Oclock in the Morning at

Elsing Green Baptised by the Revd Mr Price — God fathers the Revd Mr Price & Wm Burnet Browne — God Mothers Mrs J. Browne & Polly Nuffin Claiborne

8 Lavinia Bathurs fifth daughter of Herbert & Mary was born the 19th of January 1795 at 10 Oclock in the Morning at Elsing Green Baptis'd by the Revd Mr Price God fathers Capt William Reding of Salem N. England — and Wm Burnet Browne God Mother Mrs Browne.

9 Betty Carter Bafsett Sixth Daughter of Herbert & Mary was born the 10th of January 1799 at 7 Oclock in the Morning at Elsing Green Baptisd by Revd James Price. God-fathers John Bafsett, Wm Thomson, Capt King. God Mothers — Betsy Bafsett & Mrs Browne — and Mary Carter Burnet.

10 Augusta Brown the Seventh Daughter of Herbert & Mary was born the 23^d day of June 1800 — at two Oclock in the Morning at Elsing Green Baptisd by the Revd James Price. God Fathers Herbert Augustine Claiborne — Wm Claiborne and Wm Bafsett. God Mothers Mary Carter Burnet Claiborne Judey B Claiborne & Virginia Bafsett

11 Octavia the Eaigth Daughter of Herbert & Mary was born the 12th day of Feby 1802 at three Oclock in the Morning at E Green Baptisd by James Price. She departed this Life, July 23^d 1802 and buried at E Green by her Sister

Mary B Claiborne the Mother of the above Children Departed this life at E Green on Wednesday the 16th day of January 1805. Age 39 y

Herbert Claiborne (her husband) son of Coln Augustine — died August 1814 at the Cottage, King William County.

Herbert Claiborne Thomson, Eldest son of William and Mary H. Thomson was born July 16. 1794

FEMMITJE CLARK.
(Baptized 1681, died 1760.)

Holy Bible in English; London, Thomas Baskett and Robert Baskett, 1743.

Femmitje Clark was the wife of Alexander Clark who, from 1725 to 1760, lived on the south side of Wall Street about where the present entrance to the New York Stock Exchange is located. She was a daughter of Harmanus Van Borsum and Wybrecht Hendricks, and was baptized in the Reformed Dutch Church in Brooklyn March 20, 1681, and died September 15, 1760. The Bible has descended in direct line and is now the property of her great-great-great-great-grandson, Henry Schieffelin Clark of New York City.

Famitie Clark Her Book 1750/51.
A New Years gift for my son John Clark.

BIRTHS.

John Clark Born September 15, 1749 Died January 5th 1807

Thomas Clark Born March 14 1752 Died March 3rd 1811

My mother Fete. Clark Dyed November 15, 1760.

Scot Lawrence Clark Born September the Sixt 1753 a Quarter Befoar one in the afternoon. Died about the year 1797

Alexander Clark Born December 6, 1754 Between Ten and Eleaven at night.

December 7, 1756 David Clark Born December 7, 1756 Between three and fore (1) In the morning.

Alexander Clarke married Famitie van Borsum Jany. 13th 1714. Famitie Clark died November 15. 1760 and was buried from her House opposite the Presbyterian Church in Wall Street. into the burying Ground of the old Dutch Church in Garden Street agreeable to her request.

John Clark the Son of Famitie Died 1791/2 and was buried from the House in Wall Street left him by his mother and interred in the Family Vault of Trinity Church aged 60.

John Clark Junr. Born Sept. 15. 1749. died January 5th 1807

Thomas Clark Born March 14, 1752, died March 3, 1811

Scot Lawrence Clark, Born Sept 6, 1753, died 1797

Alexander Clark. Born Decr. 6, 1754

David Clark Born Decr. 7, 1756 died young.

Finis.

Monday 1765 January 29 Day the Popel Went over the North River the Hole Day Until Sunday being in all Seven Days,

1771 feby 9 The Wind Got Round at Nord West and Thair Continued almost 14 Days and before being Verry Modret Weather as Ever Was Known Ise Bing Verry full in North River Almost full.

This Bible being the Property of my Great Grand Mother whose name was Famitie or Euphemia, was presented by her to my Grand Father Anno. Dom. 1750. Upon the Death of my Grand Father 1792 it came into the possession of my Father, and upon the death of my mother in the year of our Lord 1810 into my Possession, being the eldest. John Clark, and I bequeath the same to Eldest son William Newton Clark. I bequeath the same to my eldest son William N. Clark Junr. Wm. N. Clark. Aug. 15th 1866. I bequeath it to my Son Henry Schieffelin Clark — Wm. N. Clark 2nd.

WILLIAM COATS.
(1741–1802.)

Holy Bible in English. Dublin, 1754.

It contains records of the Coats and Butler families of Philadelphia and is now owned by Mrs. Alice Lyman, who has deposited it for safe keeping in the Pennsylvania Historical Society. The records have been verified by Ernest Spofford, Esq., Librarian of the Historical Society of Pennsylvania.

Philadelphia

William Coats was born the thirteenth Day of May at one OClock in the Afternoon in the year of our Lord 1741. Departed this life 28 Ap^l 1802 at a quarter past six A.M.

Margaret Norris was born the twenty-third Day of February (being Thursday) in the year of our Lord 1743 and was married to William Coats on Saturday the 10th day of January 1761. Departed this life th15 of January 1828 at 12 OClock at night.

Joseph Coats the Son of William and Margaret Coats was born on the 21st Day of February being Sunday at forty-five Minutes after one OClock in the Morning in the year of our Lord 1762.

Elizabeth Coats the Daughter of William and Margaret Coats was born the 6th Day of February being Monday at four OClock in the Morning in the year of our Lord 1764. Departed this life Feby the 5th 1824.

William Pitt Coats the Son of William and Margaret Coats was born the 24th Day of March being on Monday at three OClock in the afternoon in the year of our Lord 1766.

Margaret Coats the Daughter of William and Margaret Coats was born in New Jersey the 23^d day of September being on Friday at fifty-nine minutes after nine oClock at night in the year of our Lord 1768.

Margaret Coats the Daughter of William and Margaret Coats departed this Life on the 3^d Day of December 1769 on Sunday

Morning at half past four o'Clock aged Eleven Months and two weeks.—

Mary Coats the Daughter of William and Margaret Coats was born in Philadelphia on Saturday the 29th August at twenty Minutes after four o'Clock in the Afternoon in the Year of our Lord 1772 and Departed this Life aged one Month.

Joseph Coats departed this Life June 13. 1774 on Monday a little after twelve oClock aged twelve Years three months and twenty-three days.

William Pitt Coats departed this Life June 28. 1774 on Tuesday about Seven oClock in the Evening aged eight Years three Months and four days.

Margaret Coats (the second) Daughter of William and Margaret Coats was born August the 11th friday at ten Minutes after ten OClock at night in the Year of our Lord 1775 and departed this Life aged three Weeks.

Sarah Coats Daughter of William and Margaret Coats was born the 15 decem^r on Sunday at fifteen Minutes after two OClock in the afternoon in the Year of our Lord 1776: Died 5 P.M. January 27. 1854.

Harriet Coats Daughter of William and Margaret Coats was born on friday the 5th day of March at fifty Minutes after Eleven oClock in the Morning in the year of our Lord 1779.

Elizabeth Coats Daughter of William & Margaret Coats was married to Anthony Butler on the 20th Day of April in the year of our Lord 1780.

Harriet Coats Daughter of William & Margaret Coats died on Saturday the 27 January 1781—Aged one year ten months & 22 Days.—

William Coats Butler was born the first day of february (on thursday at half after twelve oClock in the Morning) in the year of our Lord 1781 he being the Son of Anthony & Elizabeth Butler. And departed this life October 1st 1827

William Louis Coats Son of William & Margaret Coats was born on Sunday the 3rd March at three o'Clock in the Afternoon in the Year of our Lord 1782.

William Louis Coats son of William & Margaret Coats Departed this Life in September 1783 about six months old.

Margaret Butler Daughter of Anthony & Elizabeth Butler was born 28th of September 1782.

Thomas Coats son of William & Margaret Coats was Born on thursday at Eleven oClock in the morning the fourteenth Day of August in the year of Our Lord 1783.

Penelope Butler Daughter of Anthony and Elizabeth Butler was born on the 3d of March anno Domini 1785. Departed this life July 25th 1823

James Butler Son of Anthony & Elizabeth Butler was born on Sunday the 26 of August 1787 Departed this life June 28th AE. 15—1802

Harriet Butler daughter of Anthony and Elizabeth Butler was born on the 13th of October anno Domini 1789 in the afternoon.

John Mifflin Butler Son of Anthony & Elizabeth Butler was born on the first day of February A.D. 1792 between one & two oClock in the morning.

Thomas Willson Butler son of Anthony and Elizabeth Butler was Born on the Thirteenth Day of March 1793 about Twelve OClock at Noon.

Elizabeth Butler Daughter of Anthony and Elizabeth Butler was born on the 14th of April anno Domini 1797 at one OClock in the afternoon Departed this life August th 1825

Jonathan Williams Butler was born on Sunday the 22d day of march A.D. 1801 at half after 11 o'Clock at night.

Sarah Coats daughter of William and Margaret Coats was married to Samson Levy on the 5th day Sept. 1793.

Margaret Maria Levy duaughter of Samson and Sarah C. Levy. Born the first Day of August Ano—domini 1794 at twenty minutes past six oClock in the morning.

Richard W. Meade departed this life June th 25th at 5 at noon [*sic*] in 1828—

Samson Levy Departed this life—Decemer th15= 1831—at 5 O'clock at noon— [*sic*]

John Smith, Son of Elinor Smith was born on the 8th of May in the year of our Lord 1777—in the Morning at the House of Coll. William Coats—in the Northern liberties.

This Bible bequeathed by Sarah Coats Levy to Elizabeth Mary, wife of Alfred Ingraham, third Daughter of Richard W, and Margaret Coats Meade, and great Grand daughter of William & Margaret Coats.—

John Smith son of Elinor Smith born in the House of William Coats in [badly discolored and rubbed] Northern Liberties May the 8th 1777.

William Coats Departed this life 28th April 1802

Elizabeth Butler Departed this life February 5th 1824.

Margaret Coats Departed this life January 15th 1828

WILLIAM CORWIN.
(1764–1800.)

Holy Bible in English; New York, Hodge and Campbell, 1792.

This Bible contains the records of William Corwin and Leah Johnson, his wife, of Southold, Long Island, and their descendants, the Wrights and Ostranders. It now belongs to Miss Mary Ostrander of New York City, great-great-granddaughter of the original owner.

My father James Corwin was Born on longisland, southhold 1741 and departed this life November Ninth one Thousand Seven hundred and Ninty one, aged fifty years two months & Seventeen days and was Buried at goshen Near the Wallikill.

My mother, Mahetable Corwin, Daughter of William Horton was born at Southhold, longisland, September the 29th, 1743.

William Corwin was Born at Southhold, longisland, March the 19th 1764 in the year of our Lord one thousand Seven Hundred & Sixty-fore.

Leah Corwin daughter of Harman johnson was Born in New jersey Near midletown on the 11th day of may in the year of our Lord 1767.

Elizabeth Corwin was Born in New York the 28th of December 1794 on a Sunday morning between ten & eleven o'Clock.

Sarah Ann Corwin was Born in New York May the 11th, 1790 on a wednesday evening between ten & eleven o'clock.

my mother, phebe Johnson was Borne in the year of our Lord one thousen Seven hundred and fifty (1750) on the 22nd day of febuary.

My Brother, William Johnson was Borne in the year of our Lord one Thousen Seven hundred Sixty-five. 1765

My sister, Sarah Johnson was Born in october the 27 on Sunday in the morning in the year 1771.

My brother, Harman Johnson was Born in May the 25 on wensday in the moring in the year 1775.

My brother, William Johnson, Born in may the 2 tusday in the morning in the year 1780.

My sister, Phebe Johnson was Born in August 8th on Fryday in the after noon in the year 1783.

My brother Gershem Johnson Born in the year 1786 on monday att 9 a'clook in the morning the 19 day of June.

My sister Elizebeth Johnson Born in Februry the 14

My sister Hannah Johnson was born August 3rd 1793 on Friday.

John Wright, Junr., Was Born December 3rd, 1790.

Elizabeth Corwin was Born December 28th 1794.

John Wright, Junr., was married to Elizabeth Corwin on Monday evening July 13th 1812.

Sarah Ann Wright was Born 17th of January 1814 on Monday morning at 8 O'clock.

John Wright was Born 12th December 1815 on Tuesday Night at ½ past eleven O'Clock.

[A scrap of paper found in the William Corwin Bible.]

Elizabeth Wright Died on Monday Evening October 25th 1819 aged 24 years, 9 months and 28 days. Was buried in Wall Street Church vault—27.

John Wright dies on Monday morning January 19th 1817 aged 2 Years, 1 month and 5 days. Was buried in Wall Street Church Vault No. 15.

My mother, Phebe Johnson Departed this Life Sept the 4th, 1806 aged 56 years, 6 months & 13 days.

My father Harman Johnson Departed this life october 4th 1815 aged Seventy one years.

My Husband, William Corwin Departed this life February the 25th 1800 aged 35 years 11 months and Six days.

My daughter, Elizabeth Wright Departed this life monday evening, october 25th, 1819. Aged 24 years, 9 months and 28 days.

Sarah Ann Wright born 17th of January 1814 married Ferdinand William Ostrander October 1st 1833.

My grand Son John Wright Departed this Life on monday morning, January 19th 1817 aged 2 years 1 month and 5 days.

My brother, Harman Johnson Departed this Life on Sunday night Septer 18th, 1834.

Sarah A Ostrander Born Jan. 17th 1814 Died Feb. 24th 1890 about 7 A. M.

WILLIAM COVENTRY.
(1715–1774.)

Holy Bible in English; Oxford, Baskett, 1736.

On the title-page of the Prayer Book which is bound with the Bible is written, "This Book to Rosamond B. Miller is given from Elizabeth Coventry as her God Child." The records cover the Coventry, Miller, Floyd, and Van Horne families and other descendants; and the book has descended in the direct line to Mrs. Augusta Floyd Bowen of New York, a great-great-great-great-granddaughter of William Coventry.

William Coventry, born April 10 1715 on Sunday about 12 o'clock at Noon.

Elizabeth Hart, born January 29 1721/2 on Munday about 5 o'clock In the morning.

William Coventry & Eliz^a Hart were Married 0 August 28th, 1739 on Tuesday about 8 o'clock in ye Even..g.

Sarah Coventry born Septemb^r 7th 1740 about 1,o'clock in the Afternoon & baptized ye 11th of the Same Month.

Mary Coventry born July 15 1743 about 3 o'clock In the Morning & Baptized ye 7 Septemb^r follow...g

Elizabeth Coventry born — 1749 abt 6 o'clock in the Morning & Baptized ye 26 Octo^r follow..g.

Ann Coventry born April 1751 2 o'clock. in the morng. & Baptized ye 2^d May Follow..g. The foregoing was according to Old Stile.

New Stile Willi^m Coventry jnr born Jany. 14th 1754 about 12 o'clock at noon & baptiz^d ye 27 Inst. and departed this Life the 8th Septr Following abt one o'clock in the morn...g.

William Coventry Junr. was Born June 19th 1756. On Saturday about Two o'clock in the Afternoon and Baptized the 7th July following.

John Coventry Born May 7th 1758 on Sunday morning abt four o'clock in the Mng & Baptized the 19 of Same Month.

Sarah Coventry & Christopher Miller was married May 3d 1760

Mary Coventry & James Calder was married April 7" 1763

Willm Coventry Junr departed this Life August 24th 1763 abt 11 o'clock at Night aged 7 years 2 m. & 5 days.

Elizabeth Miller was born November ye 5^h 17..., on Thursday Morning about one o'clock and Baptized Satturday ye 7th Novemr and Departed this Life at 9 o'clock in the Evening.

William Coventry Calder was Born December ye 25th 1763 on Fryday morning at 3 o'clock and Baptized Jan'y ye 20^h 1764 by the Rev. Saml. Achmuty.

Sarah Coventry Miller was born Septemr 3d 1764 about 5 o'clock in the Afternoon; And Baptized the 19^h Inst by the Revd Jno Ogilvie.

Sarah Elizabeth Maria Calder was Born March 21^s 1766 about 11 o'clock in the Morning and Baptized the next Day by the Rev. Wm. Barrol — Maryland. James Calder departed this Life November 21^s 1766. About 1 o'clock in the afternoon, Aged 36 years — Maryland

Sarah Eliza Maria Calder departed this Life May the 10^h 17-7.

Elizabeth Hart Miller was born 13^h Feby 1773 baptized by the Revd John Ogilvie.

Elizabeth Hart Miller departed this life the 8th September 1775 at New York and was buried at Trinity Church behind the Governor's pew under the flat stones.

John and Ann Blackburn Miller, Twins were born the eighth Day of March 1776 at New Brunswick and baptized the 7^h April following by Rev^d Mr. Beach of said place.

Mary Calder & Floyd Daubery was married Jan 24^h 1769 by the Rev^d Mr. Ogilvie.

William Coventry Departed this life April 25^h 1774 (Aged 59 Years) at St. Christophers.

Ann Coventry & Richard Grant was married November 19ʰ 1777 by Revᵈ Benjamin Moore.

Rosamond Bend Miller was born 1ˢᵗ February 17— and was Baptized the 12ʰ March by the Revᵈ Mr. Moore of New York Mr. Grove Bend, Mrs. Daubery and Miss Elizabeth Coventry Sponsors.

Ann Blackburn Miller departed this life on Thursday the 10ʰ April 1783 at half after three in the Afternoon Aged seven years one month and two days, was put in Mr. Willets Vault on the 12ʰ.

Mrs. Sarah Miller Wife of Christopher Miller Departed this Life on Tuesday the 9ʰ of September 1783. at six in the evening of a consumtion and was buried behind the Governors pew Trinity Church aged Forty three years. (Within nine days) her daughter Ann B. Miller being first removed from Mr. Willets Vault to the same grave—near this spot is buried Elizabeth Miller; Christopher Billop Miller, Elizabeth Hart Miller children of the above lady

Sarah Coventry Miller and David van Horn was married 23 February 1788 by Revᵈ A. Beach.

Christopher Miller Departed this Life on Tuesday morning at 5 o'clock the 17th August 1802. Aged 66 years.

Richard Grant was born at Jamaica West Indies 29ʰ March 1782.

Nathaniel Philip Grant was born at New York 18ʰ November 1784 baptized by Revᵈ Mr. Moore.

Susannah Coventry was born 22ʰ September 1761 baptized by Revᵈ Mr. Ogilvie.

Mrs. Elizabeth Coventry Departed this Life on Monday the 22ᵈ of August 1803 Aged 84 years.

Dr. John Coventry Departed the Life on Wednesday the 17ʰ of June 1812 the year aged 55 years & a few days.

Mrs. Mary Daubery Departed Life on Wednesday the 6" of October Aged 70 years in the year 1813.

On Wednesday the 23ᵈ December last 1817. Departed this Life Miss Elizabeth Coventry aged 68 years.

Departed this Life the 1st of January last 1818 Miss Charlotte Coventry Daubery aged 42.

David V. Horn Departed this Life May 12" 1801. at nine in the Morning aged forty five years & nine Months.

Married on Friday evening by the Rev. Dr. Hone, Dr. Samuel Floyd to Miss Augusta Van Horne, April 26" 1817.

David Van Horne Floyd was born 1st May 1818 & Baptized September 2, by the Rev. Dr. Brownell, Miss Rosamond B. Miller & his Father, Sponsors.

Benjamin Floyd was Born October the 24" 1819. Baptized April the 13" 1820 by the Rev. Mr De Lancey. Sponsors, the Parents.

Rosamund Miller Floyd was born the 1st of September 1821 and Baptized on the 13" of February 1822 by the Right Rev. Bishop Hobart. Rosamund B. Miller & Parents Sponsors.

Died at the Island of St. Thomas on the 3^d of August in 1827 John Henry Waddell in the —— year of his Age.

Francis Lucas Waddell Born 17 March 1808.

Christopher Bilop Miller was Born the 3rd of August 1768. Departed this Life 29" June 1769.

Floyd Daubery was born on the 23" of November 174– was married to Mary Calder 24" of Jan. 1770

Floyd Saxbury Daubery was born ye 12" August 1771 Baptized ye 21" of ye same Instant.

Elizabeth Ann Daubery was Born the 2" May 1774 was Baptized the 10" Day and Departed this Life 22" of the same Month.

Charlotte Coventry Daubery Born 25" November 177– about 11 o'clock in the Morning and Baptized the 15" of December by the Rev Mr. Beach N. Brunswick.

Eliza Martin Daubery was Born 25" October 1779 about 12 of clock at Night and Baptized the 10" Novem^{br} by Mr. Inglis Rector.

Eliza Martin Daubery was Married the 8" November 1800 to Mr. Henry Waddell by the Rev. Doct. Banj'm Moore

Wm. Coventry Waddell born May 28" 1802

John Henry Waddell born June 17" 1804.

Floyd Saxbury Waddell born 12" June 1812.

Capt. Henry Waddell departed this Life July 13^h 1819 aged 52 —

Died on the 20" June 1822 Mrs. Julia Waddell the wife of William Coventry Henry Waddell.

Died on the 5" of June 1843 Sarah C. Ludlow aged 79 years and nine months.

Died on the 19" of December 1844 Blackburn Miller aged 68 years 9 months.

Married on the 8" of October 1839 David Van Horne Floyd to Elizabeth Furgeson daughter of Henry Kermit of this City.

Died on Saturday the 3^d Inst. March 1849, Henry Kermit only son of David Van Horn and Elizabeth Furguson Floyd aged 8 years and 8 months, 1849.

Died on the 11" of Jan 1852 William Ellison Miller aged 45 years. And on the 3^d of October 1842 Margaret Miller wife of Blackburn Miller aged 58 years.

Married March 1849 on Wednesday the 21st by the Revd. Wm. Berrian William Ellison Miller, M. D. to Josephine daughter of Robert Hyslep Esqr.

Henry Kermit Floyd was born 29" June 1840 and was baptized by the Rev. Edward Higbie.

Sarah Augusta Floyd was born 28" of July 1843

the two latter were the only offspring of David Van Horne and Elizabeth Furgeson Floyd.

Sarah Augusta Floyd was married to George Thomas Vingut of Cuba on the 27" Feby 1867 by Archbishop McClosky.

George Floyd Vingut was born the 10th of March 1868 and baptized the 14 of January 1869 by Archbishop McCluskey in his chapel sponsor Mr. & Mrs. T. Vingut, Madison Ave & 50th St. N. Y. C.

Harry Kermit Vingut was born the 12th of March 1871.

Maria Augusta Floyd Vingut was born the 13 of November 1873 and baptized in the N. Y. Cathedral by Father James Kelly ass't rector on Dec. 6th 1889 sponsor Miss Z. Bouvier.

Mary Elizabeth Kermit Vingut born the 29th of May 1877 and baptized in St. Patrick's Cathedral by Father James W. Kelly ass't rector on Dec. 31st 1889 sponsor her sister Maria A. F. Vingut

Benjamin Van Horne Vingut was born the 23 of December 1879 and baptized in the St. Patricks Cathedral by Father James Kelly ass't rector on Dec 31st 1889 sponsor Mary A. F. Vingut

The five latter were the only offspring of George Thomas Vingut and Sarah A. Vingut.

Elizabeth Kermit Vingut married Baron Charles d'Este of France Capt. in the French army.

Rosamund Miller Floyd died the 11th of November 1875 in the 54" year of her age.

David van Horne Floyd died 1878 was put in the Miller's Vault in the Marble Cemetary 2nd St. N. Y. City.

Frances Yzguierdo de Vingut departed of her Life on the 20th of August 1885. at 6. p.m. and was buried in the family plot at Greenwood.

Elizabeth Ferguson Floyd departed of this Life on the 11" of November 1885 & was buried in Staten Island.

Sarah Augusta Vingut departed of this life on the 20" of August 1887. and was buried in the family plot at Setauket L. I.

Frances de la Cruz Yzguierdo departed of this life on the 14" Nov. 1889 and was buried in the Vinguts Plot, Greenwood Cemetary.

Benjamin Floyd departed of this life on the 4" of March 1890 and was put in the Millers Vault Marble Cemetary 2" St. N. Y. City.

Augusta Floyd Vingut eldest daughter of George T. Vingut and Sarah A. was married the 26" February 1895 in the residence of her father 46 West 34" Street to Herbert Wolcott Bowen, Consul General at Barcelona Spain.

Thomas Van Horne Floyd Bowen son of Herbert W. Bowen & Augusta Floyd Bowen. born Dec. 6th 1895. at the Manor House Sutton Montis. England.

Thomas Vingut father of George T. Vingut was born in Cuba in the year 1815, Dec. 9" 1815.

George T. Vingut was born the 23d April in the year 1838 in Havana, Cuba.

ISAAC COVERT.
(Born, 1780; married, 1806.)

Holy Bible in English; New York, 1813.

Contains the records of Isaac Covert and Lorette, his wife, and has descended in the direct line to their great-granddaughter, Mrs. W. R. Caminoni of Oyster Bay, New York, the present owner.

MARRIAGES

Isaac & Lorette Covert was married November 6th 1806 . . .

Geo. W Townsend and Elizabeth Covert were Married Jany 10th 1832

Jacob F. Covert and Frances Townsend were married 10th Jany 1832

Butler Coles & Mary Townsend were married Oct 21st 1857

Beekman H. Townsend & Adèle Seaman were married September 22nd 1868

Loretta Coles daughter of Butler & Mary T. Coles, & William R. Caminoni were married Nov. 29th 1890.

BIRTHS

Isaac Covert was Born January 18th 1780

Lorette Covert was Born November 26th 1787

Jacob F. Covert the Son of Isaac & Lorette Covert was Born Sept. 13th 1807 . . .

Elizabeth Covert the Daughter of Isaac & Lorette Covert was Born July 12th 1812

Geo. W. Townsend son of Wm and Margaret Townsend was Born Sept. 27th 1806

Frances Townsend daughter of William & Margarett Townsend was born May 7th 1811—

Mary H. Townsend, daughter of George & Elizabeth Townsend was born 5th Dec 1832

George C. Townsend son of George & Elizabeth Townsend was Born April 13th 1834

Beekman H. Townsend was born 9th June 1836

Frances Gertrude Covert daughter of Jacob F & Frances T Covert born 19th October 1833

William F Covert son of the above named was born 15th June 1835

Elizabeth A. Coles daughter of Butler and Mary E. Coles was born June 21st 1859.

Butler Coles son of Mary & Butler Coles was born Aug. 16th 1861

George T. Coles son of Butler & Mary Coles was born Feb. 11th 1863.

Loretta Coles daughter of Butler & Mary Coles was born April 17th 1866.

Adolphus Covert was born 20th of November 1750

Hannah Covert was born 2nd of July 1744

Micah Covert was born 5th of June 1775

Isaac Covert was born January 18th 1780

Jacob Covert was born 21st of May 1782

Frost Covert was born 28th March 1785

Caleb Covert was born 9th February 1788

Ada S. Townsend daughter of Beekman H. and Adèle Townsend was born July 26th 1869.

Elizabeth Covert daughter of Beekman H. & Adèle Townsend was born Oct. 9th 1873.

Deaths

Adolphus Covert Died 24th January 1802 aged 51 years 2 months and 4 days.

Hannah Covert Died 20th of March 1827 Aged 83 years 8 months & 18 days.

Frances Gertrude Covert daughter of Jacob F. & Frances F Covert died Jany 5th 1834 aged 1 yr 2 mo 17 dys

Isaac Covert son of Adolphus Covert died 12th July 1839 aged 59 years 5 months & 24 days.

Elizabeth C. daughter of Isaac & Loretta Covert and wife of George W. Townsend died in New Haven 28th Sept. 1848 Aged 34 Years

Elizabeth Aurelia daughter of Butler & Mary Coles died Aug. 27th 1860 Aged 1 year 2 mos & 6 days.

Jacob F Covert died Feb 27th 1861. Aged 53 Years & 6 months

Butler Coles Son of Butler & Mary E. Coles died october 16th 1862 aged 1 year and 2 months.

George C. Townsend died October 10th 1863 Aged 29 years 5 mos. & 27 days.

George W. Townsend died September 1880 Aged 74 years.

Loretta Covert wife of Isaac Covert died Dec 10th 1880, aged 94 years, & 16 days

Butler Coles Died Oct 24th 1888 Aged 57 years 6 months & 14 days.

HENRY CRUGER.
(Born, 1707.)

Holy Bible in English; title-page lacking but with Book of Common Prayer, 1715, bound in.

Contains the records of Henry Cruger, son of John Cruger, Mayor of New York, and father of the Henry Cruger who was Member of Parliament for Bristol, England, and prominent in the repeal of the Stamp Act. It has descended in direct line to Walton Oakley, Esq., of New York, great-great-grandson of the original owner.

Henry Cruger Born at NYork Novemb^r 25 1707 Old Stile

Elizabeth Cruger his wife Born at Jamaica June 7th in year of our Lord 17

Hen. Cruger Marry'd to Eliz^h Harris his above wife at Legnaum [?] Jamaica by Doc^r Wm Johnston, Decr 21st 1736

Saye Harris Mother to ye Above Elizabeth wife of Hen Cruger Died at Jamaica in ye 32. Year of his Age. Feb^{ry} 2^d 1713

Mary Harris Daughter to ye Above Saye Harris Died Sepr 22 1713 Being 15 Months Old

Thomas Harris only Son to ye Above Saye Harris Died at Jamaica in ye 20th Year of his Age. Decem^r 7th 1736

Doct^r Nicholas Harris. Husband too Above Saye & father to Above Mentioned Mary. Thomas and Elizabeth. Died at Jamaica in the 57 year of his Age Decem^r 18th 1736 and was Buried with his above Deceased Wife & Children in the family Vault at Half Waytree in St Andrews Parish.

Mem^o I Saild from Port Royal Jamaica with my family in the Ship Mary Capt Robt Ratsey April 23rd 1738. and Arrived at NewYork . . . May . . 31. 1738

Mem^o Jan^{ay} 22^d 1748/9 Sunday Evening My Daughter in Law Han^h Montgom [some words illegible] Married to John Van Horn, by the Reverend Mr Hen Barclay My Above Daughter in

Henry Cruger, Sr., born 1707

Law was born in Jamaica at her [some words illegible] Kingston, November y⁰ 8ʰ 1731 as appears by a memorandum of her [some letters illegible] Patrick Montgomery writting in a Comon pray'r book.

Memorandᵐ November 17ʰ 1755 at 4 in the Morning felt a Seveir Earth Quake which Continued (by a General Computation) About 3 Minutes

Novemʳ 22 1755. at 9. in the Evening felt a Small Shock of an Earth Quake Continuing about half a minute

16ʰ 1730/31. Saild over y⁰ barr of S. Carolina in Brig Samuel Capt. Peter

Capt. Peter Morgatt & Arrived at NYork y⁰ 26. March 1731.

1731. Saild from NYork in Sloop Mary Capᵗ Jacoby Kip for Jamaica to Settle in the Island.

[Some words torn off] John Cruger Junʳ

My Son Geleman. Born at NYork Novemᵇʳ 4ᵗʰ 1740. being Tuesday Morning at 9. oClock and Baptized Novᵇʳ 25ᵗʰ 1740. by Dʳ Charleton Robt. Walton Junʳ John Cruger Junʳ God fathers. Sarah Cruger God Mother

My Daughter Mary. Born at NYork Febʳʸ 27ᵗʰ 1742/3. Sunday Morning Half an hour past twelve. and Baptized y⁰ 15ᵗʰ March 1742/3 by the Reverend Mʳ Richard Charleton. Henry Needham Esqʳ God father Anna Chambers Mary Cruger God Mothers

My Son Nicholas. Born at NYork Thursday Morning Half an Hour past four o Clock Being March 15ᵗʰ 1743/4 Baptized the 6ᵗʰ of April 1744. by the Reverend Mr. Rᵈ Charleton John McEvers John Cruger Senʳ God fathers, Rachiel Cruger. God Mother

My Daughter Elizabeth Born at NYork Sunday Morning Eight o Cloc 1747. Baptized May 28ʰ 1747. By the Reverend Mʳ Rᵈ Charl Oliver Delancy Godfather Gertrude Schuyler Hannah Montgomery God Mothers

My Daughter Mary, Married to Jacob Walton March 11th 1760 By The Revd Mr Hen. Barclay.

My Wife Elizabeth Cruger. Died the 14. April at 9 o Clock in the Morning and was Buried in trinity Church ye 15. April 1760.

My Daughter in Law Hannah Van Horne departed this Life Augt 15^h 1760 at 11 in the forenoon & was Buried ye 17^h Augt in trinity Church Near her Mother.

My Son John Harry Cruger. Marr'd to Ann DeLancy. Daughter of Oliver De Lancy at Greenwich By the Reverend Mr Hen Barclay Decr 1762.

ABRAHAM DELAMETER.[1]
(1706–1776.)

Holy Bible in Dutch; Dordrecht, Hendrick en Jacob Keur, 1690.

Contains records of Abraham Delameter and his wife Ragel Low with their descendants. Also the births of some slaves. It is now the property of the American Bible Society and is deposited for safe keeping in the New York Public Library. The records are in Dutch and have been translated by Dr. L. Bendikson.

1776 July 13 is vader Abraham Delameter gesturve up Horly omtrent middag op een Sater[dag]

1811 July 18 is Johanes DeLameter gesturven op een Donderdagh en is begraven op een Frydagh

1730 May 3 Ben ick Abraham De Lametter met myn vrouw Ragel Low getrout en ick ben gebore in jaer 1706 Juny 26 en myn vrouw is gebore in jaer 1710 October 2.

1731 October 26 is gebore myn ouste dochter en is genamt Elsje na myn moider.

1733 October 21 is myn twed dochter gebore en is genamt Jannety na myn vrou's moider en is gedoept door Peterus Vas.

1734 November 20 is myn vader Abraham De Lametter gestorve en is begrave 22.

1735 November 16 is myn soon Abraham gebore omtrent acht ure in de avont en gedopt door Dom. Manseus de 23 November.

1736/7 Februwarie 3 tuse 7 en 8 ure is myn moider Elsje DeLametter gestorve en is begrave de 6.

1736/7 Februwari 16 is myn Abraham gestorve omtrent mydernaght de 19 begrave.

1737 Desember 5 is myn dochter Ragel gebore omtrent te 7 ure in de avont en is gedopt door Domenie Manseus.

[1 The Dutch character ÿ is not cut for fonts of English type. Therefore the letter y has been used in the Dutch records where ÿ is meant.]

1737 Desember 13 is myn dochter Ragel gestorve te 3 ure in de morge en is begrave 15.

1738/9 Februwarie 18 is myn soon Abraham gebore om 8 ure in de morge, voor pet en comper alder Kierstede en syn vrouw Aryante gedop door Domenie Manseus.

1741 Agustus 17 te nege ure in de morge is gebore myn dochter Cathrinna voor comper Jacobus en Catharinna DeLametter en is te doep gehouwen door Catharinna Kirstede.

1748 Desember 4 in Nyuyorck is ons sopis meel vercocht voor een en Dertigh schelinge en nege pens wyllem borhanns in en myn en Cornelis De Lametter en Peteris smedis en Gaesbeek in voor dertigh en ses pens het hondert wight het gemenne meel is voor vier en twentigh doien vercocht.

1758 Juny Doien hade wy hier De kevers op horly by menigte
1775 Juny hade wy de kevers weer by menigte hier op horly en door het heele lant.

1743 november 21 in kingstoun is gebore myn soon Davit te 9 ure savens gedopt Door Domenie vas voor Comper en pet Davit DeLametter en syn vrouw.

1747 april 30 op horrely is myn soon Johannis gebore en is gedopt door Domenie vas voor Comper en pet Johannis De Lametter en syn vrouw marya en Door syn Dochter te Doep gehouwe Cornelya.

1749 agustus 9 op horrelye is myn Dochter Raghel gebore en is gedoept Door Domenie peterus vaes voor Comper Jan Eltinge en syn huys vrouw Raghel haesbrock voor peet.

1758 may 25 in kingstoun is myn vader abraham Low gestorve te vier ure in De morge en is begrave de 27.

1772 syptember 25 is myn huys vrouw gestorve omtrent ondergaen van de son en is begrav de 27.

1772 october 12 is myn broider Daviet De Lameter gestor . . . en begrave 14.

1748 may 4 is marey myn negerins mysie gebore

1750 may 9 is peck gebore

1754 april 1 is machhiel gebore

1757 augustus 15 is anthon gebore

1765 augustus 1 is ariaen gebore omtrent 10 ure in de morge.

1767 July 24 is denis gebore omtrent 11 ure voorm. dag

1769 mart 7 is gebor Isabel omtrent 7 ure s avens.

Abraham D. Delameter, jun.ʳ Born in the year of our Lord one thousand seven hundred and seventy four. And merried in the year one thousand seven hundred and ninety five to his dear Englittje Elmendorph who was born in the year of our Lord one thousand seven hundred and seventy six and merried in the year one thousand seven hundred and ninety five the eight of Feb.ʳʸ which was her birthday.

[TRANSLATION

[1776: July 13, died father Abraham Delameter, at Horly, on a Saturday about noon.

[1811: July 18, died Johanes De Lameter on a Thursday, and he is buried on a Friday.

[1730: May 3, I, Abraham De Lameter have taken for wife Ragel Low; and I am born in the year 1706, June 26, and my wife is born in the year 1710, October 2.

[1731: October 26, born my eldest daughter and she is christened Elsje, after my mother.

[1733: October 21, born my second daughter and she is christened Jannetij after my wife's mother, and she is baptized by Peterus Vas.

[1734: November 20, died my father Abraham De Lametter and he is buried on the 22.ᵈ

[1735: November 16, born about 8 o'clock in the evening my son Abraham and baptized on November the 23.ᵈ, by Domine Manseus.

[1736/7: February 3, died my mother Elsje DeLametter between 7 and 8 o'clock and she is buried on the 6.ᵗʰ

[1736/7: February 16, died my Abraham about midnight, buried the 19th.

[1737: December 5, born my daughter Ragel, about 7 o'clock in the evening and she is baptized by Domine Manseus.

[1737: December 13, died my daughter Ragel at 3 o'clock in the morning and she is buried on the 15th.

[1738/9: February 18, born my son Abraham about 8 o'clock in the morning, as godmother and godfather, Aldert Kierstede and his wife Aryante; baptized by Domine Manseus.

[1741: August 17, born my daughter Cathrinna at nine o'clock in the morning, as sponsors Jacobus and Catharinna De Lametter and she was presented at the font by Cathrinna Kirstede.

[1748: on December the 4th, in New York our "sopis" meal has been sold for 31 shilling and nine pence, Wyllem Borhanns', and mine and Cornelis De Lametter's and Peteris Smedis' and Gaesbeek's for 30 and 6 the hundred weight; ordinary meal was sold at that time for twenty four.

[1758: June, we had a great number of beetles at that time, here at Horly.

[1775: June, again we had a great number of beetles here at Horly, and over the entire country.

[1743: November 21, born at Kingston, my son Davit at 9 o'clock in the morning; baptized by Domine Vas, as godfather and godmother Davit De Lametter and his wife.

[1747: April 30, born at Horrely my son Johannis; baptized by Domine Vas, as godfather and godmother Johannis De Lametter and his wife Marya, and presented at the font by their daughter Cornelya.

[1749: August 9, born at Horrelye, my daughter Raghel; baptized by Domine Peterus Vaes, as godfather Jan Eltinge and his housewife Raghel Haesbroeck as godmother.

[1758: May 25, died at Kingston my father Abraham Low, at four o'clock in the morning, and buried on the 27th.

[1772: September 25, died my housewife at sunset, buried the 27th.

[1772: October 12, died my brother Daviet de Lameter, buried the 14th.

[1748: May 4, born Marey, the daughter of my negress.

[1750: May 9, born Peck.

[1754: April 1, born Machhiel.

[1757: August 15, born Anthon.

[1765: August 1, born Ariaen, about 10 o'clock in the morning.

[1767: July 24, born Denis, about 11 o'clock in the forenoon.

[1769: March 7, born Isabel, about 7 o'clock in the evening.]

EDWARD DUDLEY.
(Born, 1770.)

Holy Bible in English; New York, Collins & Co., 1821.

Contains the record of Edward Dudley of Ireland, and his two wives Mary Eves and Emma Clark, with their descendants. It passed into the possession of his nephew, William Henry Dudley, M.D., of Brooklyn, N. Y., and is now owned by his daughter, Miss Charlotte Elizabeth Dudley.

Edward Dudley born 1st, Mo. 1st, 1770, Mary Eves, Married in Dublin 11 Month 19th 1790

Their Children

Sarah Dudley Born 11 Month 10 - 1791 Died 11 Month - - - - - 1792

Ann Dudley Born 12 Month 29 - 1792 Died 8 Month - - 1807

John Dudley Born 11 Month 17 - 1794

Samuel Dudley Born 10 Month 16 - 1795

Edward Dudley Born 8 Month 30 - 1797 Deceased 11 Month 18 - 1835

William E. Dudley Born 4 Month 1 - - 1799 deceased 8th 6. 1839

Margaret Dudley Born - 4 Month 30 - - 1801 deceased 1 Mo. 9. 1842

Charles Dudley Born - - 1802 Died . . . .

Mary E. Dudley Born 11 Month 10 - 1803

Mary — wife of Edward, Died in New York - 4 Mo. 1808

Edward Dudley, Emma Clark, Married in New York 6th Month 6th 1809

Stacy B. Collins, Mary E. Dudley, Married in New York 10 Month 11th 1821

Their Children

Emma D. Collins Born 5th Month 27th 1823 died - 6 Month 18 - 1842

Anna Dudley Collins - do - 6 Month 26 - 1825

Cornelia Collins do - 7 Month 7 - 1827

Mary S. Collins do. 11 Month 3rd 1829

Sarah Collins do. 9 Month 14th 1831

Theodore Collins do 9 Month 27 1833

Anna Dudley Collins died 1 Month 7th 1834

Theodore Collins died 12 Month 28 1835

Edward Dudley Collins Born 10 Month 15th 1836

Edward Dudley Collins died 1 Month 1st 1838

Mary D. Collins died the 14th of 6th Month 1838 Aged 34 years, after a long and suffering illness through which she evinced great patience and disposal to the Divine Will, how it might terminate, her life tho' short was exemplary and pious, possessing good talents and a sweet urbanity of manners, she devoted them to usefulness, and the performance of her duties, as a Wife, Mother and Friend, and very remarkably in the Education of her Children, instilling in their young minds the most purity of morals and the sublimest views of Religion agreeable to her profession.

She was greatly beloved by a very extensive circle of acquaintance both at home and abroad, having travelled for her health —and is as greatly lamented especially by her family and near friends — For a long time before her close she often expressed her readiness and anxiety to go, that her prospects were bright, and fully assured of a happy and eternal rest, which continued to her last moments. —

She was interred in friend's Burying Ground the 17th at Milton Ulster County State of New York.

Mary D. Collins with her husband and four children left New York for Milton on the 20th of 5. ^{mo} 1838 for the benefit of purer air.

My dear Father Eleazar Dudley departed this life the 5th of 1st Month 1800. I think he said he was born in 1739.

My dear Mother Anne Dudley departed this life the 21st of 8th Month 1828, I think she used to say she was about two years younger than my dear Father. They were both interred in friends burying ground at Knackballymaher near Roscrea in the County of Tipperary, Ireland and I have no doubt are inheriting the reward of their useful well spent lives. Edward Dudley.

My dear son Edward Dudley closed a well spent life the 18th of 11 mo 1835 aged 38 years — A Character marked with many amiable and valuable traits a Dutiful, Affectionate Son, Brother and friend, whose death was in accordance with his correct life, evincing a happy resignation to the Divine will and a consoling assurance of a Glorious Admission into the Mansions of rest. May our great loss and the memory of his excellent example be sanctified to his surviving relations!

Sheldon Dudley, Elizabeth Evans, Married in Limerick in the year 1796.

Their Children

Jane Dudley Born 7 Mo. 26, 1797

Samuel Sheldon Dudley do 10 Mo 1 1799

Eleazar Dudley do 4 Mo 21 1801 - deceased

Frances Dudley do 3 Mo 14 1803

Mary Ann Dudley do 4 Mo 17 1805

John Dudley do 12 Mo 14 1806

Henry Dudley do 11 Mo 8 1808 - deceased

Edward Dudley do 6 Mo 30 1810 - do.

William Henry Dudley do 10 Mo 7 1811.

Elizabeth Dudley do 10 Mo 18 1813

Alfred Ely Dudley do 7 Mo 31 1816

Charlotte Dudley do 10 Mo 28 1818

Emma Louisa Dudley do 12 Mo 8 1820 (deceased)

Caroline Dudley do 3 Mo 29 1822

My dear Brother Sheldon Dudley (above mentioned) departed this life after a protracted illness the 4th of 11th Month 1832. E. D.

Samuel Dudley Married in New York to Mary Louise Peters, 10mo 4th 1837

Their Children

Mary Dudley, Born 8th Month 20th 1838

Edwd Dudley, Jun. Born 9 Month 4th 1840

Cornelia Collins Dudley Born 12 Month 24th 1842

Anna Peters Dudley Born 5 mo 23 1845

Our Cousin John Dudley, son of Sheldon Dudley was lost in the Steamer Manchester of which he was Captain the night of the 16th of 6 mo. 1844 in a violent storm on his voyage from Hull to Hamburgh 28 on board who all perished.

WILLIAM DYCKMAN.
(1725–1787.)

Holy Bible in Dutch; Dordrecht, Hendrick, Jacob en Pieter Keur, 1702.

Contains the records of William Dyckman and Mary Turner, his wife, and of the descendants of their son Jacobus. It has descended in direct line to Mrs. Bashford Dean and Mrs. Alexander McMillan Welch, great-great-granddaughters of the original owner; and has been deposited by them for safe keeping in the Dyckman House Museum, New York City.

William Dyckman was born August 23d, 1725, O. [S.] and died 10th of Augus 1787

Mary Turner was born February 4th 1728 O.S. and Died february 14 1802

Jacobus Dyckman Son of William & Mary Dyckman was born September 18th 1748, O.S. & Died August 20 - 1832 -

Mary Dyckman Daughter of Wm. & Mary Dyckman was Born June 2th 1752 O.S. and Died the 23 of february 1826

Abraham Dyckman, Son of William & Mary Dyckman was Born August 25th 1754 New Stile, and Died the 9th of March of a wound which he Got the 4th of March, 1782.

Michael Dyckman Son of William & Mary Dyckman was Born 9th of August 1756 and Died in January, 1808

Jane Dyckman Daughter of William & Mary Dyckman was Born 26th of June, 1759 and Died 24th of March 1772.

William Dyckman Son of William & Mary Dyckman was Born 9th of December, 1762.

Jamima Dyckman Daughter of William & Mary Dy [piece torn out] was Born 25th February 1765.

John Dyckman Son of William & Mary Dyckman was born 28 [piece torn out] and died 15th of April 1774 by Accident With a Cart.

Dyckman House, New York City
Presented to New York City in 1916 by Mrs. Dean and Mrs. Welch

Charity Dyckman Daughter of William & Mary Dyckman was Born 18th of May, 1770.

William Dyckman son of Jacobus Dyckman and Hannah Dyckman was born the [piece torn out] and died the 31st day of August 1803

Frederick Dyckman son of Jacobus Dyckman and Hannah Dyckman was born the 4 day of December 1776

John Dyckman son of Jacobus Dyckman and Hannah Dyckman was born the 10 of February 1778 and died the 9 November 1778.

Hannah Dyckman Daughter of Jacobus Dyckman and Hannah Dyckman was born the 3 day of February 1780

Abraham Dyckman son of Jacobus Dyckman and Hannah Dyckman was born the 14 March, 1782.

Maria Dyckman Daughter of Jacobus Dyckman and Hannah was bor[n] the December 25th 1786.

Jacob Dyckman, son of Jacobus Dyckman was born October 11, 1788.

James Dyckman was son of Jacobus Dyckman and Hannah Dy[ckman] was born the 1 december 1790.

Isaac Dyckman son of Jacobus Dyckman and H. Dyckman was born the 17 November 1794

Michael Dyckman son of J. D. and H. D. was born the 22 of August [date erased]

John Dyckman son of Jacobus Dy. and Ha Dyck. was born the 15 of March 1799.

CORNELIUS ELMENDORF.[1]
(1697–1790.)

Holy Bible in Dutch; Dordrecht, Jacob en Hendrick Keur, 1738.

    Contains the records of Cornelius Elmendorf and his wife Engeltije Heermans, with those of their son Jan and granddaughter, Elizabeth Cole. It was presented to the Lenox Library in 1895 by Thomas MacKellar of Germantown, Pa. The records are in Dutch and have been verified by Dr. L. Bendikson.

1697 October 20: Dan ben ick Coernelus Elmendoerph gebooren ten 4 uren na de meddagh.

1698 September 10: Dan ben ick Engeltije Heermans gebooren, huysvrou van Coernelus Elmendoerph.

1678 September 10: Dan is gebooren myn schoonmoeder Antije van Wagenen omtrent 2 uren in de naght.

1788 September is gestorven myn vrou Engeltije Elmendoerp en is begraven de 24.

1790 IJune 3 is gestorven myn vader Cornelus Elmendorph 35 menuijten na 11 uren in de naght een is begraven de 6 op een Sondagh en agtermeddagh.

1725 April 28 ben iek Jan Elmendorph geboren.

1738 Mert 18 is myn vrou Maragreta Delameter geboren.

1767 April 23 ben ick Jan Elmendorph getrut met Maragreta Delameter op een Donderdag.

1768 Februware 13 is myn son Cornelius geboren op een Saterdagh omtrent ten aght uren en gedopt by Risdyck Domene.

1769 Agustus 24 is myn son Martyn geboren op een Donderdagh 6 uren in de morgen en gedopt by Domene Keuper.

1772 April 18 is myn doghter Elisabet geboren en gedopt de 7 Mey van Domene Kock.

[1 The Dutch character ij is not cut for fonts of English type. Therefore the letter y has been used in the Dutch records where ij is meant.]

1776 Februweare 8 is myn dogter Engeltje geboren up een Donderdagh omtrent aght uren en gedopt by Domene Dull.

1781 October de 29 is myn vrou Marageta Delameter in den Heren ontslapen en 31 is sy begraven.

1720 Desember 16 Dan ben ick getroudt Coernelus Elmendoerph met Engeltije Heermans op een Vrydagh en meddagh.

1721 October 16 is myn doghter Arreantije gebooren op een Maandagh en morgen en de 22 gedoopt op een agter meddagh. ... En de 27 van Desember overleeden op een Woensdagh en morgen.

1722 October 5 is myn tweede doghter Arreijaantije gebooren op een Vrydagh en morgen en de 21 — gedoopt op een agtermeddagh. 1743 IJanneware 8 is sey overleeden op een Saterdagh en morgens en is begraaven Maandaghs 2 uren na meddagh.

1725 April 28 Dan is gebooren myn soon Jan op een Woensdagh en morgen en is de: 30: gedoopt op een agter meddagh.

1726 IJuly 28 is gebooren myn soon Coenraadt op een Donderdagh en morgen en de: 31: gedoopt op een agter meddagh.

1728 Mey 29 is gebooren myn doghter Antije op een Woensdagh en aghtermeddagh ende 2 IJune gedoopt op een agtermeddagh.

1729 is sey overleeden den 25 IJulij omtrendt meddernaght ende 27 begraaven op een agtermeddagh.

1729 September is myn soon Jacob gebooren omtrendt meddernaght ende: 15: gedoopt op een agtermeddagh.

1731 Agustus 8 is myn soon Tobeyas gebooren omtrendt meddernaght ende: 15: gedoopt op een agtermeddagh.

1733 November 25 is gebooren myn soon Coernelus omtrendt 9 uren in de naght ende: 2: van Desember gedoopt up een agtermeddagh.

1735 September 26 is gebooren myn soon Abraham op een Vreydagh omtrendt 10 uren in de naght ende: 28: gedoopt op een agtermeddagh.

1740 Feberware 18 is gebooren myn soon Beijamen omtrendt son ondergaan ende: 24: gedoopt op een aghtermeddagh.

1766 September 7 dan is myn soon Cornelus overleeden ende : 9 : begraven.

1795 June 9 gestorven ende 10 is hei begraven myn broer Abraham Elmendorph.

Elisabeth Elmendorph was born in the year 1772 April 18 and my daughter Margarit was born in the year 1793 April 2 and my son James was born in the year 1801 April 10 and my daughter Jane was born in the year 1805 Septr. 15.

(The above is the record made by Elisabeth Elmendorf, who married Cornelius Cole of her family, She was the daughter of Jan who was the sun of Cornelius Elmendorf—See preceding record. A.E.)

Elmendorf House, Hurley, New York

PETRUS EDMUNDUS ELMENDORF.[1]
(Died, 1765.)

Holy Bible in Dutch; Dordrecht, Jacob en Hendrick Keur, 1738.

Contains the records in Dutch and English of Petrus E. Elmendorf and Mary, his wife, and of some of their descendants. It has descended in direct line to their great-great-granddaughter, Mrs. French Ensor Chadwick, of Newport, R. I.

A Register of the births of the family of Petrus Edmundus Elmendorf and Mary Elmendorf his wife.

Eldest Son John born 3d Febry O.S. 1745.—

Eldest Daughter Catherine Born 1st Febry O.S. 1747.—

Second Son John born 1st April O.S. 1749.—

Third Son William born 12 May O.S. 1751.—

Second Daughter Blandina born 8 August N.S. 1753.—

Third Daughter Elizabeth born 24th23 Jany N.S. 1757.

Fourth Son William born 3rd May 1755.

Fourth Daughter Sarah born 6th April 1759. Obiit 4th Febry 1772

Fifth Son Petrus Edmundus Born 6th April 1761.—

Sixth Son Peter Edmundus born 20th Sept, 1764.—

Petrus Edmundus Elmendorf Died 13 July. 1765.

Slaves—

Dina's Daughter Jude born January 6th 1788.

her second daughter Saar born October 20th 1790.

Dina died Sept. 20th 1794 aged 28 years & 7 months.

Fransines son Jon born March 1799.

[1 The Dutch character ÿ is not cut for fonts of English type. Therefore the letter y has been used in the Dutch records where ÿ is meant.]

In't Jaer een duysent seven hondert en negen & Sestigh, den 15 May. Zyn Rutger Bleecker en Catherine Elmendorph Ten Huwelyk bevestight door den eerwaerden Heer Kuyper.

In het Jaer 1770 den 1 May, Dingsdaghs te Vier uren s'morgens, ist geboren onsen eerste Soon John, gedoopt door den eerwaerden Heer Koch — En overleeden den 14 Maert 1771 —

1771 den 20 December Vrydaghs te aght Uren s'morgens ist geboren onsen tweeden Soon John gedoopt den 22 — dooe den eerwaerden Heer Westerlo —

1774 den 8 September Donderdaghs te Elf Uren en den Naght is geboren onsen derden Soon Peter, Edmund, gedoopt den elfden door den eerwaerden Heer E. Westerlo. Departed this life the 18 Day of September at one o Clock past noon 1793

1777 den 3 October Vrydaghs Te Veyf Uren in den Morgen is geboren onsen Doghter Elizabeth gedoopt den sevenden door den Er. W. Heer Barent Vrooman.

1780 den 18 September Maandagh te Veer Uren na Middagh is onse tweden Doghter geboren. Gedoopt den door de Eerwaerde E. Westerlo, Maria.

1783 Den 1 October teen Uren in den Avant is geboren onsen derde doghter, gedroopt door Domine E. Westerlo den Dagh van de ulfden Maent en genoomt Blandina.

1788 16 January wednesday night between 11 & 12 O Clock was born the fouth Daughter baptized by Dominé E. Westerlo March and named Sarah Rutger. and departed this life 10th Decem^r 1793 ¾ after 12 O Clock at night.

Departed this Life on the 4th Octr 1787 ¼ after 11 at night my brother Rutger Bleecker, he was born 6th June 1745 Old Style Aged 42 years 3 months & 17 days,

Departed this Life on the 18th Septr 1793 at 1 Oclock the afternoon Peter Edmund Bleecker, aged 19 years, 10 days.

    [I hereby testify that Cornelia Jones Chadwick appeared before me this day January 5th., 1916, and testified that to her best knowledge and belief that the above is an exact copy of the entries in the Elmendorf Bible owned by her.
    (SEAL)   [FREDERICK H. PAINE,
    [*Notary Public*]

REBECCA PALMER FISH.
(Married, 1743.)

Holy Bible in English; Oxford, John Baskett, 1739.

Contains the records of Rebecca Palmer and her husband, Daniel Fish, with some other Palmer and Crary entries. It is now the property of Mrs. Frederic R. Lefferts, Flushing, Long Island, who is the great-great-great-granddaughter of Nathan Palmer, a brother of Mrs. Rebecca P. Fish.

March the 5th. 1742/3 Rebeckah Fish her Bible Given her by her Loving Mother [piece torn out] Lars Mrs. Maria Palmer. Cost £1-15-0.

My honred Father Departed this Life August ye 13th 1751.

My honred Mother in law Departed this Life Farbuary ye 3rd 1762.

Daniel Fish and Rebekah Palmer was marred February the 17th 1742/3

Rebekah Fish died J July the 12 1786

Danniel Fish died April the 11 1788

Nathan Palmer his bible Given him by Mrs. Sarah Fish Decr. ye 15 1788.

Docr. Nathan Palmer Departed this Life the 27th March 1795 suppose in 85th year of his age.

11 days difference between old and New Stile.

Peter Crary was born 16 June. 1748 O.S. 27 June N.S.

Lucretia Palmer was born 16th Octr. 1751. O.S.

Peter Crary & Lucretia Palmer was married 8th Decr. 1771.

Phebe Crary was born 10th May 1773.

Edward Crary was born 10th March 1775.

Lucretia Crary was born 21st July 1779 and departed this life 9th Septr. 1780.

Peter Crary Jnr. was born 12th Febry. 1781

John S. Crary was born 18th March 1785.

Giles R. Crary was born 17th Septr. 1790, and departed this life Augt. 1795.

Lucretia Crary wife of Peter Crary departed this life April 26 1822 at ¼ past 3 P.M.

Brick house built by Major Thomas Jones in 1696

RICHARD FLOYD.
(Born, 1665.)

Holy Bible in English; London, Charles Bill, 1701.

This Bible contains the records of Richard Floyd, Senior, and has come down in direct descent through six generations to the present owner, Edward H. Floyd-Jones, of Massapequa, New York, who has verified the entries.

Richard Floyd senior was born ye 12 day of may Ano 1665

Margret Floyd senior was born ye 30 day of may Ano 1662

Sewsana Floyd was born ye 25 day of may Ano 1688

Margret Floyd was born ye 25 day of aprell Ano 1690

Charity Floyd was born ye 6 day of aprell Ano 1692

Ewnes Floyd was born ye 16 day of may Ano 1694

Richard Floyd was born ye 14 day of november Ano 1696

Ruth Floyd was born ye 6 day of agust Ano 1699

Richard Floyd dececed was born ye 5 day of may Ano 1701

Richard Floyd jewnier was born ye 29 day of december 1703

Nicol Floyd was born ye 27 day of agust Ano 1705

Elisibeth Floyd the wife of Richard Floyd was born March 28 ano 1709

Richard Floyd Son of Richard Floyd Junior was Born Feb^{ry} 26:th Anno 1731/2

Elizabeth Floyd was born June the 4th Anno 1733

John Floyd was Born Decem^{br} 4:th Anno 1735

Margretta Floyd was born the 3^d day of Decem^{br} Anno 1738

Benjamin Floyd was born the 4.th Day of Decem^{br} Anno 1740

Gilbert Floyd was born the 21^{rst} day of Aprill Anno 1743

William Samuell Floyd was born the 16 day of August 1745

Mary Floyd was born the 29 day of October 1748

Ann Floyd was born the 4 day of March 1751

William Samuel Floyd Departed this Life October the 6 1762

Gilbert Floyd depearted this life april ye 30 1760

Benjamin Floyd was born December th 4 Day Anno 1740

Ann Floyd the wife of Benjamin Floyd was born December th 25 Anno 1745

Margaret Floyd Daughter of Benjamin and Ann Floyd was Born October the 31: 1768

Richard Floyd was Born December the 22: 1769

Gilbert Floyd was born July the 21: 1771

Samuel Floyd was Born May th 19^d 1773

Margretta Floyd daughter of Benjamin Floyd esq^e Departed this life 1770

Ann Floyd wife of Benjamin Floyd Departed this life May 1773

Co^{ll} Richard Floyd Departed this life Aprile 25st Anno 1775

Mrs Elizabeth Floyd wife of co^{ll} Richard Floyd Departed this life April 1778

Fort Neck House, Massapequa, Long Island (originally Tryon Hall)
Built by Judge David Jones for his son Judge Thomas Jones in 1770

RICHARD FLOYD, Jr.
(1731-1771.)

Holy Bible in English; London, Mark Baskett, 1763.

The Bible contains the records of the family of Col. Richard Floyd and some of his descendants. It has descended in direct line to his great-great-grandson, Thomas Floyd-Jones, of Nutley, New Jersey, the present owner.

Richard Floyd Junior was Born february th 26 1731-2

Arrabella Jones was Born December th 7 on Saterday 1734. and was marred to Richard Floyd Junior on Wednefday th2 day of November 1757.

Richard Floyd Jr. was born 26th February 1731-2

Arrabella Daughter of David Jones was born 7th December 1734.

Richard Floyd Jr. & Arrabella Jones were married on the 2nd November 1757.

Their children were.

Elizabeth, born August 8th 1758

David Richard, born November 14th 1764 &

Anna Willett, born 17th August 1767.

Richard Floyd Junior was born February th 26 day 1731-2

Arrabella Floyd wife of Richard Floyd Junior was Born December 7th day 1734.

Elizabeth Floyd Daughter of Richard Floyd Junior was born August 8th day 1758

David Richard Floyd was born November 14th day 1764

Anna Willitt Floyd was born August 17th, 1767.

David Richard Floyd was married to Miss Sally Onderdonk Daughter of Hendrick Onderdonk 20th day of September 1785.

Elizabeth Floyd was married September 28th day 1785 to Mr. John Delancey.

Anna Willett Floyd was married December 3rd day 1784 to Mr. Benjamin Nicoll.

Coll Richard Floyd Departed this Life April th21, 1771.

David Jones, Esqr. Departed this Life October th11, 1775. Aged 76.

Arrabella Floyd wife of Richard Floyd Junior Departed this Life May 29th day 1785 Aged 51 years.

David Thomas Floyd was born the 25th day of April 1787 and departed this life June 12th day 1787 Aged 2 months and a half.

Thomas Floyd was born July 23th 1788.

Arrabella Floyd Jones departed this life May 5th, 1790, aged 3 month

General Thomas Floyd Jones of Fort Neck died Augt. 23, 1851.

Henry F. Jones was born January the 3rd 1700 [a mistake for 1792] and died December 20, 1862.

David Richard Floyd Jones Junior was born April 6th 1813.

David Richard Floyd Jones born April 6, 1813.

Ann Willett Nicoll wife of Benjamin Nicoll of Shelter Island departed this life June 8, 1813.

Elizabeth Delancy wife of John Peter Delancey departed this life May 7, 1820 aged sixty two years.

William F. Jones was born March 10, 1815.

Sarah Maria Floyd Jones was born December 10th 1819

Elbert Floyd Jones was born Feby. 7, 1817.

Thos. Floyd Jones was born March 21, 1841 at Fort Neck Massapequa, L. I.

David Richard Floyd Jones of Fort Neck Lieut. Govr. Died Jan. 8, 1871

William Floyd-Jones died Feby. 7, 1896.

Elbert Floyd-Jones died Feby. 17, 1901.

Sarah Maria Floyd Jones wife of Coleman Williams died Jan. 2, 1892.

Sons of David Richard Floyd Jones and One Daughter.

David Thomas Floyd was born 25th of April 1787 and departed this Life June 12th, 1787 aged 2 months and a half.

Thomas Floyd was born July 23rd 1788.

Arrabella Floyd was born February 6th, 1790. and departed this life May 5th, 1790 aged 3 months.

Henery Onderdonk Floyd Jones was born January 3th, 1792.

Andrew Onderdonk Floyd Jones was born January 9th, 1794 and departed this life February 11, 1794 aged one month & 2 days.

Pegga Tredwell born Juoly Ye 31, 1728

Phebe Tredwell born Juoly ye 12, 1730

John Tredwell born August ye 3, 1732

Benj. Tredwell born May ye 11, 1735.

Phebe Tredwell Deceast January ye 18, 1738

Sarah Tredwell born January ye 1, 1740

Samuel Tredwell born May ye 28, 1743

William Tredwell born December ye 11, 1747.

Benj. Tredwell - - - - born September ye 27, 1702

Gloranah Tredwell born November ye 2, 1751.

Gloranah Tredwell deceast April ye 19, 1753.

Elizabeth Tredwell born September ye 8, 1753.

Elizabeth Tredwell deceast October 20th, 1770.

Sarah Tredwell deceast April 11th 1782

James Tredwell born the 15th day of Jany. A Friday 1768.

Henry Tredwell born the 6th day of March on Wednesday 1771.

JACOB FROST.
(1752–1837.)

Holy Bible in English; New York, Duyckinck, Collins & Co., 1815.

  Contains the records of Jacob Frost. It has descended to his great-great-great-niece, Mrs. W. R. Caminoni, of Oyster Bay, Long Island, the present owner.

The Property of Jacob Frost, Born Ap¹ 2ᵈ 1752 Died Mar 17th 1837.

The Following is the Dates of Joseph and Martha Frosts Children when Born

Amey Frost Born January 16th 1735

Micah Frost Born November 2ᵈ 1738

Elizabeth Frost Born February 24th 1741

Hannah Frost Born July 2ᵈ —— 1743

Wright Frost Born September 28th 1746

Caleb Frost Born June 18th 1749

Jacob Frost Born April 2ᵈ 1752

Sarah Frost Born June 16th 1755

Joseph Frost Departed this Life January 17,,1774 - - - -

Grace Frost Wife of the above named Jacob Frost Died Sept. 16,, 1797 Aged 25 years 6 months and 21 Days - - -

Jacob Frost died March 17ᵗʰ 1837 aged 84 years 11 months and 15 days

JAMES GILLILAND.
(Married, 1762.)

Holy Bible in Dutch; Dordrecht, Jacob en Hendrick Keur, 1741.

Contains the records of James Gilliland and Judith Roose, his wife. It is now the property of the American Bible Society and is deposited for safe keeping in the New York Public Library.

New York, 7th July being a very thundery evening was married or bound in matrimony James Gilliland & Judith Roose by Rothenbuler who was minister in this citty at that time Anno Dommini 1762.

James Gilliland aged 21 years, the woman was aged 14 years.

1772 August the 22 was born our 5th daughter Judith

1774 August 8 was born our 4th son Nicholas.

COLONEL JACOB SANDERS GLEN.[1]
(1691–1762.)

Holy Bible in Dutch; Dordrecht, Hendrick en Jacob Keur, 1686.

    This Bible was originally owned by Col. Jacob Glen, the grandson of Alexander Lenders Glen, who founded Schenectady. It contains the records, written by Col. Glen, of his ancestors as far back as 1648, including an account of the sack of Schenectady by the French and Indians in 1690 and the sparing of the Glen house by order of the Governor. It contains records from that date to the present and is now the property of a direct descendant, Mrs. W. W. Galbraith, of Washington, D. C. Part of the records are in Dutch and have been translated by Dr. L. Bendikson.

Annoe 1648 de 5 november is myn vader Johannis Sanders Glen gebore

1658 Is dese plaet angevaet By Benoom van Korlaer Alexander Sander Lenders Glen & Willem Teller

1684 de 12 augustes is myn grooetmoeder Caethrinae dounken in de heere gerust

1685 de 3 ocktobr is myn oom Jacob Sand: Glen in den heere gerust

1685 de 13 november is myn grooetvader alexsander lenders glen in de heere gerust

1690 tussche de 8 & 9 feberewari is de droevige mort gedaen hir op schonechtaede by de franse & harre welde & alles verdesterrewert & verbrant op 5 huys nae maer hir op schotisyae geen quaet gedaen by eckspresse order van haer Governuer voor het goet daet, myn grooetvader myn vader en oem aen een gevange paep priest & verschyd andere gevangen gedan hade in de orelogh tussche onse welde & de franse

1688 de 5 november is myn huysvrou Sarah Wendell gebore

[1 The Dutch character ÿ is not cut for fonts of English type. Therefore the letter y has been used in the Dutch records where ÿ is meant.]

[90]

First page of the Glen Record

1690 is myn vader & moeder getrout—(2ᵈ wife Maria Wemp (See Date))

1691 de 29 desember ben ick Jacob Glen gebore in Albany

1695 de 16 aprel is myn oem Alecksander Glen in de heere gerust

1694 de 18 feberewari is myn broeder abraham glen gebore

1696 de 8 yuny is myn suster maregretae Glen geboore

1697 de 19 Jannewari is sy in den heere gerust

1697 de 28 desember heft de patroen Kelyaen van renselaer & davit Schuyler hier het blyde nies gebroght van de vreede God sy gedakt

1717 de 15 desember ben ick Jacob Glen met Sarah Wendell in de huwelycken staet getrede

1721 de 9 junij is onse doghter geboore en genaemt debora

1724 de 10 april is moeder in den heere grust

1731 de 6 november is myn vader in den heerre gerust was out 83 Jarre & een dagh

1762 N S Den 15ᵈᵉ Augustis is Collº Jacob Glen in den Heer Gerust op Sondagh te 12 Euren op Den Dagh En in de kerck De 17ᵈᵉ Dagh Begraven

1762 Den 19ᵈᵉ Augustis Is Myn Schoon moedʳ Sara Glen in den Heer Gerust op Donderdagh Vief Euren in den Morgen En in de kerck de 20ˢᵗᵉ Dagh Begraven

1782 Den 13ᵈᵉ September is John Sanders in Den Heer Gerust op Vridagh fiftien Minouten na Drie Euren na Den Midag and is in Harty Begraven op Sondag was in die De 15ᵈᵉ Ter Vier Euren na Den Midag out Synde Eght en sestigh yaren een maendt Drie en Twintigh Dagen

1786 Mai 8 Is Deborah Sanders (huysvrow Van de overlede John Sanders) in de here ontslapen op een woensdag tien uren in de avont en is de Elfde in de kerk op Schᵈʸ begraven out synde Vier en Sestigh ya[er] Eight maenden en Sestien dagen

1671 de 2 maij is myn vade Joh: Sanderse Glen met syn erste vrou antye peeck getrout

1672 de 23 maert is mij halve suster Catrinae Glen geborre

1674 de 9 may is myn suster Jacquemyna Glen gebore

1676 de 30 november is myn broer Alexsander Glen geborre

1679 de 21 mart is mijn suster mariae Glen geboore

1681 de 2 november is myn sustr helenae Glen gebore

1683 28 september is myn broeder Johannis Glen gebore

1686 de 27 feberewari is myn broeder Jacob Sanders Glen gebore

1688 de 19 desember is mijn suster annae Glen gebore

1696 de 17 desembr is myn broeder Alexsande Glen in den here grust in madegaskoe out 21 Jarre

1709 de 5 desmbr is myn broeder Johannis Glen in den heere gerust

1709 de 2 Septembr is myn broeder Epharim Wenck in den here gerust

1712 de 12 Jannewari is myn suster Susannae wenck in den heere gerust

1731 de 6 feberewari is myn suster Jaquemyna Glen in den here gerust & de 15 ditoe is myn suster Catrinae Glen in den here grust

1777 Feby: 24 Ben Ick John Sanders Ju^n in den howliken Staat getreden met mine huisvrow Deborah Sanders en Getrout Door Domine Elardus Westerlo In Albanie

1777 Decr 20 Is my een Dogter Geboren ten Vier Uren in De morgen en Gedoopt Door Domine Bar^t Vrooman en Genaent (Elizabeth) als Getuygen myn Vader En moder John en Deborah Sanders

1779 July 12 Is my een Soon Geboren te tien Uren in Den Avont en Gedoopt Door Don^l Bar^t Vroonan en Genaemt (Barent) als Getuygen John Ja: Beeckman en Syn huisvrow Maria

1781 Septr 8 Is my een Soon Geboren en Gedoopt Door Dom^e Barent Vroman en Genaemt (Robert) Als Getuigen Philip Van Ranselaer en syn huisvrow Maria

1783 Aug⁸ 28 Is my een Dogter Geboren te Elf uren in Den Avont en Gedoopt Door Don⁵ Bart Vrooman en Genaent (Sara) als Getuygen John S: Glen en Syn huisvrow Sara

1782 Sepr 13 Is myn Vader John Sanders in Den here gerust op Vryday aftermidagh just na Drie Uren en op Sondagh te Vief Uren na middagh in Den kerk op Schonectade begraven out 68 yaren 1 mant 23 Dagen

1783 Octr 25 Is myn Soon Robert in Den Here gerust op Vridagh twlf Uren op Den Middagh en is op Sondagh te Vief Uren hier op Scotia in het Niwe Begraefplaes Begrave

1785 Octr 10 Is my een Dogter geboren en Gedoopt Door Dominie D Romeyn en Genaent (Catrina) als Getuygen Elizabeth Sanders & Robt Sanders Van Renselaer

1786 Mar 8 Is myn Moeder Deborah Sanders in den heer Gerust op een Woensdag tien Uren in den Avont en is de Elfde in de kerk op Sch^y begraven Out Sinde Vier en Sestigh Jaer Eght maenden en Twaelf Dagen

1787 July 18 Is myn derde Soon Geboren en Gedopt door Domine D Romyn Genaemt (Robert) als Getuygen Myndert S Ten Eyck & Elsie Syn huysvrow

1789 April 21 Is myn Vierden Soon geboren en Gedoopt door Domine Dirck Romeyn is genamt (Jacob Glen) als getuygen myn Suster Margareta Sanders & Jacob Sanders Glen

1792 Feby 17 Is myn Viefden soon geboren vier uren in den aftermiddag en is gedoopt door Dom Dirck Romeyn genaent (Peter) als getuygen myself & Vro[uw]

1793 Nov. 28 Is myn huysvrow Deborah in den here gerust op donderdag Elf uren in de voor middag en is op de volgende maendag hier op Scotia in het niwe begraeveplats gelegen out synde vief in dertig yaeren negen maenden on twentig dagen

1800 Aug⁸ 30 Is myn doghter Elizabeth in de Howliken Strat getreden met Doct^r William Anderson

1800 Nov 30 Ben ick getrout met Albertina Ten Broeck my twede vrouw in Clermont Columbia County doghter van Dirck W: Ten Broeck

1801 Aug 8 Is myn vrow verlost van een doot kint, het was een doghter

1802 Dec' 27 Is my een Soon geboren Seven uren in de morgen

1804 Octob 20 Is myn sevende Soon geboren ses uren in den after middag en in huys gedoopt den 28ste door dominie Meyers als getuyen myn soon Peter ende myn doghter Caty ende is genaemt *Dirck Wesselse*

1810 April 9de Is myn doghter *Cathrina* in den Huilike Straet getreden met *Gerard Beekman* van New York soon van James Beekman

1810 June 9de Is myn soon *Barent* in den Huilike staet gertreden met *Catlina* Doghter van Jacobus Bleker van Albanie

1811 Augt 30 Is myn schoonson Doctor William Anderson gestorven aenboort van het Schip Captn Winekoop op de ries no huys Van Neu Orleans in Louisiana

1824 February 3de Is myn soon Peter in den Huiliken Staet getreden met Maria doghter van Peter Elvendorp in Albanie

1826 October 2de is myn soon John in den Huiliken staet getreden met *Jane* doghter van Walter T. Livingston in Clermont the county van Columbia

[TRANSLATION

[Anno 1648, November the 5th, born my father Johannis Sanders Glen.

[1658: This place is founded by Uncle Ben van Korlaer, (Alexander) Sander Lenders Glen & Willem Teller.

[1684: August 12, died in the Lord my grandmother Caethrinae Dounken.

[1685: October 3, died in the Lord my uncle Jacob Sand: Glen.

[1685: November 13, died in the Lord my grandfather Alexsander Lenders Glen.

[1690: between February 8 and 9, took place, here at Schonechtaede [Schenectady] the sad murder by the French and their savages (Indians) and everything was devastated or set on fire, with exception of 5 houses; but here at Schotisyae no harm was done by special order of their Governor for the kindness shown by my grandfather, my father and my uncle to a captive Roman Catholic priest and several other prisoners during the war between our savages and the French.

[1688: November 5, born my housewife Sarah Wendell

[1690: Father and mother married.

[1691: December the 29th, I, Jacob Glen, am born at Albany.

[1695: April the 16th, died in the Lord my uncle Alecksander Glen

[1694: February the 18th, born my brother Abraham Glen.

[1696: June the 8th, born my sister Maregretae Glen

[1697: December the 28th, Patron Kelyaen van Renselaer and Davit Schuyler have brought here the glad news of the peace; thank the Lord.

[1717: December the 15th, I, Jacob Glen am united in matrimony with Sarah Wendell

[1721: June the 9th, born our daughter and christened Debora

[1724: April the 10th, mother died in the Lord.

[1731: November the 6th, died in the Lord my father, in the age of 83 years and one day.

[1762: (New Style) August the 15th, Sunday at 12 o'clock noon, died in the Lord Col. Jacob Glen and buried in the church, on the 17th day.

[1762: August the 19th, Thursday at 5 o'clock in the morning, died in the Lord my mother-in-law Sara Glen and buried in the church on the 20th day.

[1782: September the 13th, Friday, fifteen minutes past 3 o'clock in the afternoon died in the Lord John Sanders and buried in Harty on Sunday the 15th day at 4 o'clock in the afternoon, in the age of sixty-eight years, one month, twenty-three days.

[1786: May the 8th, died in the Lord on a Wednesday at 10 o'clock in the evening Deborah Sanders (housewife of the late

John Sanders) and buried in the church at Sch[enecta]dy on the 11th, in the age of sixty-four years, eight months and sixteen days.

[1671: May the 2d, is my father Joh: Sanderse Glen united in matrimony with his first wife Antye Peeck.

[1672: March the 23d, born my half-sister Catrinae Glen.

[1674: May the 9th, born my sister Jacquemyne Glen.

[1676: November the 30th, born my brother Alexsander Glen.

[1679: March the 21th, born my sister Mariae Glen.

[1681: November the 2d, born my sister Helenae Glen.

[1683: September 28, born my brother Johannis Glen.

[1686: February the 27th, born my brother Jacob Sanders Glen.

[1688: December the 19th, born my sister Annae Glen.

[1696: December the 17th, died in the Lord my brother Alexsander Glen, in Madegaskoe, in the age of 21 years.

[1709: December the 5th, died in the Lord my brother Johannis Glen.

[1709: September the 2d, died in the Lord my brother Epharim Wemp.

[1712: January the 12th, died in the Lord my sister Susannae Wemp.

[1731: February the 6th, died in the Lord my sister Jaquemyna Glen and on the 15th of the same month my sister Catrinae Glen died in the Lord.

[1777: Feb. 24, I, John Sanders Jun. am united in matrimony with Deborah Sanders, my housewife; married by Domine Elardus Westerlo at Albany.

[1777: Dec. 20, born unto me a daughter at 4 o'clock in the morning, baptized by Domine Bart: Vrooman and christened Elizabeth; as sponsors my father and mother John and Deborah Sanders.

[1779: July 12, born unto me a son, at 10 o'clock in the evening, baptized by Domine Bart: Vroonan, and christened Barent; as sponsors John Ja: Beeckman and his housewife Maria.

[1781: Sept. 8, born unto me a son, baptized by Domine Barent Vroman, and christened Robert; as sponsors Philip van Ranselaer and his housewife Maria.

[1783: Aug. 28, born unto me a daughter, at 11 o'clock in the evening, baptized by Domine Bart: Vrooman, and christened Sara; as sponsors John S: Glen and his housewife Sara.

[1782: Sept. 13, died in the Lord, on Friday afternoon a little after three o'clock my father John Sanders, buried on Sunday at 5 o'clock in the afternoon in the church at Schenectady, in the age of 68 years, 1 month, 23 days.

[1783: Oct. 25, died in the Lord, on Friday at 12 o'clock, noon, my son Robert, buried on Sunday here at Scotia at 5 o'clock at the new cemetery.

[1785: Oct. 10, born unto me a daughter, baptized by Domine D. Romeyn and christened Catrina; as sponsors Elizabeth Sanders & Robert Sanders Van Renselaer.

[1786: March 8, died in the Lord my mother Deborah Sanders, on a Wednesday at 10 o'clock in the evening; buried on the 11th in the church at Schenectady, in the age of sixty-four years, eight months and twelve days.

[1787: July 18, born my third son, baptized by Domine D. Romyn and christened Robert, as sponsors Myndert S. Ten Eyck & Elsie, his housewife.

[1789: April 21, born my fourth son, baptized by Domine Dirck Romeyn and christened Jacob Glen, as sponsors my sister Margareta Sanders & Jacob Sanders Glen.

[1792: Feb. 17, born my fifth son at four o'clock in the afternoon, baptized by Domine Dirck Romeyn and christened Peter, as sponsors myself & [my] wife.

[1793: Nov. 28, died in the Lord on Thursday at 11 o'clock in the forenoon, my housewife Deborah, buried on the following

Monday here at Scotia at the new cemetery in the age of thirty-five years, nine months and twenty days.

[1800: Aug. 30, my daughter Elizabeth is united in matrimony with D^r. William Anderson.

[1800: Nov. 30, I am united in matrimony at Clermont, Columbia County, with my second wife, Albertina Ten Broeck, daughter of Dirck W. Ten Broeck.

[1801: Aug. 8, my wife was brought to bed with a still born child; it was a daughter.

[1802: Dec. 27, born unto me a son, at 7 o'clock in the morning.

[1804: Oct. 20, born my seventh son, at six o'clock in the afternoon, baptized at home on the 28th by Domine Meyers, as sponsors my son Peter and my daughter Caty, and christened Dirck Wesselse.

[1810: April the 9th, my daughter Cathrina is united in matrimony with Gerard Beekman of New York, son of James Beekman.

[1810: June the 9th, my son Barent is united in matrimony with Catlina, daughter of Jacobus Bleker of Albany.

[1811: Aug. 30, my son-in-law Doctor William Anderson died on board of the ship Capt. Winekoop, on the way home from New Orleans in Louisiana.

[1824: February the 3^d, my son Peter is united in matrimony with Maria, daughter of Peter Elvendorp, at Albany.

[1826: October the 2^d, my son John is united in matrimony with Jane, daughter of Walter T. Livingston, at Clermont, the county of Columbia.]

1829 January 20th Is my son Theodore M. Sanders entered into the marriage state at Bethleham with Margaret R eldest daughter of William N. Sill & Marget Mather his wife

1834 March 30th John Sanders of Scotia Glenville Died and was Buried on his Estate In the Burial Ground aged 76 Years 5 M^o and 28 Days

1840 July 23ᵈ Albertina Sanders 2ᵈ wife of John Sanders deceased & Mother of John and Theodore W. Sanders, died at the residence of her son Theodore W. in the Village of Scotia, aged 79 yrs 7 mos 25 ds - - & is interred in the family burying ground -

1840 Novᵇ 5th Died my brother Robert Sanders 23 - minutes past 7. o.clock On the evening of that day, at the house of his friend Job Hedden in the Town of Glenville; on the 6ᵗʰ he was removed to his late residence at East Scotia, & from thence was taken to the Dutch Church near Scotia village, where an immense concourse tesfied their high regard for his worth; & after appropriate funeral services, his remains were interred on the 8ᵗʰ at 1. o.clock P.M. on the right hand side of his mother Deborah Sanders, in the Scotia family burying ground. He was aged 53 years 3 mos & 18 days - Kind by nature, amiable in his deportment, strictly just, & wisely generous. None knew him, but to love him. None named him, but to praise.

Omitted

1835 Octb 15th Died my sister Catharine Beekman wife of Gerard Beekman Esq of the city of New York, aged 49 years 11 mos & 25 days, and was interred on the 17th in the Dutch Church Burying ground, on 2ᵈ Street at the city of New York, she left an only child James W. Beekman Esq —

1847 June 30ᵗʰ I, Jacob Glen Sanders of Glenville Schenectady County, was married with Catharine Mary Cox, only surviving daughter of Isaac B. Cox, & Cornelia Beekman of the city of New York, at the said city, by the Revᵈ Phillip Milledoler D.D. of Said City

For marriage of Jacob Glen Sanders, of Albany, the only son of Jacob G. Sanders above said and Catharine M Cox [some words cut off]

Family Record of Jacob G Sanders

1850 April 27ᵗʰ Born at Albany My Son Jacob, Glen, Sanders about 10 O,Clock P.M Baptised in the Scotia Church by the Revᵈ Edwin Vedder, Sponsers Myself & Wife

1850 May 12ᵗʰ Died at Sotia Schenectady County My Brother Peter Sanders at 1 O.Clock P.M & was buried in the Scotia Family Buriing ground. He was Born 17th February 1792. He left Two Sons Charles & Peter Edmund

1850 June 21st June Died My Sister Eliza Anderson Relict of William Anderson M. D at 5 P.M at her residence in The City of Schenectady. Born 1777 Decr 20th Left No Children

1867 March 26th Died at his residence 150 State Street in the city of Albany Jacob G. Sanders. Aged 79 years 10 mos 4 days, his remains were subsequently removed to his former place of residence Scotia near the city of Schenectady and interred in the family burying ground of the Glen & Sanders families Of whom he was a direct and much honored descendent

1871 Decbr 1st Died at her residence 150 State Street in the city of Albany ---- Mrs. Catharine M. Sanders relict of the late Jacob G. Sanders aged 65 years 4 months and 15th days, her remains were conveyed to Scotia, & intered beside those of her honored husband in the Glen & Sanders family Cemetery, this lady was deeply mourned by all who knew her extreme benolence and Christian graces. For she was eminently a mother in Israel; adorned by every virtue that could distinguish an eminent Christian, an affectionate wife, a tender mother and a devoted friend; and who knew her, declares unhesitatingly — that this admirable lady lived without a fault, & died without an enemy.

1870 October 11th At Mount Holly the capitol of Burlington County, New Jersey, Jacob Glen Sanders of Albany, was married by the Reverend C. M. Perkins of the Episcopal Church, at the residence of the brides father, to Janie daughter of Hon John C Ten Eyck of Mount Holly — late United States senator.

1881 August 25 Born at Albany my daughter Catharine Mary Sanders About 9 Oclock A M Baptised at 150 State Street Albany by the Rev Rufus W Clark Sponsors

1885 September 15 Born at Albany my daughter Jane Ten Eyck Sanders about O clock W Baptised at 150 State Street by the Rev David Schwartz Sponsors myself & wife & Mrs Schwartz

1907 Jan 19th Married at Hotel St Regis city of New York, by the Rev. Walter E. C. Smith Katharine Mary Sanders daughter of Jacob Glen Sanders, and Jane Ten Eyck to Sherfe Coffin Rose.

1912 September 15th Died at Riverside Calif. Sherfe Coffin Rose

1907 Nov 29th Born at Denver Colorado George Sherfe Rose son of Sherfe Coffin Rose of Denver and Katharine Mary Sanders of Albany N Y.

1914 Married at Church of Transfiguration, City of New York October 24th 1914 Katharine Mary Sanders Rose & William Winton Galbraith U. S. N.

1886 Died May 21 — 1886 Jane Ten Eyck Sanders aged eight months and six days

1891 Died Jacob Glen Sanders aged forty one years five months and one day — at Albany New York September 28th 1891 —

BEEKMAN VERPLANCK HOFFMAN.
(1789–1834.)

Holy Bible in English; Saratoga Springs, G. M. Davison, 1826.

 Contains the records of Beekman V. Hoffman and Phœbe Wilmot Townsend, his wife. It is now the property of Mrs. W. R. Caminoni, of Oyster Bay, the greatniece of Mrs. Phœbe Townsend Hoffman.

BIRTHS.

Beekman Verplanck Hoffman was born the 28 of November 1789.

Phoebe Wilmot Townsend was born the 7 of November 1799.

Margaret Townsend Hoffman the daughter of Beekman and Phoebe Hoffman was born the 5 of December 1818.

Gertrude Verplanck Hoffman the Second daughter of Beekman and Phoebe Hoffman was born the 29 of March 1821

Mary Cromline Hoffman the third daughter of Beekman and Phoebe Hoffman was born the . . . of December 1825

Gertrude Verplanck Hoffman daughter of William and Gertrude Uhlhorn born September 23^d 1844

Beekman Verplanck Hoffman son of William and Gertrude Uhlhorn June 24th 1848.

MARRIAGES

Beekman Verplanck Hoffman was united to Phoebe Wilmot Townsend the 29th of November in the year of our Lord 1817

William C Uhlhorn to Gertrude C. V. Hoffman Oct 25th 1843

DEATHS

Mary Cromline Hoffman the daughter of Beekman and Phoebe Hoffman died January 1827

Beekman Verplanck Hoffman died Dec^c 10th 1834

JEREMIAH HOUGHTALING.
(Born 1766.)

Holy Bible in Dutch; Leyden, J. Elzevier, 1663.

Contains the marriage notice of Jeremiah Houghtaling and Mary Roosa, his wife, with their birth dates. It was presented to the American Bible Society by Thos. Houghtaling of Hurley, N. Y., in 1842, and is now in the New York Public Library.

Jeremiah Houghtaling Jun[r] his Bible, February 10th 1795; and was born in the year of our Lord 1766, May 17. . . . was married with Mary Roosa, October 16th, and she was born January 28, 1766.

ADAM HUDE.
(Died 1746.)

This record is from a Bible which formerly belonged to Rev. Ravaud Kearny Rodgers, a great-great-grandson of Adam Hude and Marion, his wife. We have not been able to locate the Bible nor identify the edition.

Adam Hude & Marion his wife sailed from Leith, Scotland Sept. 5th 1685, in the Ship Henry & Francis He is supposed to be one of those who had refused the oath of Allegiance to the King; & was sent to East Jersey with many others. In 1695 he resided on Staten Island, during that year he purchased land in Woodbridge, New Jersey; in 1718 he was appointed one of the Judges of the Court of Common Pleas of Middlesex Co. and acted in the capacity of Presiding judge as late as 1733. He was also Master in Chancery, and enjoyed in a great degree the confidence of his fellow Citizens.

The Tombstones of himself, his wife & his son Robert are still to be seen in the Presbyterian Churchyard at Woodbridge, N. J. bearing the following inscriptions.

"Here lies the body of Mrs. Marion Hude, wife of Adam Hude Esq. for ye space of 46 years, dearly beloved in Life & Lamented in Death. She lived a Pattern of Piety, Patience, Meekness & Affability, & after she had served her Generation in ye love & fear of God, in ye 71st year of her Age, Fell asleep in Jesus, ye Nov. 20th 1732."

"Here lyes ye Body of Adam Hude Esq. Departed June 27th 1746 in ye 85 year of his age."

"Here Lyes ye Body of Robert Hude Esq. Deceased Jan'y ye 30th 1748 in ye 58th year of his age."

Oct. 1710 Judge Hude (Adam) was admitted to the membership of the Presbyterian Church, Woodbridge N. J. Rev. Mr. Wade Pastor.

The children of Adam Hude & Marion his wife were as follows:

John	Hude was born in the year	1687	in July	the	23d.
Agnes	Hude " "	1689	" Oct.	"	29th
Robert	Hude " "	1691	" Sept.	"	25th
Andrew	Hude " "	1693	" July	"	13th
James	Hude " "	1695	" Aug.	"	14th
Mary	Hude " "	1696	" July	"	27th.

So that in the year 1711 as every of the days of the month come about, the age of my children is as followeth, viz.

> Agnes   is 22 in Oct. 29th
> Robert " 20 " Sep. 25th
> Andrew " 18 " July 13th
> James   " 16 " Aug. 14th
> Mary   " 15 " July 27th

This Computation is made the 9th day of May 1711 by me — (Signed) Adam Hude Marion Hude.

My Allow deer Wiff departed this life the 20 day of November 1732, the 70 year & nine months of her age — She & I lived 46 years together Man & Wiff, in sweet Society, & as she lived in sweet peace & quiet, fel asleep in Jesus, at 5 of the Clock, in the morning of the said day, above s,^{d} — & as she sleepeth in Jesus, God will bring her to him when he shall appear in the clouds with the holy Angels & Saints with the Lord Jesus, in glorious appearance, Ameane!

(John the first mentioned son died early, 1 Nov. 1687, & Andrew is marked as having died in Dec. 1716 Robert died Jan. 30th 1748.)

(This record on 3d & 4th pages, was copied from Book in possession of Rev. Ravaud Kearny Rodgers, a great, great grandson of Adam & Marion Hude.)

AUGUSTE JAY.*
(Born 1665.)

Holy Bible in French; Amsterdam, Desbordes, Mortier & Brunet, 1707.

Contains the records in French of Auguste Jay and Anne Marie Bayard, his wife, and of their descendants to 1739. There are also copies of the birth certificates of Pierre, Isaac and Auguste Jay, sons of Pierre and Judith Jay, who were baptized at Rochelle, France, from 1633 to 1666. The Bible is now in possession of a direct descendant, Pierre Jay, Esq., of New York.

Auguste Jay Est né alaRochelle dans Le Royaume de france le 23/13 mars 1665 —

a new york ce 28: octob 1697 old stille Jay Espousé anne marie Bayard, fille de baltazard bayard e —

Le mardy 29: aoust 1698: Environ Les deux heure du mattin Est née ma fille Judith Jay, Elle a Eu pour parain Son grand pere Baltazard bayard et Sa femme marie bayard p⁻ maraine baptisee' aL esglise hollandoise par m^r Selinus —

Le Samedy 31: aoust 1700 — Environ 11 heure Et minuit Est née ma fille marie Jay, a Eu pour parain m^r paul Droither Et mad^{selle} Leboiteux p⁻ marainne, baptisee' alEsglise françoise par m^r peiret Le 4e Sept⁻ Suiuant —

Le Jeudy 26: febrier 1701/2 Est née ma fille francoise Jay Sur Les neuf Et dix heures du soir baptisee' alesglise francoise par

---

* Extrait du Registre des Baptêmes faits au Temple de la Ville Neuve de La Rochelle depuis le 1er Janvier 1660 jusqu'au 13 juin 1666.

Folio 133.

Le dimanche au matin 6e May 1663 ont esté baptisez par Monsieur Lortie Pierre fils de Pierre Jay, marchant & de Judith François. P. François de Baussay marchant. M. Marie François. Il est né le 3e dudit mois. Debaussay. I. Papin, Ancien.

Folio 166.

Le dimanche 30e de Mars 1664 après midy ont esté baptisez par Mons. de Caniebaratz, Isaac, fils de Pierre Jay et de Judith François P. Mre. Isaac François, pasteur de l'Eglise de Surgères. M. Marguerite Jay. Il est né le 26e dudit mois. (François) (I. Papin, Ancien). françois J. Papin Ancien.

Folio 202.

Le mesme jour (le Dimanche 29 de Mars 1665) au catéchisme, ont esté baptisés par Monsieur Lortie Auguste, fils de Pierre Jay et de Judith François. P. Mr. Isaac Manigaud M. Elisabeth François. Il est né le 23 du présent Mois. Isaac Manigault Lortie Massiot, ancien & Scribe du Cong.

Title-page of the Bible of Auguste Jay, 1707

mʳ Peiret a Eu pʳ parain Jacobus bayard mon beau frere, et magaritte bayard pʳ maraine , Le mercredy 4: mars suiuant —

Le vendredy 3: nouemb 1704 Est né mon fils pierre Jay Sur Les trois heure du matin baptise' a Lesglise hollandoise Le 22: Suiuant par mr. Gualtus Dubois a Eu pour parain Jacobus bayard Et ariantie Verplanck pʳ marainne. —

Le Jeudy 6: mars 1706/7 Est née ma fille anne Jay sur Les quatre heure aprais-midy, baptisee' a Lesglise hollandoise Le mercredy 12: Suiuant p mʳ gualtus Dubois , a Eu pʳ parain, mʳ Samuell bayard Et Judith bayard pʳ marainne — ma belle soeur —

Le 24: dessemb. 1707: Sur Les 10: heure du matin Est decedée ma fille anne, et Enterrée Le 26ᵉ Suiuant au smetierre anglois —

Le 29: Jeuin 1723: ma fille marie a Espousé mʳ pierre Vallete —

Le 19: Januie 1723/4 ma fille francoise a Espousé mʳ frederick Cortlant —

1723/4 march 23: Lundy ma fille Vallete a accouché dun Garcon Sur Les 7 a 8 heure du matin a este baptise Le dimanche Suiuant 29: p mʳ Roux a Eu pʳ. parain augᵗᵉ Jay Et Sa femme pʳ marainne   Es nommé Stephen.

1726/7 march yᵉ 3ᵗʰ Jacobus Van Cortlant Est né sur Les 8: heure du mattin a Esté baptisse' alEsglise hollandoise par mʳ Du Bois Le 12: Ditto, a Eu pʳ parain Jacobus Van Cortlant, Et pʳ maraine anna maria Jay —

5: Dᵒ Est né Auguste Vallette Sur Les 3: heure du matin a Eu pʳ parain pierre Jay — Et Judith Jay pʳ maraine baptise' al Esglise françoise par mʳ Louis Rou Le 19— Suiuant —

1727/8 Samedy 20ᵗʰ Januier mon fils pierre Jay a Espouse' marie Van Cortlant fille de mʳ Jacobus van Cortlant Sur Les huit heure du soir p. mʳ Gualtus dubois — min:

1728: aoust 3ᵒ: Sur Les 11: heure Et demie du Soir Est né Augustus Van cortlant a esté Baptise' a LEsglise hollandoise par mʳ Bõelle Le 14: Suiuant a Eu pour parain Augᵗᵘˢ Jaÿ Et annatie van CortLant pʳ maraine —

nouemb. 8: Sur Les 8: heure dumatin Est née Eue Jay a Esté baptisée a Lesglise hollandoise p.m^r Du Bois a Eu p$^-$ parain Jacobus Van Cortlant, Et anne maricke Jay p$^-$ maraine —

1729: Jeuillet 27: dimanche Environ minuit Est né peter Vallete a Esté baptise' Le ... aoust Suiuant par m^r Vesy a Eu p$^-$ parains peter Vallete Jac$^-$v cortland Et frances Vancortland p$^-$ maraine

1730: mars 28: Samedy Sur Les 11: heure dusoir Est né frederick Van Cortlandt a Esté baptisse' a Lesglise hollandois Le ... : auril par m^r hendrik Boele, a Eu p$^-$ parain peter Jay, Et Judith Jay — pour marraine, —

1730: Auril Le 6me Sur Les deux heure du mattin Est né Augustus Jaÿ a Esté paptisé Le ... : Suiuant par m^r Wm Vesy, a Eu p$^-$ parain aug^{tus} Jay & Et frederik v Cortlant a Eu p$^-$ marraine anne mary Jay

1731: aprill 27th Sur Les 6: a 7: heure du matin Est né Jacobus Jay baptissé Le 13th: maÿ par m^r Vēsey a Eu p$^-$ parins m^r peter Vallete & abr: Depeyster Et margarite Depeyster p$^-$ maraine baptisé chez m$^-$ Jacobus Van Cortlandt —

Sept$^-$ 29th: 1731, Stephen Vallete est mort Sur les 11: heure du soir. — Octob: Est deessedé James Jay —

28. march 1732: Est née Eüe Van Cortland a Eu pour parain m^r Jacobus Van Cortland Et annatie van Cortland p$^-$ maraine —

1732: octob 16: Sur les Six heure dumatin Est né Jacobus Jay a Esté baptisse' Le ... suiuant part m^r: Vesÿ a Eu p$^-$ parains adolph Phillips & Phillip Stuÿvesant, p$^-$ maraine Judith Jaÿ —

Laus Deo: n: ÿork Julÿ y^e 10th:1733 — This day at 4: oclock In y^e morning Dÿed Eua van Cortland vas buried y^e next day, y^e 12th in my vault at m^r Stuyvesant about six and seuen oclock In y^e afternoon —

This daÿ Sunday y^e 17th: of march 1733/4 was borne anne vallete was baptised the 27th off ye month by m^r Veseÿ — had for Godfather augustus Jay and his wiffe annemary for godmother and matte Jay, in ye English Church.

1735: aprill 6: this daÿ Easter was my daughter Judith Jay married wth Corneille Van horne, son of Gerit Van horne —

First page of the Auguste Jay Record

July 28: at 1: oclock after midnight, Dÿed Anna Vallette aged abo⁻. 16: mo^th 11: daÿs

1736: aujourdhuy 22: may ma fille frances Van Cortland Est acouchee' dune fille sur Les 3: heure aprais midy a Este' baptisée Le . . . a Eu pour Parain peter Vallete Et marie Sa femme p⁻ marainne, a Este' baptissee' a LEsglise hollandoise par m^r Boelle.

1736: aujourdhuy Vendredi 30ᵉ: Jeuillet Est ne' Auguste Van horne Sur Les trois heures aprais midy a Este' Baptise' Le 8: aoust suiuant a Lesglise holland. p. m^r Boelle a Eu p⁻ parain auguste Jay Et anne marike Jay p⁻ marainne —

1737 — aujourdhuy mardy 5th Jeuillet Est né Stephen Vallete Sur Le midy a Este' baptise' a lEsglise Engloise par m^r Vesey Le 13: suiuant a Eu p⁻ parain corneille Van horne Et peter Vallete Et anne marie Jay p⁻ marainne.

1737: Jeudy 20: octob. Est née anna marike Jay Sur les . . . heure a Esté baptisee Le 26ᵉ D⁰ par m^r Vesey a Eu p⁻ parain auguste Jay Et sa femme anne marieke et francoise Van Cortlandt p⁻ maraines.

1737/8 January 22: aujourdhuy dimanche 22th ma fille Judith Van horn est acouchée Entre 7: et 8: heure dusoir Dun Garcon, Corneille, a Este' baptise' Le 5: febrij suiuant p. m⁻ Boelle a Eu p⁻ parain peter Vallete et . . . Johnson p⁻ marainne

1739: juin 7: Sur Les 11: heure dumatin Est decede' Steph: Vallete age Environ 23: mois, Est mort Dune puissante piquotte

August 18: about 11: oclock is my daughter Judith Vanhorne brought to bed of a son wch was baptised at ye dutch Church p. m^r Boelle had for godfather . . . and . . . for godmother, y^e . . . of this Instant —

February 14th 1745 — lend to m⁻ peter Vallete £200 of our currency —

PETER AUGUSTUS JAY.
(1776–1843.)

Holy Bible in English; Philadelphia, Carey & Lea, 1823.

Contains the records of Peter A. Jay, son of John Jay, and of Mary Rutherfurd Clarkson, his wife; with those of their descendants to the present day. It is now the property of Dr. John C. Jay, of New York, grandson of the original owner.

Marriages—

John Jay was married to Sarah V. Livingston (fourth daughter of Wm. Livingston Esqr) on the 28th day of April in the year of our Lord 1774 by the Rev. Mr. James Caldwell of Elizabethtown.

Maria Jay was married to Goldsborough Banyer junior Esqr. at Albany the 22nd day of April 1801 by the Revd. Thomas Ellison Rector of St. Peters Church in that city.

Peter Augustus Jay was married to Mary Rutherfurd Clarkson (eldest daughter of Mathew Clarkson Esqr) at New York the 29th day of July 1807 by the Right Revd. Bishop Moore.

Mary Rutherfurd Jay (eldest daughter of Peter Augustus Jay Esq.) was married to Frederick Prime (youngest son of Nathaniel Prime Esq) at New York the 30th of April 1829 by the Revd William Richmond.

W. Jay (youngest son of John Jay) was married to Augusta McVicker.

Sarah Jay 2nd daughter of P. A. Jay, was married to Wm. Dawson Feb. 11th 1836.

Peter A. Jay son of J. C. & L. Jay was married to Julia daughter of Alfred C. Post M. D. in New York March 30th 1869 by Rev. Dr. Prentiss & Rev. R. F. Alsop.

John Clarkson Jay, son of J. C. & L. Jay was married to Harriette Arnold daughter of Maj. Gen. D. H. Vinton in New York Dec. 12th 1872 by the Rev. Dr. Alexander H. Vinton & Rev. Peter A. Jay.

John Clarkson Jay M. D. was married to Laura Prime youngest daughter Nathaniel Prime on the 8th November 1831 by the Rev. Dr. Wainwright

John Jay son of William Jay was married to E. R. Field daughter of H. W. Field 23rd June 1837.

Fred^k Prime was married a second time to Lydia, only daughter of Robt Hare of Philadelphia in August 1838.

Catherine Helena Jay, 3rd daughter of P. A. Jay was married to Henry Augustus Du Bois, M. D. on the 17th Dec. 1835, the Great Fire in N. Y. began in the evening of Wednesday the 16th Dec. —35.

Peter Augustus Jay son of Peter A. Jay was married to Miss Josephine Pearson youngest daughter of the late Joseph Pearson of Brentwood near Washington D. C. on the 13th Jan. 1848 by Rev. Mr. Pyne.

Anna Maria Jay daughter of Peter A. Jay was married to Mr. Henry E. Pierrepont, youngest son of the late H. B. Pierrepont of Brooklyn N. Y. on the 1st Dec. 1841 by the Rev. P. S. Chauncey.

Susan Matilda Jay was married to Mathew Clarkson, eldest son of David Clarkson on the 14th April 1852 by Rev. Dr. Hawks.

Laura Jay was married to Charles Pemberton Wurts on the 8th Feb. 1854 by Rev. E. C. Bull in the old Church at Rye.

Mary J. Jay daughter of J. C. & L. Jay married to Jonathan Edwards on the 5th of June 1861 by the Rev. J. C. White at Rye.

BIRTHS.

Peter Augustus Jay (son of John Jay) was born in Elizabeth Town in New Jersey the 24th day of January 1776.

Susan Jay born at Madrid the 9th day of July 1780.

Maria Jay born at Madrid the 20th day of February 1782.

Ann Jay born at Passy near Paris the 13th day of August 1783.

William Jay born in the City of New York the 16th day of June 1789.

Sarah Louisa Jay born in the City of New York the 20th day of February 1792 (all the above were children of John Jay and Sarah V. Livingston)

Goldsborough Banyer born at Albany the 30th day of September 1804.

Sarah Jay Banyer born the 29th day of November 1805 (The last two were Children of G. Banyer junior Esq. and Maria Jay) The following 8 are the children of P. A. Jay and Mary R. Clarkson.

John Clarkson Jay born the eleventh day of September 1808 in the City of New York.

Mary Rutherfurd Jay born in the City of New York the 16th day of April 1810.

Sarah Jay born the 19th day of December 1811, in the City of New York.

Catherine Helena Jay born at New York the 11th day of June 1815.

Anna Maria Jay born at New York the 12th day of September 1819.

Peter Augustus Jay Junior born at New York the 23rd day of October 1821.

Elizabeth Clarkson Jay born at New York the 2nd day of July 1823.

Susan Matilda Jay born at New York the 29th day of November 1827.

Laura Jay Born at Hell Gate N. Y. the 10th day of August 1832. Was baptized by the Rev. Mr. Hawks. Her Father Mrs. Jay and Mrs. Prime were sponsors.

John Jay (second child of J. C. Jay) was born in New York Nov. 14th 1833 was baptized by Rev. Mr. Hawks, his Father & Mother were sponsors.

Augustus Jay born Oct. 14th 1835 in New York baptized by the Rev. Mr. Hawks Nov. 27th 1835, P. A. Jay, N. Prime & Mrs. Prime were sponsors.

Mary J. Jay daughter of J. C. Jay was born 3rd day June 1837 in New York City was baptized Sep^t 16th 1837 by Rev. Dr. Anthon Mrs. M. Banyer, Mrs. P. A. Jay & her father being her sponsors.

Cornelia Jay daughter of J. C. Jay was born 3rd April 1839 in New York she was baptized by Rev. Dr. Anthon, her father & Mother and Mrs. Prime being her sponsors.

Edith Van Cortlandt, daughter of John C. & Harriette A. Jay born June 2nd, 1875 in New York City.

John Clarkson Jay (3rd) son of John C. & Harriette Jay born Jan. 20th 1880, N. Y. City, both baptized by Dr. Howland.

Peter Augustus Jay son of John C. Jay was born 16th June 1841 was baptized by Rev. Dr. Anthon July 23rd 1841 his Grandfather & Father & his Aunt Anna Maria were sponsors.

Ann Maria Jay daughter of John C. Jay was born 16th Feb. 1843 was baptized by Rev. P. S. Chauncey at Rye—Elizabeth C. Jay, Mrs. H. E. Pierrepont & her Father being her sponsors.

John Clarkson Jay son of John C. Jay was born 20th October 1844 was baptized by Rev. P. S. Chauncey at Rye—His Father & Uncle, Peter A. Jay & his sister Laura Jay were his sponsors.

Alice Jay daughter of John C. Jay was born 12th July 1846 was baptized by Rev. P. S. Chauncey at Rye her Mother & Grandmother & Father were sponsors.

Sarah Jay daughter of John C. Jay was born 21st Jan. 1848 was baptized on 19th Feb. 1848 by Rev. P. S. Chauncey Her Aunt E. C. Jay & her Mother & Father were sponsors

Matilda Coster Jay daughter of John C. Jay was born July 5th 1850 was baptized on 10th Sep^t 1850 by Rev. Mr. Bull of Rye, Miss Harriet Sands, her sister Mary J. Jay & her Father were sponsors.

John Jay (child of Peter Jay) was born 12th Dec. 1745—

Augustus Jay the son of Pierre Jay was born 23rd March 1665

Peter Jay son of Augustus Jay & father of John Jay was born 3rd Nov. 1704

Laura Prime youngest child of Nath. Prime was born Feb. 17th 1812.

John Jay son of William Jay was born at Bedford in June 1817.

Mary Rutherfurd Clarkson daughter of Mathew Clarkson & afterwards wife of P. A. Jay was born July 2nd 1786.

Augustus Jay son of P. A. Jay and Josephine Pearson was born in Washington City D. C. 17th Oct. 1850.

Mary Rutherfurd Prime was born 24th August 1830.

Harriet Prime was born Sept. 11th 1832.

Helen Jay Prime was born Aug. —22 1835 Married 16th Oct. 1856. F. T. Garrettson

William Pudsey Dawson born Feb. 14th 1839

Mary Jay Dawson born Nov. 10th 1842

John Wurts, 1st child of Chas. P. Wurts was born July 10th, 1855

Rudolph Wurts, 2nd child of C. P. Wurts was born Dec. 1st, 1856.

Charles P. Wurts, born May 30th, 1859.

Alexander Wurts, born March 3rd 1862.

Martha Haskins Wurts, born June 17th 1863.

Pierre Jay Wurts, born at Nice, France, July 6th, 1869. Baptized in the English Church by Reverend C. Childers.

Pierre Jay, son of Peter A. Jay, born in Warwick, N. Y. May 4th, 1870. Baptized at Rye by Rev. R. F. Aslop Sept. 11th 1870.

Mary Rutherfurd, daughter of Peter A. Jay, born in New Haven, Conn. Aug. 16th 1872. Baptized in Grace Ch — N. Haven by her father,

Maria Arnold Jay, daughter of John C. Jay Jr. born in New York Sept. 18, 1873. Baptized in Trinity Chapel by Rev. Peter A. Jay.

John Jay, son of Revd. Peter A. Jay born in New York, Nov. 19th 1875, Baptized in the Ch. of Heavenly Rest, by Dr. Robert Howland, May 9th 1876.

DEATHS.

Mrs. Sarah Jay died on the 28th of May 1802 at Bedford in the 46th of her age.

Goldsborough Banyer Junior Esq., died on the 6th day of June 1806 at New York remains removed to Rye Jan. 1846

Goldsborough Banyer (son of the former) died the 26th day of October 1804 at Albany.

Sarah Jay Banyer died at Albany on the 8th day of October 1808.

Susan Jay died at Madrid on the 4th day of August 1780.

Sarah Louisa Jay died at New York on the 22nd day of April 1818.

John Jay died on the 17th day of May (Sunday) at Bedford in the 84th year of his age — 1829.

Mary Rutherfurd Prime died at Hellgate New York on the 9th of September 1835 in her 26th year.

Augustus Jay died in 1751 in his 86th year.

Augustus Jay son of J. C. Jay died 27th June 1837. at Hellgate, N. York was buried at Rye N. York.

Mary Rutherfurd Jay wife of P. A. Jay died in the Island of Madeira on the 24th day of December 1838.

John Jay son of John C. Jay died in N. York on the 16th day of June 1841 & was buried at Rye.

Peter Augustus Jay son of John Jay died in N. York Feb. 20th 1843 and was buried at Rye aged 67 years.

Sarah Jay wife of Wm Dawson died Jan. 9th 1846 was buried at Rye.

Wm Dawson died March 12th 1852 was buried at Rye.

Maria A. Jay, daughter of John C. & Harriette Jay died Jan. 2nd 1878, aged four years —

Josephine wife of P. A. Jay died at the house of Mrs. Banyer in N. York on the 3rd Jan. 1852 & was buried at Rye.

Wm Pudcey Dawson died 12th March 1851 aged 12 years & was Buried at Rye.

Nath. Prime died 26 Nov. 1840 aged 72.

Cornelia widow of Nath Prime died April 21st 1852 aged 78 & 5 months about — Buried in Family vault at Eastchester.

Peter Augustus Jay grandson of Gov. Jay died in New York Oct. 30th 1855.

Matilda Coster Jay died December 28th 1856 at Rye aged 6 years & 5 months 23 days.

Ann Maria Jay daughter of John C. & Laura Jay, died in N. York Dec. 3rd 1858.

Rev. Peter Augustus Jay died Oct. 11th 1875 aged 34 years son of John C. & Laura Jay.

Sarah Jay daughter of John C. & Laura Jay died April 24th 1883.

Laura Jay wife of John C. Jay died Monday July 30th 1888 Aged 76 buried in Family cemetery at Rye.

John Clarkson Jay, son of Peter Augustus Jay & grandson of John Jay died at Rye Nov. 15th 1891 in the 84 year of his age Buried in the Jay cemetery at Rye.

Elizabeth Clarkson Jay daughter of Peter Augustus Jay & Granddaughter of John Jay died at New York Oct. 26th 1895 in the 73rd year of her age. Buried in the Jay cemetry at Rye.

Ann Jay daughter of Gov. Jay died November 13th 1856 in N. Y.

Maria Banyer, the last daughter of Gov. Jay died November 21st 1856 at her residence in N— Y—.

Augusta Jay Wife of Wm. Jay died April 26th 1857 & was buried at Bedford

Wm. Jay son of Gov. Jay died at Bedford Oct. 14th 1858 & was buried there beside his wife.

Cornelia Jay daughter of John Clarkson & Laura Jay died at her residence 155 W. 58th St. New York City on Friday Oct. 18th 1907 in her 69th year Buried in Jay cemetery Rye N. York.

Susan Matilda Clarkson. On Wednesday, June 20th 1910. Wife of Mathew Clarkson & daughter of the late Peter A. Jay died at 160 Central Park South. Interred at Tivoli-on-Hudson.

Laura Wurts. On Sep. 17th 1910 in Honolulu Hawaii of Pneumonia; Widow of Charles Pemberton Wurts of New Haven, Conn. & eldest daughter of the late John Clarkson Jay of Rye N. York in her 79th year Interment in Jay Cemetery at Rye on Oct. 1st 1910.

Mary Jay Edwards, widow of Jonathan Edwards, & daught. of John C. & Laura Jay, died at Ridgefield Conn. June 27th 1897 buried in Jay cemetery.

Jonathan Edwards, born Nov. 6, 1821, died at New York May 30th 1882, Buried in Jay cemetery.

Harriette Arnold Jay, wife of Dr. John Clarkson Jay, born Oct. 3rd, 1849, died May 8th, 1914, buried in the Jay cemetery at Rye, N. York, May 11th, 1914 — Died at Worcester, Mass, suddenly, while visiting her brother, she was the daughter of the late Maj. General D. Hammond Vinton.

MARRIAGES.

John Clarkson Jay Jr. was married April 20th 1903 in the Pine St. Presbyterian Church at Harrisburg Pennsylvania to Marguerite Montgomery Solèliac, daughter of Mr. & Mrs. Charles Solèliac by the Reverend George S. Chambers.

BIRTHS.

Sarah Livingston Jay, daughter of John Clarkson Jay Jr. was born at New York 13th of March 1904. Baptized by her great-uncle, Rt. Rev. Alexander H. Vinton, D.D.

Alice Jay 2nd, daughter of John Clarkson Jay Jr. was born at Pelham, N. York, November 5th, 1908.

John Clarkson Jay 3rd, son of John Clarkson Jay Jr. & Marguerite M. Jay was born at Detroit, Mich. December 11th 1915.

CATTRIN JOHNSON.
(Born, 1703.)

Holy Bible in Dutch; Dordrecht, Jacob Canin, 1614.

Contains some record of the Johnson family. It is now the property of the American Bible Society and is deposited in the New York Public Library.

Cattrin Johnson 2 day of April 17(0)3.

John Johnson born 25 day December 17(0)3.

Nicholas Johnson born 20 day of Nouember anno D. 17(0)9.

Lena Johnson born 16 day of October 1713.

Kattren Iohnson is in the 23 day of Yun in year 17(0)9, 22 year old.

In the year anno 1706/7 in the 12 day of Fabbry, Alex Iohnson is 20 year old.

In the year anno 1706 an de 11 day of March Lena is 14 year old.

In the 5 day of October in the sam year Will Ionhe is 17 year old.

And in the sam year and in the 24 day of September then Margr. Ionsen was a 11 year old.

Peter Johnson marryed to Sary Creed Novembr ye 4, 1775.

Nelley Johnson born Octobr 4, 1775.

Peter Johnson born April 23 = 1756.

Sarah Johnson born September ye 10, 1756.

SAMUEL JONES.
(1734–1819.)

Holy Bible in English; New York, Hodge & Campbell, 1792.

Contains the records of Samuel Jones and Cornelia Haring, his wife, with their descendants. It belonged to their great-great-granddaughter, the late Mrs. Wilmot T. Cox, of New York, and is now deposited with the New York Historical Society.

Samuel Jones Son of William Jones, Son of Thomas Jones of Fort Neck Long Island, of Oyster Bay West Neck in Queens County on Nassau Island in the Province of New York, was born the 26th Day of July 1734.

Cornelia the Daughter of Elbert Haring of the City of New York Gent. was born the 15 Day of February 1741 and the 7 Day of July 1768 the said Samuel and Cornelia intermarried. The Ceremony was performed at the House of Alderman Cornelius Roosevelt by Johannes Ritzema Minister of the Dutch Church in New York.

William Jones the first Child of the said Samuel and Cornelia Jones was born the 25 Day of April 1769 between four and five of the clock in the morning and was baptized the 12 of May following at the House of the said Samuel Jones by Johannes Ritzema Minister of the Dutch Church in New York, Evert Banker one of the Elders of the Church being present, The Sponsers were Elbert Haring the Grand-Father and Cornelia Jones, the Mother of the Child.

Samuel Jones the second child of the said Samuel and Cornelia Jones was born the 26th Day of May 1770 between five and six of the clock in the morning and was baptized the 17th of June following at the Old Dutch Church in the City of New York. The Sponsers were Cornelius Roosevelt and Elizabeth Haring the GrandMother of the Child.

The 30th Day of September 1770 at Six of the clock in the Evening William the first Child of the said Samuel and Cornelia Jones died of Small Pox.

William Jones the third child of the said Samuel and Cornelia Jones was born the 4 Day of October 1771 between three and four of the Clock in the Morning and was baptized the 20 Day of the same Month of October at the new Dutch Church in the City of New York. The Sponsers were Elbert Haring and Elizabeth his wife the Grand Father and Grand-Mother of the child.

Elbert Haring Jones the fourth Child of the said Samuel and Cornelia Jones was born the 6 Day of August 1773 at Six of the Clock in the Morning and was baptized the 15 Day of the same Month of August at the New Dutch Church in the City of New York. The Sponsers wer John De Peyster Junor and Mary Herring.

Thomas Jones the fifth child of the said Samuel and Cornelia Jones was born the 7 Day of August 1773 at Eleven of the Clock in the Morning and was baptized the 15 Day of the same Month of August at the new Dutch Church in the City of New York. The Sponsers were Samuel Kip and Sarah Herring. Elbert and Thomas were twins.

Elbert Haring the Father of the said Cornelia Jones died the 3d Day of December 1773 aged 67 Years.

David Jones the Sixth Child of the said Samuel and Cornelia Jones was born the 3d Day of November 1777 at half an Hour Eleven of the clock in the Morning.

William Jones the Father of the said Samuel Jones died the 29 -
Y. M. D.
Day of August 1779 aged 71. 3. 18. being born 25th April 1708.

Walter Jones the Seventh Child of the said Samuel and Cornelia Jones was born the 13 Day of March 1781 at ten of the clock in the Morning and died the 14 Day of September following at ten of the clock in the Morning.

Elizabeth Haring the mother of the said Cornelia Jones died the 10 July 1787 aged 73 years.

Phebe Jones the Mother of the said Samuel Jones died the 10th of May 1800 Aged 85 Years.

Samuel Jones the Elder died at West Neck aforesaid on the 25 day of November 1819.

Cornelia Jones Widow of said Samuel Jones last mentioned died the 29th Day of July 1821.

David Jones (who wrote his name David S. Jones) died in the city of New York on the 10th day of May 1848 in the 71st year of his age.

William Jones son of said Samuel and Cornelia Jones died at his residence Coldspring Long Island on the 16th day of September 1853 in the 82d year of his age. He was buried on the 19th September 1853 in the Family burying ground on West Neck South Oyster bay Long Island.

Thomas Jones son of said Samuel and Cornelia Jones died at the residence of his son Thomas W. Jones, South Oysterbay L. I. on the first day of February 1852 in the 79th year of his age. He is buried in the family burying ground on West Neck L. I.

Samuel Jones son of said Samuel and Cornelia Jones died at the residence of his brother William Jones, Cold Spring Long Island on the ninth day of August 1853 in the 84th year of his age. He is buried at Rhinebeck Dutchess County N. Y. Re-interred at South Oyster bay.

John Bleecker Miller married Cornelia Jones 26" Dec. 1850 at St. George's ch. Schenectady.

John Bleecker Miller, son of John Bleecker & Cornelia Jones Miller, married Mary Berthenia Dunn 9th Sept. 1893. Daughter Rev. Ballard Dunn & Elizabeth Stansbury Dunn.

Cornelia Stansbury, daughter of John Bleecker & Mary Berthenia Miller born 22^d November (Sunday morning 7 A.M.) 1896.

John Bleecker, son of John Bleecker Miller & Mary Berthenia Miller born 29 January 1899 (Sunday at 1.10 p.m.)

Cornelia Jones daughter of John Bleecker & Cornelia Jones Miller married Commander French Ensor Chadwick U.S.N. 20" Nov. 1878.

John Bleecker Miller, son of John Bleecker Miller & Mary Berthenia Dunn Miller died at Long Beach 14" September 1900 aged 17 months.

Maria Duane Bleecker Miller daughter of John Bleecker Miller & Cornelia Jones Miller married 26" December 1896 to Wilmot

Townsend Cox son of Townsend Cox & Anne Helme Townsend Cox of Glen Cove & Mill Neck Long Island.

Saturday 7" Dec. 1901, Cornelia Jones Miller daughter of Samuel William Jones & Maria Bowers Duane and widow of John Bleecker Miller at 58 West 9" Street New York and is buried in the Miller lot in Utica New York.

William Jones Son of Samuel Jones was born the 4th Day of October 1771 between three and four of the Clock in the morning. Kezia the Daughter of Daniel Youngs of the Township of Oyster Bay was born the 12th Day of February 1773. And the 14th Day of October 1790 the said William and Kezia intermarried.

Samuel William Jones the first child of the said William and Kezia was born the 6th day of July 1791.

David William Jones the second child of the said William and Kezia was born the 3d Day of May 1793

Cornelia Haring Jones the first Daughter and third child of the said William and Kezia was born the 22d Day of April 1796.

Susan Maria Jones the second Daughter and fourth Child of the said William and Kezia was born the 20th Day of April 1802.

Elbert W. Jones the fifth child of the said William and Kezia was born the 17th Day of July 1803.

Eleanor Jones the sixth child of the said William and Kezia was born the seventh Day of May 1805.

Hannah Amelia Jones the seventh Child of the said William and Keziah was born the tenth day of June 1807.

Daniel Youngs Jones the eighth Child of the said William and Kezia was born the 9th day of July 1809.

Also a Daughter born in 1811 August the 7th.

Elbert W. Jones above named died January 14th 1826 in the 23d year of his age.

Cornelia H. above named died 29th December 1839 then being the wife of Thomas Floyd Jones—in the 43 year of her age.

Kezia Jones above named died on the first day of May 1847 aged Seventy four years two months nineteen days at her residence Cold Spring.

Susan Youngs the mother of Kezia Jones died at her residence at Oyster bay Cove on the 22d September 1847 in the 96th year of her age. Born 21st April 1752.

Hannah Amelia above named wife of the Rev. Samuel Seabury D. D. of New York died at her residence in that city on the 18th September 1852 in the 46th year of her age.

William Jones above named died 16th September 1853 in the 82^{d} year of his age.

Samuel W. Jones above named died first day of Dec. 1855 in the city of New York in the 65th year of his age. He was buried on the 3d of December 1855 in the family burying ground on West Neck South Oysterbay Long Island.

Maria B. Duane wife of Samuel W. Jones died at Geneva N. Y. Dec. 23d 1858 in the 67th year of her age; and buried in St. George's Church Schnectady Dec. 25th, 1858.

Marianne Duane Jones, daughter of Saml W. Jones and Maria B. D. Jones died in New York City January 10th 1887. Buried in Utica, New York.

James Duane Jones son of Saml W. Jones & Maria B. D. Jones died in Schenectady December 31st 1879. Buried in Cemetary Schenectady N. Y.

Daniel Jones son of Saml W. Jones & Maria D. B. Jones died of wound fever near Jacksonville Florida July 1864 buried on Col. Drummond's place. He fought in the Confederate Army.

On the 28th January 1812 Cornelia H. Jones the eldest daughter of William and Kezia Jones was married to Thomas Floyd-Jones son of David Richard Floyd-Jones and Sarah his wife, by the Rev. Seth Hart of Hempstead, Long Island.

On the 26th of November 1816 Samuel W. Jones the Eldest son of the said William & Kezia was married to Maria B. Duane the eldest daughter of James C. & Mary Ann Duane by the Rev. Cyrus Stebbins of the city of Schenectady.

On the 10th of December 1818 Susan Maria the second daughter of the said William and Kezia was married to James H. Weeks son of James and Miriam Weeks by the Rev. Marmaduke Earle of Oyster bay L. I.

On the 7th of May 1823 Eleanor Jones, the third daughter of the said William and Kezia, was married to William Sidney Smith son of William and Hannah Smith, by the Revd Seth Hart of Hempstead.

On the 17th day of November 1835 Hannah Amelia fourth daughter of the said William and Kezia was married to the Revd Samuel Seabury son of the Revd Charles Seabury & Ann his wife, by the Rev. Wm. A. Muhlenberg D. D. of Flushing, L. I.

John Bleecker Miller, son of Morris Smith Miller & Maria Bleecker his wife, of Utica, New York Married 26th December 1850 Cornelia Jones daughter of Samuel William Jones and Maria Bowers Duane his wife.

John Bleecker Miller, son of John Bleecker Miller & Cornelia Jones his wife, married 9th of September 1893 Mary Berthenia Dunn daughter of Rev. S. Ballard Dunn & Elizabeth Stansbury his wife, of Maryland.

Cornelia Jones, daughter of John Bleecker Miller & Cornelia Jones his wife, married 20th November 1878 French Ensor Chadwick, Lt. Commander U. S. Navy, son of Capt. Daniel Chadwick & Eliza Evans his wife of Morgantown, West Virginia, by the Rev. William Jones Seabury.

Maria Duane Bleecker, daughter of John Bleecker Miller & Cornelia Jones his wife, married 26th December 1896 Wilmot Townsend Cox son of Townsend Cox & Anne Helme Townsend, his wife, of East Island, Glen Cove, Long Island. Married at 58 West 9 Street, New York, by Rev. Percy Grant.

Cornelia Stansbury Miller, daughter of John Bleecker Miller & Mary Berthenia Dunn his wife was born the 22 November 1896 at 7. A. M. Sunday.

John Bleecker Miller son of John Bleecker Miller & Mary Berthenia Dunn Miller was born 29 January 1899 at the residence of his parents 56 West 9 Street, Sunday at 1.10 p.m. He died at Long Beach: Long Island 14 September, 1900.

Maria Duane Bleecker Cox, beloved wife of Wilmot Townsend Cox, died on the 16th day of December, 1915.

Old Knickerbacker Homestead, Schaghticoke, New York
Built by John Knickerbacker, Jr., about 1770, to replace the original house

COL. JOHANNES KNICKERBACKER.[1]
(1723–1802.)

Holy Bible in Dutch; Dordrecht, Jacob en Hendrick Keur, 1741.

Contains the records in Dutch and English of Col. Johannes Knickerbacker and Rebecca Fonda, his wife, with their descendants for three generations. It passed into the hands of strangers but was purchased from them by Miss Katheryne Knickerbacker Viele, a great-granddaughter of Col. Knickerbacker, who has presented it to the New York State Library at Albany, N. Y.

Joh⁸ Knickerbacker zyn boeck of Bybil Gekogt van pietrus Kurtineus to new york Pris £. 3:13: Siptember Den 19, 1763.

1723th Mart 17th Es gebooren John = Knickerbacker en mir Vrou Rabeckka Fonda is geboren in Het Yar 1718 April 14th in wi zin getrout in het yar

1750 Februware 17th; 1751 Jannewary 29, na De oude Styl is Gebooren myn Soon Johannis,

1753 Jannewary 19th de Newe Styl is gebooren myn Dockter Annatie

1754 november 19 na De newe Styl is geboren myn Twe Docktors Neiltie en Eliesabeth.

Abraham Viele en Annaie Knickerbacker Getrout July 5: 1771 En Mine Son Johannis Geboren in het yar 1774 (20th March - - - - En Myn Doghter Eva Geboren 27th Jany 1779.

Be it Remembered that Annaie Viele, wife of Abraham Viele Departed this Life on the 15th of Febuary A.D. 1826 at 11o'clock in the Morning aged Seventy Three Years and twenty six Days.

Be it Remembered that Abraham Viele departed this (life) on the 18th August 1829 at 12 of noon aged Eighty four years and two Days.

[1 The Dutch character ij is not cut for fonts of English type. Therefore the letter y has been used in the Dutch records where ij is meant.]

Be it Remembered that Johannis Knickerbacker departed this life on the 16th Day of August 1802 at a Quarter past ten in the Morning aged Seventy Nine Years fore Months and twenty one Days. and his Wife Rebecca on the 6 Day of Jan'y 1800 About 8 o'c in the Morning.

Abraham Viele Born August 16th1745.

JOHANNES HERMENSEN KNICKERBACKER.[1]
(Born 1679.)

Holy Bible in Dutch; Amsterdam, de Groot, vander Putte, van Heereren, & Hasbroek, 1718.

This Bible originally belonged to Johannes H. Knickerbacker, son of the first American Knickerbacker, who married Anna Quackenbos of Albany. It descended from him to his grandson, known as Col. Johannes Knickerbacker, Jr. (1751-1827), and contains his records in Dutch. It has descended in a straight line from him to the present owner, Col. Charles Knickerbacker Winne, of Albany.

J:K: Backer Albanij 1721 augustus 3 mals hoogh water gehat dat er veel winter koren weg draf in orten in haver 11 - 18 - 26 - augustus

Rebecka Fonda Housvrow Van John Knickerbacker is geboren 1718 Den 14 April en gestorven den 8 Januwary 1800 out Synde 81 Yaer 8 Mante & 6 dagen

1751 ben ik Geboren John Knickerbacker Jun[r] 29th Januwary by de oude Stiel

1752 April 6th is geboren myn vrou Elisebeth & wy syn getrout 1769 February 29 te Albany

1826 November 10th Died Elizabeth Knickerbacker aged Seventy four Years Seven Months and four Days.

10th November 1827 Died John Knickerbacker at four OClock in the Morning

Albany Mert 16th anno 1679 is Johannes Knickerbacker Geboren en syn vrou is Geboren Anno 1681 de 4th Mert en is Getrout Met Ante Quackenboss den 19th van Octover Anno 1701 en har ouste Doghter Libete is Geboren Anno 1702 den 1 dag van November

Nelte is Geboren Anno 1706 den 24 dag van June

Harmen is Geboren Anno 1709 den 19 dag December

[1 The Dutch character ij is not cut for fonts of English type. Therefore the letter y has been used in the Dutch records where ij is meant.]

Wouter is Geboren Anno 1712 den 27 October

Cornelia is Geboren Anno 1716 den 16 September

Johannes is Geboren Anno 1723 den 17 Mert en is Gestorven den 20th October 1802 oudt Synde Negen en seventig Jaer Vijf Maante en 22 Daagen

1768 Septem[r] 18th is Harmen Knickerbacker Overleden Out Synde 58 Years 8 Manden en 18 dagen

Schactekook Fabruwary 29th 1769 Ben ik Getrowt Johannes Knickerbacker Jun[r] Met Elizebeth Winne

1769 December 17th is Geboren my Erste Son Harmen omtrent Sondag Midag

1771 November 28 is Geboren myn tweden Soen William omtrent 11 Uren in de avont

1772 July 28th is Gestorven myn Soen William omtrent midag Oud Synde 8 Manden

1773 May de 9 is Geboren my Son William Winne omtrent 11 Uren in de morgen

1775 May the 9th is Geboren myn Erste doghter Rebecken omtrent 2 uren na de midag

1777 Mert the 23th is Geboren myn tweden doghter Marytie omtrent 2 uren na de midag

1777 October de 16th is Gestorven myn Oudste Soen Harmen omtrent 10 uren, vor midag Oudt Synde 7 Jaer en 10 manden

1779 July de 27th is Geboren Myn soen Harmen omtrent 7 uren in de morgen

1781 June 16th is Geboren Myn Doghter Dirke omtrent midag

1782 April de 21th is Gestorven myn Doghter Dirke out synde 10 Mande en ses dagen

1783 Januwary de 27th is Geboren my Twede Doghter Dirke omtrent 4 Uren in De morgen

1784 December de de 7th is Geboren my Son Johones omtrent 5 Uren in de morgen

[1786]* October 19 is Geboren myn Dochter Annatie omtrent an helf ur voor medag

[1788 Au]*gust 18 is Geboren myn Dochter Elizebeth omtrent 9 uren [in de]* Avont

[1790 Ju]*ne 12th is Geboren myn Dochter Neltie omtrent 7 Uren [in de]* morgen

[1792 A]*ugustus 23 is Geboren myn Dochter Katlyne omtrent [2 ure]*n in De morgen

1796 is Geboren myn Son Abraham omtrent 2 Uren Na de midag April 7

William W Knickerbacker was born May 9th 1773

Diricke Van Veghten born February 12th 1778

Schaghtikoke May 19 1792 Was I William W Knickerbacker Maried to Mr Diricke Van Veghten of Schaghtikoke by the Reverend Lambartus De Ronde

Johannis Kneckerbacker Min Bibel Goot Segent Ons ByDe Amen

FRANCIS LEWIS.
(Born 1750.)

Holy Bible in English; Oxford, T. Wright and K. Gill, 1777.

> Contains record of Francis Lewis and Elizabeth Ludlow, his wife, with their children. We have not been able to locate the present owner of the Bible, nor to verify the records.

Francis Lewis Junr., Eldest Son of Francis Lewis of ye City of New York, Merch't. Born in New York ye 28th. Feby 1750 O.S. ------ Married in New York ye 8th. May 1775 to Elizabeth Ludlow youngest Daughter of Gabriel and Elizabeth Ludlow Born in New York the 15th. July 1755 ----- Their Issue -----

Eliza, born 22d. July 1776 at one O'clock P.M. at the Seat of Geo. D. Ludlow's Hempstead Plains, Long Island. Baptized ye 11th. Aug. 1776 by the Revd Mr. Cutting. Sponsors Elizabeth Ludlow, Francis Ludlow, Francis Ludlow, Junr. Died Sunday 5th. Octobr 1777 at four O'clock P.M. at Baltimore, Maryland.

Morgan, born Thursday 11th. Septemr. 1777 at half past eight A.M. at Baltimore. Baptized 15th. Octobr 1777 by the Revd Mr. Chase. Sponsors. Morgan Lewis. Francis Lewis, Junr. Ann Ludlow. (Rich'd Carson, proxy Elizabeth Lewis.)

Juan Francis, born Thursday, 16th. Septr 1779 at four O'clock A.M. at Philadelphia. Baptized ye 26th. Octobr 1779 by the Revd. Mr. White. Sponsors. Don Juan D. Miralles Francis Lewis, Junr. Jennett Montgomery.

Edmund Ludlow, born Sunday 30th. Septemr. 1781 at Twelve O'clock A.M. at Philadelphia. Baptized 8th: Novemr. 1781 by the Revd. Mr. White. Sponsors. Francis Lewis, Junr. John Craig. Margta. M. Craig. Died Saturday 20th. Aug. 1782 at five O'clock P.M. at Philadelphia.

Ann Dashwood, born Friday 9th. May 1783 at six O'clock A.M. at Philadelphia. Baptized 7th. Septr. '83 at Flushing by the Revd. Jos'a Bloomer. Sponsors. Elizabeth Ludlow. Arabella Ludlow. Daniel Ludlow.

Eliza, born Thursday 25th. Aug. 1785 at half after nine O'clock A.M. at New York. Baptized 19th. Nov. 1785 by the Revd. Jos'a Bloomer at Flushing, Long Island. Sponsors. The Father & Mother.

Gabriel Ludlow, born Wednesday 4th. July 1787 at 7,O'clock P.M. at New York. Baptized 19th. August 1787 at Flushing, Long Island, by the Revd. Jos'a Bloomer. Sponsors. Francis Lewis, Junr. Morgan Lewis. Gertrude Lewis.

Louisa Elizabeth, born Monday 16th. March 1789 at nine O'clock P.M. at Flushing, Long Island. Baptized 10th. April 1789 at Flushing by the Revd. Jos'a Bloomer. Sponsors. Eliz'h Crommelin. Sarah Aspinwall. Robert Crommelin.

Cecilia Goold Lewis, born Wednesday 12th. January 1791 at 7-O'clock P.M. at Flushing, Long Island. Baptized 22d. March 1792 at Flushing, by the Revd. William Hammel. Sponsors. Francis Lewis, Jr. Eliz. Lewis. Ann D. Lewis, Proxy for Sarah Goold.

Horatio Gates Lewis, born Sunday, 17th. Feby. 1793 at 6-O'clock A.M. at Flushing, Long Island. Baptized 19th. November 1793, at Flushing, by the Revd. William Hammel. Sponsors. Francis Lewis, Jr. Elizabeth Lewis.

Emma Frances, born Saturday 7th. March 1795 at 5-O'clock P.M. at the House of William Prince, Flushing, Long Island. Baptized 10th. July 1795 by Bishop Prevoorst. Sponsors. Francis Lewis, Jr. Elizabeth Lewis.

George Edwin, born 5th. November 1797 at 10-O'clock P.M., at the house No. 42 Pine Street, New York. Baptized 22nd. Aug. 1798, by Revd. Mr. Beache. Sponsors. Francis Lewis, Jr. Juan F. Lewis. Elizabeth Lewis.

May his fame be Renowned in History; and Gloriously die in the love of God.

PHILIP PHILIP LIVINGSTON.
(1741–1787.)

Holy Bible in English; Cambridge, Archdeacon, 1768.

Contains the records of Philip P. Livingston and Sarah Johnson his wife. It has descended directly to the present owner, Oswald J. Cammann Rose, Esq., of Geneva, N. Y., the great-great-grandson of Philip Livingston.

RECORD.

Philip Ph. Livingston & Sarah Johnson. Married in Jamaica the 29th day of June 1768 by the Rev^d Mr. John Poole Rector of St. Andrews.

Philip Ph. Livingston born the 28th day of May 1741. O. S. is the 8th of June N. S. Died in New York 2 Novr 1787

Sarah Johnson born the 23^d day of March 1749. O. S. is the 2^d of April N. S. Died in New York 6 Novr 1802

Christina Livingston. (the 2nd daughter of the above named) born on Tuesday the 26th day of September 1774. at ten minuites after 12 O'Clock in the Morning (A.M.) at New York in North America. Baptized by the Reverend Mr. John Livingston on the 18th day of November 1774. Godfather Mr. Abraham Livingston, Godmother Miss Sarah Ph. Livingston. (Married 29 March to J. N. Macomb 1797.)

Sarah Livingston (the 3^d daughter of the above named) born on thursday the 29th day of february 1776 at half past ten O'Clock P.M. at Kingston Jamaica. Baptized by the Rev^d Mr. Coxeter 16th of June 1776. Godfathers Mr. John Cargill and Mr. Muscoe Livingston. Godmothers Mrs. Thomas Cargill and Mrs. (Muscoe) Livingston. Died in New York 12th April 1797.

Philip Henry Livingston, Son of Philip Ph & Sarah Livingston, born the 30th October (being Monday) at three quarters of an hour after 2 o'Clock in the Morning 1769, Baptised by the Reverend Mr. Thomas Coxeter Rector of Kingston Jam^a, on the 26th November 1769. Godfathers, Henry Livingston, Daniel Moore & Nathl Grant Esqs. Godmothers, Mrs. Mary Burke and Mrs. Mary

Fitch. Married to Maria Livingston daughter of Walter L. 8 May 1788. She died in August 1828 at New York.

George Livingston born on Monday the 14th day of October (at three quarters of an hour after 10 o'Clock in the m [tear in paper] in the year of our Lord 1771. Baptized by the Revd Mr. Coxeter on the 6th January 1772. Godfathers, Mr. Jasper Hall, Mr. Richard Cargill, Mr [tear in paper] Mr. Joseph Fitch, Mr. Eliphalet Fitch, and Mr. Charles Da- [tear in paper] Godmothers, Mrs. Catherine Van Rensselear, Mrs. Fran [tear in paper] Orgill, Mrs. Ann Grant, & Mrs. Frances Ingles.

Catherine Livingston, born on Tuesday the 13th day of October (at five minuites after three o'Clock in the afternoon) in the year of Our Lord 1772. Baptized by the Revd Mr. Coxeter 6th Jany 1773. Godfather Philip Livingston Junr of Pensacola, Esqr Godmothers Mrs. Eliza Cargill, Mrs. Sarah McDonell and Miss Margaret Livingston. (Married to John Saunders 13 Octr 1796, at New York. Died 20th of March 1819 at St. Mary's Jamaica. Mr. Saunders died in Jamaica December 1818.)

ROBERT LIVINGSTON.[1]
(1654–1728.)

Holy Bible in English; (London), 1683.

Contains the records of Robert Livingston, first Lord of the Manor of Livingston, and of his wife, Alida Schuyler. The Bible descended in the direct line to Mrs. Mary E. Livingston Wilson, who presented it to the New York Historical Society in 1913. The records are in Dutch, with an English translation.

Robert Livingston his Bible, sent by his mother from Rotterdam, A. D. [1689]

Den 9 July 1679 oude Stÿl Ben ick Robt Livingston in den Howelyken Staat bevestigt met myn Waarde Huysvrow Alida Schuÿler gewesene Wed⁻. wÿlen Dom: Nicolaus van Rensselaer in de gereformeerde Kerke te albany in america op een woonsdagh voor de Middagh door Dom: Gideon Schaets God v⁻leene ons dat hem Eerlyk ons Ons Saligh is amen

A°. 1680 den 26 aprill zynde 's maandags 's morgens tuschen 8 & 9 uyren is myn Oudtse Soon Johannes gebooren, de heer will hem in deughde laeten opwassen; hy is nae myn Vader Salg⁻ genoemt & den 2 mey zynde Sondaghs gedoopt, d' Compeers waeren myn Schoonvader C: Phillip Schuyler & Dirk Wessels & ten doop gehouden van myn Schoonmoeder Juffr: Margareta Schuyler doch vader Schuyler op d' Vlakte zynde was v⁻hindert van d'Extreem hooghwater hier te comen so dat Broed⁻ Pieter in zyn Plaats als getuyge gestaan heeft.

A°. 1681 Den 5 Decemb⁻ zynde 's maendaghs 's morgens ontrent 6 uyren is myn Oudtse Dochter Margareta geboren, d' heere will haer segenen nae Siele & lichaam, zy is nae myn Schoonmoeder genoemt & op den 11 d^{to} van Do: Gideon Schaets gedoopt, d' getuygen waren myn Sch ... vader C: Phill: Schuyler & myn Schoonmoeder die haer ten doop heeft gepresenteert.

A°. 1683/4 p^{mo} februarÿ zynde Vrydaeghs 'S morgens ontrent 7 uyren is myn Twede Dochter Johanna Philippina geboren;

[1 The Dutch character ÿ is not cut for fonts of English type. Therefore the letter y has been used in the Dutch records where ÿ is meant.]

d' heere will haer zegenen & in deughde laeten opwassen, Sy is naer myn moeder & myn Schoonvader salg⁻ genoemt & op den 3 d⁰ van D⁰. Gideon Schaets gedoopt, Dom. Godevridus Dellius leesende t Formulier, de getuyge waren oom David Schuyler en Broed⁻ Arent Schuyler & is ten doop gedraege van Suster Engeltie Schuyler.

A⁰. 1686 Den 9 July zynde Vrydagh savonts te 10 uyren is myn Twede Son Philip geboren Godt will hem in deughde laeten opwassen, hy is naer myn Schoonvader genoemt & op den 25 d⁰. gedoopt van D⁰. Gideon Schaets D⁰. Godevridus Dellius lesende t Formulier d'Coompeerst waeren oom David Schuyler & Broed⁻ Phillip Schuyler & is ten doop gepresenteert van Suster Cornelia Broed⁻ Brants huysvrou ick was te N: Yorke gecommitteert met Br: Pʳ om d Charter

A⁰. 1688 Den 24 July zynde dynsdaghs te 3 uyre 'S achtermiddaghs is myn huysvrouw v⁻lost van myn derde Soon Robert, d heere will hem zegenen dat hy in deughde magh opwassen in d' oprechte gereformeerde Religie is op Sondagh den 29 gedoopt van D⁰ Godevridus Dellius, d Compeers waeren oom David Schuyler & Br. Johannes Schuyler en is ten doop gepresenteert van Suster Margareta Schuyler: Ick was met gov⁻ Dongan nae N: York v⁻trocken weg: d Reck⁻ van d Soldaeten optemaeken die hier v⁻lede winter in garnisoen laegen & door my onderhouden

A⁰. 1689/90 Den 3 maart zynde 's Maendaghs te 5 uyren 'S morgens is myn Vierde Soon geboren genaemt Gysbertus nae myn huysvrows Broed⁻ Salg⁻ de heere will hem & ons altemael bewaeren in dese gevaerlyke oorloghstyden is op woonsdagh den 5 d⁰ gedoopt van D⁰ Godevridus Dellius, is ten Doop gedraage van Suster Jenneke Schuyler de Compeers waaren Livinus van Schaÿk & ...... Ick was gecommitteert van d Conventie nae de Colonyen van N: Engelandt om assistentie van Volk en ammunitie tegens de franse, die Shennechtady op den 9 feb⁻ lestleden . hebben offgelopen geen waght gehouden zijnde 't Volk zynde v⁻deelt door usurpatie van eenen Jacob Leysler Coopman tot N: Yorke die zich de Regeering van dese Provintie assumeerde Sonder Commissie. N.B. is ook voor een v⁻raeder gexecuteert te N: Yorke in Mey 1691

1690 Den 24 Junÿ So is onse Lieve Dochter Johanna Philippina in den Heere ontslaapen te N: Yorke & naest haer Engeltje meut begraeven, ick was te hartford aldaer te v͞blyven gedurende de tydt van d Revolutie & disorders, ick quam in July tot albany met Maj͞ Gen¹ Winthrop & werde siek van d Coors v͞trock in Septemb͞ nae Stratford myn huysvrouw Volgde in decemb͞ den 15 arriveerde zy met d kinders te norwok gingen te fairfeild woonen dese winter. Ondertuschen arriveerde Maj͞ Richd Ingoldesby met de Soldaeten uyt Engelant & naederhant Col henry Sloughter gov͞ gen¹. Doch Jacob Leÿsler & zyn factie Resisteerde de Coninklycke authoriteyt & wilde t fort niet overleveren, naderhant d' Canallie hem afvallende liet hem & zyn Raaden in d Peekell om alles te v͞antwoorden waerom 8 zyn gecondemneert voor hoogh-v͞raet om te sterven, Leysler & Milborn gehangen als de hoofden, d Rest in gevankenisse tot dat d Coning zyn believe bekent wort.

1679 den 9 July oude Styll Ben ick Robert Livingston in den houelyken......tigh met myn Waerde huysvrow Alida Schuyler gewesene wed͞ wylen Dom ... Nicolas Van Renselaer in d gereformeerde kerk van albany in america op Woensdagh voor d Middagh door Dom: gideon Schaets Godt v͞leene ons dat...... Eerlyk en ons Saligh is amen

1680 den 26 aprill zynde S maendaghs S morgens tushen 8 & 9 uren is myn soon...... geboren d heer will hem in deugde laeten opwassen hy is naer myn Vad^r Salg͞. ...naemt & den 2 meÿ zynde Sondaegs gedoopt waerover als getuygen zyn m... shoonvad͞ Phillip Schuyler & Dirk Wessels is ten doop gehouden van .... schoenmoed͞ Juff͞. margrieta Schuyler doch vader Schuyler op d Vlakte sy... was v͞hind^t van d Extreme hooge water hier t komen soo dat Broe... Pieter in zyn Plaets (in zyn Plaets) als getuyge gestaen heeft

1681 den 5 Decemb͞ S maendaegs S morgens ontrent 6 uren is myn oudtste Doghter margareta geboren; d heere will haer segenen naer ziel en lichaem zy .... naer myn shoenmoed͞ genaemt en op den 11 d° van Dom shaets gedoopt getuygen waeren myn shoonvad͞. Phillip Shuyler en mÿn shoonm... die haer ten doop heeft gepresenteert

1683/4 den Erste February zynde Vrydaegs S morgens ontrent 7 uren is m... Doghter Johanna Phillipina geboren: Godt will haer met zyn geest en in Deugde laten opwassen, sy is naer mÿn moed- & myn Shoonm... Salg- genaemt & op den 3 d° van Dom: shaets gedoopt Dom: godevr... Dellius leesende t formulier, d getuygen waren oom David Shuy.... Broed-. arent Schuyler & is ten doop gepresenteert van Suster Engel... shuyler: NB. zy is in den heere gerust te N: Yorke van d kinder Pocke gestorven, Juny 1690.

1686 Den 9 Jully zynde Vrydaegs avont ... 10 uren is myn Twede ... Phillip geboren, godt will hem ... deaugde laeten opwassen ... naer myn shoonvader genoemt en op den 25 d° gedoopt van .... Dom: godevridus Dellius lass het formulier, d. Compeers waren ... David Schuyler & Broder Phillip Schuyler & is ten doop gepresenteert .... Suster Cornelia Schuyler Broed- Brants huysvrow, ick was t N: York gecommitteert weg: d Charter.

1688 Den 24 Jully zynde Dynsdaeg ten 3 uyren achtermiddaghs .... huysvrowe v-lost van myn derde soon Robert D heere will hem zyn zeegan v-leene dat ghy in deugde magh opwassen in d oprechte ge...meerde Religie is op Sondagh den 29 gedoopt van Dom: godev... van Dell: d Compeers waren David oom & Johannes Shuÿler ... doopt gepresenteert van Suster Margerata Shuyler Ich was .... Excell. Tho: Dongan Capt Genl naer N: Yorke v-trocken w... Rek- d. militia belangende op te maken -

1689/90 Den 3 maert zynde Maendagh te 5 uyren 's morgens is myn waerde pant v-lost van myn ... Soon Gysbert, d Almaghtige will hem bewaren in dese gevaerlyke Tyden & hem .... maken int Ewige Paradys is op Woonsdagh den 5 d° gedoopt van Dom: godevrid... d Compeers waren Br: Peter Shuyler d mayor & alderman Livinus Van Sh[aick] Peet was Suster Jenneke Shuylers.

1692 Den   maert is geboren myn Vyffde Soon Willhem godt geve hem geluk & sa ... hy is gedoopt van D° Dellius waarover als Compeers stingen

d° Den 5 november is myn Soon willem in d heere ontslaepen & was begra ... van N: Yorke arriveerde

1694 Den 10 Decem⁻. is geboren myn derde Dochter Johanna zynde maendagh 'S avondts, (op dieselfden dagh ging ick & myn Johannes d Sandt Punt uyt in de Ship d Charity Lancaster Syms Shipper) zy is gedoopt van D° godev . . . Dellius . . . . waren Collonel Richard Ingoldesby & Maj P⁻ Shuyler & is ten doop . . . . van Juffrow Dellius [some words cut off]

1699 Den 13 Feb⁻ is onse soon Robert

1698 Den 22 maÿ is geboren onse Vierde Dochter Catharina en is 2 weeken daernae gedoopt Door Dom⁻ godevridus Dellius d Compeers waren Capt Brant Schuyler & Collonel Abraham de Peÿster en d Countess d' Gravinne van Bellomont was Peet die haer ten doop hiel

1699 Den 6 Decemb⁻ ontrent 8 uyren 's avonts is onse Dochtertie Catharina in den heere ontslapen en op den 9^{den} daeraen in de kerk begraven by haer grootvader Capt Phil: shuyler zalg⁻

1700 Den 20 Decemb⁻ is myn oudtste Dochter Margareta getrowt met Capt Samuel Veitch tot onsen in huys door D° Johannes Lydius met een Lycence. de heere will haer zyn Segen geven in dese werelt & d' Ewighe Vreucht hiernamaels amen

[TRANSLATED FROM THE DUTCH BY DINGMAN VERSTEEG

[On July 9, 1679, Old Style I, Robert Livingston, was married to my worthy wife Alida Schuyler last widow of the deceased Domine Nicolaus Van Rensselaer, in the Reformed Church at Albany in America on a Wednesday in the forenoon, by Dom. Gideon Schaets. May God grant us to Honor Him, toward our salvation, Amen.

[1680 April 26, being Monday morning between 8 and 9 o'clock my eldest son Johannes was born; may the Lord grant him to grow up virtuous; he was named for my deceased father, and baptised on May 2, being a Sunday. The witnesses were my father in law Cap Phillip Schuyler and Dirk Wessels, and was presented for baptism by my mother in law Mrs. Margareta Schuyler. But Father Schuyler, being at the Flatts, was prevented by the extremely high water from coming hither, and Brother Pieter acted as witness in his father's stead.

[1681, December 5, being Monday morning about 6 o'clock my eldest daughter Margareta was born; may the Lord bless her both spiritually and physically she was named for my mother in law and was baptised on the 11th of the said month by Dom. Gideon Schaets. The witnesses were my father in law Cap Phill. Schuyler and my mother in law who has presented her for baptism.

[1683/4 February first, being Friday morning about 7 o'clock, my second daughter Johanna Philippina was born; may the Lord bless her and grant her to grow up virtuous; she was named after my mother and my deceased father in law, and was baptized on the 3rd by D° Gideon Schaets, Dom. Godevridus Dellius reading the Formulary. The witnesses were uncle David Schuyler and Brother Arent Schuyler, and was presented for baptism by Sister Engeltie Schuyler.

[1686, July 9, being Friday evening about ten o'clock, my second son Philip was born; may God grant him to grow up in virtue; he was named for my father in law, and on the 25th was baptized by Dom. Gideon Schaats, D° Godevridus Dellius reading the Formulary. The Witnesses were uncle David Schuyler and Brother Phillip Schuyler, and was presented for baptism by Sister Cornelia Schuyler, wife of Brother Brant. I was at New York as Commissioner for the Charter, with brother P^r.

[1688 July 24, being Tuesday at 3 o'clock in the afternoon my wife was delivered of my third son Robert, the Lord will bless him that he may grow up in virtue in the true Reformed Religion; was baptised on Sunday the 29th by D° Godevridus Dellius. The witnesses were Uncle David Schuyler and Brother Johannes Schuyler, and was presented for baptism by sister Margareta Schuyler. I had departed with Governor Dongan for New York, in regard to making out the account for the soldiers garrisoned here last winter, and supported by me.

[1689/90 March 3d being Monday at 5 o'clock in the morning my fourth son was born; named Gysbertus after my wife's deceased brother; may the Lord protect him and us together in these dangerous times of war. Was baptised on Wednesday the 5th by Dom. Godevridus Dellius. Was presented for baptism by sister Jenneke Schuyler. The witnesses were Levinus Van Schayke & .... I was deputed by the Convention to the New England

Colonies, to request assistance of people and ammunition against the French, who on February 9 last had surprised Schenectady, no guard having been kept, the people being divided on account of the usurpation of one Jacob Leysler, merchant at New York, who, without a commission, assumed the government of this Province. N.B. Was also executed as a traitor at New York in May 1691.

[1690 June 24, Our beloved daughter Johanna Philippina slept in the Lord at New York, and was buried next to Engeltje. I was at Hartford intending to stay there during the period of revolt and disorder. I arrived in July at Albany in Company with Maj. Genl Winthrop, and was taken sick with fever. Departed in September for Stratford. My wife followed in December, and on the 15th she with the children arrived at Norwalk. We went to live at Fairfield for the winter. Meanwhile Majr. Richd Ingolsby arrived with the soldiers from England, and afterward Col. Henry Slougter, gov^r Genl. But Jacob Leysler and his faction resisted the royal authority and was unwilling to surrender the fort. Afterward the mob falling away from him left him and his Councillors in a pickle, to answer for everything. On account hereof eight have been condemned to death on a charge of high treason; Leysler and Milborn hung as the ringleaders. The remainder imprisoned till the King's pleasure shall be known.

[1679 July 9 Old Style, I Robert Livingston was married to my worthy wife Alida Schuyler last widow of the deceased Domine Nicolas Van Renselaer, in the Reformed Church of Albany in America, on a Wednesday in the forenoon by Dom. Gideon Schaets. May God grant us to honor Him, for our salvation, Amen.

[1680 April 26, being monday morning between 8 and 9 o'clock my son . . . was born. May the Lord grant him to grow up virtuous. He was named for my deceased father, and baptised on May 2 being a Sunday, at which there were witnesses my father in law Philip Schuyler & Dirk Wessels. Was presented for baptism by my Mother in law Mrs. Margareta Schuyler. But Father Schuyler being on the Flatts, was prevented coming here by the extremely high flood, so that Brother Pieter stood in his stead as witness.

[1681 December 5, being Monday about 6 o'clock in the Morning, my eldest daughter Margareta was born; may the Lord bless her spiritually and physically; she was named for my mother in law, and on the 11th of the said month was baptised by Dom. Shaets. Witnesses were my Father in Law Phillip Schuyler and my mother in law who presented her for baptism.

[1683/4 February 1, being Friday morning about 7 o'clock my daughter Johanna Phillipina was born; may God endow her with His Spirit and grant her to grow up in virtue; she was named for my mother and my deceased father in law and was baptized on the 3d by Dom. Shaets, Dom. Godevridus Dellius reading the Formulary. The witnesses were Uncle David Shuyler, Brother Arent Shuyler and was presented for baptism by Sister Engeltie Schuyler. N.B. She rested in the Lord at New York, dying with small pox, June 1690.

[1686, July 9, being Friday evening at 10 o'clock my second son Phillip was born; may God grant him to grow up in virtue. He was named for my father in law and baptised on the 25th of the same month by Dom. Shaets. Dom Godevridus Dellius read the Formulary. Witnesses were uncle David Schuyler & Brother Phillip Schuyler, and was presented for baptism by Sister Cornelia Schuyler, Brother Brant's wife. I was at New York, as Commissioner regarding the Charter.

[1688, July 24, being Tuesday at 3 o'clock in the afternoon my wife was delivered of my third son Robert.; the Lord will bless him that he may grow up in virtue, in the pure Reformed religion. Was baptised on Sunday the 29th by Dom. Godevridus Van Dell. The witnesses were Uncle David and Johannes Schuyler. Presented for baptism by Sister Margareta Schuyler. I had gone to New York with His Excellency Tho: Dongan, Captain General, in order to make out the accounts concerning the Military.

[1689/90 March 3, being Monday at five o'clock in the morning my dear life partner was delivered of my son Gysbert. May the Almighty guard him in these dangerous times and make [obliterated] in the eternal Paradise. Was baptised on Wednesday the 5th by Dom. Godevridus. The witnesses were Brother Peter Schuyler, the mayor, & Alderman Levinus Van Shaick. Sister Jenneke Shuylers was godmother.

[1692 March — Was born my fifth son Willhem. May the Lord grant him happiness and prosperity. He was baptised by Do. Dellius and as witnesses stood . . .

[November 5. My son Willem slept in the Lord. He was buried when I arrived from New York.

[1694 December 10. Was born my third daughter Johanna, being Monday in the evening. (On the same day I and my Johannes passed the Sand Point in the ship The Charity, Lancaster Syms, skipper) She was baptised by Dom. Godevridus Dellius. Witnesses were: Colonel Richard Ingoldesby and Maj. Pr Shuyler, and Mrs. Dellius presented her for baptism.

[Here follows one line which is entirely obliterated]

[1698 May 22 Was born my fourth daughter Catharina, and two weeks later was baptized by Dom. Godevridus Dellius. The witnesses were Capt. Brant Schuyler and Col. Abraham De Peyster. And the Countess Gravinne Van Bellomont was the godmother, presenting her for baptism.

[1699 December 6, about 8 o'clock in the evening our little daughter Catharina slept in the Lord, and was on the 9th following buried in the Church next to her grandfather Capt. Phil Schuyler, deceased.

[1700 December 20. My oldest daughter Margareta was married to Capt. Samuel Veitch, in our house by Do. Johannes Lydius, with a licence. May the Lord grant her His blessings in this World, and eternal joy hereafter, Amen.]

GOVERT LOOCKERMANS.[1]
(Married 1641.)

Holy Bible in Dutch; Amsterdam, Paulus van Ravesteyn, 1624.

Contains the records of Govert Loockermans and Ariaentie Jans, his wife, who were married in New Amsterdam (New York) in 1641. It is now the property of the American Bible Society and has been deposited in the New York Public Library. The records are in Dutch, with an English translation by Dr. L. Bendikson.

Laus Deo in Amsterdam a 1641. Is getrout Govert Loockermans met Ariaentie Jans den 26 Feb. op Dinsdagh.

1641 den 3 November Sondaghs smorgens ten 3 uren is gebooren Maria Loockermans int schip "De Coninck Davit" onderweegen Christoffel en Nieu Nederlant

1643 den 23 September is gebooren Jannetie Loockermans smorgens ten 7 uren in Amsterdam in N: Nederlant.

1664 den 12 November is getrout Balthasaer Bayard en Maria Loockermans in N.Amsterdam in N.N.

1665 den 20 September morgens ten 3 uren heeft Maria Loockermans haer eerste soone gebooren en den 28 ditto is hy Samuel gedoopt de Compeers waren zyn grootvaders Govert Loockermans en ......

1667 18 November smorgens te drie uren is myn huysvrou Maria Loockermans verlost van een jonge dochter en den 20 dito aende Manhatans gedoopt Ariaentie. Haer peetoom is N.Bayard en peetmoey Marretie Jans.

1670 den 6 Meert nieuwe styl is geboore Anna Maria; haer peters syn Hendr. Vande Waater en Petrus Bayard, haer peet is haer meutie Anna Maria Bayard; en gedoopt den Meert tot N.Yorck.

1672 den 14 Junij is gebooren Samuel Bayard; syn peetooms syn Mr. Hans Kierstede en Baltelasaer Stuyvesant, syn peetmeuy is Jannetie Kierstede tot N:Yorck.

[1 The Dutch character ÿ is not cut for fonts of English type. Therefore the letter y has been used in the Dutch records where ÿ is meant.]

1677 den 31 Jann. nieuwe styl is gebooren Judith Bayard en den 10 dage daeraen gestorven. Haer peetom was Oloff Steevense van Cortlant en haer meutie Judith Varlet huysvrou van Nicolaes Bayard . . .

[TRANSLATION

[Laus Deo. Amsterdam, anno 1641. Married on Tuesday, February the 26th, Govert Loockermans and Ariaentie Jans.

[1641: November 3d, Sunday, born at 3 o'clock in the morning Maria Loockermans on board the ship "De Coninck Davit" on the way from Christoffel to the New Netherlands.

[1643: September 23d, born at 7 o'clock in the morning Jannetie Loockermans, at Amsterdam in the New Netherlands.

[1664: November 12th, married Balthasar Bayard and Maria Loockermans, at New Amsterdam in the New Netherlands.

[1665: September 20th, Maria Loockermans was brought to bed with her first son at 3 o'clock in the morning and on the 28th inst. he was christened Samuel; the godfathers were his grandfathers Govert Loockermans and ......

[1667: November 18th, my housewife Maria Loockermans was brought to bed with a daughter at 3 o'clock in the morning and she was christened Ariaentie on the 20th inst. at Manhattan. Her godfather is N. Bayard and [her] godmother Marretie Jans.

[1670: March 6th new style, born Anna Maria; her godfathers are Hendr. Vande Waater and Petrus Bayard, her godmother is her aunt Anna Maria Bayard; she was christened at New York on March ......

[1672: June 14th, born Samuel Bayard; his godfathers are Mr. Hans Kierstede and Baltelasaer Stuyvesant, his godmother is Jannetie Kierstede, at New York.

[1677: Jan. 31 new style, born Judith Bayard and she died on the 10th day thereafter. Her godfather was Oloff Steevense van Cortlant and her godmother Judith Varlet, housewife of Nicholas Bayard ......]

WILLIAM MACEY.
(Born 1614.)

Holy Bible in English; Printed by the Printers to the Universitie of Cambridge, 1637.

Contains fragments referring to the Macey family, John Ball and others. One page of manuscript and part of another are so confused and obliterated that they have not been copied. The Bible is now the property of the American Bible Society and is stored there.

William Macy was bourn in 1614 | Joane the daughter of William | Macy was Bourn the 204 day | of June in the yeare of our | lord god noon 1647 jay dorlsh | Joane Macey the daughter of William | Macey was bourn 204 day | of June in the yeare the of our | Lord God noon 1647 | Joane the daughter of William | Macye was Baptized the 207 of | June 1647 | John Ball, his hand and Pen 1687 | Jone the daughter of William Macy | was baptized 207 of June 1647 | Joane Mac | Joane the daugter of William Macey | was born the twenty four day of | June in the yeare of our Lord God 1667 | In Yorleke | William Macy his book | 1688 | Abraham Hole was born the | 9th day of May 1709 | John Ball his | paid to Elizabeth Curtis — 3 . . . | John Ball his | paid to John Rusele . . . 3 . . . 0 | paid to Bartholomu   4 . . . 0 | paid Roger harden . . . 2 . . . 5 | John Ball | the 10 day of May | paid to Elizabeth Curtis — 3 . . . 0 | John Ball | paid to John Rusele . . . 3 . . . 0 | paid to bartholomu   4 . . . 0 | paid to Roger harden Jone Ball 2   0 | harden John Ball 1687 | John Ball this is his   John Ball 1687 | Book God give him | Grace therein to look and when the Ole | for him doth tole the Lord of heaven | Recive his Soul. John Ball made this | 1689 | William Macy 1689 | his Book God give grace | therein to look and when | Ole for him doth tole the Lord | of heaven recive his Soul 1687 | John Ball 1700 | Oliver Ellsworth Lindsey was born on Wednesday | the twenty third of December A.D. 1807 | at a quarter past one in the afternoon. | and named in honor of Chief Justice Oliver Ellsworth | of Windsor New England. | He died on Sunday January the third | 1808 at 8 o'clock P.M. | Charles Lindsey was married on Sunday | Evening January the 27th 1811 to Aurelia Mitch | a Daughter of Isaac Mitchell of | Poughkeepsie.

ISAAC MAZŸCK.

Holy Bible in French; Amsterdam, 1680.

Contains the records of the births and deaths of the children of Isaac and Marianne Mazÿck, who came to America in 1686. It is now in the possession of the Charleston Library, Charleston, South Carolina.

En Charlestown En Carolina 1694 Liste Dela Naisace et mort Demes Enfans; et Leurs Batesme.

1: Le 17: may 1694: Est Né ma fille marianne a 2: hure apres midy, & a Este batise le 7 Juin; Elle a heu pour Parain; Henry Noble; son oncle & Pour maraine marianne Mazÿck; sa mere — mort 1695 Le 27 septembre mafille marianne Est morte; sur la minuit agee de 16: mois 10: jours; Elle a este Entairee le Lande-main; un samedi a 4 hure apres midy den le Simetiere; de Lesglises françoise De Charlestown. —

2: Masegonde fille marianne Est Nee le 15 mars 1696: un dimanche a [ ] hure du matain; & a Este batisee le 21: Dudit mois; un dimanche; Elle a heu pour Parin; Isaac Mazyck; son Pere; & pour maraine Caterine Noble Satante materneille —

3: Le 8 aoust 1698: Est ne mafille Elizabet est Nee a 8 hure dumatain & a Este batisee le 4 septembre; Elle a heu pour Parain Jacque Boyd & pour maraine marianne Mazÿck sa mere —

4: Le 6: mars 1699/1700: Est né mon fils Isaac Mazyck a 2: hure apres midi un mercredy; et a Este batisé le 7: dudit mois, Il a heu pour Parain Jacque le Sierurier; son oncle maternel; et pour maraine mariee le Seirurier Satante —

5: Le 5: octobre 1702: est né mon fils Paul Mazÿck a 4: hure du-matain & [ ] Este batisé le 19 Nouembre; Il a heu pour Parain; Pierre de St Jullien son oncle; et pour maraine marianne Mazÿck sa mere —

6 Le premier de Janvier 1704/5: un Lundy; Est ne mafille Suzon a 10: hure dujour; et a Este batise le 25. Dudit mois un judy Den lesglise françoise de Charlestown; Elle a heu pour parain Arenos france son Cousin jermain Paternel; et pour maraine; Damearis St Jullien; Satante maternelle —

7: Le 6: septembre 1707: un samedy Est né mafille Mariee a 8 hure dusoir; Elle a Este batisee le 15 du Courent un Lundy; Elle a heu pour Parain; Pierre Seirurier; son Cousin Jermain materneil et pour maraine sa Cousine Suson le Noble materneille germaine —

8: Le 8: Janvier 1709/10: un dimanche Est ne ma fille Penelope a 2: hure du [ ] et a Este batisse le . . . Par M^r lescot; sur ma plantation; Elle a heu pour Parain; le gouverneur Edward Tent; et pour maraine; madame Lescot; representant, mafille marianne Mazyck Sa soeur —

mort Le 22: feuvrier 1712 un Vendredy ma Chere fille Suson Est dessede a 1 hure et demiec apres midy; dune petite vairolle; agee de 7 ans un mois & 22 jours; & a Este Entairee Le 23: a 11 hure du matain Den le Simetiere De lesglises françoises de Charlestown —

9 Le 30 mars 1712: a 2 hure après minuit un Dimanche Est ne ma fille Suson; dont jeluy ay Donne le Non desa desfunte soeur; pour sa mainmoire; Elle a Este batisee le Judy le 24: auril; Elle a heu pour Parain Isaac Mazÿck; son Perre; et pour maraine Marianne Mazyck sa mere —

10: Le 29: Janvier 1713/14: un Vendredy a une hure du matain; Est né mon fils Pittre Mazÿck; et a Este batisee le 14 feuvrier; alesglises fra[ ] un dimanche; Il a heu Pour Parain, Monsr Pittre Renew; delondre; Monsr Pittre de St Jullien; la presente; pour Luy et pour maraine Elizabet Mazÿck sa soeur —

mort Le 7 aoust 1714: un samedy machere fille Penelope est Decedee a ½ hure apres midi; agee de 4 ans 7: mois; Causé par les nairs & a Este e[ ]ree le 8: dudit mois Den le Simetiere de Notre Esglises a 6: hure [ ] soir —

Le 17: Dessembre 1715: un Samedy a 3 hure apres midi Est né mon fils Benjamain Mazÿck; et a Este batise le 19 Janvier 1716: un Judy Den Lesglises françoise; Il a heu Pour parain; Benjamain Godin & Pour maraine Marianne Mazÿck sa soeur —

12: Le 27: Nouembre 1718: un judy a 3 hure et demiee du matain Est Ne mon fils Estienne Mazÿck; et a Este batise le 12 Dessembre un Vendredy; par Monsr Lescot; ministre de Lesglises françoises; Il a heu Pour Parain Mr Benjamain Dela Conseilliere; Pour maraine — Damearis St Jullien; sa Cousine Germaine Materneille —

13: Le 5 aoust 1730 Est ne Isaac Mazÿck a 8 hure dusoir; fils de Isaac Mazÿck; & a Este batise le jour en suivant par Mr Gar[ ] Ministre; Il a heu Pour Parain; Isaac Mazÿck; son Grans Pere Pour marain marianne Mazÿck; sa grans Mere —

mort Le 3 et 4: auril 1732: Lundy a 1 hure apres minuit ma Chere famme Est [ ] auec qui Jay Jouis 40: ans Demariage. Elle Estoit agee de [ ] 7 ans [ ] Est morte dune Cruelle & fachuse Langeur qui la Reduit a na[ ] Lapos et Lesos; Causé par un Cours deuentre; quelle a garde san[ ] Larester Plus de 18 mois; Elle a Este Entairee mercredy suivant [ ] du soir Den le Simetiere De Les glises francoises — M: She was Born at St Quinte . . . In Picardy [ ] October 1675.

mort Le 27: Octobre 1732 a 11½ hure de la nuit mon Cher fils Pitre Mazÿck est mort; a dubeling; Chay son oncle age de 18 ans 9: mois; Il est mort d'un sansible et Noir Chagrain; et Tristesse Dauoir Laisé son Pere & frere & soeur; surtout son pere; je remarque par la lettre de mon fre quil Doit auoir Este atagué; deson Itropisiee; estant chagrain & ne voulant pas parle

mort Le 13 Janvier 1732/3 un Samedy; machere fille marie Chardon Est morte a 6½ hure du jour; Dune fachuses et Longue maladiee dun Cours deuentre, Comme sa Pauvre mere; Elle estoit grose de Pres de 7: mois; Elle auoit 26: ans 6: mois quent elle est morte & a soufert de grande Doulleurs; Elle a este entairee le 15 du couran den le Simetiere, de lesglises françoises —

[ ]rt Le 30 auril 1735: un mercredy a 1: hure Dumatin Machere fille Suson [ ]eword Est morte (agee de 23 ans 3 mois). Dune fachuse & violente Couche; Dun Enfans — quon atué volontairement quon atire avec un Instrumans; ayant tué Lenfans a force de pétrin Sateste & Trop Presé Sacouche; Elle est morte 9 jours apres Estre Delivree Causé — Par une violente fievre & une opresion; qui la Estoufe; ne pouvant Respirer; et son uentre Enfle comme un tanbour; qui me fait Croire quon luy afait mal auec Linstrument on Laise quelque Chose — De lariere faix; Elle a Este entairee le meme jour a 7: hure du soir Den Notre Simetiere

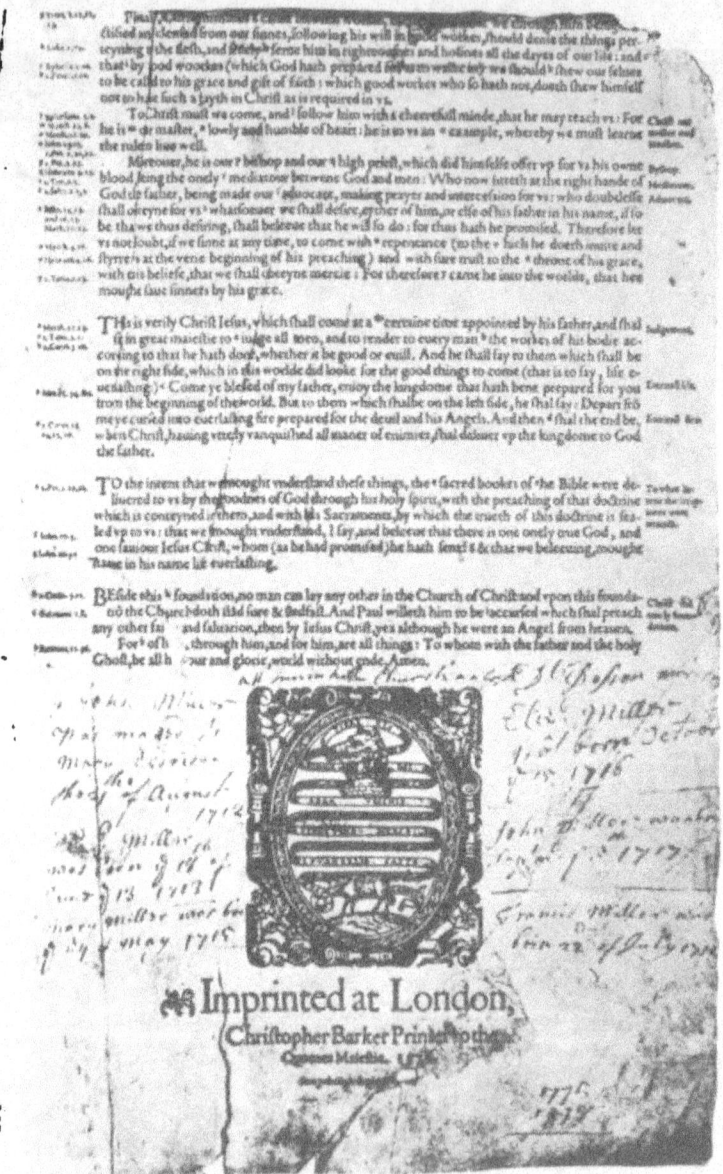

Colophon and records in the Bible of John Miller, 1578

JOHN MILLER.
(Married 1712.)

Holy Bible in English; London, Christopher Barker, 1578.

This Bible lacks the title-page but has the colophon; it contains the records of John Miller and his wife, Mary Eldridge, with their children. Parts of the records are repeated on a second leaf. The Bible is now the property of the American Bible Society and is stored at their rooms.

I. John Miller & Mary Eldridge was marrd at Suninhill Church, by Dockt. Dawson August ye 21st in ye year 1712: - - -ye 1 was

Elizb. Miller was born ye 18th of June, 1713.

Mary Miller was born May ye 24th 1715.

Elizb. Miller was born Octobr. ye 15th 1716.

John Miller was born Septbr. ye 3th 1717.

Francis Miller was born July ye 22th 1718

Mary Miller was born Septb. ye 30th 1719

Richd. Miller was born Januy. ye 31 1720/1

Ann Miller & Charles Miller twins was born Decemr. ye 22th. 1721.

Danl. Miller was born Juhn. ye 25, 1722.

Mary Miller was born Nobr. ye 12, 1724.

Feb. ye 11th, 1728 was born Elizb. Miller

I John Miller, att Suninhill Church by Dtr. Dofson marrd. was marrd to Mary Eldridge the 21st of August 1712.

Elizb. Miller was born ye 18th of June ye 13 1713

Mary Miller was born ye 24 of May 1715.

Elizb. Miller was born Octobr. ye 15 1716

John Miller was born Septmb. ye 3th 1717

Francis Miller was born 22d. of July 1718.

JUDGE LEWIS MORRIS.
(1698–1762.)

Holy Bible in Dutch; it is probable that this is the edition published at Dordrecht by Jacob and Pieter Keur in 1714 but we have not been able to verify the imprint or the records, as the Bible is in storage.

> Contains the records of Col. Lewis Morris, Judge of the Admiralty, and his two wives, Trintje Staats and Sarah Gouverneur, with their descendants. It is now the property of Alexander Rutherfurd, Esq., of Old Lyme, Conn., a great-great-grandson of Col. Morris.

I begin the Year the 25th of March

I was born at Tinton In New Jersie in the year 1698 the 23rd of September my wife was born at New York the 4th of April in the year 1697.

I was married by William Vesey the 17th day of March 1723 to Mrs. Trintje Staats Daughter to Dr. Samuell Staats.

My Daughter Mary was born the first day of November 1724 after one of the clock in the morning christened by John Bartow, my father godfather my mother and my sister Coymans godmothers.

My Son Lewis was born the 8th day of April 1726 at half an hour after ten of the clock at night, was christened by Robert Jenny Mr. Weymans and Capt Vincent Pearse godfathers Sister Gouverneur godmother.

My Son Staats Long was born the 27th day of August 1728 at a quarter after one in the morning was christened by Parson Ovens chaplain of the garrison cap^t Robert Long and my Brother John godfathers My Sister Ann Elizabeth Schuyler godmother.

My Son Richard was born the 15th Day of August 1730 at a quarter after Eight in the Evening, was christened by parson Ovens chaplain of the garrison Mr. Joseph Murray and Mr. Gilbert Willett godfathers and my Sister Mary Pearse godmother.

Lewis Morris, II, 1698–1762

Trintje Staats, wife of Lewis Morris, II

My wife departed this life the Eleventh Day of March 1731 aged 35 years after a violent Illness for nine days.

My daughter Mary was married the 9th Day of March Ano Dom 1743 to Thomas Lawrence Jun^{or} of Philadelphia by Thomas Standard Minister of the parish of Westchester.

The 3rd Day of November 1746 I was married To Mrs. Sarah Gouverneur by Thomas Standard minister of the Parish of Westchester.

The 3rd Day of February 1747/8 my wife was Delivered of a Daughter at half an hour after Eleven of the clock at night was christened by Thomas Standard Named Isabella My Mother and Mrs. Margarett Gouverneur godmothers and my Brother Robert Hunter Morris godfather.

The twenty Third of November 1749 my wife was Delivered of a Daughter at half an hour after four of the clock in the afternoon. She was christened by Thomas Standard The 10th of December 1749 Named Sarah Mrs. Low and my Son Lewis's wife stood godmothers and my son Lewis godfather.

The 30th of January about half an hour after one of the clock in the Morning in the year 1752, according To The alteration of The Stile by act of Parliament, my wife was Delivered of a son he was christened The 4th of May 1752 and Named Gouverneur after my wifes father, Nicholas Gouverneur and my Son Staats were his godfathers and my Sister Antill his godmother. Parson Achmuty christened him.

The 10th Day of September 1753 at five of the clock in the morning My wife was Delivered of a Daughter. She was christened The 8th Day of October 1754 and Named Euphemia after my Sister Morris My Sister Morris and Sister Graham were her godmothers and my son Richard her godfather Moley Ashfield Stood Proxy for Mrs. Morris and I stood proxy for my Son Richard he being Sick at York, Parson Achmuty christened her

The 30th Day of January 1757 at 15 minutes after Nine of The clock in the morning my wife was delivered of a Daughter She was christened The Second Day of March 1757 and Named Catherine after the Dutchess of Gordon The Dutchess of Gordon and my Daughter Lawrence were godmothers and my Son in [law] Lawrence her godfather Mrs Sarah Low stood proxy for the Dutchess of Gordon and Mrs. Margarett Governeur stood proxy for my Daughter Lawrence and my Son Richard for Thomas Lawrence She was christened by Doctor Johnson.

Col. Lewis Morris Judge of the Admeralty died July 3rd 1762 at Morrisania aged 64 - a'3 of ͭ Clock A. M.

On the first day of December in the year 1776 Catherine Morris departed this life aged 19 years and 10 months.

On the fourteenth day of January 1786 Mrs. Sarah Morris relect of Col Lewis Morris died at Morrisania aged 71 & 3 months.

On the twenty second day of January 1798 Lewis Morris of Morrisania died aged seventy one years nine months & fourteen days.

The ages of the Children of Lewis and Mary Morris the time they were Married and by whom.

I was married to Mary Walton on the 25th of September 1749 by Henry Bartley - She was eldest Daughter of Jacob Walton. I was born at old Morrisania April 8th 1726 and my wife was born at New York May 14th 1727.

My daughter Mary born September 6th 1750 forty five minutes after five of the Clock in the afternoon Christened by Henry Bartley.

My daughter Catherine born March 3rd 1752 at half an hour after ten of the Clock at Night - Christened by Henry Bartley -

My Son Lewis born May 3rd 1754 at six o'Clock in the Morning and Christened by Henry Bartley, Godfathers Richard Morris and William Walton Jun[or] Godmother Magdalane Johnston.

My Son Jacob born December 28th 1755 at 7 o'Clock in the morning christened by Henry Godfathers David Johnston and Jacob Walton - Godmother Catherine Thompson.

My Daughter Sarah born December 20th 1757 at 9 Clock at night Christened by Parson Huss. Godfather Capt. William Little Godmothers my wife's mother and my Brother in Law William Walton's wife.

Ross Hall, Raritan, New Jersey

The home of Mrs. Edward Antill, who was Ann Morris, sister of Lewis Morris, II

My Son William Walton born April 28th 1760 ten o'Clock in the afternoon Christened by Parson Aucmudy Godfathers Thomas Walton and Thomas Hays. Godmothers my Brother Richards' wife.

My Daughter Magdalane born November 20th 1761 twelve o'clock in the morning Christened by Parson Miller Godfather Isaac Wilkins Godmothers Mrs Graham and Isabella Morris.

My Son Staats born June 30th 1763 between the hours of 8 & 9 at night Christened by Parson Miller - Godfathers Mr. Isaac Willet and Col^n Staats Morris.

My son James born August 25th 1764 eleven o'Clock at Night Christened by Parson Miller - Godfathers Abraham Walton and Thomas Lawrence his Sister Mary Godmother.

My son Richard Valentine born 8th March 1768 Christened by Parson Seabury Godfathers Gerard Walton & John Marston Godmother Rachael Marston.

CHIEF JUSTICE RICHARD MORRIS.
(1730–1810.)

Holy Bible in English; London, Thomas Baskett, 1769.

Contains the records of Richard Morris, Chief Justice of New York State, and Sarah Ludlow, his wife, with some of their descendants to their great-grandchild, the father of the present owner, Mrs. William B. Morrison, of Denver, Colorado.

The records have been verified by Miss Sophie Morris, a sister of Mrs. Morrison.

I was born the 15th August 1730 old stile * I was married on Wednesday the 13th day of June 1759 to Sarah Ludlow eldest daughter of Henry Ludlow & Mary his wife (her maden name Mary Corbett) by the Rev. Mr. Barclay.

My son Lewis was born the 2nd November 1760 two o'clock A. M. My father & Mr. W. Wickham & Mr. Ludlow stood for him.

My son Robert born 20th of June 1762 eleven o'clock A.M. My brother Lewis Uncle R. H. Morris and my sister Lawrence stood for him.

My daughter Mary born 2nd of August 7 o'clock A. M. 1763 Lewis Morris' wife my wife's sister Mary Ludlow, god mothers G. H. Ludlow God father.

* My wife was born 15th September 1730 old stile.

My daughter Catherine born 6th of June 1765 at 7 o'clock P. M. Mary Ashfield the Duchess of Gordon (by proxy) god mothers & Mr. Henry Ludlow Sen. God father. She died the 22nd of July 1765 burried in the vault at Morrisania.

My daughter 2nd Catherine born the 9th of June 1766 at 2 o'clock A. M. Mrs. Sarah Hoffman & Mrs. Martha Ludlow God mothers and Mr. William N. Ludlow Godfather. She died the 13th of Aug. 1767 forty minutes after eight A.M. burried in the family vault at Morrisania.

My wife died on Fryday the twenty eighth day of October 1791 at half after eight in the evening & was interred Monday the 30th in a vault I had built for my family in Trinity Church yard.

My father Richard Morris died at Scarsdale in the County of Westchester on Wednesday the eleventh day of April 1810 about one o'clock P. M. in the eightieth year of his age and was burried in his vault Trinity Church yard New York on Friday the thirteenth of the same month.

My father Lewis R. Morris died at Springfield in the County of Windsor & state of Vermont on Thursday the 29th day of December 1825 at half past eight o'clock P. M. in the 66th year of his age and was burried in the burrial ground at Charlestown N. H. on Sunday the 1st day of Jan. 1826.

I was born November 2nd 1760 & on the 30th of July 1801 was married to Ellen, the eldest child of Jonathan and Leveriah Hunt of Vernon Vermont — who was born on the 19th of October 1781 and died at Springfield, County of Windsor, state of Vermont on Thursday August 24th in the eighty fifth year of her age and was buried in the burial ground at Charleston N. H. on Sunday the 27th of August 1865.

My father Richard H. Morris was born at Springfield Windsor Co. Vt. on the 16th of May 1803. He was married to Mary P. Emerson, daughter of Hon. Thos. Emerson of Windsor, Vt. Father died (on his return from the Floridas) at Pederton Georgia Nov. 4th 1837 and was buried in the burial ground at Charleston N. H.

His wife Mary P. Morris was born --- and died and was buried at Ann Arbor Michigan Ap. 30th 1860 aged 57 yrs.

Lewis R. Morris eldest son of R. H. Morris was born at Norwich Vt. Nov. 22nd 1831. Was married on Dec. 22nd 1853 at Cleveland Ohio to Mary Stillman who was born at Euclid Ohio 14 Nov. 1834 He died Ap. 24th 1877 at Detroit Michigan & was buried in the family burial ground at Cleveland Ohio.

RICHARD VALENTINE MORRIS.
(1768–1815.)

Holy Bible in English; New York, Collins, Perkins & Co., 1807.

Contains the family records of Richard V. Morris and Anne Walton, his wife, whose name, "Anne Morris," with the date 1809, appears on the title-page. The records cover the family to the third generation; the Bible now belongs to Henry Lewis Morris, Esq., of New York City, a grandson of the original owner.

MARRIAGES.

At Ballstown January the twenty-fourth in the year of our lord one thousand seven hundred and ninety seven Richard Valentine Morris to Anne Walton.

At New York 8th October in the Year of our Lord One Thousand eight hundred and twenty-seven Gerard Walton Morris to Martha Pyne.

At Canandaigua N. Y. On the 11th day of October in the year of our Lord one thousand eight hundred and thirty one Henry Morris to Mary N. Spencer.

At New York by Rev. J. W. Moore in the Church of the Ascension on the 5th May 1852 Francis J. Barretto to Honora S. daughter of Gerard W. & Martha P. Morris.

At the Residence of Gerard W. Morris 5th Avenue on the 19th December 1854 by the Rev. J. W. Moore Jonathan Edwards to Minny P. Morris.

BIRTHS.

Richard V. Morris born at the Manor of Morrisania 8th March 1768

Anne Walton born in New York 24 Jan. 1773

Lewis born at Morrisania on the seventh day of December in the year of our lord one thousand seven hundred and ninety seven. Baptized by the Rev. Mr. Ireland on the 13 April year following. Sponsors Col. Lewis Morris, Sarah Morris.

Gerard Walton born in New York on the eleventh day of July in the year of our lord one thousand seven hundred and ninty nine. Baptized by the Rev. Mr. Bisset the 27th of August following. Sponsors Gerard Walton. Henry Walton Eliza Walton

Richard Valentine born in the Island of Malta on the ninth day of June in the year of our lord one thousand eight hundred and three Baptized by the Rev. Mr. Cossevat the 9th July following. Sponsors John Haris Cruger, William Loughton Smith, Anne Cruger.

Henry born at Morrisania on the twenty second day of August in the year of our Lord one thousand eight hundred and six. Baptized by the Rev Mr. Wilkins the 21 July year following. Sponsors Col. Lewis Morris Gen. Jacob Morris Matilda C. Walton.

Isabella Pyne born at New York on the 28th day of July in the year of our Lord one Thousand eight hundred and twenty eight Baptized by the Rev. Manton Easburn. Richard V. Morris Anne Morris Martha P. Morris, Sponsors.

Anne Walton born at New York on the 13th Dec. 1829. Baptized by the Rev. Manton Eastburn in the Church of Ascension the 27th June following.

Honora Smith born 2nd Sep. 1831 in New York Baptized at Middle Town Connecticut by the Rev. Smith Pyne.

Gerard Walton born in New York 3rd December 1833 Baptized by Mr. Eastburn in the Church of Ascension.

Mary Pyne born May 1835 New York Baptized by the Rev. Mr. Eastburn

John Pyne born in New York 13th January 1837. Baptized by Rev. Mantun Eastburn.

Richard Valentine Born in New York 22nd Aug. 1838 Baptized by the Rev. Mantun Eastburn.

Henry born in New York 27th October 1839 Baptized by Rev. M. Eastburn.

Arthur born in New York on the 4th June 1846 Baptized by the Rev. Mr. Bedell.

Henry Lewis, the Son of Henry Morris born at New York the 8th of August 1845 Baptized by Rev. Henry Anthon.

Mary Natelie born in New York the 10th of December 1848 Baptized by the Rev. Mr. Taylor.

Born at New York the 11th of February 1853 Gerard Morris Barretto Baptized by Rev. John W. Moore.

Born the 2nd Nov. 1854 Annie Barretto Baptized by the Rev. Bedell

Born Jan. 2nd 1856 Gerard Morris Edwards of Jonathan & Mary P. Edwards.

Born Frances Barretto March 22nd 1857 of Francis I. & Honora Barretto.

Born April 16, 1857 Mary Morris Edwards of Jonathan & Mary P. Edwards

DEATHS.

Lewis died the 12 September 1798 aged nine months and five days

On Saturday the 13th of May 1815 died Richard Valentine Morris aged forty seven years and two months.

On the 18th of December 1836 died John C. Spencer Son of Henry and Mary N. Morris aged two months twenty five days.

On Saturday the ninth day of December 1843 died Richard Valentine Morris son of Richd V. and Anne Morris aged forty years and six months.

On 22nd Feb'y 1850 died Anne Walton Daughter of Gerard W. & Martha P. Morris aged 20 years 2 mos. & 9 days.

On 24th March 1850 died Richard V. son of Gerard W. & Martha P. Morris aged 11 years 6 mos.

On 28 August 1851 Isabelle P. Daughter of Gerard W. & Martha P. Morris aged 23 years 1 month

On June 1852 Martha P. wife of Gerard W. Morris aged 46 years.

On the 10th January one Thousand Eight hundred & Fifty four died Henry Morris Son of Richard V. & Anne Morris aged Forty Seven years 5 months.

Died Sept 28th 1856 Anna C. Barretto aged 1 Year 10mth. & 26 days.

Died April 27th 1857 Mary P. Edwards aged 21 years 11 months & 24 days.

Died April 18th 1858 Anne Walton Relict of Richard V. Morris Decd. aged 85 years 2 months & 25 Days.

THOMAS MORRISON.
(1792–1879.)

Holy Bible in English; Philadelphia, John Edwin Potter, 1864.

 This Bible contains the records of Thomas Morrison and his family. It was given to the present owner, Mrs. George B. Holland, of Walpole, New Hampshire, by her parents, David H. and Harriet J. Morrison. They received it from Mr. Morrison's uncle, Samuel R. Morrison, of Indianapolis, Indiana, who wrote the record it contains. It is supposed that he copied it from an older Bible.

MARRIAGES.

*Thomas Morrison and Sarah H. Humfreville were married in Dayton, Ohio, February 20th A.D. 1817, By Rev. Doct^r Welch.

Robert J. Skinner and Mary Hollis were married in Philadelphia, Pa, November 7th A.D. 1818, By Rev. Wm Staughton.

David H. Morrison and Harriet J. Skinner were married in Waupaukonnetta, O. November 11th A.D. 1840, By Rev. J. Alexander,

Children of the Above.

Charles Carroll Morrison, and Libbie Jones, were married Nov 21st A.D. 1867

†James Hollis Skinner Morrison, and Daisy Skinner, were married ... in Shelbyville, Ind^a.

‡Julius Curtis Morrison, and Maggie Maie Goodwin, were married February 7th, A.D. 1882.

Sarah Eliza Morrison, and George B Holland, were married November 5th, A.D. 1879.

Harriet Gest Morrison, and William T. Rankin, were married November 29th A.D. 1877.

Samuel Robert Morrison, and Virginia Updyke, were married October 26th A.D. 1881.

†James H. S. Morrison, and Susan Knight, were married Apr¹ 2nd 1881.

*Thomas Morrison, and Mrs Ann Downs, were married Nov, 4th 1852

‡Julius Curtis Morrison and Emma Darrow, were married Apr¹ 14th 1896

Births.

Thomas Morrison, son of Ephraim and Nancy Morrison, was born Aug. 9th A.D. 1792, in Pa.

Sarah H. Morrison, daughter of David and Elizabeth Humfreville, was born Octr 1st A.D. 1798, in N.Y.

Robert J. Skinner   March A.D. 1792

Mary Skinner, daughter of James and Phebe Hollis was born in Lancaster Co Pa.

David H. Morrison, son of Thomas and Sarah H Morrison was born in Dayton, Ohio December 19th A.D. 1817.

Harriet J Morrison, daughter of Robert J. and Mary Skinner, was born in Dayton, Ohio, March 25th A.D. 1821.

Children of David H. and Harriet J. Morrison.

Adrian Clifford Morrison, was born February 2nd A.D. 1842.

Charles Carroll Morrison, was born October 12th A.D. 1843.

David Harry Morrison, was born August 10th A.D. 1845.

Anna Mary Morrison, was born September 3rd A.D. 1847.

§ James Hollis Morrison, was born October 25th A.D. 1850.

Julius Curtis Morrison, was born November 21st A.D. 1852.

Sarah Eliza Morrison, was born October 7th A.D 1854.

Harriette Gest Morrison, was born September 8th A.D. 1856.

Samuel Robert Morrison, was born February 5th A.D. 1860.

Thomas Rollin Morrison, was born March 14th A. D. 1863.

Note. The first two children were born in Wapaukonnetta, O.; all the others in Dayton, Ohio.

5th James Hollis *Skinner* Morrison.

DEATHS

Robert J. Skinner, died in Dayton, O. June 26th A.D. 1849.

Mary Skinner, died in Dayton, O, June 29th A.D. 1849.

Sarah H. Morrison, died in Dayton, O. June 28th A.D. 1849.

Adrian Clifford Morrison, died in Dayton O. June 28th A.D. 1849.

Anna Mary Morrison, died in Dayton. O. June 26th A.D. 1849.

All died of Asiatic Cholera.

David Harry Morrison, Fell in defence of his Country, near Greenville, S. C. May 18th A.D 1865.

Thomas Morrison, died in Dayton, O. March. 23rd A D 1879, Aged 86 years, 7 months and 14 days.

Thomas Rollin Morrison, died August 9th A.D. 1880, aged 17 years, 4 months and 27 days.

David H. Morrison, died July 21st A.D. 1882, in Dayton, O.

Harriet J. Morrison, died November 27th A.D. 1898, in Walpole, N. H.

Mrs Ann Morrison, (T, M,'s 2nd wife) died Septr 29th A.D. 1882.

Julius Curtis Morrison, died, October 28th A.D. 1907.

Memoranda.

Samuel Morrison[2], son of John Morrison[1]; who was born in Scotland A.D. 1639 and married there, date & to whom not known; emigrated to N. of Ireland, 1660.

2.—was born in Ireland, Dec'r 25th 1699, O.S. married Mercy Maize (of Scotch descent) A.D. 1735, emigrated in 1740, to America, & settled in Pennsylvania.

Ephraim[3], son of Samuel & Mercy Morrison, was born in Bucks county, Penna, June 5th 1759; married Nancy Foster, July 1st A.D. 1787, by Rev. Isaa Grier

Emigrated west and settled in Dearborn county, Inda Feb. 14th 1796.

Nancy Morrison, was born in Pa, A.D. 1754, and died in Dearborn Co. Inda Decr 18th A.D. 1803.

Ephraim Morrison[3], was a soldier in the Revolution, and wounded in the battle of Brandywine, died of an injury received at a house-raising in Clark Co. O. Feb. 2nd 1806

The above work was done by Samuel Morrison[4], in his 88th year of age, since the 1st of March, 1885; now, May 1st 1885.

Note. The figures at the end of a name, denote the Generation they are of, counting John Morrison First.

[This record was sworn to by Sarah E. Holland.]

GENERAL WILLIAM NORTH.
(1755–1836.)

Holy Bible in English; New York, Collins, Perkins & Co., 1807.

    Contains the family records of General North and his wife, Mary Duane, with their descendants. The present owner, William M. Austin, of Elizabeth, New Jersey, is the great-great-grandson of General North.

Family Record

MARRIAGES.

Wm. North & Mary Duane, 14" Oct. 1787

Wm. Aug. S. North & Margaret Bridge, Sept. 25, 1820

Mary C. North & Daniel C. Weston, Oct. 4 1842

Henry Saunders (of the U. S. Army) to Delia, (youngest daughter of Genl. Wm. North) 3^d Sept. 1828

BIRTHS. DEATHS.

Mary Catharine daughter of Wm. Aug. S. North, born Apr. 14, 1822 [died] Aug. 4, 1882.

Hannah Elizabeth, [born] Dec. 15 1823 [died] Mar. 13–1888

Delia born Aug. 26 1825 [died] July 11 1826

1. Wm. Henry (Son of H. Saunders & Delia North Saunders) Born June 1 1829 at old Point Va.

2. Eliza North Saunders Born 18" March 1831 at Old Point, Va.

3. Delia North Saunders Born 7" of Dec. 1833 at Fort Trumbull Ct.

DEATHS

Wm. Henry Saunders Died Aug. 8, 1829 aged 2 months & 8 days.

Eliza N. Saunders Died 18 Jan. 1837 at Fort Washington Md. Aged Five years & ten Months

Died at Fort Sullivan, Eastport Md. our dear & only child Delia N. Saunders, on 14" of Dec. 1843 aged ten years & seven days. God Will be done.

The 20" of Feb. 1876 Henry Saunders at Leesburg Va. all with Christ but the poor sufferer who is left.

BIRTHS.   DEATHS.

Gen. Wm. North born 1755 [died] Jan. 3 1836

Frederick Wm. Steuben 14 July, 1788 [died] 1789

James Duane 28 Jany 1791 [died] May 1792

Maria 12 Aug 1789 [died] June 8, 1812

Wm. Augustus Steuben Feb. 2 1794 [died] Nov. 7 1845

Elizabeth 1793 [died] June 8 1845

Adelia (called Delia) 1795 [died] Feb. 1878

Margaret Bridge wife of Wm. Aug. S. North was born Feb. 12 1802 [died] Dec. 31 1882.

Daniel Cony Weston born At Augusta Maine Feb. 24–1815 died Washington D.C. Mar 20. 1903

Daniel C. Westons 6 children

Wm. North born Aug 20 1843 d Apl 23 1847

Geo. Melville b May 4 1845   d May 16 1883

Duane b Apl 2 1847   d Jan 12 1850

Henry Livingston b Jan. 29. 1849   d Jan 29 1850

Mary North Weston B May 25 1851.

James . b Mch 28. 1854   d Mch 28 1854

Mary North Weston Born May 25 1851   Married June 5 1872 Francis B. Austin b June 11 1847

Children

Wm. Morris b Nov. 30 1876.

Mary Livingston   b. Dec. 26 1880   d Nov. 11. 1913

Births & Marriages

Wm Morris Austin b Nov 30 1876 Married Apr 10, 1901 Pauline Dexter Foss, b Jan 7,

Children

Wm Morris b. Feb 16 1902

Francis Duane b May 23 1905

Frederick Foss b Jan 20 1909

Mary Livingston Austin b Dec 26 1880 d Nov. 11. 1913. Married June 3 1902 Charles Longstreet Poor, b Oct. 1. 1873

Children

Mary Lindsay b May 14. 1903 d Nov 19. 1904

Charles Longstreet b Aug 12 1905 d June 4 1906

Chas Austin b Feb 25 1908 d Nov 18 1915

Richard Longstreet b Dec 28 1910

[State of New Jersey County of Union.

[Mary N. Austin, being duly sworn on her oath, says that the records sent by her to the Society of Colonial Dames were copied by her from the family Bible of General William North, and are correct and accurate in every particular to the best of her knowledge and belief.

[Mary N. Austin.

[Sworn and subscribed before me this 4 day of November 1915.

[Arthur W. Hicks, Notary Public for N. J.

[seal]

MOSES OGDEN.
(Married 1746; died 1768.)

Holy Bible in English; London, Thomas Baskett, 1756.

The Bible contains the records of Moses Ogden and his family and has descended directly to his great-granddaughter, Miss Amy Edwards, of Elizabeth, New Jersey, who is the present owner.

Moses Ogden & Mary His Wife Was Married the 3^d Day of November 1746.

1 Son Aaron Ogden Born November 3^d 1747 Dyed the 28 Day of Jany 1747/8

2 Mary Ogden: Born January 8 1748/9 Dyed the 15th of Feby 1748/9

3 Frances Ogden: Born Feby 7th 1749/50 Died at New Haven 7th July 1800.

4 John Cosens Ogden: Born November the 15th 1751 Died at Chestertown Maryland Sep. 1800.

5 Moses Ogden: Born March 22d 1754 Dyed Sep^t 16th 1756.

6 Barne Ogden: Born January 14th 1756.

7 Anne Ogden: Born April 18th 1758

8 Moses Ogden: Born August 25 1760 the above Taken out of a small Bible.

9 Aaron Norton Ogden Born Sep^t 15th 1762

10 Mary Cosens Ogden Born November 25 1764

11 David Ogden Born December 17th 1766

Mr. Moses Ogden Died October the 14th 1768 in the 46 year of His Age.

Benoni Ogden was born November 17 1768

Benoni Ogden Died June 16: 1774

Francis Ogden Married to Pierrpont Edwards

Born unto them Polly Susana, John Starks, Henery, Ogden, Alfred, Henrietta.

John Cosens Ogden Married to Polly Worster, born unto them Polly, David, Aaron.

Benoni Ogden Married to Nancy Sale April 26th 1778.

Born unto them Betsy & Polly twins Feb. 3 1780

Betsey died Feb. 13 aged 10 days

Polly Cosens died Feby 23rd age 20 days.

Moses Ogden Killed in the Action of Connecticut Farmes June 7th 1780 aged 19 years 10 months 7 days.

Aaron Norton Ogden Died Decr 12 1780 in the 18 yr of his age.

Hendrick Onderdonck, 1724–1809

HENDERICK ONDERDONCK.[1]
(1724–1809.)

Holy Bible in Dutch; Dordrecht, Pieter en Jacob Keur, 1729.

Contains the family records in Dutch of Henderick Onderdonck and Phœbe Tredwell, his wife. The Bible descended by marriage to the Floyd-Jones family and is now the property of Edward H. Floyd-Jones, Esq., of Massapequa, N. Y., the fifth in descent from the original owner.

Henderick Onderdonck Syn Boeck den 31 Augustus Anno Domini 1751 to B. Onderdonk to Maria Onderdonk to Henry Floyd-Jones

Phebe Onderdonck is overleeden den 2 dag van July 1758

Vaader Andries Onderdonck is overleeden den 21 dag van November 1758

Henderick Onderdonk is overleeden den 31 dag van Maert 1809 AET. AN. 85ta

Henderick Onderdonck is geboren den 11 Desember Anno 1724

Phebe Tredwell is geboren den 12 July Anno Domini 1730

Desen Syn te Samen Getrout den 20 mey Anno Domini 1750

Benjamen Onderdonck is geboren den 13 April Anno Domini 1751

Geertruy Onderdonck is geboren den 11 February Anno Domini 1753

Phebe Onderdonck is geboren den 2 Augustus Anno Domini 1754

Andries Onderdonck is geboren den 6 van May 1756

Sara Onderdonck is geboren den 26 van Maert 1758

Henderick Onderdonck is geboren den 1 Daag van February 1760

[1 The Dutch character ÿ is not cut for fonts of English type. Therefore the letter y has been used in the Dutch records where ÿ is meant.]

Maria Onderdonck is geboren den 22 daag van November 1761

Johannis Onderdonck is geboren den 22 daag van Augustus 1763.

Phebe Onderdonck is geboren den 2 daag van June 1765

William Onderdonk is geboren den 12 daag van January 1767

Samuel Onderdonk is geboren den 31 Daag van Augustus 1770

Benjamin Onderdonk is geboren den 25 daag van January 1776

[State of New York, County of New York, ss.:
[I, Edward H. Floyd-Jones, of Massapequa, Nassau County, New York, do hereby certify that the paper writing hereto annexed is a true and correct copy of the record of births and deaths etc. written in a certain Holy Bible in my possession, having the appearance of age, on the title page of which is printed: "Te Dordrecht Bij Pieter en Jacob Keur Anno 1729." The said copy has been carefully examined and compared by me with the original and is a complete and accurate copy of said written record and of each and every part thereof, and that the appearance of the writing indicates that all of the entries thereof are old.

[EDWARD H. FLOYD-JONES.

{Sworn to before me this 10th day of March, 1913.
[CHARLES AUFINKOLK, JR., Notary Public.]

JOHN PARKER.
(Married 1721.)

These records were copied by the late James Parker, Esq., President of the New Jersey Historical Society, who died in 1868. He took them from his sister's papers, which were apparently copied from original Bible records destroyed by the Hessians. The records are given as furnished by Mrs. William Bedlow Beekman, a granddaughter of James Parker, Esq.

(From an original paper in the handwriting of Gertrude Parker (1856))

John Parker was married to Jennet Johnston at the City of Perth Amboy, by Mr. Edward Vaughan the 16th day of September Anno Domini 1721.

1. John Parker born the day of June 1722 was Christened by Mr. William Skinner, Doctor John Johnston, & Major John Johnston, Godfathers and Mrs. Elisha Parker Godmother. He died the 30th day of April 1725.

2. Elisha Parker born the Second day of March 1723/4 was christened by Mr. Wm. Skinner. Col. John Hamilton & Mr. Lewis Johnston Godfathers & Mrs. Catharine Johnston Godmother. He died the 14 day of March 1751.

3. James Parker born the 29th day of January 1725/6 was christened by Mr. Wm. Skinner, Dr. John Johnston & Mr. Andrew Johnston Godfathers & Mrs. Ursula Parker Godmother.

4. Mary Parker born the 27 day of October 1727 was christened by Mr. Wm. Skinner- Mr. James Johnston Godfather & Mrs. Mary Johnston & Mrs. Mary Parker Godmothers.

5 John Parker born the 7th day of November 1729 (was christened by Mr. Wm. Skinner, Mr. John Watson & Mr. Robert King Godfathers & Mrs. Mary Foster Godmother. He died the 10th February 1762.

6 Lewis Johnston Parker born the 9th day of December 1731 was christened by Mr. William Skinner, Mr. John Parker & Mr.

Wm. Skinner Godfathers & Mrs. Anne Morris Godmother. He died February 2, 1760.

James Parker died 4 October 1797

Mary Parker died 25 February 1813 unmarried.

Memorandum.

2 Elisha Parker married Catharine daughter of James Alexander who survived him. He left no child. His widow afterwards married Walter Rutherfurd.

3 James Parker married Gertrude Skinner in 1763 and died Octo. 4th 1797. His widow died February 10th 1811.

> (From a paper in the handwriting of James Parker — except the last item. (Cortlandt Lewis Parker) written on a bit to supply a part torn off)

James Parker & Gertrude Skinner were married the 13 Feby. 1763 by the Revd. Robert McKean.

1. John Parker was born 14th November 1763 Baptised by Mr. Robt. McKean, Mary Parker, Lewis Johnston, & Cortlandt Skinner Esq Sponsors.

2. Elizabeth Parker was born the 16th Aug. 1765 Baptised by Mr. McKean Elizth Skinner, Susanna Delancey, & John Skinner Esq. Sponsors.

3. Jennet Parker was born 27 December 1766, Baptised by Mr. McKean, Catharine Skinner, Ann Johnston, & Stephen Skinner Esq. Sponsors.

4 Gertrude Parker was born the 15 day of January 1770 baptised by Mr. John Preston, Gertrude Beekman, Catharine Barbarie, & John A. Johnston Sponsors.

5. Maria Parker was born the 29 September 1771 baptised by Mr. John W. Preston, Susanna Kearny, Mary Johnston & John Smyth Esq. Sponsors.

6. Susanna Parker, was born the 4th December 1772 baptised by Mr. John Preston, Cortlandt Skinner & his lady, & Gage by their Proxies, Stephen Skinner, Cath Skinner, & Mary Parker, Sponsors.

7. William Parker was born 19 April 1774 Baptised by Mr. John Preston, Cortld. Skinner, & Samuel Kemble Esq. by their proxies Cortlandt Skinner and James Kearny & Mrs. Susanna Smyth Sponsors.

8. James Parker was born the 1st March 1776 Baptised by Mr. William Frazer, Henry Cuyler, & James Parker the elder, & Mrs. Sarah Skinner by her proxy Mary Parker, Sponsors. Born & Baptised at Shipley, in the County of Hunterdon, N. J.

9 Catharine Montgomery Parker, was born the 31 January 1778. Baptised by Mr. Wm. Frazer, Catharine Rutherfurd, Janet Montgomery, & Walter Rutherfurd Esq. Sponsors. Born & baptised at Shipley in the County of Hunterdon, N. J.

10. Cortlandt Lewis Parker was born 15 June 1781 Baptised by the Rev. William Frazer, Richard Kemble, & John Rutherfurd Esq. & Miss Ann Kemble, Sponsors. Born & baptised at Shipley in the County of Hunterdon, N. J.

Gertrude Parker—widow of James Parker died at Perth Amboy February 10 1811.

Memorandum.

1 John Parker married in 1789 Ann, daughter of John Lawrence. He died at New Brunswick, 11 October 1801. His surviving Children.

Gertrude born in December 1789

Maria married in 1818 to Edward Dunham, died at New York of Cholera in 1834, leaving Issue four sons, Edward, John, James, Carroll, and a daughter Ann.

2. Elizabeth Parker died unmarried Octo. 21 1821.

3. Jennet Parker married Edward Brinley, died at Perth Amboy Dec. 18 1804, leaving issue daughters, Gertrude Aleph, Elizabeth, Maria, Catharine, & a son Francis W. Brinley.

5. Maria Parker married in 1793 Andrew Smyth, died without issue Octo. 14 1798.

6. Susanna Parker died unmarried April 23, 1849.

7. William Parker, died 29 October 1783

10. Cortlandt Lewis Parker married Anne Elizabeth, daughter of Anthony Gouverneur, of Curacoa. He died there Feb. 12, 1826 leaving several children,

4. Gertrude Parker died at the residence of her brother James Parker, April 11, 1856 unmarried.

8. James Parker married first Penelope Butler, daughter of Anthony Butler Esq and second Catherine Morris Ogden, daughter of Col. Samuel Ogden

9. Catherine Parker married James Kenny, and left issue, two daughters

Family of Dr. John Johnstone

(Taken from a Manuscript Paper in a handwriting well known in the possession of Gertrude Parker.)

"John Johnstone married Eupham Scott 18 April 1686

"Eupham born^d Jany 18th, 1686/7 about noon dyed 16th 7br. "1723 baptised by Mr. Archibald Ridell.

"Isabell bornd 10 Aug. 1688 dyed the 15th.

"Kathrin bornd 16 September 1689 dyed 7 July 1690.

"John bornd May 7 1691, 10 in the morning, baptised by Mr. "Thom. Bridges.

"Margaret bornd 12 Feb. 1692–3, 8 at night, baptised by Mr. "Bridges.

"Andrew bornd December 1694, 11 in the morning, baptised by "Mr. Bridges.

"Wm. bornd 3 xbr 1696 dyed April 7, 1698 baptised by Mr. "Woodbridge.

"Jennet bornd 7 April 1699, 5 in ye afternoon, baptised by Mr.
"Williams

"James Bornd Tuesday xbr 3, 1700, between 3 and 4 in the
"morning.

"George bornd 7br. 3 1702 Baptised

"Lewis Bornd 10 xbr 1704

"Isabel bornd 16 July 1707, died July 1708

"Mary bornd 12 7br 1710, 4 in the afternoon.

(Note by James Parker—I do not know the name of the writer from whose memorandum the above is copied, but it is familiar to me, and has every appearance of being genuine.)

Obituary Notice in the Philadelphia Mercury.

"Perth Amboy Sept. 19. 1732. On the 6th instant and in the 71st
"year of his age, Doctor John Johnstone, very much lamented
"by all who knew him, and to the inexpressible loss of the Poor
"who were always his particular care."

Notes.

7 Andrew Johnstone married Catharine daughter of Stephanus Van Cortlandt.

9. Jennet Johnstone married John Parker Sept. 16 1721

12. Lewis Johnstone an Eminent Physician married Heathcote he died in 1773.

(From a paper said to be in the handwriting of Ursula Parker in the possession of Gertrude Parker.)

My father dyed June the 30, in the year one thousand seven hundred and seventeen on a Saturday at 10 o'clock of the night. He was a good Father, a kind master, and a sincere Christian. He gave convincing proofs in his last Illness, by his patience and Resignation to the will of his Maker. He easily parted with everything but his Children, and in that particular, nature got the better as we had reason to think. His last hours was employed in petition for our good in this world, and the happiness in the next, He bid us depend on God, for all our Wants, as he had done, and need not fear being provided for—and pray God I may follow this advice and never forget the words of a dying Father.

The name of her Father is not mentioned. It was Elisha Parker (no doubt) who purchased the lot on which the Homestead of the Family Stands in 1715 his son John Parker purchased the Garden lot in 1718 the year after his fathers death.

(From a paper said to be in the handwriting of Ursula Parker in the possession of Gertrude Parker.)

My brother Elisha Parker was taken ill of "Pleurisai" on a Friday the Seventh of April, and died the sixteenth at four o'clock in the afternoon, on a Sunday, in the year One thousand Seven hundred and twenty Seven.

He was in the twenty-third year of his Age, was very willing to dye. In his sickness he armed himself with Resolution, and willingly resigned his Soul to God, he put his trust in him, and pleaded his Saviours merits, for a pardon of all his sins and acceptance with God; he was patient under his greatest pain, and did not let it make him forget his God, he willingly renounced the World, for his desire was fixed on heaven which made him choose death rather than life. He had all his Senses all the time of his sickness, till the day he died.

"Grant O my God that I may make a right use of this affliction, and learn from this, not to set an immoderate value on anything here but live as if every day was my last, never let me want thy Assistance to conquer myself, in this, and everything else, that is against thy positive Command."

JOSEPH PETTES.
(1757–1811.)

Holy Bible in English; New York, Collins and Perkins, 1806.

Contains the records of the Pettes and Prescott families and has descended in the female line to the present owner, Miss Elizabeth Prescott Hale, of Yonkers, New York. She is the great-great-granddaughter of the original owner.

Family Record.

MARRIAGES.

Joseph Pettes married to Charlotte Wales April 18th 1782.

Frederick Pettes marr'd September 25th 1814 to Harriet Mynderse.

Mary Pettes married October 15th 1816 to Samuel Prescott.

John Pettes married to Lucy Richards of Dorchester, Massachusetts, January 20th 1820.

Lucy Richards Prescott married Nov. 11th 1847, Edward Mott Moore.

Isham Green Searcy married Sept. 4th 1837 to Charlotte Pettes Prescott.

Mary Elizabeth Searcy born June 22nd 1838.

Lucy Frederic Searcy born Sept. 27th 1840.

Charlotte Pettes Searcy born Feb. 21st, 1842.

Lucy Frederic Searcy married 24th February 1870 to Thomas Hale—in Windsor, Vt.

Thomas Hale Jr. married on the 27th November 1901 Elizabeth Hall Henderson in Yonkers, N. Y.

BIRTHS.

Joseph Pettes born July 22nd 1757

Charlotte Pettes born November 24. 1761

Mary Pettes born January 20th 1788—Sunday.

Frederick Pettes born February 17th 1789—Tuesday

John Pettes born March 17th 1793, Sunday

William H. Pettes born December 24th 1815.

Harriet Mynderse born August 20th 1791

Charlotte Pettes Prescott was born May 22nd 1818 Tuesday

Joseph Pettes Bottiswood was born December 7th 1809

Charlote Pettes Prescott was born Friday May 22d. 1818

Lucy Richards Prescott was born Monday April 17th 1820.

William Richards Pettes born Nov. 7th 1821.

Mary Elizabeth Pettes born June 18th 1823

John Pettes born Nov. 4th 1825

Frederick Dudley Pettes was born Sept. 28th 1827.

Edward Pettes born Aug. 3rd 1829.

Lucy Ellen Pettes born March 14th 1831.

Robert Thaxter Pettes born June 21st 1833.

Mary Elizabeth Searcy was born at Tallahassee Florida June 22nd 1838

Lucy Frederic Searcy was born at Tallahassee Florida, September 27th 1840

Charlotte Pettes Searcy was born at Tallahassee Florida February 21st 1842.

Charlotte Elizabeth Prescott Hale, born Dec. 5th 1870 in New York City.

Thomas Hale Jr. 4th Feb. 1874 in Yonkers, N. Y.

Elizabeth Hall Henderson born 13th Feb. 1878

Elizabeth Hale born in Yonkers N. Y. Wednesday, 13 November 1902.

Thomas Hale 3rd July 12th 1904 in Yonkers.

Lucy Prescott Hale, born January 3rd, 1910.

Lucy Richards was born at Dorchester Mass. June 7th 1798

Charlotte Lucy Prescott Moore was born June 10th 1861 at Rochester, New York.

Mary Pettes Moore was born at Rochester New York Sept. 6th 1848.

Edward Mott Moore was born at Windsor Aug. 25th 1850.

Lindley Murray Moore was born at Rochester March 19th 1852

Samuel Prescott Moore born at Rochester January 3rd 1854

Richard Mott Moore was born at Rochester N. Y. Nov. 23rd 1855.

Abbie Joy Moore, born at Rochester, Aug. 23rd 1857.

Frederick Pettes Moore, born March 16th 1859.

DEATHS

Joseph Pettes died December 5th 1811

Harriet Pettes died October 21st 1816

Samuel Prescott died at Mantanzas on the Island of Cuba, Sept. 1822.

Frederick Pettes died at Detroit, Michigan, Thursday October 25th 1838 at 1-¼ A.M. at the National Hotel kept by A. Wales.

Charlotte Pettes died April 21st 1849

Lucy Richards Pettes died May 27th 1849

Charlotte Lucy Prescott Moore died April 15th 1863

Mary Pettes Prescott Sergeant, died June 15th 1863

Lucy Richards Prescott Moore died Aug. 1902 in Rochester, N. Y.

Dr. Edward Mott Moore died in 1900 Rochester N. Y.

Mary Elizabeth Searcy died in N. Y. 18 Jan. 1897

Charlotte Pettes Prescott Searcy, died in Yonkers, N. Y. 11th April 1907.

Lucy Frederic Searcy Hale died in Yonkers 10th Dec. 1909

Lucy Ellen Pettes Sabine died in Windsor Vt. 6th March 1911

Isham Green Searcy died in New Orleans, La. of Yellow Fever 24th July 1841

BENJAMIN RHOADES.
(1704–1773.)

Holy Bible in English; Edinburgh, Alexander Kincaid, 1762.

Contains the records of Benjamin Rhoades and Rachel, his wife, and descended to the present owner, Miss Elizabeth Prescott Hale, of Yonkers, New York. She is the great-great-great-great-granddaughter of the original owner.

Joseph Pettes was Born July 22nd 1757

Charlotte Pettes Born Novr. 24th 1761

were married the 18th day April 1782

Joseph Pettes died December 5th 1811

Benjamin Rhoades Died June 25 1773, aged 68

Rachel Rhoades Died March 25, 1782 aged 83

John Pettes D'd June 20th 1790 in the 81st year of his age.

Benjamin Rhoades was born the 12th Day of June 1704

Rachel Rhoades was born 1698 October the 28 - - Day.

Benjamin Rhoades His Bible 1769.

Amherst, Nov. 10th 178(7), Dick Bottiswood was born

Sunday Jany. 20th 1788, Polly Pettes was born.

Tuesday, Feby. 17th 1789. 20 mts. after 7 o'clock P.M., Frederick Pettes was born.

John Pettes born Sunday March 17th 1793

Freder'k Pettes married September [piece torn out here] 1814.

[Piece torn out of the following four lines]

   H. Pettes born December

  arriet Mynderse born (Say Pettes)

    August 20th 1791, married to F.

   Pettes Sept. 25th 1814

Harriet Pettes died October 22nd 1816.

[Note by present owner, Miss Hale.]

The Rhoades family came from England about 1746. This Bible was owned by Benjamin & Rachel Rhoades John and Rachel (Rhoades) Pettes, Joseph and Charlotte (Wales) Pettes, Mary Pettes (M. 1st,) Prescott, (2nd,) Sergeant, Charlotte Pettes Prescott Searcy, Lucy Frederic Searcy Hale, Charlotte Elizabeth Prescott Hale.

CHRISTOPHER ROBERT.
(Married 1743.)

Holy Bible in English; Oxford, Thomas Baskett, 1747.

The Bible contains the date of the marriage of Christopher Robert and Mary Dyer, his wife, and of the births of their children. The record is repeated on a second page. It has descended directly to the present owner, T. J. Oakley Rhinelander, Esq., of New York City, who is the great-great-grandson of Christopher Robert.

On the 28 of October 1743 Was Maried Christopher Robert to Mary Dyer by the Rev. Richard Charlton

On ye 28th July 1744 was born at 1 oclock the first Daughter of Christr. & Mary Robert named Christian who Departed this Life ye 14th August 1745

On ye 27th January 1745/6 was born the First Son of Christr. & Mary Robert named Daniel.

On ye 29th July 1748 Was born Mary the Second Daughter of Christr. & Mary Robert and departed this Life October 18th 1752.

On ye 2th September 1749 was born Christopher the Secon Son of Christr. & Mary Robert.

On ye 18th Juin 1751 Was Born Susannah the third Daughter of Christr & Mary Robert an Died ye 30th Juin 1752.

On the 22 of May was born Mary Elizabeth fourth Daughter of Christopher & Mary Robert 1753

On the 4 of June 1755 Was born Mary fifth daughter of Christopher & Mary Robert.

April 22 was born John the 3 son of Christopher & Mary Robert.

January 30th was born William forth son of Christopher & Mary Ro [some letters cut off] who d - - - -

The 28 October 1743 was Married Christopher Robert to Mary Dyer by the Revd. Mr. Charlton

1744 July 28 was born Christian the first Daughter of Christopher & Mary Robert and Departed this Life August 14 day 1745

1745/6 January 27 was born Daniel the first son of Chrstr. Mary Robert.

1748 July 29 Was born Mary Second Daughter of Christr. and Robert and Departed this Life October 18 day 17— [some figures cut off]

1749 Sepm. 2 was born Christopher second son of Christopher and Mary Robert.

1751 was born June 18, susanna Third daughter of Christor. and Mary Robert departed this Life June 30th 1752

1753 May 22 was born Mary Elizabeth fourth daughter of Christopher & Mary Robert.

1755 June 4 was born Mary fifth daughter of Christ. and Mary Robert

1757 April 22 was born John third son of Christopher & Mary Robert.

1760 January 30 was born William fourth son of Christopher and Mary Robert & Departed this Life January the Eight 1763.

HENDRICK RUTGERS.[1]
(Married 1732.)

Holy Bible in Dutch; Dordrecht, Pieter en Jacob Keur, 1730.

    Contains the records of Hendrick Rutgers and Catharina De Peyster, his wife, with their children. The Bible has descended through eight generations to the present owner, Mrs. Mary Crosby Brown, of Woodmere, N. Y. The records are in Dutch and have been translated by Dr. L. Bendikson.

Niew York Juny Den 9 A 1732 —

Ben Ick Hendrick Rutgers Met Catherina DePeyster Getrout Door myn Oome Den Eerwaerde Petrus Vas Predikant tot Kingston in Esoapes De Heer Geve Daar Toe Zyn Zeegen, Amen

1732 Octob^r 2 is Onse Eerste Doghter Catharina Gebooren op Sondagh Omtrent Elve Uren S' morgen's en Gedoopt in De Niewe Kerk op Sondagh Den 8 Dezer, Door Domanie Gaultheru[s] Du Bois, en Tot Compeer Vader Harmanus Rutgers & Peet Moeder Catharina Rutgers.

1734 Decemb^r 28 is onse Eerste Zoon Johannis Gebooren op Saterdagh Omtrent Negen Uuren S. morgens, en Gedoopt in De Neiwe Kerk op Neiwe Yaers Dagh, Door Domanie Hendrickus Boel tot Compeer Broeder Wellem De Peyster & tot Peet Moeder Anna De Peyster

1736 Dec 30 is Onse Tweede Doghter Anna Gebooren up Donder Dagh S. avendt. Omtrent Elf Uuren en in De Neiwe Kerk Gedoopt op Sondagh Den 9th Jan^{ry} 1736/7 Door Domanie Hendrickus Boel, Tot Compeer Broeder Abraham Boelen & tot Peet Suster Elizabeth Boelen

1738 Octob^r 14 is Onse Tweede Zoon Harmanus Gebooren op Saterdagh. S avondts Omtrent Elf Uuren en in De Neiwe Kerk Gedoopt op Sondagh Den 22" Deser Door Domanie Gualtherus DuBois en tot Compeer Broeder Harmanus Rutgers en to Peet Suster Elsie Marshall

[1 The Dutch character ÿ is not cut for fonts of English type. Therefore the letter y has been used in the Dutch records where ÿ is meant.]

1739 Augusto 8 Is Onse Tweeden Zoon Harmanus in Den Heere Ontslaapen De Heere Geven hem een Zalighen Opstandighen, Amen.

1741/2 January 5 Is onse Derden Doghter Elizabeth Gebooren Op Dingsdagh Avondts Omtrent 8 Uren en Gedoopt in De Neiwe Kerk Door Domanie Henricus Boel tot Compeer Broeder Harmanus Rutgers en peet Suster Elizabeth Rutgers —

1742 May 24 Is Onse Eersten Zoon Johannis in Den Heere Ontslaapen Op Maendagh Omtrent Drie Uren Na Middagh De Heere Geven hem een Zalighen Opstandinghe, Amen.

1743 Novemb^r 19. Is Onse Derden Zoon Harman Gebooren Op Saterdagh Avont Omtrent 7 Uren en Gedoopt in de Neiwe Kerk op Sondagh Den 27 Dezer Door D.... en tot Compeer Vader Harmanis Rutger en tot Peet Suster Eva Provoost.

1745 Octob^r 7 Is Onse Vierden Zoon Hendrick Gebooren Op Mandagh Avondt Omtrent Negen Uren en gedoopt in den Neiwe Kerk Op Sondagh Den 20 Dezer Do[or] Domanie Johannis Ritsma tot Compeer Broeder John Marshall en Peet Suster Catharina Van Horn

1746 April 22 Is onse Zoon Harman in den Heere Ontslaap[en] op Dingsdagh Omtrent Twaalf Uren op Den Dagh, Den Heere Verleenen hem een Zaligh Opstandingh, Amen

October ye 26 1747 is onse Maria Geboren tusse 6 en 7 uren Mandagh Agter Migdagh is gedoopt door Domeni Ritsema tot Compeer John Prevoost en tot Peet Onse Doghter Catharena Rutgers

September ye 12 1749 Is Onse Zoon Harmanes Gebooren Dingesdag Smorgens te 3 Vren en Ge Doopt Door Doomene Deuboos tot Compeer Wellem Bedlow en tot peet onse Dogter Catharena Rutgers Huis Vrou Van Wellem bedlow

Maria gedoopt den 1st Novr 1747

Harmanus D. . . . 4 Octob^r, 1749

[TRANSLATION OF ABOVE.

[New York, June the 9th Anno 1732. I, Hendrick Rutgers have been married to Catharina De Peyster by my uncle the Reverend

Petrus Vas, minister at Kingston in Esopus. May the Lord give his blessing thereunto. Amen.

[1732: Oct. 2, born on Sunday about 11 o'clock in the morning our first daughter Catharina and baptized in the New Church on Sunday the 8th inst. by Domine Gualtherus Du Bois, as godfather Harmanus Rutgers, and as godmother Catharina Rutgers.

[1734: Dec. 28, born on Saturday about 9 o'clock in the morning our first son Johannis; baptized in the New Church on New Year's Day by Domine Hendrickus Boel, as godfather brother Wellem De Peyster and as godmother Anna De Peyster.

[1736: Dec. 30, born on Thursday evening, about 11 o'clock our second daughter Anna, and baptized in the New Church on Sunday. Jan. the 9th 1736/7, by Domine Hendrickus Boel; as godfather brother Abraham Boelen and as godmother sister Elizabeth Boelen.

[1738: Oct. 14, born on Saturday evening about 11 o'clock our second son Harmanus and baptized on Sunday the 22^{d} inst. in the New Church by Domine Gualtherus Du Bois; as godfather brother Harmanus Rutgers and as godmother sister Elsie Marshall.

[1739: August 8, died in the Lord our second son Harmanus. May the Lord grant him a blessed resurrection. Amen.

[1741/2: January 5, born on Tuesday evening about 8 o'clock our third daughter Elizabeth and baptized in the New Church by Domine Henricus Boel; as godfather brother Harmanus Rutgers and as godmother sister Elizabeth Rutgers.

[1742: May 24, died in the Lord our first son Johannis, on Monday about 3 o'clock in the afternoon. May the Lord grant him a blessed resurrection. Amen.

[1743: Nov. 19, born on Saturday evening about 7 o'clock, our third son Harman and baptized in the New Church on Sunday the 27th inst. by D . . . as godfather Father Harmanis Rutger and as godmother sister Eva Provoost.

[1745: Oct. 7, born on Monday evening about 9 o'clock our fourth son Hendrick and baptized in the New Church on Sunday the

20th inst. by Domine Johannis Ritsma; as godfather brother John Marshall and as godmother sister Catherina van Horn.

[1746: April 22, died in the Lord our son Harman on Tuesday about 12 o'clock at noon. May the Lord grant him a blessed resurrection. Amen.

[1747: October ye 26th, born on Monday between 6 and 7 o'clock in the afternoon, our Maria; baptized by Domine Ritsema, as godfather John Prevoost and as godmother our daughter Catharena Rutgers.

[1749: September ye 12th, born on Tuesday at 3 o'clock in the morning our son Harmanes; baptized by Domine Deuboos; as godfather Wellem Bedlow and as godmother our daughter Catherena Rutgers, housewife of Wellem Bedlow.

[Maria baptized Nov. 1st, 1747.

[Harmanus D.... Oct. 4, 1749.]

GEORGE RYERSON.

Holy Bible in Dutch; Dordrecht, Pieter Keur, 1719.

This Bible originally belonged to George Ryerson and has his name in it, dated 1781. It contains various entries of the Ryerson family and their slaves, and on another page is a series of entries referring to the Van Der Voort family. Whether they first owned the Bible and it afterwards went to the Ryersons, or whether the Van Der Voort record was copied in, we have not been able to determine. The Bible now belongs to the American Bible Society and has been deposited in the New York Public Library.

My negro boy born the 10 February, 1783.

Samuel Ryerson son of George Ryerson and Elizabeth born the 23 of April 1784.

Polly Ryerson born 23 of December 1785 and died the 20 of June 1803.

Hannah Ryerson born the 5 of September 1788.

> George Ryerson his Bible Book.
>   God give him grace therin to look;
> Not only look but understand,
>   For learning is better than house and land.
> When house and land is gone and spent
>   Then learning is most excellent.
>   October the 18, 1781.

Mary Ryerson wife of John Francis Ryerson born the 12th day of October, 1729.

Ellen the daughter of Mary Tice Ryerson was born the sixt day of November one thousand eight hundred and two at one o'clock.

John the sun of Mary Tice Ryerson was born the seventh day of September at six o'clock in the afternoon, 1804.

Genny the daughter of Mary Tice Ryerson was born 1st day of July one thousand eight hundred and six at ten o'clock of the evening.

De 1 Mert 1752 is geebore Heelena Van Der Voort.

De 1 My 1754 is geebore Samuel Van Der Voort.

De 30 Mert 1756 is geebore Jan Van Der Voort.

De 23 December 1757 is geebore Jacobus Van Der Voort.

De 13 Augustus 1759 is geebore Maria Van Der Voort.

De 11 October 1761 is geebore Sarel Van Der Voort.

Yores Ryerse zine Bible.

George Ryerson his Bible, October the 17th 1781.

JOHN SCHUYLER.[1]
(Married 1723.)

Holy Bible in Dutch; Dordrecht, Pieter Keur, 1719.

Contains the records of John Schuyler and Cornelia Van Cortlandt, his wife, with some of their descendants. The Bible contains some additional entries which are in the nature of personal memoranda and not genealogy; these have been omitted at the request of the family. The Bible is now owned by Dr. John Van Rensselaer, of Albany, N. Y.

1723 October Den 18th been ick in Den Houwelyken Staat getreden Mett Cornelia Van Cortlandt

1724 Augustes den 18th is gebooren onse eerste Dochter genamt Gertruydt op Degensdaght.

1725 Decr Den 30th : is gebooren onse eerste Zoon genamt Johannes op Donderdaght Vor getuyge

1727 Septr Den 30th : is gebooren onse Twede Zoon genamt Stephanes, op. Saterdagh & is gestorven Van June 1729

1729 Desember Den 20th is gebooren onse Derde Zoon — Genamt Stephanes

In hett Jaar 1723 ben Ick Johannis Schuyler in Den Houwelicken. Staet getreden Mett Cornelia V. Cortlandt Den 18th Van October

In hett Jaar 1724 Den 18th : Augustes is geboren ons Eerste Kindt een Dochter genamt Gertruydt getuyge Jo. Schuyler & Will bayard

In hett Jaar 1725 Den 30th December is geboren onse twede Kindt een Zoon genamt Johannes, getuygen Moeder Elizth Schuyler & Phill: Van Cortlandt

In hett Jaar 1727 Den 30 September is geboren onse twede Zoon genamt Stevanes getuygen Anna Delansey & Phllip Schuyler, overled June 1729

[1 The Dutch character ij is not cut for fonts of English type. Therefore the letter y has been used in the Dutch records where ij is meant.]

Schuyler House, Belleville, New Jersey
Erected about 1710

In hett Jaar 1729 Den 20 December is geboren onse Derde Zoon genamt Stevanes, getuygen Coll⁰ Phillip Schuyler & Zyn huysvrow Margreta Schuyler -- Overlede Den 15ᵗʰ Desember in het Jaar 1731

In het Jaar 1731 Den 13ᵗʰ Octʳ is gebore onse Vierde Zoon Genamt Phillip getuyge Vader Johˢ Schuyler & Moder Eizath Schuyler, Overleder Den December 1732

In het Jaar 1733 Den 10 Novʳ is geboren onse Vyfde Zoon Genamt Phillip Getuyge Deepatrone & Zyne Moeder Marya Miln

In het Jaar 1735 Den 21ᵗʰ July is geboren onse Sesde Zoon genamt Cortlandt tot getuyge Coll⁰ Phill Schuyler and Gertruydt Beeckman

In het Jaar 1737 Den 12ᵗʰ Augᵗ is Gebore onse Sevende Zoon Genamt Stephanes tot Getuyge Stevanes Van Ranssear and Suster Cataline Cuyler

In het Jaar 1738 Den 5ᵗʰ Octʳ is Gebore ons Negende Kint Een Doghter Genamt Elizᵗʰ tot Getuyge Isaack Wendell and Margreta Schuyler, Een is overlede 26ᵗʰ June 1741

In het Jaar 1741 febʳʸ 15ᵗʰ is Gebore ons Tiende Kint Een Zoon Genamt Oliver Tot Getuyge Cornˢ Cuyler and Elizᵗʰ Ransselar Een is overlede Den 22ᵗʰ July 1741

1741 November den 5ᵗ Is de voornoemde Johannis Schuyler Overleden, Ende op den 9ᵗʰ October 1762 is overleden den Voornoemde Cornelia Schuyler, Lieflyke waeren sy in haer leven, den heer gieft dat sy salig syn Gestorven

1763 September den 19ᵉⁿᵉ is Geboren ons sesde kint genaemt John Bradstreet. Gedopt by Domini Eliardus Westerlo, Getuyge Colonel John Bradstreet & Judah Van Renselaer, rynighhem. [?] O Godt met het bloed Van a verkoun Sone.

1764 Augustus den 10ᵉⁿ is onse Sone John Bradstreet overleeden, Alles na u welbehagen O! heer.

1765 July den 12ᵉⁿ is Geboren ons Sevende kint Genaemt John Bradstreet. Gedopt by Domini Eliardus Westerloo, Getuyge Colo. John Bradstreet & Judah VanRenselaer doct by hem heer na u Wilbehagen, Ende zy hy aen u in leven andy in Sterven

1768 January den 20ᵉⁿ Is geboren ons Achgsten kint Genaemt Philip Jeremiah, gedoept by Domini Eliardus Westerlo Getuyge Robert Van Renselaer & Barabar Schuyler, Den Heer wett geven dat hy op mach wassen, tot den eere Godts ende syne wellusk

1770, July 17 - - - - - - iverden Geboren drie kinderens tusce doot ende een levendige, hit wellige Stierf den saluden day

1773 January 29 in geboren onse twalfden Kint genaemt Rensselaer guft hem O' Heer unser Sagge dat hy op Magd Wasschen In u vaesse, gedoept by Domini Eliarden Westerloo Getuyge, Meyn Vader Johannes VRenselaer & myer Dockler Engeltge Schuyler

1775 Decʳ 22ᵈ is Geboren onse derteenen Kind genaemt Cornelia Lynch den Heere wielt Hoor Segeren Ende tot ben mach sipwaasr Getuyge Cornelia Livingston Myn [illegible]

1778 May 14 is Geboren onse vertienden Kind Genaemt Cortlandt. syt genadegh tot him O Heer Ende Segonte alle Syn duechsame megon, Getuyge myn Dochter Elizabeth, overlede Octo: 17ᵈ/

1781 is Geboren Onse vyftienden kind Genaemt Catherine Van Rensselaer, Sach haer O Heer up mapen in dugdelychie heyh and tot une Em - Getrage [several words in this record are illegible]

CHARLES SHELDON.
(Married 1783.)

Holy Bible in English; Worcester, Mass., Isaiah Thomas, 1791.

Contains the records of Charles Sheldon and Elizabeth Bellamy, his wife, with their descendants. It is now in the possession of their great-grandson, Charles L. Sheldon, Esq., of New York City, but is in storage, so we have not been able to verify the entries.

Charles Sheldon son of Capt. Daniel Sheldon of Hartford was married to Miss Elizabeth Bellamy daughter of the Rev. Joseph Bellamy D. D. of Bethlehem in Woodbury on the 23rd day of February, in the year 1783.

The time of the Births of their children & their names are as follows, viz.

Elizabeth Sheldon born Feb. 20th 1785

Charles Sheldon Jr. Born March 23rd 1787

Frances Sherman Sheldon born Sep. 19th 1789.
"   "   "   Died May 4th 1848.

Henry Sheldon born Aug. 5th 1796. Isabel Woodbridge Sheldon Born June 12th, 1800.

(Was married (the 2nd time) to Miss Elizabeth Parsons daughter of Mr. Linas Parsons of Springfield on the 25th day of Oct; 1795.)

October 31 - 1792 Died Mrs. Elizabeth Sheldon at West Suffield by the small Pox which she took by noculation the 16th Inst. in the 33rd year of her Age.

May 4th 1848 died Frances Sherman Sheldon wife of Dr. Josiah Noyes of Clinton New York.

April 13th 1855 Died Charles Sheldon Jr.

Alicia Lawrence wife of Charles Sheldon Jr. died Nov. 27th 1866.

Record of the family of Charles Sheldon Jr.

Alicia Sheldon born May 18th 1813

Elizabeth Bellamy Sheldon born January 29th 1815.

Jane Sheldon born June 25th 1816.

Sarah Sheldon born Aug. 12 1818.

Charles Henry Sheldon born Sep. 11th, 1820

William Lawrence Sheldon born March 13th 1823.

Edward Sheldon born Sep 19th 1825

Catharine Sheldon born March 31st 1827

George Sheldon born May 17th 1829

Henry Lawrence Sheldon born July 19th 1831.

George Sheldon died May 21st 1830

Catharine Sheldon died Feb. 3rd 1840.

William Lawrence Sheldon died March 13th 1843

Charles Henry Sheldon died Nov. 24th 1873

Edward Sheldon died March 26th 1886

Alicia Sheldon died Aug. 3rd 1900.

LAWRENCE SMYTH.

Holy Bible in English; London, Cooke, n.d.

The records commence with Lawrence Smyth, whose dates are not given, but whose wife, Margaret Johnston, was born in 1694. The Bible is now the property of the Colonial Dames of the State of New York, and is deposited in the Van Cortlandt House, New York City.

Domestic Chronology—

Lawrence Smyth, (Born [?]) married Margaret Johnson (Born 1694. Died 1762. Daughter of Andrew Johnston and Catherine Van Courtlandt—Andrew Johnson was one of the children of Dr John Johnson, the first emigrant who arrived in N.Y. from Scotland Dec^{br} 1685 - - and died in Perth Amboy, Sept. 1732.) both died in Perth Amboy leaving an only Son John Smythe.

John Smyth Born 1724. Clerk to the board of East Jersey.—proprietor and treasurer of the province when the Revolution commenced.—died in London 12 January 1786. in the 64th year of his age. buried in Mary le Bone Churchyard near London. married Susannah Moore Born May 24th 1725. the 10th daughter of Col. John Moore, and Frances Lambert. Died 1803. aged 78 years—was interred in the family Vault in Trinity church yard. their only child Andrew Smyth Born June 21st 1765. Died August 3^d 1827 aged 62 years, one month, and eleven days.—Burried at St. Michaels Church yard. Bloomingdale—reinterred in Greenwood Cemetery 1867—

married, 1st Maria Parker Born at Perth Amboy. Married to Andrew Smith December 29th 1793, by the Rev. Richard Channing Moore—she departed this life October 14th 1798. no issue

2d Maria Livingston Born September 22^d 1777. Daughter of Philip John Livingston & Frances Bayard. married to Andrew Smyth Sept. 30th 1801 by the Rev Isaac Wilkins. died August 13th 1856, aged 73 years, 3 months, & 22 days. burried in Greenwood Cemetery.

1st child John Livingston Born September 20th 1802. baptized by Rev C. Jones. died July 30th 1803. Aged 10 months.

2nd, Frances Susan Born December 21st 1804. Married Aug. 1838 to Charles I. Aldis. baptized by Rev. A. Beach.

3d, John William Born July 28th 1807 Baptized by Rev. I. Wilkins.

4th, Maria Ann Born Sept 16th 1811 Baptized by Rev. I. Wilkins. Died May 12th 1813 aged 20 months.

John William Smith The only surviving son of Andrew Smyth and Maria Livingston Born July 28th 1807. Son of Andrew Smyth & Maria Livingston married Sept 9th 1835, died December 10th 1866, aged 59 years, 4 months and 13 days. burried in Greenwood Cemetery

Married Mary Anne Coggill Born April 29th 1808. in Leeds, England. daughter of George Coggill & Anne Atkinson—Married to John W. Smyth Sept. 9th 1835 by the Rev. I. M. Forbes in St. Luke's Ch. N.Y.

Georgina Maria Smyth Born September 23d 1840.—daughter of J. W. and M. A. Smyth, baptized by Rev. Charles Aldis at St. Peters church Nov. 15. 1840. Chelsea N. York—Sponsors—George Coggill, Frances S. Aldis and her Mother. Married to John William Payne, Oct. 7th 1879.

Henry Coggill Smyth Born November 1st 1843—only Son of J. W and M. A. Smyth. baptized by Rev Hugh Smith, at St. Peters church Chelsea—N.Y.—on Christmas Day, 1843 Sponsors, Henry Coggill Ann Eudora Coggill, and Charles I. Coggill died at Schenectady N.Y. August 10th 1847 aged 3 years 9 months and 10 days—burried in Greenwood Cemetery.

Bot. Feby 11th, 1792 £2. 18. 0.

Beneath this Stone, lies the remains of John Smyth Esqr only son of Lawrence Smyth & Margaret Johnson of Perth-Amboy in the Provence of New Jersey, North America—Who departed this Life 12th January 1786—in the 64 year of his Age

The above is the Inscription on a Tomb Stone, I caused to be placed over my Father's Grave in Marybone Church Yard, near London, the 5th of May 1791

Andrew Smyth died August 3ᵈ 1827 62 years 1. mo & 11 days only son of John Smyth.

John W. Smyth only son of Andrew Smyth died December 10ᵗʰ 1866. aged 59 years 4 mo & 13 days.

Henry Coggill Smyth only son of John William Smyth, died August 14ᵗʰ 1847, aged 3 years, 9 mo & 13 days.

Letter from Rev. Richard Channing Moore (afterwards Bishop of Virginia), to his Aunt Mrs. John Smyth (formerly Susanna Moore) on the occasion of the Marriage of her only son Andrew

December 30ᵗʰ 1793

Staten Island—Decʳ 30.93

I embrace the early opportunity that has offered to inform my dear Aunt, that I last evening joined *her beloved Andrew*, in the bonds of Matrimony with my aimable friend *Maria Parker*—a young lady whose virtues are truly extensive, and whose domestic accomplishments authorize me to think that She will prove to him a source of most unfading Pleasures.

on last Thursday she dedicated herself to the Almighty at his *Altar*. May that God in whose Service she has engaged, *bless her* with effusions of his Spirit and crown her with the richest favors of his Providence & grace. Give my love to *Fan* tell her that she possesses the *kindnest regards* and best wishes, of your truly affectionate *nephew*

Richard Chang. Moore

I congratulate my dear Aunt on the Nuptials of both her Children—Andrew & his Bride will be in Town to morrow

(Addressed)

Mrs. Smyth Beekman Street New York   Favor'd by Mr. Whaites

SAMUEL STIMSON.
(1782–1852)

Holy Bible in English; Charlestown, Mass., Samuel Etheridge, 1803.

This Bible contains the family records of Samuel Stimson and his wife, Mehitable Ellithorp. It also contains the records of a number of marriages performed by Mr. Stimson as Justice of the Peace. It has descended in the direct line, and belongs to the estate of the late Miss Margaret Stimson of New York City.

This Bible Is the Property of Samuel [&] Polly Stimson 1st Jany 1808.

Marriages.

Samuel Stimfon Jr. was married to Mehitable Ellithorp the First of January, 1803.

Births.

Samuel Stimson Jr. was Born August the 1st 1782.

Mehitable Stimson his wife was Born June the 18. 1787

the children

Sufannah M. Stimfon there children was Born the 27 of November 1805

Earl L. Stimson was Born February 12th 1807

Azariah Stimfon was Born July th9 , 1809

Samuel Leonard Stimfon was Born march 29 1812

Abigail Anny Stimson was Born April 29th, 1815

Solomon Leonard Stimson was born February 8th, 1820.

John Fay Stimson was born 22 of November 1824

Eliphas Day Stimson was born the 1st of September 1827.

Mary Elizabeth Stimson was born April 9th 1830

Alexander F. Armstrong was born August 14 1826

E. L. Ellithorp Born Dec. 6, 1840

Wiley Ellithorp born friday march 19 1784

John Ellithorp born April 7 1785.

Betsey Ellithorp born July 21 1792.

Isaac Ellithorp, born may 6 1795

Abigail Ellithorp, born Octo 1th 1797

Azariah Ellithorp, born May 28 1790

Solomon Ellithorp born Oct 16 1797.

Azariah Feabruly married Sept. 10, 1815

Jacob Ellithorp born Dec. 18 1816

Sally Ellithorp, born Sept. 13 1818

Zenis Ellithorp born Nov. 25 1820

Eliz Ellithorp born August 16 1826.

Emily Ellithorp born May 1 1828

Wiley Ellithorp, born April 12th 1830

Twins, Abby Ann, Mary Anne, were born July 11 - 1833.

DEATHS

Samuel Stimson departed this life April 20" 1852 Aged 69 years 8 months and 20 days.

Samuel Leonard Stimson Died the 20" of September 1813 aged 1 year 5 months 24 Days.

Eliphaz Day Stimson Died the 3d Day of August 1830 aged 2 years Eleven month and three Days.

Earl Geo. Earl L. Stimson departed this Life October 11" 1830 aged 23 years 8 months Low 1 Day.

Memorandum of the persons whom I have married whilst in place of a justice of the peace. J. Samuel Stimson

1819   1819   On the 3 of September Mr. John Hinds to Rebecki Mc Card Boath of the Town of Edinburgh

On the 19" of September 1819 Mrs Mr. Richard Bridwer of Hadley Lavina Fraker of Edinburgh.

On the 7 of November 1819 Mr. Isaac Ellithorpe to Mrs. Effa Rufsell Both of Edinburgh

On the 11 of march 1820 Mr. Ebenezer Beckerr to Mrs. Sally Turk Both of the town of Concord.

On the 19th of march 1820 Mr. John Ash to Mrs. Dolly Perry Both of the town Concord, Saratoga

On the 21 of March 1820 Mr. Sumner Smith to Mrs. Mosther Van Vleck Both of town of Edinburgh Saratoga County.

On the 30" of march 1820 Mr. Obediah Perry to Mrs. Betsey Hills[3] Both of the town of Concord, Saratoga County.

on the 7" May 1820 Mr Stephen Stedmond to Mrs. Jemima Hunt Boath of town of Corinth

on the 10" August 1820 Mr. Thomas Foraker to Mrs. Betsey Clute Boath of the town of Concord

On the 24 of September 1820 Mr. Peter Bumore to Betsey Colson Boath of the town of Concord.

On the 24 of January 1821. Mr. Joseph Flansburgh to Betsey Flansburgh Boath the town of Concord.

On the 1st Day February 1821 Mr. Jacob Turk of Concord Mrs. Abigail Bloggett of Corinth.

On the 18 Day February 1821 Mr. William Wooley to Concord Mrs. Rachel McDonnald atholl

On the 20 Day of August 1821 Mr. Petter Stedman to Soriah ann Vonnuter Both of the town of Concord.

On the 17th Day of February 1822. Mr. Benjamin Hosley to Rectina Copelin Both of the town of Concord.

On the 24" of February 1822 Mr. John Clute to Mrs. Mariah Wooley Both of town of Concord.

On the 24" February 1822 Mr. Beriah Phelps of Hadley to Mrs. Esther Clute of Concord.

On the 6" March 1822 Mr. Josiah Martin of Northampton montgomery County to Miss Lois Hewit of Edinburgh, Saratoga County.

on the 26 of may 1822 Mr. Ira D. Mosher of corinth to Mrs. Fanny Johnson of Concord.

On the   octob. 1823 Mr. David Gilbert to Mariah Flansburgh Boath of the town Concord

on the 18" of May 1824 Mr. Edward Tabor of Vermont to Mrs. Nancy Cook of Concord.

Nehemiah Wing to Sophia Day

Mr. John Cannon to Sally Cook Both of Concord.

A. T. Ellithorpe to Ann Day Both of town of Edinburgh.

On the 15" of July 1824 Mr. Daniel Catheson to Mrs.   Mac Cumber Both of Concord

on the 15" of September 1824 Mr Gran Wart of providence to Mrs. Pheby Potter of Concord.

on the 14 of November 1824 Mr. Henery Blackwood of —— to Mrs. Rebecky Dorling of Concord.

on the 19" march, march 1825 Mr. Daniel Allen to Mrs. Sally Wait boath of the town of Concord.

Luke Gilbert to Ruth Wait.

Renslow Mathew to Saly Thayer

JUDGE SELAH STRONG.
(1737–1815.)

Holy Bible in English; New York, T. Allen, 1792.

Contains the records of Judge Strong and his wife, Anna Smith, with their descendants. It has descended in a straight line to the present owner, Benjamin Strong, Jr., of New York City, the great-great-grandson of Judge Strong.

Selah Strong—born 25th December 1737 — Anna Smith, born April 14th 1740 and were Married, November 9th 1760.

They had Issue —

Keturah, born November 4th 1761, Married to James Woodhull, September 10th 1782, and Died, August 13th 1790 —

Thomas Shepard, born May 26th 1765

Margaret, born May 2d 1768 —

Benjamin, born April 14th 1770 —

Mary — born October 23d 1773 — and died November 12th 1773 —

William Smith, born January 24th 1775 and Died 26th September 1794 at 10 Minutes past 2 o Clock P. M—

Joseph, born December 1st 1777 —

George Washington, born January 20th 1783 —

Joseph, Married Esther Jones, January 19th 1805 —

Anna, Strong died August 12th 1812 —

Selah Strong, died July 4th 1815 —

Revd Selah Strong Woodhull — D. D. son of James W. and Keturah S. died at New Brunswick N. J. February 27th 1826 — he was one of the Professors in Rutgers College, and had entered on its duties, about three months previous —

Thomas S. Strong, Died April 18th 1840 at 20 Minutes past 7 — A. M. —

Dr. Romyn born 8th Novr 1776

Dr. Romyn, Died 22d February 1825 —

Mrs. Romyn, Died 22d October 1825 —

Jotham Weeks, born 24th Aug — 1731 — Sally Huggins, born 10th February 1738 and were Married 5th April 1756 —

Mrs. Weeks, Died with the Small Pox, the 16th December 1794, at ½ past 8 o Clock P. M—

Jotham Weeks, Died the 3d July 1807 Aged 75 years — 10 Ms & 9 Days —

Amy Hand, (Wife of Captain Isaac Hand) Died the 19th of April 1805 in the 35th year of her Age — born Aug. 14 1770—

Mary Hand (Second Wife of Capt. Isaac Hand) died Sept 6th 1810 = *1811* Born Aug. 14, 1770

Margaret Smith, Died Sept. 25th 1756—

William Smith, Esq. Died Octr 2d 1776

1847 Aug. 24. Cornelia Van Cleve Woodhull—Youngest daughter, of Selah Strong Woodhull, was Married to Josiah L. Pickard, of Platteville, Grant County, Wisconson—

Benjamin Strong, born April 14th 1770

Sally Weeks, born July 5th 1765= 1765 and were Married February 4th 1792

They had Issue —

Charles Lloyd — born August 15th 1794, at 9 o Clock A. M— died in Cincinnati March 24, 1864

Sally Huggins, born March 8th 1796 at 3 o Clock A. M.

Oliver Smith, born February 5th 1797, at 7,o Clock on Sunday evening —

Anna Smith, born November 24th 1798. at 8 o Clock, on Saturday evening—

Harriet Thompson, born February 16th 1801 at 6 o Clock, on Monday Morning — died Feby 25/64

Edward Augustus, born June 16th 1803 at 5 o Clock, on Thursday Morning—

Eliza, Templeton, born December 7th 1804 — at 20 minutes past, one — Friday Morning died in N. Rochelle, April 22/69

Oliver Smith Strong, died March 26th 1806, at 3 o Clock A. M. Aged 9 years, 1 Month & 21 Days—

Oliver Smith, Born the 11th December 1806 — on Thursday 5 o Clock P M— Died Apl 17 1874.

Sarah Strong, Died May 11th 1843 at 5 o Clock P M— Aged 77 years, 10 Months & 6 Days

George Strong Baxter, was born November 21st 1845 —

Benjamin Strong, died January 27th 1851 at 20 minutes before 12 midnight, aged 80 years 9 months and 13 days.

Charles Lloyd Strong, was married to Jeannette Amy Bradley April 7th 1817—

Eliza T. Strong, was Married to Andrew S. Snelling, April 9th 1829

Anna S. Strong, was married to George Baxter, January 21st 1829 —

Edward A. Strong was Married to Marianne Clay, the 5th October 1831 —

Harriet T. Strong was Married to Robert D. Weeks — April 27 — 1832

Oliver Smith Strong was Married to Margaret McIntyre, January 2d 1834

Sarah H. Strong, was Married to Dr. Nicoll H. Dering — October 1st 1844

Margaret, (the Wife of O. S. Strong) Died at Jersey City, on the 4th February 1845 — at 7 o Clock P M—

Charles Edward Strong, was Married to Eleanor Burrill Fearing the 18th April 1850

Georgianna Snelling, was Married to Dr. John C. Peters, the 16th May 1849

Julia Weeks Strong, was Married to Theodore Armstrong Bailey May 9th 1850

[State of New York } ss.
County of New York }

[This is to certify that the accompanying records from the Benjamin Strong Bible have been compared with the originals, corrected and are now as perfect as they can be made.

[SEAL] BENJ. STRONG, JR.]

SAMUEL SWAN.
(1720–1808.)

Holy Bible in English; Edinburgh, John Mosman & William Brown, & Assigns of James Watson, 1729.

Contains the records of Samuel Swan of Charlestown, Mass., and his wife, Joanna Richardson, with their descendants. The Bible has descended directly to their great-great-grandson, William L. Swan, Esq., of Oyster Bay, who is the present owner.

Samuel Swan of Charlestown (1720–1808) writes:

My Brother Timothy Swan Died the year 1745.

My Honoured Father Died in the year 1747.

My Honoured Grand Mother Austin Died November in the year 1746.

My Honour Mother Died in March the 11 (?), 1754.

Daughter Mehitable (2nd) Born January 17, 1765, 12 o'clock at noon. Daughter Mehitable Died March 9, 1765.

Son Joseph Born August 20, 1766. Died November 8, 1767.

Son Daniel Died August 4, 8 o'Clock in ye Morning, 1780. By clensing a Watter Cistern & haled up by Mr. Isaac Mallet. Dead in a few minnits after he went down. he Lived Desired and agreeable by Relatives and friends & acquaintance, & Died very much Lamented.

Son Timothy Died January 21, 1788, In Washington, North Carolina. he was married their and a Doctor their by information a Carecter good as a Doctor & acquaintance.

Died July 4th, 1796, Monday Mornin. My Dearly Beloved wife; she Lived with Relations & friends beloved, died Lamented by me very much and by all that was acquainted with her.

Daughter Joanna died December 9, 1791. A Cripal for 13 years befor she died 8 o'clock in ye morning beloved very much by her

Parents & Brothers & acquaintance. lived Beloved died Lamented pray God to Santifie it our everlastin Good.

Died my wife Anna Swan February 25 Wednesday 3 o'Clock afternoon, by me Lamented & all & pray God to santifie it for my everlastin Good. Lived beloved & died Lamited greatly.

Brister a negro, had when very young & died 1793 much lamed. by ye Family & others.

Samuel Swan Married To Joanna Richardson, March ye II, 1746. My Beloved wife Died July ye 4, morning 5 o'Clock, 1796.

Son Saml. was Born August the Six, Between nine & ten o'Clock in the Evening in the Year 1747.

Son Samuel Died September ye 29, 1749, about nine o'Clock in the Evening.

Son Samuel the Second was Born January ye 17th Between one & two o'Clock in the Morning in the Year 1749/50

Son Daniel Born October ye 4, 1752 N.S. in the Evening between 8 & Nine o'Clock.

Son Caleb, Born July ye 6th, 1754, N.S. Between Eleven & Twelve o'Clock in the Day.

Daughter Joanna, Born ye Eleventh Day of March, Thursday, Between Seven & Eight of ye Clock in ye Evening, 1756 N.S.

Daughter Mehitable Born ye Twenteth-fourth day of July, Sabeth Evening, Between Twelve & One o'Clock, N.S.—1757

Daughter Mehitable Died with ye Measelles — March 10, 1759, about 6 o'Clock Morning.

Samuel, Daniel, Caleb, Joanna had ye Measelles.

Son Timothy Born December 21, 1759, in ye morning, Between 4 & 5 o'Clock.

All previous records are supposed to have been burnt at the Conflagration of Charlestown, by the English, at the battle of Bunker Hill, 17th June, 1775.

Timothy Swan of Charlestown, was married to Miss Mehitabel Austin, daughter of Samuel and Sarah Austin, of Charlestown, Nov. 1, 1715, by Revd. Joseph Stevens, their Minister. She was born May 7, 1696, and Christened the 10th of the same month.

He died 1746, aged ... he was an only child

She died March 11, 1754 aged 58

Their children:

Timothy born Oct 9, 1716 Christened Oct 21, 1716 died 1745, aged 33
Abigail   "   "   July 12, 1719
Samuel   "   "   Oct   8, 1721
Caleb   "   "   Nov 12, 1727

Samuel Swan of Charlestown their Son, married Miss Joanna Richardson of Woburn, 2d March, 1746.

She died July 4, 1796 — in recording her death, he calls her "my dearly beloved wife"

He died Augt 6, 1808, aged 88

Their Children.

Samuel born August 6, 1747 died Sept 29, 1749

[Memorandum referring to the following four children:] All had the measles

Samuel 2d [born] Jany. 17, 1750 married Miss Hannah Lamson Daughter of Joseph Lamson of Charlestown 5th March, 1778.

Daniel [born] Oct 4, 1752 [married] Miss Elizabeth Tufts, dr. of Peter Tufts of Winter Kill Augt 21, 1777. he died in a Cistern Augt 4 1780. she died at their Son Joseph's farm in South Malden, Sept. 1753, having been 73 years a widow. She was an excellent woman.

Caleb [born] July 6, 1754 M. Miss Sarah Semple from London - 1780 She came out on a visit to her uncle Mr. Burt of Boston. ... He died in Woburn March 1816, aged 62 She died in Woburn Autumn 1820. Merchants in Boston

Joanna [born] March 11, 1756 died Dec 1791, aged 35 unmarried— 12 years a Cripple from rhumatism. She was much beloved and respected ... Mrs. Withington of Medford, when a girl, went to my grandfather's to take care of her. My Sister Hannah was very fond of her.

Mehitabel [born] July 24, 1757 died March 10, 1759, of measles.

Timothy [born] Dec. 21, 1759 [died] Jany 21, 1788 married ... an eminent Physician in Washington, N. C.

Mehitabel 2d [born] Jany 17, 1765 died March 9, 1765

Joseph [born] Augt 20 1766 [died] Nov 8 1767

Oct 12, 1797 he married Miss Anna Whittemore, of Charlestown (a near neighbor for many years) much beloved by all who knew her. My Sister Hannah Said She was a pious, lovely Christian woman. She died 25th July 1807, aged 76 ... they lived very happily. (Caleb Swan went from Boston to her funeral) Dr. Morse performed the funeral Service.

My Grandfather was a devout religious man ... every morning after breakfast, after reading a Chapter in the Bible, he made a prayer ... standing behind his high back chair.

He lived in a large house in Charlestown Square. when the town was burnt by the British troops at the battle of Bunker Hill 17th June, 1775, the inhabitants dispersed to the neighboring towns. He went with his family to Concord. When the English army evacuated Boston March 1776, he returned, with the other inhabitants, and built his house near "the Neck", between the main road, and the West Side of Bunker Hill, with a pleasant garden in front where he lived until his death in August 1808, aged 88. The house and barn are still standing in good preservation (1864–1868) though surrounded by modern houses.

The new mown hay used by the Americans for a breastwork in the battle (between two lines of rail fence) was mowed on his land the day before the battle. (D.S.) He had a fine orchard of Apple trees on the slope of Bunker Hill, which were all cut down by the British troops for fuel, the following winter. (D.S.) He said his Father was an only child, and therefore that he himself had neither Uncle, Aunt, nor Cousin.

That his father had been a dissipated man, and was disinherited by *his* father, who was rich, and he could not therefore give his Children so good an education as he had himself (H.S.)

He had 2 or 3 Slaves who were freed by the law of Massachusetts about 1780, one was a young woman said by Sister Hannah to be very handsome, ... one a man, wanted to come back if he did not like being free. he told him no, he must decide now; he might remain if he chose, but if he left, he could not come back. after some time, he finally concluded to go.

* * * * * * * *

Samuel Swan of Medford, Son of Samuel Swan of Charlestown married Miss Hannah Lamson, daughter of Joseph Lamson of Charlestown 5th March 1778. they removed from Charlestown to Medford, August 1791. He died 14th Nov, 1825 aged 75. She died 18th Nov. 1826 aged 70.

Their Children.

Samuel born 9th May 1779 married Miss Margaret Tufts dr. of Samuel Tufts of Medford, April 1809 his vessel lost at Sea in a storm along the coast 31 March 1823—on his homeward voyage from Princes Island Africa— aged 44. She died in Medford 29th Nov 1863, aged 84.

Daniel [born] 17th Feby 1781 married Miss Sarah Preston, youngest dr. of Remember Preston of Boston and Medford May 19, 1824.—m. by Revd. Andrew Bigelow. He died in Medford 5th Dec 1864 aged 83. She died in Medford 26th May aged 64 [both] buried in his Father's Tomb.

Joseph [born] 8th Sept 1784 married Miss Ann Rose from London, now of Medford / Jany 6, 1817. He died in Medford 21 Jany 1853 aged 69 She died in Medford 23d March 1860 aged 72.

Hannah [born] 13 Augt 1785 died in Medford 8th Augt 1862 aged 76 & 11 months. She was buried in her fathers tomb—her 3 brothers Daniel, Benjamin, Caleb were at the funeral.

Benjamin Lincoln [born] 15th June 1787 married Miss Mary Childs Saidler of New York Jany 23, 1816. She died in New York 27th Feby 1857 aged 57. He died in New York 31 March 1866 aged 78.

Timothy [born] 8th Nov 1788 lived 15 years in England from 1814 - - died in St. Croix island 30th Jany 1830, unmarried. He went to St Croix for his health, October 1829 — with his brother Caleb — his remains were brought home in April, and placed in the family tomb. Daniell, Joseph, and Caleb being present.

Caleb [born] 23rd June 1790 married Miss Harriet Stone, N. York daughter of the late Moses Stone of Watertown, Mass. 29th Sept 1830. She died in New York Dec. 20, 1867, aged 65 very suddenly, buried at Greenwood in his brother Benjamin's Vault.

> [The asterisks indicate the omission of a few entries which repeat some of the original records given above.]

JOHANNES TEN EYCK.[1]
(Married, 1746.)

Holy Bible in Dutch; Dordrecht, Jacob en Hendrick Keur, 1738.

Contains the records, in Dutch, of Johannes Ten Eyck and his wife, Sara Ten Broek, with their children. It has descended to Miss Margaret Ten Eyck Pruyn of Albany, New York, the present owner. The translation is by Dr. L. Bendikson.

Albany 26 may 1746. Ben Ick Joh^s H. Ten Eyck In den Echten Staaet getreden mett Sara Ten Broek. God geeve ons Syn Segen na Siel en Licham en getrout van Dominie Schuyler.

1748 April 12 Dinsdags morgens Breekke van den dag is geboren onsen Eersten Soon Hendrick. En is in den Heer gerust den 19 outt seijnde 6 Dage

1749 mey 5 is geboren onsen Tweede soon Hendrick op mandagh morgens omtrent 8 uure. En is in den Heere gerust den 26 Juni.

1751, Juni 11 is geboren onsen Derden Son En was doot

1752 is geboren onsen Eersten Dochter den 25 July En Cam doot op die werlt.

1754 Juni 20 is geboren onsen vierden Soon Hendrick op woensdagh omtrent vier ure meddagh

1756 Augustus 10 is myn Son Hendrick in den Heere gerust op mandagh morgens omtrent 2 a 3 ure En is Begrave den 11 Agustus.

1758 April 14 is geboren myn 2 Dochter En is gedoopt margreta En is in den Heere gerust op den 2 mey.

1725 Mey 26ste is Gebooren Sarah Dochter van Dirck Ten Broek.

1801 February de 16de is Sarah Ten Eyck Huys Vrouw van Joh^s. H. Ten Eyck door een Haastige ende onverwachtse Doot in

---

[1 The Dutch character ij is not cut for fonts of English type. Therefore the letter y has been used in the Dutch records where ij is meant.]

den Heer Ontslaapen op Stillwater ten Huyse Van Abraham Livingston & is Begraaven in het duytsche kerk hof te Albany.

1794 July 30ste is Johannis H. Ten Eyck in den Heer Ontslapen.

[TRANSLATION

[Albany, May 26th, 1746.

[I, Joh⁸ H. Ten Eyck have taken as wife Sara Ten Broek. May the Lord bless our bodies and our souls. Married by Domine Schuyler.

[1748 April 12th, Tuesday, born in the morning at day-break our first Son Hendrick; he died in the Lord on the 19th, being 6 days old.

[1749 May 5th, born our second Son Hendrick on Monday morning about 8 o'clock. He died in the Lord June 26th.

[1751 June 11, born our third son [who] was still born.

[1752 July 25th, born our first daughter [who] was still born.

[1754 June 20th, born our fourth Son, Hendrick, on Wednesday afternoon, about 4 o'clock.

[1756 August 10th, Monday, died in the Lord my Son Hendrick, about 2–3 o'clock in the morning, and he is buried on August 11th.

[1758 April 14th born my second daughter, christened Margreta; she died in the Lord May 2d.

[1725 May 26th, born Sarah, daughter of Dirck Ten Broek.

[1801 February 16th, died in the Lord Sarah Ten Eyck, house wife of Joh⁸ H. Ten Eyck, suddenly and unexpectedly at the house of Abraham Livingston at Stillwater and buried in the Dutch Cemetery at Albany.

[1794 July 30th died in the Lord Johannis H. Ten Eyck.]

HARMANUS TEN EYCK.
(1749-1828.)

Holy Bible in English; New York, Collins & Co., 1821.

Contains the records of Harmanus Ten Eyck and his wife Margaret Bleecker, and their descendants. It is now the property of Miss Margaret Ten Eyck Pruyn, of Albany, New York, who is the great-granddaughter of the original owners.

Family Record.

I, Harmanus Ten Eyck was born January 9, 1749 Old Style

Was born my Wife Margaret Bleecker, October 31, 1755 New S

Was born our first child May 22, 1777, named Catalina and departed this life October 6, 1777

Was born our second child October 12, 1778 named Catalina

Was born our third child Feb 9, 1781 named Jacob for sponsors Henry Ten Eyck and Anna Mancious

Was born our Fourth child Anna March 26, 1783 for Sponsors Dr. William Mancious & Margaret the wife of Henry Ten Eyck

Was born our fifth child February 22, 1786 named Henry for Sponsors Nicholas Bleecker and Nelly his wife

Was born our sixth child April 29, 1788 named Margaret for sponsors Henry Bleecker & Caty Bleecker And departed this life June 15 1789

Was born our Seventh child July 22, 1791, named Margaret

Was born our Eight child named Herman October 22, 1793.

Was born our ninth child February 10, 1796 named Catharine and departed this life August 25, 1797

Was born our Tenth child September 30, 1798 named Catharine.

Departed this life our Son Henry, July 1st 1794, aged 8 years 4 months and 6 days.

Harmanus Ten Eyck, 1749-1828

Was born our first granddaughter Margaret Ten Eyck Foster, at New York March 30 1820

Was born our first grandson Herman Ten Eyck Foster, March 1st, 1822 at New York

Was born our second Granddaughter Margaret Ten Eyck April 29, 1822 at Geneva.

Was born our Third Granddaughter Margaret Ten Eyck Burr, March 28, 1827 at Cazenovia

Was born our second grandson Jacob Post Girard Foster April 8, 1827 at New York

Was born our third Grandson William M. Burr, Jr.

Was born our fourth Grandson Jacob H. Ten Eyck Jr.

Was born our fourth Granddaughter Anna Foster Burr.

Was born our fifth Granddaughter Catalina Ten Eyck

I Harmanus Ten Eyck was married to Margaret eldest daughter of Henry Bleecker Junr March 10 1776

March 1st 1819 was married our daughter Anna to Andrew Foster of the City of New York

May 7, 1821 was married our son Herman to Eliza the daughter of Herman H Bogart of Geneva.

November 14, 1825, was married our daughter Catharine to William M. Burr of Cazenovia

Nov. 9 1818 Departed this life Our Mother Catalina Cuyler Widow of Henry Bleecker Junr aged 87 years, 2 months, 17 days mother of Mrs. Margaret Ten Eyck

Departed this life January 27, 1828 on Sabbath afternoon at half past 4 O'clock, our dear Father Harmanus Ten Eyck aged 78 years 11 days

Departed this life August 30, at half past 12 O'clock at night 1834, Our dear Mother Margaret Ten Eyck, aged 78 years 10 months

Departed this life December 26th 1849 — Andrew Foster, aged Seventy-seven years and six months

Departed this life July 13 1851 — Ann, relict of the late Andrew Foster, and daughter of the late Harmanus and Margaret Ten Eyck, aged 68 years, 3 months and 17 days.

Departed this life June 29th 1853 Margaret daughter of the late Harmanus and Margaret Ten Eyck aged 61 years 11 months and 7 days.

Departed this life Oct 8 1872, Jacob H. son of the late Harmanus & Margaret Ten Eyck, aged 92 years

Departed this life July 5 1853 — Eliza, wife of Herman Ten Eyck aged 50 years, 1 month and 4 days.

Departed this life January 2nd 1855 Catalina, daughter of the late Harmanus and Margaret Ten Eyck aged 76 years, 2 months and 21 days.

Died Herman Ten Eyck, 1861

Departed this life May 28 1865 Catharine wife of William M. Burr and daughter of the late Harmanus and Margaret Ten Eyck aged 66 years, 7 mos. and 28 days.

Departed this life April 17 1861 Herman, son of the late Harmanus & Margaret Ten Eyck.

HERMAN TEN EYCK.
(1793–1861.)

Holy Bible in English; New York, Collins & Co., 1821.

Contains the records of Herman Ten Eyck and his wife Eliza Bogert, with their descendants. It is now the property of their granddaughter, Miss Margaret Ten Eyck Pruyn, of Albany, New York.

Herman, third son of Harmanus and Margaret Ten Eyck, born October 22nd, 1793

Eliza, second daughter of Herman H. and Dolly Bogert, born Wednesday June 1st, 1803

Married, May 8th, 1821 at Geneva, by Revd. Aaron Lane, Herman Ten Eyck to Eliza, daughter of Herman H. Bogert.

Margaret, first daughter of Herman and Eliza Ten Eyck, born April 29th, 1822.

John Bogert, first son of Herman and Eliza Ten Eyck born May 3rd, 1824.

Jacob H. Second son of Herman and Eliza Ten Eyck born August 17th, 1833.

Cornelia Dorothea, second daughter of Herman and Eliza Ten Eyck, born December 11th, 1835

Cathalina, third daughter of Herman and Eliza Ten Eyck born January 24th, 1840

Cornelia Anna, fourth daughter of Herman and Eliza Ten Eyck born July 17th, 1845.

John Bogert, first son of Herman and Eliza Ten Eyck departed this life July 23rd, 1825 aged fourteen months and twenty days

Cornelia Dorothea, second daughter of Herman and Eliza Ten Eyck, departed this life, of Scarlet Fever, November 8th 1841, aged five years ten months and twenty seven days

Cornelia Anna, fourth daughter of Herman and Eliza Ten Eyck departed this life, August 15th 1845, aged twenty nine days.

Eliza Bogert, wife of Herman Ten Eyck, departed this life, July 5th 1853, aged fifty years, one month and four days.

Herman Ten Eyck departed this life May 17th, 1861, aged sixty eight years six months and twenty five days.

Margaret T. E. Robison Widow of John A. Robison departed this life March 10th 1891 at Washington, D.C. aged sixty eight years 10 mths., 10 days.

Jacob H. Ten Eyck departed this life March 24th, 1898 aged 64 yrs. 8 mths. & 7 days.

Married, May 28th, 1844 at Albany by Revd. Duncan Kennedy, John Alexander Robison of Syracuse, N.Y. to Margaret, daughter of Herman and Eliza Ten Eyck.

Herman Ten Eyck, first son of John Alexander and Margaret Robison, born December 20th, 1845

Hugh, second son of John Alexander and Margaret Robison, born December 3rd, 1847

John, third son of John Alexander and Margaret Robison, born November 3rd, 1849.

William, fourth son of John Alexander and Margaret Robison, born August 7th, 1851.

Married September 17th 1866 at Albany by Rev. Dr. R. W. Clark, Augustus Pruyn to Catalina daughter of Herman & Eliza Ten Eyck

Married April 11th, 1867 at Albany by Rev. I. Livingston Reese at St. Pauls Church Jacob H. Ten Eyck Jr. to Matilda Eliza Bleecker daughter of G. V. S. Bleecker.

GEORGE TOWNSEND, II.
(1687–1762.)

Holy Bible in English; London, Assigns of Thomas Newcomb & Henry Hills, 1712.

This is known as the "Duck Pond Bible" and was originally owned by George Townsend, II, of Oyster Bay. The entries by him are followed by those of his descendants, including some by the name of Cock. The Bible has descended directly to Mrs. W. R. Caminoni, Oyster Bay, N. Y., who is the great-great-great-great-granddaughter of the original owner.

The following entries are by the 2nd George Townsend, the owner of this (Duck Pond) Bible.

m	Memorandum that George Townsend ye Eldest
s	fon of George Townsend of Oysterbay, Deafed was
b	Borne In Oysterbay ye 18th Day of October
a	annoy Domini 1687 —
m	Memorandum that Roseannah Coles Eldest
D	Daughter of Nathaniel Coles Ju^n of Oyster bay
w	was Borne In Oysterbay ye 2th Day of October
a	Annoy Domini 1691 —
m	Memorandum that ye above Named George
T	Townsend & Roseannah Coles was Joyned
T	Togather In Holy Matrimony ye 18th Day
O	of March Annoy Domini 1710/11
Mem R	Roseannah Townsend Daughter of ye above
n	Named George & Roseannah was Borne
I	In oysterbay ye 14th day of March
A	Annoy Domini 1711/12

Mem w William Townsend fon of ye above named

g George & Roseannah Townsend

w was Borne in Oysterbay ye 13th Day of

f ffebruary annoy Domini 1715/16

g George Townsend ye Son of ye above named George &

R Roseannah Borne in Oysterbay ye 13th

D Day of November annoy Domini 1720

J John Cock the fon of Hezekiah Cock & Grandfon to y^e

a above Named George Townfend was Born In Oysterbay

M March ye 27th annoy Domini 1731

P Penn Cock fon to ye fd Hezekiah Born

I In oyster Bay ye fixth Day of May 1733

T The above Named John Cock Departed this

L Life the 31th Day of January anno: Domini 1735/6

Memorandom that Rosannah Townsend Departed this Life the 29th of June 1757 in the 66th Year of her age

Memorandom that George Townsend the son of George and Rosannah Townsend Departed this Life January ye 20th 1761 in the 42^d Year of his age

Memorandom that George Townsend departed this Life May ye 11th 1762 in in the 76th Year of his Age

Departed this Life the 5th day of may 1777 in the sixty second year of his age William Townsend Esq son of Geo. & Rofeanna Townsend

Departed this Life the 30 Nov. 1794 Elizabeth Townsend wife of William Townsend

Entries by Geo Townsend 2ᵈ

Memorandum that James Townſend the Son of William & Elizabeth Townſend was Born In Oysterbay the 26ᵗʰ Day of April 1742

Memorandum that Roseannah Townſend Daughter of yᵉ ſd William & Elizabeth Townſend was Born In Oysterbay the 4ᵗʰ Day of September 1751

Memorandum that Prior Townſend yᵉ Son of George Townſend Juⁿ & Mary Townſend was Born the 11ᵗʰ Day of December 1749

Memorandum that Hannah Townsend the Daughter of George Townsend & Mary Townsend was Born the 21ᵗʰ Day of May 1755

Be it Remembred that Daniel Cock son of James Cock and Roseannah Townsend Daughter of William and Elizabeth Townsend was Joined in Matrimony on the twentieth day of December in the Year of Our Lord Seventeen hundred and sixty Eight 1768

Be it Remembered that Elizabeth Cock Daughter of Daniel and Rosannah Cock Was Bornd December the Seventh 1769

Be it Remembered that James Cock Son of Daniel and Roſeannah Cock Was born January the 12 1772

Notice that Townſend Cock ſon of Daniel and Roſeannah Cock was born the fourth Day of December 1773.

Deborah Cock was born February the fifth Day 1776 the Daughter of Daniel and Roſeannah Cock

William Cock son of Danˡ & Roseannah Cock was Born the 22ⁿ day of August 1780

Thomas Cock son of the above was born the 12ᵗʰ day of January 1783

Phiany Cock daughter of the above was born the 23ʳ day of April 1785

The Entries on this and the 1ˢᵗ page, by William Townsend— 1st, of Duck Pond to 1776.

Memorandom that James Townsend the Son of William & Elisabeth Townsend was Born the 26ᵗʰ Day of April 1742

Memorandom that Freelove Townsend Wilmot the Daughter of Walter & Freelove Wilmot was Born ye 25th Day of February 1744

Memorandom that James Townsend & Freelove Townsend Wilmot was join'd in the Holy bands of Mattrimony the 4th Day of Febuary 1762

Memorandum that John Cock the fon of Hezekiah Cock & Roseannah Cock was Born In Oyster bay the 10th Day of November annoy Domini 1735

Violetah Cock the Daughter of ye fd. Hezekiah & Roseannah Cock was Born In Oyster bay the fifth Day of January anno Domini 1737/8

Dorothy Cock the Daughter of the faid Hezekiah & Roseannah Cock was Born In Oysterbay the 5th Day of June annoy/ Domini 1742

Sarah Cock the Daughter of ye said Hezekiah & Roseannah Cock was born in Oysterbay the 14th Day of Febuary Annoy Domini 1750

Gabriel Cock the Son ye s'd Hezekiah and Roseannah Cock was born ye 15th Day of December anno Domini 1753

Memorandom that Walter Wilmot Townsend the son of James & Freelove Townsend was Born December ye 18th 1762

Notice that John Townsend a son of the above J. T and F. T was born March the 17th 1765

Notice that Elizabeth Townsend Daughter of the above James and Freelove Townsend was born the forth of May 1767

Notice that William Townsend the son of James and Freelove Townsend was Born the twelvth day of September anno Domini 1769

Notice that Judith Townsend daughter of the above J & F. T was Born the thirteenth day of June 1772

Departed this Life on July the 5th 1774 the above mentioned Judith Townsend

Roseannah Townsend Daughter of James and Freelove Townsend was born April the first day 1775. Departed this Life May 13th 1824 aged 49 Years.

Sarah and Esther Townsend Daughters of James and Freelove Townsend was born the 12th day of March 1778

Sarah Frost, daughter of James & Freelove Townsend died March 1853.

Esther Coles, daughter of James & Freelove Townsend died April 2nd 1854

William Townsend son of James & Freelove Townsend Died August 23rd 1834

Margaret, wife of the above William Townsend, and daughter of Dr. Jas Townsend died Oct 11th 1818

Charlotte Coles Daughter of Nathl Coles & Hannah Coles was born the 19th of May, 1765.

Walter W. Townsend & Charlotte Coles was married the 19th of May 1785

Charlotte Townsend, daughter of Walter W. & Charlotte Townsend was born at Duck Pond the 31st March 1786

James Townsend, son of Walter W. & Charlotte Townsend was born at Duck Pond the 17th February 1788

John Townsend son of Walter W. & Charlotte Townsend was born at New York the 18th November 1790

Departed this Life, Walter W. Townsend, fon of James & Freelove Townsend the 7th of December 1793 in the 31st Year of his Age.

Walter W. Townsend, Son of Walter W. Townsend & Charlotte was born the 29th of January 1794. - - -

William Townsend & Margaret Townsend was married the 8th of February 1792

Esther Townsend daughter of James & Frelove Townsend was married to Thomas Coles Son of Jarvis & Abigail Coles the fourth day of February 1812

John Townsend Coles Son of Thomas & Esther Coles was born the 12th day of May 1813 Departed this Life September 27th 1815

Nathaniel Coles of Dosoris, born March 23rd 1763. Died March 10. 1824

Elisabeth Coles, wife of Nathl Died March 13, 1838.

The following Entries by Wm Townsend of Oyster Bay

Departed this Life the 12th of Decr 1798 in the Fifty seventh year of his age James Townsend Esqr Son of Willm and Elizabeth Townsend

Departed this life on the 21 of July 1809 in the 66th year of her age Freelove T Townsend relict of the late James Townsend & daughter of Walter & Freelove Wilmot

John Townsend fon of James & Freelove Townsend was Married to Phebe Townsend Daughter of Doctor James & Margaret Townsend on the 20th January 1789.

Phebe Townsend Wife of John Townsend aforesaid departed this Life 15th May 1790 aged 24 years

John Townsend was Married a fecond time to Rebecca Franklin Daughter of John & Deborah Franklin of New York the 7th January 1793

Walter W. Townsend Son of John & Rebecca Townsend was born 31st January 1794 & departed this Life 11th February following aged 11 Days.

Walter Franklin Townsend Son of John & Rebecca Townsend was born 31st May 1795.

Elizabeth Townsend Daughter of James & Freelove Townsend was Married to Nathaniel Coles Son of Nathaniel Coles & Hannah on the . . . July 17

Sarah Townsend Daughter of James & Freelove was Married to William Frost Son of Stephen & Sarah Frost on the . . . of March 1796

JAMES TOWNSEND.
(1729–1790.)

Holy Bible in English; London, Mark Baskett, 1766.

Contains the records of James Townsend and Mary Hicks, his wife, and their children; also a memorandum of the earlier Townsend ancestors. It is now the property of Mrs. W. R. Caminoni of Oyster Bay, New York, a great-great-granddaughter of the original owner.

John Townsend 1st emigrated with his two brothers, Henry and Richard, from England, Norwich County Norfolk. He died in Oyster Bay in 1668 and was buried on his place on Fort Hill. Elizabeth his wife, the date of whose death not known, was living in 1671.

John Townsend, son of John 1st moved to Jericho, his second wife, the mother of his children, was Susannah Harcourt, of Oyster Bay; the date of his death not known, but he was living in 1715 when he was not less than eighty years old. It is not known where he and his wife were buried but it is supposed at Jericho.

James, son of John 3rd married Audrey Almy, date of his marriage not known, but his oldest son was born in 1692. He died between 1729 and 1733. It is supposed he lived on the place belonging to the family of Samuel Underhill, and was buried there.

Jacob, son of James (above) was born in 1692 married Phebe Seaman, He died Dec. 30th, 1742 and was buried in the family burying ground on the place of Samuel Underhill, where his tombstone still stands; His wife died April 14, 1774 aged 75.

James, son of Jacob, see his family record on next page, commenced by him.

James Townsend was born Decemb^r 17th 1729

Mary Hicks was born July 16 - - - - - 1730

They were married ye 2nd Day of April 1757.

Their first Child Mary Townsend was born Novr 16th 1759

2nd .. Martha Townsend was born Decb^r 26 - - - 1761

3rd -- James Townsend was born Octb^r 16th 1763

4th -- Phebe Townsend was born Sep^t 26 1765

5th -- Almy Townsend was born Ap^rl 18 --- 1768

6th -- Samuel Townsend Born Mar 20th --- 1770

7th -- Margret Townsend Born Feb^ry 6th -- 1772

Benjamin Underhill, Son of Townsend & Almy Underhill, was born March ^th 18. 1789.

Mary Townsend died May 7th 1790. on friday evening.

Samuel Townsend, died May 12th 1790. on wednesday

Almy Underhill, died May 12th 1790. on wednesday evening.

Phebe Townsend, died May 14th 1790 — on friday night.

James Townsend, May 24th 1790 — on Monday morning.

Mary Townsend, wife of James Townsend, died 2nd of July 1796.

Martha Willis, wife of Edmend Willis, and daughter of James and Mary Townsend, died January 23rd 1810.

Margaret Townsend, wife of William Townsend and daughter of James & Mary Townsend, died oct 11th 1818.

Almy Townsend, died August 11th 1811.

James Townsend, son of James and Mary — died at Newark, 1831.

Tombstones.

Tombstones in the rear of Samuel Underhill's house at Jericho, copied by James C. Townsend, June 4th, 1864.

Jacob Townsend, Died Dec. 30th 1742, aged 50, Phebe Townsend, Died April 14th 1774, agd. 75 (on one stone)

James Townsend, Died at Sea Feb. 13th, 1790 agd. 39

Benj. Townsend, Died Sept. 18, 1789, agd. 66

Frost Townsend, Died July 18, 1770 agd. 21, Benj Townsend, Died June 2, 1758 agd. 2 (on one stone)

Our grand Father Dr. James Townsend and his family, who died in the great sickness in 1790 were all buried there but there are no monuments to show. J. C. T.

WILLIAM TOWNSEND.
(1769–1834.)

Holy Bible in English; New York, Hodge & Campbell, 1792.

Contains the records of William Townsend and Margaret, his wife, with some of their descendants. The Bible is known as the "Oyster Bay" Bible and is now in the possession of Miss Marguerite Valentine of Glen Cove, Long Island.

William Townsend was Born September 12th 1769

Margaret Townsend was Born February 6th 1772

William and Margaret Townsend were Married February 8th 1792

James Townsend the Son of William and Margaret Townsend was Born June the 15, 1793.

William Townsend the Second Child of William & Margaret Townsend was born October 21st 1795.

James Townsend the Oldest Son of William and Margaret Townsend Deceased October 30th 1796

Mary Townsend the third Child of Willm. & Margaret Townsend was born June 20th 1797. Died June 8. 1881

Phebe and Almy Townsend born Novr. 17. 1799 Daughters of Willm. and Margaret Townsend

Almy Townsend Daughter of Willm. & M. Townsend Deceas'd Decr. th 5. 1799.

Almy Townsend Daughter of Willm. & M. Townsend born January th. 1 1802.

James Townsend son of William and Margaret Townsend was born 15th June 1804

George W. Townsend son of William and Margaret Townsend was born 27th Sept. 1806.

Margaret E. Townsend Daughter of William and Margaret Townsend was born 21 March, 1809 (Died February 14th 1879)

Frances Townsend Daughter of William and Margaret Townsend was born 7th May 1811.

Samuel H. Townsend Son of William and Margaret Townsend was born 22d. July 1814.

Gertrude Townsend Daughter of William and Margaret Townsend, was born 21st January 1818.

Gertrude Townsend Daughter of William and Margaret Townsend died 5th October 1818

Margaret Townsend, Wife of William Townsend died 11th October 1818

Wm. W. Townsend, Son of Wm. & Margaret Townsend, Died 10th September 1828. William Townsend husband of Margaret Townsend died August 23d. 1834.

Wm. Winder Polk, of, William, was born in Somerset County in the state of Maryland on the 9th day of august, 1787

Almy U. Townsend was born 1st january 1802

William and Almy were married on the 29th Novr. 1817

Wm. Winder Polk, son of Wm. & Almy was born February 5th 1819

Mary Townsend Polk daughter of Wm. Winder and Almy U. Polk was born Septm. 8th 1822.

Margaret Townsend Polk, Daughter of William & Almy U. Polk was born March 12th 1825.

Gertrude Polk Daughter of Wm. Winder & Almy Polk was born 14th March 1827   Deceased th August 1828

Francis James Polk Son of William & Almy U. Polk was born 5th october 1829   Deceased 10th october 1831

James Black Polk Son of Wm. and Almy Polk was born Sept. 3d 1832

Jacob F. Covert, and Frances Townsend, were married 10th January 1832   Jacob F. Covert was born 13th September, 1807.

George Townsend and Elizabeth Covert were married 10th January 1832.

Mary Townsend Daughter of George and Elizabeth Townsend was born 5th December 1832.

William W. Townsend married Fanny Seaman, Feb. 12th, 1817. He died Sept. 10th, 1828, She May 27th, 1854. Issue, Billopp, Margaret, William, Matilda, Henry. Wm. died in California.

Almy U. Townsend and Wm. W. Polk, see entry in preceding page. He died in the morning; she in the evening of Feb. 13, 1856 in Frederick City, Md. and were buried there. Issue, Winder, Mary, Margaret, Frank, Gertrude, James, and Louisa. Frank & Gertrude died in infancy.

Phebe W. Townsend md. Beekman V. Hoffman, U.S.N. Nov. 29, 1817. He died Dec. 10, 1834. Issue, Margaret, Gertrude, Mary. The last died in infancy.

George W. Townsend md. Elizabeth C. Covert Jan. 10, 1832. She died Sept. 28, 1846. He Sep. 5, 1880. Issue, Mary E, George C, Beekman H. George C died Oct. 10, 1863.

Margaret E. md. Dr. James C. Townsend, Decemr. 5th 1838. She died Feb. 14 1879. Issue, Julia M, James H.

Mary H. Townsend, Died June 8th, 1881

George W. Townsend, Died Sept. 5, 1880

Frances M. Townsend md. Jacob F. Covert Jan. 10. 1832. He died Feb. 27, 1861. Issue Francis, William, Margaret, James, Aurelia. Frances and James died in infancy. William died April 29, 1853.

Samuel H. Townsend md. Louisa Parish. Issue, Fanny, Wm., Anna, Henrietta, Louisa, Samuel, Charlotte, Mabel. Charlotte died in infancy

James C. Townsend married Aurelia C. Winder Nov. 14, 1846.

Mary E. Townsend married Butler Coles. issue, Lizzy, Butler, George, T, Loretta C, Nathaniel, the two first and last died in infancy.

Beekman H. Townsend married Adele Seaman. Issue, Ada, Elizabeth,

Aurelia W. Townsend was born May 14th 1820, died April 16th, 1885

Samuel H. Townsend Died Oct. 13, 1886.

DANIEL TOWNSEND.
(1798–1860.)

Holy Bible in English; London, Samuel Bagster, 1841.

Contains the records of Daniel Y. Townsend and Sarah Titus, his wife, with their descendants to the present day. It is now the property of Edward M. Townsend, Jr., of Oyster Bay, New York, a grandson of the original owner.

MARRIAGES.

Daniel Youngs Townsend, Sarah Titus, Married in New York by the Revd. Edward Mitchell, November 29, 1820.

Edward Mitchell Townsend, Belinda Rockwell, Married in New York by the Rev. Dr. Anthon May 31st. 1853

August Phillipe Montant, Hannah Maria Townsend, Married in New York at 19 East 22nd Street by the Rev. Ducey, November 5th 1883.

Frederick John Kingsbury Jr., Adèle Townsend, Married in Trinity Church New York, Nov. 11th 1886 by the Revs. Mess. Geer & C. B. Smith.

Edward M. Townsend, Sarah Day Johnson, Married at Trinity Church Dec. 4th 1886, by Rev. Dr. Dix.

Edward M. Townsend Jr., Alice Greenough, Married at Grace Church April 20th, 1892, by the Rev. W. R. Huntington & Rev. Dr. Van de Water.

Robert Cooper Townsend, Louisa Anna Johnson, Married at St. Bartholomew's Church May 22nd, 1894, by the Revs. David H. Greer and William M. Geer

Howard Rockwell Townsend, Therese Firth, at South Orange, N.J. January 28, 1905.

Louis Townsend Montant married Alice Anderton, Cedarhurst Sept. 16, 1911

Marie Adèle Montant and Huntington Norton, Oyster Bay, June 16 1906.

BIRTHS.

Daniel Youngs Townsend born at Oyster Bay, L. I. June 29, 1798

Sarah Titus born in Ridgefield Conn. January 12th 1791

Hannah Maria Townsend, born at North Salem, September 6th 1821

John Titus Townsend, born in New York, June 9, 1823.

John Joseph Townsend, born in New York, May 8, 1825

Edward Mitchell Townsend born in New York October 7, 1829.

Children of Belinda & Edwd. M. Townsend.

Sanford Coley Townsend born in New York Jany. 27, 1855.

Hannah Maria Townsend, Born in New York Dec. 19, 1856

Edward Townsend Jr. Born in New York Sept. 29, 1861.

Adèle Townsend, Born in New York, Aug. 23, 1863.

Walter Townsend Born at Scarborough on Hudson, July 14, 1865

Robert Cooper Townsend, Born in New York April 9, 1869.

Howard Rockwell Townsend, Born at Oyster Bay, Aug. 10, 1871.

Ruth Kingsbnry, b. Waterbury Ct. Aug. 29, 1887.

Marie Adèle Montant Sept. 9: 1884 N.Y.

Louis Townsend Montant, Dec. 27. 1885 N.Y.

Edward Mitchell Townsend 3rd. Feby. 13, 1893 N.Y.

Greenough Townsend, March 4th, 1895 N.Y.

Ingersoll Day Townsend May 28, 1895 N.Y.

Frederick John Kingsbury 3d. Sept. 10, 1895, Fairfield Conn.

Howard Rockwell Townsend Jr. March 23, 1907, Boston,

Thérèse

DEATHS.

John Titus Townsend died June 19, 1824, aged 1 year & 10 days. interred at Oyster Bay, L.I.

Hannah Maria Townsend, died December 12. 1853, aged 32 years 3 mo. 6 ds. interred at Oyster Bay, Long Island.

Daniel Youngs Townsend died December 15 1860 aged 62 years, 5 mo. & 17 days. interred at Oyster Bay, L.I.

Sarah Titus Townsend died Feby. 24th 1867, aged 76 years 1 mo. & 12 days interred at Oyster Bay, L.I.

Sanford Coley Townsend, died Sept. 7, 1867, aged 12 years 7 mo. & 11 days. Interred at Oyster Bay, L.I.

Walter Townsend died Dec. 24, 1869, aged 4 years 5 mo. & 10 days. interred at Oyster Bay, L.I.

Belinda Rockwell Townsend, wife of Edw. M. Townsend, died in New York April 13 1882. aged 50 years 1 mo. & 18 days interred at Oyster Bay, L.I.

Robert Cooper Townsend, died in New York April 1st, 1897 in the 28 year of his age. Interred at Oyster Bay, L.I.

Edward Mitchell Townsend, died in New York, Feby 2nd, 1904, in the 75th year of his age. Interred at Oyster Bay.

Sarah Eliza Day (widow of William Johnson) widow of Edward M. Townsend died at Pittsfield, Mass. Feby. 28th, 1916, aged 73 years. Interred in Johnson vault, Greenwood cemetery.

Remarks.

Belinda Rockwell, wife of Edwd. M. Townsend was born at Ridgefield Conn Feby. 26, 1832. died in New York April 13, 1882 in the 51st year of her age.

Sarah Day Johnson wife of Edward M. Townsend was born in New Orleans July 18, 1843 Louisiana.

F. J. Kingsbury Jr. b. Waterbury Conn. July 7, 1863 Son of F. J. & A. R. Kingsbury of the same place.

Auguste P. Montant born in Paris, France, April 4, 1856.

Alice Greenough wife of Edward M. Townsend Jr. was born in Quincy Mass. March 24, 1872, daughter of Wm. & A. M. Greenough.

Louisa Anna Johnson wife of Robert Cooper Townsend was born in New York June 3rd, 1870, daughter of Sarah E. Day and William Martin Johnson

Therese wife of Howard R. Townsend daughter of Emilie Lesher and John Firth.

Louis Townsend Montant married Alice Anderton daughter of William B. Anderton and Elizabeth Palmer his wife September 16, 1911 Cedarhurst Long Island

Alice Anderton born 26 December 1887.

Louis Townsend Montant 2nd, born July 19 1912.

MARY TOWNSEND.
(Died, 1807.)

Holy Bible in English; Edinburgh, Alexander Kincaid, 1769.

Inside front cover is the statement: "Mary Townsend's Bible price 20 / Bought of Hugh Gaine @ New York, 1st August, Anno Domini 1775. Mary Townsend, Deceased February 7th, 1807." The book contains other records of the Townsend family and their slaves and is now the property of Miss Marguerite Valentine of Glen Cove, Long Island.

"Deborah Townsend's Book, presented her by her Aunt Hannah Valentine February 1807".

Deborah Townsend was Born October 17th, 1776.

Hannah Townsend was Born October 18th, 1783. Hannah Townsend Deceased February 6th, 1808 aged 24 years 3 months 13 days.

Elizabeth Townsend, Wife of Jacob Townsend, Died June 23d. 1811, aged thirty four years, five months and eleven days.

Jacob Townsend, Died January thirteenth, 1841, aged 69 years, 10 months and 8 days.

An acct. of the Birth of Prior and Sarah Townsend and their children.

Prior Townsend was Born December 21st 1749

Sarah Townsend was Born August 27th 1750

George Townsend their first son was Born December 21, 1768

Jacob Townsend their second son was Born March 5th, 1771

Hannah Townsend third child was Born September 7th, 1774.

Deborah Townsend, fourth child was Born October 17th day 1776

Hannah Townsend their fifth child was Born October 18th, 1783.

Prior Townsend Deceased December 8th 1803

Sarah Townsend Deceased September 11th 1833 aged 83 years

Black Boy Crodus was Born February 8th the eighth in the year 1767

Jerod Crodus Son was Born Novembr. 3d. 1807.

ADAM TREADWELL.
(1772–1852.)

Holy Bible in English; Philadelphia, John Thompson & Abraham Small, 1798.

> Contains the records of Adam Treadwell and Jane Moore, his wife, with their descendants, including the Sackett family. It is now the property of their great-grandson, Mr. Clarence Sackett, of Rye, New York.

Jane Treadwell, presented by her brother, John H. Moore.

Adam Tredwell was born the Twelfth Day of November One Thousand Seven Hundred and Seventy-two. 1772

Jane Moore was born the Twenty-fifth Day of May One Thousand Seven Hundred and Seventy-eight. 1778, and were married the Ninth Day of April One Thousand Eight Hundred and One. 1801.

Their Children.

Gertrude Tredwell born 22nd April 1802.

Elizabeth Kissam Tredwell born 5th May, 1803.

Benjamin Moore Tredwell born 9th October, 1804.

Lambert Holland Tredwell born 27th January, 1808.

Their Grand Children.

Adam Tredwell Sackett born 13th January 1828.

Gertrude Elizabeth Titus born 6th March 1831.

Their Great Grand Children.

Clarence Ostrander Sackett born 4th August 1856.

Gertrude Tredwell Sackett born 8th October 1858.

George Edward Sackett born 9th December 1861.

Mary Moore Sackett born 15th August 1863.

Helen Louise Sackett born 9th November 1865.

Ferdinand William Sackett born 16th August 1867.

Benjamin Lambert Sackett born 20th January 1869.

Grenville Alfred Sackett born 17th November 1873.

MARRIAGES.

Gertrude O. Tredwell was married to Clarence D. Sackett 19th December 1826.

Elizabeth K. Tredwell was married to James H. Titus 9th February 1830.

Adam Tredwell Sackett was married to Sarah Elizabeth Ostrander 18th May 1854.

DEATHS.

Gertrude O. Sackett died 14th January 1828 and was buried in the old Episcopal burying ground Brooklyn, L. I.

Gertrude E. Titus died 28th January 1832 and was buried in the old Episcopal burying ground Brooklyn, L. I.

Jane Tredwell died 23rd October 1837 and was buried in the old Episcopal burying ground Brooklyn, L. I.

The remains of the above were removed to the burying ground of Christ Church Manhasset, Queens Co., L. I. 9th June, 1852.

Adam Tredwell died 3rd June 1852   Buried at Christ Church, Manhasset, L. I. 7th June, 1852.

Lambert H. Tredwell died 13th March, 1859   Buried at Christ Church, Manhasset, L. I. 16th March, 1859.

Benjamin M. Tredwell died 23rd April, 1859.   Buried at Christ Church Manhasset, L. I. 28th April, 1859

Elizabeth K. Titus died 20th January, 1869.   Buried at Christ Church, Manhasset, January 23rd, 1869.

Clarence D. Sackett died 8th March, 1858. Buried at Greenwood Cemetery 11th March 1858.

Grenville Alfred Sackett died 2nd March, 1874. Buried at Woodlawn Cemetery March 5th, 1874.

Adam Tredwell Sackett Died December 9th, 1878. Buried at Woodlawn Cemetery December 12th, 1878.

James H. Titus died April 23, 1882. Buried at Manhasset, April 26 1882.

Mary Moore Sackett died January 11, 1886. Buried at Woodlawn Cemetery January 14 1886.

George Edward Sackett died 22 November 1893. Buried at Woodlawn Cemetery November 25 1893.

Ferdinand William Sackett died November 26 1893 Buried at Woodlawn Cemetery November 29, 1893.

Sarah Elizabeth Sackett died April 2 1909. Buried at Woodlawn Cemetery April 5, 1909.

Benjamin Lambert Sackett Died July 3 1912 Buried at Woodlawn Cemetery July 6 1912

DANIEL UNDERHILL.
(1798–1886.)

Holy Bible in English; Oxford, T. Wright & W. Gill, 1770.

Contains the records of Daniel Underhill and Mary Ann, his wife, with their descendants and collateral lines to the present day. It belonged to the late Miss Judith Underhill and the record was furnished by Mrs. Edward M. Townsend, Jr., of Oyster Bay, New York.

Presented to the children of Joseph & Hannah Townsend by Susannah Cock their Aunt.

Daniel Underhill was born March 4th 1798.

Daniel and Mary Ann Underhill were married June 19th 1821

Susanna T. Underhill was born March 22d 1822.

Samuel Edward Underhill was born June 22d, 1824.

James T. Underhill was born in the city of New York June 2d, 1826.

Judith Townsend Underhill was born October 17, 1828.

Joseph William Underhill was born February 5. 1831.

Daniel Isaac Underhill was born February 8 1833.

Mary Amelia Underhill was born May 19th 1835

John Fleet Underhill was born June 1st 1837.

Margery Phelps — Died Nov. 16th 1884.

Samuel Townsend, Died Feb. 28th 1747 In the 56th year of his age.

Sarah Townsend his wife (Daughter of Robert Cooper) died March 3rd 1751 age 53.

Joseph Townsend their son was born Feb. 17th 1728 Died 1812. He married Hannah Youngs who died in 1761.

Susannah Cock, donor of this book was the sister of the above Hannah Townsend. She was born Sept. 28th, 1722 — Died Feb. 3d 1804.

Joseph Townsend son of the above Joseph was born March 16th 1761. Died August 19th 1843. Hannah Youngs born May 24th 1770 Died November 25th 1859.

Joseph Townsend and Hannah Youngs were married Feb. 26th 1786.

Judith Townsend born Sept. 22nd 1787. Died July 23d 1872.

James Townsend born Sept. 10th 1790. Died July 3. 1861

Susan Townsend born Oct. 15. 1795, Died June 26th 1839.

Daniel Y Townsend born June 29th 1798. Died Dec. 16th 1860.

Mary Ann Townsend born Feb. 18th 1803. Died Nov. 24th 1883

James Fleet born Nov. 9th 1784. Died Aug. 12th 1852

James Fleet and Judith Townsend were married May 17th 1815.

John J. Fleet was born Sept. 15th 1816. Died Nov. 22d 1880.

Joseph F. Fleet, born Nov. 26th 1818. Died Jan. 18th 1861.

Arnold Fleet born Dec. 11th, 1823

John J. Fleet & Mary E. Bates were married

Mary E. Bates was born 1865. Died Dec. 5th 1888.

Susan F. Fleet born Dec. 23d 1838

Mary W. Fleet born March 27th, 1841.

James Fleet, born Aug.   1843. Died

George B. Fleet born April

Roswell C. Fleet born Sept. 13th 1848. Died Aug. 9th 1878.

Roswell C. Fleet and Clara A. Street were married Feb. 21st 1871

Clara A. Street was born Jan. 22nd 1848.

Mellicent Townsend Fleet Born June 10th 1872.

Ernest Crosby Fleet, Born Mar. 15th 1875.

Joseph F. Fleet and Susannah T. Underhill were married Oct. 25th 1849.

Susannah T. Underhill was born March 22nd 1822 and died March 4th 1866.

Samuel U. Fleet born Feb. 12' 1851.

Elizabeth E. Fleet born Oct. 18th 1854.

Elizabeth E. Fleet was married to Joshua Cocks Oct. 5th 1881.

Arnold Fleet and Maria P. Seaman were married June 8th 1848.

Maria P. Seaman born Dec. 13th 1822 died Mar. 5th 1886.

Mary A. Seaman adopted daughter of Arnold and Maria Fleet born

Mary A. Seaman was married to William C. Townsend Oct. 24th 1879.

James Townsend and Margaret Underhill were married Feb. 24th 1841.

Margaret Underhill was born Nov. 25th 1821 and died July 4th 1856.

James E. Townsend born Jan. 2nd 1842.

Joseph Townsend born June 30th 1844

Daniel Townsend born Sept. 23d 1846 died April 12. 1877.

Mary A. Townsend born June 1st 1849.

Susan R. Townsend born Nov. 30th 1852.

Margaret Townsend born June 9th 1856. Died Aug. 20th 1856.

Susan R. Townsend was adopted by Joseph and Mary A. Ireland of Bridgeport Conn.

Mary A. Townsend was married to Sidney McCoun May 29. 1873.

Rebecca Y. McCoun born May 31. 1874.

James T. McCoun born Jan. 5. 1877

Sidney born   1888.

Susan Townsend Ireland Married Wm. W. Starr. Oct. 1. 1874.

William Wright Starr was born Jan. 12 – 1848.

Margaret Townsend Starr born Nov. 25. 1875.

William Ireland Starr born May 26. 1877.

Mary Amelia Avery Starr born Aug. 10. 1880.

Susan Hotchkiss Starr born Aug. 23. 1882.

Daniel Y. Townsend and Sarah Titus were married Nov. 29th 1820

Sarah Titus was born Jan. 12th 1791. Died

Hannah M. Townsend born Sept. 6th 1821 and died December 12th 1853.

John T. Townsend born June 9th 1823 and died June 19th 1824.

John J. Townsend born May 8th 1825 Died Dec. 5 1889.

Edward M. Townsend born Oct. 7th 1829 died Feb. 2. 1904.

John J. Townsend and Catherine R. Bronson were married Dec. 21st 1854

Ann Eliza Townsend born Sept. 28th 1855

John J. Townsend born June 19th 1858

Charlotte B. Townsend born June 21st 1861. Died Feb. 25th 1863.

Arthur B. Townsend born July 8th 1864

Catherine B. Townsend born March 24th 1866.

Edward M. Townsend and Belinda Rockwell were married May 31st 1853.

Belinda Rockwell born Feb. 26th 1832 Died Ap. 13. 1882.

Sanford C. Townsend born Jan. 27th 1855. died Sept. 7th 1867

Hannah M. Townsend born Dec. 19th 1856.

Edward M. Townsend Sepr. 29th 1861

Adèle Townsend born Aug. 23d 1863.

Walter Townsend born July 14th 1865. Died Dec. 23d 1869

Robert C. Townsend born April 9th 1869.

Howard Townsend born 10 August 1871

Hannah Maria Townsend was married to Auguste Phillippe Montaunt Nov. 5th 1883.

Adèlle Townsend was married to John Frederick Kingsbury Nov. 11th 1886

Edward M. Townsend was married to Sallie Day Johnson Dec. 1886.

Daniel Underhill born March 4th 1798, died Dec. 20th 1886

Daniel Underhill and Mary A. Townsend were married June 19th 1821. Mary A. died Nov. 24th 1883.

Susannah F. Underhill born March 22nd 1822. and died March 4th 1866.

Samuel E. Underhill born June 22nd 1824 died June 23d 1895.

James T. Underhill born June 2nd 1826 died Aug. 26. 1885.

Judith T. Underhill born Oct. 17th 1828

Joseph W. Underhill born Feb. 5th 1831.

Daniel I. Underhill born Feb. 8th 1833. Died Sept. 2nd 1868

Mary A. Underhill born May 19th 1835 Died Feb. 24. 1903.

John F. Underhill 1st born June 1st 1837. Died Aug. 28th 1838

John F. Underhill 2nd born June 22nd 1839.

Albert H. Underhill born July 11th 1841.

Hannah Y. Underhill born June 11th 1843, died May 11th 1906.

Francis K. Underhill born April 6th 1845.

Abigail K. Underhill born Sept. 30th 1847.

Samuel E. Underhill and Elizabeth Bayles were married Sept. 3d 1850.

Elizabeth Bayles, born   Died March 20th 18

Samuel E. Underhill and Mary J. Seaman were married July 18th 1855.

Mary J. Seaman was born March 29th 1829. Died Dec. 1st 1858.

Clarence E. Underhill born May 6th 1856.

Arthur Underhill born Nov. 29th 1858. Died Dec. 11th 1858

Samuel E. Underhill and Almira E. Craft were married Jan. 1st 1863.

Almira E. Craft was born Dec. 10 1827. Died Oct. 20th 1883.

Eleanor A. Underhill born May 27th 1867.

Marian Underhill born Dec. 12th 1869, died Feb. 3. 1888.

Clarence E. Underhill and Fanny H. Muddell were married Dec. 3d 1884. Fanny H. Muddell was born March 8. 1866.

Maude F. Underhill — Born Aug. 20. 1885.

Arthur Underhill Born May 9. 1887. Died Aug. 31. 1887.

Clare Underhill.

James T. Underhill and Esther Seaman were married May 13th 1851. Esther Seaman born   Died Aug. 4th 1852.

James T. Underhill and Luisa Matilda Trutie were married April 3d 1858. Luisa Matilda Trutie born March 23rd 1843 died Oct. 19th 1880.

Luisa Emilia Underhill born Jan. 1st 1859

Marianna Natalia Underhill born Dec. 1st 1860

Antonio Ricardo Underhill born March 29th 1862

Atala Arcadia Underhill born Jan. 12th 1867 died March 23. 1884.

James T. Underhill died at sea. Aug. 26th 1885.

Luisa E. Underhill was married to Dr. James A. Hathaway Jan. 26th 1881. Dr. James A. Hathaway died Mar.   1892.

James Henry Son of James A. & Luisa E. Hathaway was born Oct. 19. 1881. died Feb. 18. 1882.

Harold B. Hathaway born Aug. 24, 1883.

Joseph W. Underhill and Sarah B. Mount were married Feb. 19th 1856. Sarah B. Mount was born Sept. 15th 1834.

Mary A. Underhill born Dec. 13th 1856.

Shepard B. Underhill born June 11th 1858 lost at sea 1884.

William H. Underhill born Sept. 22nd 1863 died   1891.

Margaret T. Underhill, born Jan. 22. 1865.

Albert Underhill born July 7th 1869.

Margaret T. Married Joseph W. Elberson, 1889

Marian Underhill daughter of Joseph and Margaret T. Elberson born 1890.

John F. Underhill and Delia Seaman were married Oct. 29th 1867. Delia Seaman was born August 12th 1836.

William A. Hall born Aug. 11th 1843. William A. Hall and Abigail K. Underhill were married Oct. 3rd 1866.

Isaac F. Hall born July 13th 1867. Died Aug. 8th 1867.

Edward A. Hall born Aug. 1st 1868.

Ida Louise Hall born June 4. 1871. Died April 20 1872.

Arthur William Hall born January 16. 1873, Died July 17th 1878.

Agnes Louise Hall born July 31. 1875. Died Sep. 8th 1875.

Florence Underhill Hall born April 4th 1880.

Gilbert Phelps Hall born Oct. 15th 1884.

Edward A. Hall married Norma Ammack June 6. 1894. Norma D. Anmack born May 3rd 1870.

Theodore Edward Hall born April 23rd 1898.

Francis K. Underhill and Mary Elizabeth Whitson were married Oct. 27th 1875. Mary Elizabeth Whitson was born Feb. 13. 1848.

Herbert Whitson Underhill born Sept. 18. 1876.

Wilbur Townsend Underhill born Mar. 27th 1880 died Sept. 4. 1881.

Joseph Townsend was born March 16th AD. 1761.

Hannah Townsend was born May 24th AD. 1770

Joseph and Hannah Townsend were married February 26th 1786

Judith Townsend was born September 22nd AD 1789

James Townsend was born September 10th AD 1790

Susan Townsend was born October 15th AD 1795

Daniel Y. Townsend was born June 29th AD 1798

Mary Ann Townsend was born February 18th AD 1803

James Fleet was born November 9th 1784

James and Judith Fleet were Married May 17th 1815.

John James Fleet was born September 15th 1816

Joseph T. Fleet was born November 26th 1818

Arnold Fleet was born December 11th, 1823

Susan Townsend daughter of Joseph and Hannah Townsend died, January 26th, 1839, aged 43 years, 2 months, 11 days.

Joseph Townsend husband of Hannah Townsend died August 19" 1843 aged 82 years, 5 months 3 days.

Hannah Townsend wife of Joseph Townsend died Nov. 25th, 1859 in the 89th year of her age.

Daniel Y. Townsend died Dec. 16th 1860

James Townsend died July 3rd 1861.

MARIA VAN BEVERHOUDT.
(1752–1791.)

New Testament and Psalms in Dutch; Amsterdam, A. Hasebroek, I. van der Putte, I. van Heekeren, 1723.

Contains part of the records of the children of Maria Van Beverhoudt and her husband, James Barclay; the existing record begins in the middle of the notice of their first son and it is probable that there was an earlier leaf of records which is now lost. The Testament passed to Mrs. Maria Van B. Barclay's nephew, Andrew Barclay Bache, and it has descended directly from him to his great-granddaughter, Miss Charlotte Elizabeth Dudley, of Brooklyn, N. Y., who is the present owner.

... Church the Sponsors were my Father Andrew Barclay Susanah Marshal of New York Gaut. Sp' De Wint and his wife Elizabeth De Wint of the Island St. Thomas.

On Friday Morning One O Clock 24 Sep 1774 was born my first Daughter Margaretta and Baptized in Trinity Church by the Rev Charles Inglis the Sponsors my Brother Thomas Barclay Ann Dorothy Bache and Margaretta Duncan.

On Tuesday ¼ before 7 o Clock the 19 March 1776 at New Barbadoes Neck, N. Jersey was born my second Daughter Maria and Christened in Mynanunck Church by the Rev. Mr. Schoonmak(er) the Sponsors were Thos. Duncan Catherine Van Cortlandt and Elizabeth Bayard.

On Sunday Morning 1 O'clock 26 Oct. 1777 at New York was born my third Daughter named Helena and Baptized in St. paul's Church by the Rev. Benjamin Moore the Sponsors were my Brother Andrew D. Barclay Sarah Lispenard and Mary Burke.

On 7 April 1779 at New York was born my Second Son named James and Baptized in St. paul's Church the Sponsors A. Lispenard, John Hill, Chas. Bailey and on the 10' July it pleased the Lord to take him aged 3 months and 3 Days.

On Sunday the 5 Nov. 1780 was born my fourth Daughter Ann Dorothy and Baptized in St. paul's Church the Sponsors were

Doctor Richard Bailey Stephen N. Bayard and Charlotte Amelia Bailey.

On the 9th Day of Decem. 1781 was born my third Son named James and baptized in St. paul's Church the Sponsors were John Ritson, John Barclay and Elizabeth Ritson and the 12th of Feb. 1782 it pleased the Lord to take him to himself aged 2 months 3 Days.

On the 3 Day of Decem 1782 was born my Fourth Son named Fred^k Jay and Baptized in St. pauls Church by the Rev. Doctor English the Sponsors Fred. Jay John Ritson and Ann Maginetes Jay.

On 22 April 1784 was born my twin Daughters Charlinne Elizabeth and Sarah Amelia and baptized in St. paul's Church by the Rev. Mr. Marshal of Connecticut the Sponsor to Elizabeth John De Wint, Mrs. Henry White and Mrs. Bleecker. to Emilia Leonard Lispenard, Mrs. Mc Evers & Helena Cortlandt and on the 20 of Sept 1786, 9 O'Clock in the Evening it pleased the Lord to take to himself my Daughter Amelia aged 2 years — Months and 6 Days.

On the Fifth May 1785 was born my Fifth Son named Johannes Van Beverhoudt and Baptized in St. pauls Church by the Rev. Benj. Moore the Sponsors were Helena Lispenard, Mrs. De Wint the Rev. John Marshal Peter Hall and John Barclay.

On the 6th May 1786 was born my Seventh Daughter named Juliana Susanah and baptized in St. pauls Church by the Rev. Benj. Moore the Sponsors were Mr - - - Bullon of Amsterdam, Miss Mary Hill and Helena Roosevelt.

On the 6" Day of Jan'y 1788 was born my Eight Daughter named Sarah Amelia and baptized in St. paul's Church the Sponsors were Henry White, Mrs Mc Evers & Helena Cortlandt and on 22' Aug. it pleased the Lord to take her to himself aged 7 months 15 Days.

On the 12' of April 1788 was born my 9th Daughter named Charlotte Matilda and Christened in St. pauls Church by the Rev. Mr. Moore the Sponsors were James Bleecker, J. C. Mc Evers and Ann D. Bache.

JANE BEEKMAN VAN CORTLANDT.
(Married, 1801; died, 1841.)

Holy Bible in English; Brattleborough, John Holbrook, 1816.

Contains scattering notices of the Beekman, Van Cortlandt and other families. It descended collaterally to the late William Bedlow Beekman, Esq., and is now the property of Mrs. Beekman, New York.

April 6th 1807 Departed this life father James Beekman aged 75 yrs 6 days.

August 15th 1808 Departed this life brother William Beekman aged 54 yrs.

Feb'y 7, 1817 Departed this life mother Jane Beekman ages 83 yrs.

September 30th 1839 Departed this life Stephen Van Cortlandt aged 89 yrs 1 month and 6 days.

July 20th 1841 Departed this life Jane Van Cortlandt aged 81 yrs 3 mos & 15 days.

Died April 21st 1854 Wm de Peyster aged 66 years

MARRIED.

On the 21st of May 1801 by the Reverend John Abeel Stephen Van Cortlandt of Belleville New Jersey to Jane Beekman daughter of James Beekman Esq of New York.

On Friday, Nov. 26th 1858 by the Rev. D. D. Morgan John Neilson to Catherine Foulke Daughter of Joseph Foulke & Lydia Beekman.

KILIAEN VAN RENSSELAER.[1]
(Born 1663.)

Holy Bible in Dutch; Dordrecht, Hendrick, Jacob en Pieter Keur, 1702.

Contains the records of Kiliaen Van Rensselaer and Maria Van Cortlandt, his wife, with their children; also some earlier entries have been written in. It has descended to the present owner, Eugene Van Rensselaer, Esq., of Washington, D. C., who is the great-great-great-grandson of the original owner. The records are in Dutch and have been translated by Dr. L. Bendikson.

1645: 20 julij Donderdagh quartier voor eene is gebooren onse Dochter *) Maria van Cortlandt N. S.

1674: 12 oct^r: op sondagh is mijn vader jeremias van Rensselaer in Den Heer ontslaepen en op Den 15 dito begraven N. S.

1688/9: 24 janua is mijn Moeder Maria van Rensselaer in den Heer ontslaepen. O. S.

1663: 24 Augu op frijdagh en ochgent te achten is gebooren Kiliaen van Rensselaer en op sondagh daer aen gedoept N. S.

1665: 1 augu is gebooren Anna van Rensselaer. Oude stijll.

1667: 23 octo: is geboren Hendr: van Rensselaer oude stijll.

1672: 25 Octo: is Maria van Rensselaer gebooren

1701: 15 octo. ben ick Kiliaen van Rensselaer getrout outt 38 jaer Met Maria van Cortlandt outt 21 en ½ jaer. Godt will ons sijne seegen verleene en geeue ons een saligh ijnde.

1702: 21 julij op frijdach en ochgent tusschen 4 a 5 ure is gebooren mij Dochter Maria van Rensselaer Door D°: Lidius gedoopt en tot Compeer C: pieter Schuijlder & Miladie Correnberrie tot peett

1703: 4 octo. op Maendach en ochgent tusschen 4 a 5 ure is onsse tweede Dochter geertruij van Rensselaer gebooren tot getuijgen

[1 The Dutch character ij is not cut for fonts of English type. Therefore the letter y has been used in the Dutch records where ij is meant.]

Hendr: van Rensselaer en olif van Cortlandt tot peet Catrina van Rensselaer: Den 9 Mij Daeraen is onse Dochter geertruij in de Heer ontsla[pe]

1704/5 10 Maert is onse outste soon gebooren op sondagh in de achter mijddagh tuschen 4 a 5 ure: en de sondagh daer aen gedoopt den 25 ditto Door Do. Lidius gedoopt tot Compeer Hendr: van Rensselaer & Maria Schuijlder tot peett genaemt jeremias De Heer will hem seegenen en in Deuchde laeten opwasschen tot freuchde van sijn familie

1706/7: 17 Maert op Maendach en ochgent breeke Dach is myn tweede soon gebooren en den 23 dito Sondagh daer aen gedoopt door Do. Lidius & genaemt steefen tot Compeer philip Schuijlder tot peeten Moeder Cortlandt & Elizabett Johanne Schuijlder die hem droech

1708: 10 Desem op vrijdach en nacht een ur is Mijn derde soon gebooren tot peett suster Nickels en Nicht Maria van Rensselaer hem gedrage tot Comper jan Coll[ens] gedoep Door D°: Lidius & genaemt johannis 30 Ditto is hey in den heer ontslaeppen en 2 jan begrae[ven]

1710: 28 August op Mandagh Met breeke Dagh is mijn derde docht[er] geboore ♯ en den 2 september op saeterdach in den heere ontslaepen.

1711: 15 Nouem op donderdagh tusschen 11 en 12 ure in de Nacht is onse fierde soon gebooren in Albanie en gedoopt Door D° Baerlie tot Compeer jan Schuijlder en jan Collens en tot peet Margrite Collens genaemt johannis 9 Desem op Sondagh in den heere ontslaepen.

1713: 29 Maert op sondagh half achten in de avont is mijn 5 soon gebooren en op vrijdagh voor paeschen gedoep Door D°: Van Driessen en genaemt jacobis tot Compeer jacobis van Cortlandt & philip Cortlandt broed: Rensselaer voor haer gestaen en tot peet Margrita Beyert en Margrita Liffeston die hem droegh De Heere will hem in Wisheyt laete op wasschen tot sijner sile saligheyt

1714: 1 octo is gebooren onse vierde Dochter op Vrijdagh te achten in de avont en gedoep de sondagh daer aen Door d° van

Driessen en ten doop gehoude Door suster geertruij van Cortlandt en tot Compeers stefanis van Cortlant en Robbert Leffeston junr en genaemt Geertruij Die heere will haer in Duchde laete opwassen tot tot frucht van haer familie en haere siele salygheijt

1716/7: 29 Jannuarij op Dijnsdagh en morgen tussen een en twee uren is gebooren onse sesde soon genaemt Jan batis nae mijn faeders broeder ten dooep gehoude door juffr. Collens voor juffr. Liffeston haer suster tot Compeer jan Collens en door D⁰ van Driessen gedoept De heere wilhem in de freese Godts laeten op wassen tot sijne Eere

1718/9 Den 1 Jannua is gebooren onse fijfde Dochter Anna× ×een quartier nae neegen in de morgen en ten Doop gehoude Door j.... Rensselaer voor haer en suster Delansie en tot Compeer Broeder Beyert waer filip Schuijlder voor stont en Door D⁰ van Driessen gedoept Die heere will haer in Deuchde laeten op wassen tot harer siele saligheijt

[TRANSLATION

[1645: July 20th, Thursday, born at a quarter to one our daughter Maria van Cortlandt. (New Style).

[1674: Oct. 12th, Sunday, died in the Lord, my father Jeremias van Rensselaer, and he is interred on the 15th of the same month (New Style).

[1688/9: Jan. 24th, died in the Lord, my mother Maria van Rensselaer (Old Style).

[1663: Aug. 24th, Friday, born at eight o'clock in the morning, Kiliaen van Rensselaer and baptized on the following Sunday (New Style).

[1665: Aug. 1st, born Anna van Rensselaer. (Old Style)

[1667: Oct. 23^{d}, born Hendr. van Rensselaer. (Old Style)

[1672: Oct. 25th, born Maria van Rensselaer. (Old Style)

[1701: Oct. 15th, I, Kiliaen van Rensselaer, 38 years old, have married Maria van Cortlandt, 21½ year old. May the Lord give us his blessing and grant us a blessed end.

[1702: July 31ˢᵗ, Friday, born between 4 and 5 in the morning, my daughter Maria van Rensselaer; baptized by Domine Lidius; as godfather Pieter Schuylder and Milady Cornbury as godmother.

[1703: Oct. 4ᵗʰ, Monday, born between 4 and 5 in the morning, our second daughter, Geertruy van Rensselaer; as witnesses Hendr. van Rensselaer and Olif van Cortlandt; as godmother Catrina van Rensselaer. — On May the ninth, following, our daughter Geertruy died in the Lord.

[1704/5: March 8ᵗʰ, Sunday, born, between 4 and 5 in the afternoon, our eldest son, and baptized on the following Sunday by Domine Lidius; as godfather Hendr. van Rensselaer and Maria Schuylder as godmother — christened Jeremias. May the Lord bless him and may he grow up in virtue, a comfort to his family.

[1706/7: March 17ᵗʰ, Monday, born in the morning at daybreak my second son, baptized on Sunday the 23ᵈ inst., by Domine Lidius, and christened Steefen, as godfather Philip Schuylder, as sponsors, mother Cortlandt, and Elizabett Johanne Schuylder, who presented him [at the font].

[1708: Dec. 10ᵗʰ, Friday, born at one o'clock in the night my third son, as godmother sister Nickels and cousin Maria van Rensselaer [who] carried him, as godfather Jan Coll[ens], baptized by Domine Lidius and christened Johannis. — On the 30ᵗʰ of the same month he died in the Lord and is buried on January the 2ᵈ.

[1710: August 28ᵗʰ, Monday, born at daybreak my third daughter ‡ [she] died in the Lord on Saturday, September 2ᵈ.

[1711: Novemb. 15ᵗʰ, Thursday, born between 11 and 12 in the night, our fourth son, in Albany, and baptized by Domine Barclay; as godfather Jan Schuylder and Jan Collens and as godmother Margrite Collens; christened Johannis. — Dec. 9ᵗʰ, on Sunday [he] died in the Lord.

[1713: March 29ᵗʰ, Sunday, born at half past seven in the evening, my fifth son, and baptized on Friday before Easter by Domine van Driessen, and christened Jacobis; as godfather Jacobis van Cortlandt and Philip Cortlandt [but] brother Rensselaer stood for him; and as godmother Margrita Beyert and Margrita Liffeston, who presented him [at the font]. May the Lord grant that he grow up in wisdom, that his soul may come to blessedness.

[1714: Oct. 1st, Friday, born at eight o'clock in the evening, our fourth daughter, and baptized on the following Sunday, by Domine van Driessen; presented at the font by sister Geertruy van Cortlandt and Robert Leffeston, jun^r. and christened Geertruy. May the Lord grant that she grow up in virtue, a comfort to her family, and that her soul may come to blessedness.

[1716/7: Jan. 29th, Tuesday, born between one and two o'clock in the morning our sixth son, christened Jan Baptist after my father's brother, presented at the font by juffr. Collens, for juffr. Liffeston, her sister; as godfather Jan Collens and baptized by Domine van Driessen. May the Lord grant that he grow up in the fear of God in His honour.

[1718/9 Jan. 1st, born at a quarter past nine in the morning, our fifth daughter Anna, and presented at the font by j.... Rensselaer for herself and sister Delansie, and as godfather brother Beyert, whose place was filled by Philip Schuylder and baptized by Domine van Driessen. May the Lord grant that she grow up in virtue, that her soul may come to blessedness.]

STEPHEN VAN RENSSELAER.
(Married, 1764.)

Holy Bible in English; New York, Hodge and Campbell, 1792.

Contains the records of Stephen Van Rensselaer and Catherine Livingston, his wife, with some of their descendants. It is now the property of Mrs. Grace Schuyler de Luze, of New Rochelle, a great-great-granddaughter of the original owner.

[Bible records copied by Grace Schuyler de Luze, March 7th, 1917.]

1764 January 23d. Stephen Van Rensselaer was married to Catherine Livingston, daughter of Philip Livingston Esq. of New York

1765 November 1st. Was born our first son at New York and Baptized by the Revd. Arch. Lardla [?] Stephen. My Father in law & Mother in law Philip & Christina Livingston Godfather & Godmother.

1766 April 15th Was born my second son at Water Vliet & Baptized by the Revd. Elardus Westerlo, Philip, my brother in law Abm. Ten Brouk & wife, Godfather and Godmother.

1768 Aug. 15th Was born my Daughter at Water Vliet & Baptized by the Revd. Barent Vrooman, Elizabeth, my brother & sister in law Abm. Ten Brouk & wife, Godfather & Godmother.

1769 Oct. 19th It pleased the Lord to take unto himself Stephen Van Rensselaer, He departed this Life at his house, in Water-Vliet & his Body was buried in the family Vault.

1775 July 19th Elardus Westerlo was married to Catherine Van Rensselaer widow of Stephen Van Rensselaer.

1776 May 6th Was born a son, & baptized by his Father, (name) Rensselaer, our Eldest son Stephen & daughter Elizabeth Godfather & Godmother.

1778 Aug. 23d. Was born a Daughter & Baptized by her Father, Catherine, John W. Ten Eyck & his wife Sarah Godfather & Godmother.

1783 March 13th Was born a Daughter & Baptized by her father, Johanna, John W. Livingston & Margaret Jones my brother & sister in Law, Godfather & Godmother.

1783 June 6th Stephen Van Rensselaer was married to Margaret Schuyler, daughter of General Philip Schuyler.

1784 July 6th Was born their first child & Baptized Catherine Schuyler, his Father & mother in law, Godfather & Godmother

1786 June 6th Was born their son Stephen, departed this Life

1789 March 29th Was born their second son Stephen Philip S. Van Rensselaer & Catherine Westerlo, Godfather & Godmother.

1787 April 15th Philip S. Van Rensselaer was married to Ann Depeyster Van Cortlandt Daughter of the Honble. Pierre V. Cortlandt

1787 Sept. 18th John B. Schuyler & Elizabeth Van Rensselaer were married

1788 Oct. 26th Was born a son & Baptized Philip Schuyler.

1790 May 4th Was born a son & Baptized Stephen Van Rensselaer Schuyler Died May 25, 1790

1795 Aug. 7th John B. Schuyler arrived at his House in Saratoga from the Westward, taken sick on Wednesday the 12th of a Billious Fever, Died the 7th of August 1795. Buried in the Vault of Stephen V. Rensselaer Esq. at Water-Vliet 20th August 1795

1800 Nov. 17th John Bleecker & Elizabeth Schuyler (widow of John B. Schuyler) were married by the Revd. John B. Johnson

1803 Jan 5th Was born a son, Baptized by the Revd. John Basset, Stephen Van Rensselaer, Stephen Van Rensselaer Esq. & Catherine Westerlo Godfather & Mother.

1804 Oct. 16th Was born our second son, Baptized by Revd. John Basset, John Rutse Bleeker, James Bleeker & Elizabeth Bleeker, GodFather & Mother.

1809 Oct. 1st Was born our daughter, Baptized by the Revd. John M. Bradford Catherine Westerlo, Rensselaer Westerlo & Catherine Westerlo GodFather & Mother

1826 April 16th Stephen V. R. Bleeker died aged 26

1832 July 19th John R. Bleeker Junr. died Aged 27

1833 Dec. 29th John Bleeker died, aged 70

1842 March 23d. Elizabeth Van Rensselaer, widow of John B. Schuyler & wife of John Bleeker died, aged 74 years, & buried [paper torn off] Vault at Water Vleet, leaving her son Philip Schuyler & daughter Catherine.

PETER VAN SCHAACK.
(Married, 1765.)

Holy Bible in English; London, Baskett, 1768.

Contains the records of Peter Van Schaack and his wives, Elizabeth Cruger and Elizabeth Van Alen, with their children. The Bible has descended to his granddaughter, Miss Anna Van Schaack, of Kinderhook, New York, the present owner.

Peter Van Schaack, Elizabeth Cruger, Married 2 October 1765.

Eldest son Cornelius, born at Kinderhook 12 February 1767 Godfather and Godmother, Cornelis Van Schaack and Lydia Van Schaack.

Second son Henry Cruger born at New York 8 October 1768 GodFathers Henry Cruger and John Cruger Esq^{rs} God Mother Anne Cruger.

A Daughter born in March 1770 Elizabeth, who lived but a few days.

March 1771 A Son born, who was baptized John and died the Day after his Birth.

February 1772 Another Son born who lived but a few Hours after his Birth.

1773 July 16 Daughter Ellin born — God-Father Henry Cruger Jun. Esqr and God Mothers Mary Cruger, Jane Van Schaack. On Thursday the 6th of October 1774, at about four o'clock in the Afternoon, after five Days Illness, died our Daughter Ellin! She was mine; and I was—was most blest—Gay Title of the deepest Misery!

1774 December 8th at two o'clock in the Morning was born our Son John. God Fathers John Harris Cruger & Leonard Gansevoort—Junr God Mother Mrs. Dorothea Cruger.

1775 July 19th between two and three o'clock in the Morning died at my Father's House at Kinderhook (whither he was taken for the Recovery of his Health) our eldest Son Cornelius a most promising Child! aged 8 y. 5 M & 6 Days.

And on the 22ᵈ of the same Month died at New York our Son John, of which we received the Account at Kinderhook a few Days afterwards by the Sloop which we expected would have brought him up.

1776 April 14ᵗʰ at one o'clock in the Morning — (Sunday) was born at Kinderhook our Son Cornelius and was baptized by the Rev. Mr. Fryenmoet the 5 May, Henry Van Schaack & Cathᵃ Van Schaack God Father & God Mother.

1776 Octobʳ 30ᵗʰ Wednesday near four o'clock P.M. died at his own House in Kinderhook my much honored Father Cornelis Van Schaack Esqʳ having completed the Seventy first year of his Age on the 11ᵗʰ Day of the same Month O.S.

1777 June 23ᵈ Monday Morning between one and two o'clock was born at Kinderhook my Daughter Elizabeth who was baptized at Albany by the Revᵈ Mr. Monro. God Father & God Mother Cornelis Van Schaack Margaret Van Alen.

1778 April 20ᵗʰ Monday Eveng. about ten o'clock died at Kinderhook my Wife Elizabeth Van Schaack!

1780 February 5ᵗʰ died in Bristol my Father in Law Henry Cruger Esqʳ

1785 July 19 I returned to my native Country and landed at New York, when I was first informed of the Death of my honored Mother which happened May in this year.

Peter Van Schaack, Elizabeth Van Alen, married 27 April 1789

1790 March 8 was born a Son baptized by the Name of John.

1791 March Died my Sister Margaret Van Alen.

July 26 Died our Son John!

1791 October 30 Was born our second Son who was baptized by Domine Labagh the 27 November by the name of Johannes, or John God Father Johannes L. Van Alen God Mother Christina Van Alen.

Decʳ 20.   at New York died John Cruger Esqʳ aged 82.

1793 Dec 9ᵗʰ was born our son David, God Father & God Mother David Van Schaack & Lydia Van Schaack.

1795 October 19th was born our Son Peter. God Father & God Mother Henry C. Van Schaack & Elizabeth Van Schaack.

1798 July 4 Born our Daughter Lydia. God Father & God Mother H. V. Schaack & Jane Silvester.

1800 July 2d Born our Daughter Cristina. God Father & God Mother Lucas I. V. Alen & Maria Van Vleck.

1802 April 3d was born our Son Henry Cruger. God Father & God Mother Henry H. Cruger Junr & Elizabeth V. Schaack.

1804 November 7th was born our son Lucas Van Schaack.

1807 June 9th was born our daughter Margaret Van Schaack. God Father & Mother Lucas Van Alen & Heletie his wife.

[Copied and sworn to by Mrs. Benjamin W. Franklin.]

ANTHONY VAN SCHAYCK, Jr.[1]
(1682–1759.)

Holy Bible in Dutch; Dordrecht, Jacob en Pieter Keur, 1714.

Contains the records of Anthony Van Schayck, Jr., and his two wives, Susanna Wendel and Anna Cuyler, with his descendants by his second wife. The records are in Dutch and English, and the Dutch records have been translated by Prof. Edward Delavan Perry, of Columbia University. The Bible has descended to Mrs. Caroline M. Swartwout, of Stamford, Conn., a great-great-granddaughter of the original owner.

1682. Albany. Juny 3. Ben ik Anthony Van Schayck [or: Van Schaijck] Junyer geboren tot Watervliedt in d Collony Rensselaerswick Smorgens te 8 uren Volgens Aentykening van Myn Vader Anthony Van Schayck

1707 Decembr 16 Ben ik getroudt med Susanna Dochter van Johan Wendel Myn Schoon vad Salgr getrouydt door Dom Johs Lydins

178/9 Janny 20 Is Myn Huysvrou in den heere ontslapen in arbyd van d Kraem savons te 8 uren out Synde 29 Jaer en 35 Dagen

1685 Novem 26 Is geboren Anna Doghter van Johas Cuyler volgens Syn Aentykening

1712 May 29 Ik war getrout met Anna Cuylers Voorschreve door Dom Petrus van Driesen

1713 Decem 2 Is geboren ons Soon Anthony Myn Vader Comper by Moeder Maria Van Schayck ten Doop getragen

1715 Jully 29 Is geboren onse Dochter Else Vridagh Smorgens omtrent 8 uren Myn. Schoon Vader Comper by Moeders Cuylers te Doop gedragen gedoopt door Petris Van Drissen

1716 Mardt 25 Is onse Dochter Else na Droef Marte aan de Pocken in den her ontslapen Smorges te 5 uren Is gedragen door Jacob Ver Planck

[1 The Dutch character ij is not cut for fonts of English type. Therefore the letter y has been used in the Dutch records where ij is meant.]

1716 Decemb 4 Is onse Eerste gebore Soon Anthony in den her ontslapen omtrent 6 uren gesmort an de lonpipen gedragen door Jacob Ver Planck en Davidt Groebeck en Davidt Van Dick en Harmanis Schueler

1717 Jully 12 Is geboren 2 Soon Anthony Vridagh ½ ur son Myn Vader Comper Bey Moeder Van Schayck te Doop gedragen gedopt door Petries Van Driessen

1718 Novembr 4 Is geboren ons Soon Johannes Myn Schoon Vader Comper bei Moeder Cuylers te dop gedragen

dato 15 Is onse soon Johannes in den heer ondtslapen savons 11 uren Is gedragen door Cornelis Ver Planck

1719 Jully 2 Is onse soon Anthony de 2 in den heer ontslapen Gedragen door Cornelis Ver Planck en Davidt Groesbeck en Harmans Schuyler en Jacob Wendel

1719 Novembr 9 Is geboren ons 2 dochter Else Min Schon Vader Comper bei Moeder Cuyler te dop gedragen

1722 October 21 Is geboren onse 4 dochter Anna sondagh savons omtrent 7 uren bro Cornelis Cuiler Comper by Sustr Cristine Cuilers te dop gedragen gedop door pitris van driese

1724 October 16 Is geboren onse viefde dochter Catrina Vridagh safons 9 uren br Gosen Van Schayck Comper bey Sustr Gertie ten Eyck te dop gedragen

1727 1 Jannywar Is geboren onse sesde dochter Cristiena smandagh omtrent 9 uren swager Johannes Cuiler Comper bey Sustr Cristina Cuiler Sara Hansen te dop gedragen

[Year obliterated] Janniw 31 Is myn Vader Anthony Van Schayck in den heer ontslapen ouyt sinde in syn 82 Jaer

1740 May 9 Is onse dochter Else in den heer ontslapen

1740 Jully 20 Is myn Schoon Vader Johannes Cuiler in den heer ontslapen

1741 Jully 10 Is myn Huisvrou in den heer ontslapen

1743 Mart 25 Is myn Moeder Marya Van Schayck In den heer ontslapen ouydt synde in Haer 82 Jaer

1743 April 16 Is myn dochter Catriena in den her ontslapen

1744 Desember 26 Is geboren Sammel Ten Broeck Soon Van myn Dochter Anna Ten Broeck

1759 Augustus 13 Is Vader Anthony Van Schaick Salgr In Den heer ontslapen des maendaghs morgens tusschen seven & aght uren & des Woensdaghs begraven Oudt 77 Yaer & 2 Maenden

[TRANSLATION[1]

[1682. Albany, June 3. I, Anthony Van Schayck, Jr., was born at Watervliedt in the Colony of Rensselaerswick, at eight o'clock in the morning, according to the record of my father Anthony Van Schayck.

[1707. Dec. 16. I was married to Susanna, daughter of Johan Wendel, my father-in-law deceased; married by Dom. Johannes Lydius.

[1708/9. Jan. 20. My wife fell asleep in the Lord, in childbirth, at eight o'clock in the evening, aged 29 years and 35 days.

[1685. Nov. 26, was born Anna, daughter of Johannes Cuyler, according to his record.

[1712, May 29, I was married to Anna Cuyler, above mentioned, by Dom. Petrus Van Driesen.

[1713, Dec. 2, was born our son Anthony; godfather, my father; carried to baptism by Mother Maria van Schayck.

[1715, July 29, was born our daughter Else, Friday about eight o'clock in the morning. Godfather, my father-in-law; carried to baptism by Mother Cuyler; baptized by Petris van Drissen.

[1716, March 25, our daughter Else fell asleep in the Lord, after dreadful suffering, of small-pox, at five o'clock. Carried by Jacob Ver Planck.

[1716, Dec. 4, our first born son Anthony fell asleep in the Lord, about six o'clock, of bronchitis. Carried to burial by Jacob Ver Planck and Davidt Groebeck and Davidt Van Dick and Harmanis Schueler.

[1717, July 12, our second son Anthony was born, about half past twelve o'clock in the afternoon. Godfather, my father;

[[1] Note: The spelling of all proper names is retained without change. The records show the variations common in such documents. For example, Driesen, Drissen, Driessen, and Driese are all the same name, and all pronounced alike.]

carried to baptism by Mother van Schayck; baptized by Petries van Driessen.

[1718, Nov. 4, was born our son Johannes. Godfather, my father-in-law; carried to baptism by Mother Cuyler.

[—— Nov. 15, our son Johannes fell asleep in the Lord, at eleven in the evening. Carried to burial by Cornelis Ver Planck.

[1719, July 2, our son Anthony the second fell asleep in the Lord. Carried to burial by Cornelis Ver Planck and Davidt Groesbeck and Harmans Schuyler and Jacob Wendel.

[1719, Nov. 9, was born our second daughter Else. Godfather, my father-in-law; carried to baptism by Mother Cuyler.

[1722, Oct. 21, was born our fourth daughter Anna, Sunday about seven o'clock in the evening. Godfather, Brother Cornelis Cuiler; baptized by Pitris van Driese.

[1724, Oct. 16, was born our fifth daughter Catrina, Friday at nine o'clock in the evening. Godfather, Brother Gosen Van Schayck; carried to baptism by Sister Gertie ten Eyck.

[1727, Jan 1, our sixth daughter Cristiena was born, Monday about 9 o'clock. Godfather, my brother-in-law Johannes Cuiler; carried to baptism by Sister Cristina Cuiler and Sara Hansen.

[[Year obliterated] Jan. 31, my father Anthony van Schayck fell asleep in the Lord, in the 82d year of his age.

[1740, May 9, our daughter Else fell asleep in the Lord.

[1740, July 20, my father-in-law Johannes Cuiler fell asleep in the Lord.

[1741, July 10, my wife fell asleep in the Lord.

[1743, Mar. 25, my mother Marya van Schayck fell asleep in the Lord, in the 82d year of her age.

[1743, Apr. 16, my daughter Catriena fell asleep in the Lord.

[1744, Dec. 26, was born Sammel Ten Broeck, son of my daughter Anna Ten Broeck.

[1759, Aug. 13, Father Anthony van Schayck Salger[1] fell asleep in the Lord, Monday morning between seven and eight o'clock, and was buried Wednesday; aged 77 years and 2 months.]

I Anthony Ten Broeck Son of Henry Ten Broeck Is Born In the year 1756: November the 2 day

Anthony Ten Broeck are Maryed to Christina Ten Broeck in the year 1782: October the 13

In the year 1783 September the 28 Is Born our first Child named Anna

November the 12 1785 Is Born our Daughter Caty

March the 25 1787 Is Born our Son Henry

1759 June 5th Was born Mary daughter of Henry Ten Brook & wife of Aaron Lane—Died January 1827

1751 Den 21 September Heb ik Anthony G. Van Schaick mynselve In den Houweliken Staet Begeven Met myn Nigte Christina Van Schaick Door De heer Theodorus Vreelinghuysen

1752 Den 19 Juny Is Geboren Onse Erste Geboorne Soon Goose te 10 Uuren Vrydaghs des Morgens Den 21 Do. Gedoopt tot Compeer en preet Myn Schoonvader Anthony Van Schaick En Moeder Deborah Beekman

N° St. Den 27 Decr Is Onse Soon Goose in Den heer Gerust Oudt Synde Vyf Maende en 28 Dagen Gedragen door John Beekman jun. Gestorven Woensdags des Avonts te negen Uuren en Vrydaghs Begraven

[TRANSLATION

[1751, Sept. 21, I, Anthony G. Van Schaick, entered the state of holy matrimony with my niece Christina Van Schaick; married by Mr. Theodorus Vreelinghuysen.

[1752, June 19, was born our first-born son Goose, at 10 o'clock Friday morning. Baptized Thursday, 21st; godparents, my father-in-law Anthony Van Schaick and Mother Deborah Beekman.

[[1] Note: Salger (like the German selig) is added to the name of a deceased person.]

[N⁰ St. Dec. 27. Our son Goose was taken to rest in the Lord, aged five months and 28 days. Carried to burial by John Beekman, Jr. Died Wednesday evening at 9 o'clock and buried Friday.]

1797 March 23 Married Henry Ten Broeck to Patty Cumstock

1798 February 21 Is Born Our first Child Henry

1785 September 10 Is Born Maria B. Ten Broeck Daughter of John C. Ten Broeck

1787 December 29 Is Born Anna Van Schaick Ten Broeck Daughter of John C. Ten Broeck

1790 June 26 Is Born Caty Ten Broeck Daughter of John C. Ten Broeck

1800 August 23 Departed this life Samuel Ten Broeck Son of Henry Ten Broeck

1789 April 3d Is Born Cornelius P. Ten Broeck Son of Anthony Ten Broeck

John C. Ten Broeck was born in Claverack Columbia County N Y March 15 1755 Died August 10th 1835 in the 81st year of his age

Anna Ten Broeck wife of J. C. Ten Broeck born May 9 1754 at Claverack — Died May 9 1838 aged 84 years

Maria Ten Broeck and Joseph Ketchum Married 22d Sept 1804

Thomas Hillhouse and Anna Ten Broeck married Oct. 8, 1812

Rev. Maurice W. Dwight & Catherine Ten Broeck married May 9th 1825 [May 9th 1825 added in pencil]

Joseph Ketchum 3d Son of Joseph Ketchum and Maria Ten Broeck Married Sarah Hannah Keeler January

Cornelia Anne, 4th daughter of Joseph and Sarah Ketchum, married Henry Seaman Howard at Stamford, Conn., Nov.

Ten Broeck, only son of Cornelia A. and Henry S. Howard, born Feb

Joseph Ketchum died Nov

Last record made by Caroline M. Swartwout 2d daughter of Joseph and Sarah Ketchum at Stamford, Conn., Sept. 3, 1891.

GUERT VAN SCHOONHOVEN.[1]
(1718–1783.)

Holy Bible in Dutch; Dordrecht, Hendrick, Jacob en Pieter Keur, 1702.

Contains the records, in Dutch, of Guert Van Schoonhoven and his wife, Anna Lansingh, with some other Van Schoonhoven entries. It has descended to the present owner, Frederic V. S. Crosby, of New York, who is the great-great-grandson of Guert Van Schoonhoven.

Ick Guert Van Schoon Hoven ben geboren in yaer onses heeren 1718 den 9 maart

1743 den 3 februwarie is Guert Van Schoon hoven en Anna Lansingh in den heuwelyken staat getreden dit is de ouderdom van haer kint

1744 den 17 februwarie is myn Soon Jacobus gebore

1744 den 28 februwarie is myn vrou Anna Lansingh in den heere gerust en den 2 maert begraven

1748/9 den 24 Jannewarie is myn vader Jacobus Van Schoonhove in den heere gerust en de 26 begraven out synde 78 yaer min 4 maenden

1757 den 4 Jannewarie is myn suster Anna Van Schoonhove in den heere gerust en den 6 begraven out synde 33 yaer en een maent

1760 is myn moeder in den heere gerust Septerber de 22 en de 24 begraven out synde 73 yaer min 3 maenden 8 dage

Above dates were under old style. Add 12 days to above dates to correspond with present style (viz.: adding 11 days for original alteration and 1 day after the year 1800).

[1 The Dutch character ij is not cut for fonts of English type. Therefore the letter y has been used in the Dutch records where ij is meant.]

DIRCK TUENISEN VAN VECHTEN.[1]
(1634–1702.)

Holy Bible in Dutch; Amsterdam, Jan Evertz, 1603.

This Bible contains the records, in Dutch, of Dirck Tuenisen Van Vechten and his wife, Jannetie. It also contains, in English, the records of Jeremiah Field and Mary Van Vechten, his wife. The Bible was presented to the American Bible Society by Peter D. Vroom in 1817 and is now deposited in the New York Public Library.

Derck van Veghten

Janniete van Veghten

Dirck Tuenisen gebooren in jaer 1634 onses Heere en Saligmaeker Jesum Christi, Anno 1634 's Maendaghs nae Vastelavondt oude styl in Feruwary omtrent tusschen 9 en tien uere — in 't Sticht van Utrecht en is den Heer ontslapen in jaer 1702 den 25 November.

Jan Tuenise gebooren — in 't Sticht van Utrecht tot Kersten Anno 1637 in Desember Kersavont omtrent een ure nae son oude styl.

Jannetie Tuenise dochter gebooren int jaer onses Heere Anno 1639 in Nieu Nederlant, aent Fort over in de Colonie Renselaers Wyck, den 16 Februwarius 's morgens omtrent 9 en tien ure nieuwe styl.

Cornelis Tuenisen gebooren inde Colonie Renselaers Wyck Anno 1640 int eerste van September nieu styl.

Dochter Pietertie Tuenisen gebooren in de Colonie Renselaers Wyck anno 1644 in de maent van July omtrent Sint Jan, nieuwe styl.

Gerret Tuenisz gebooren in de Colonie Renselaers Wyck anno 1647 den 16 a 17 September nieu styl.

[1 The Dutch character ij is not cut for fonts of English type. Therefore the letter y has been used in the Dutch records where ij is meant.]

First page of the Van Vechten Record, 1634

Anno 1704 in Meert Gerrit Tuenissen in den Heer ontslapen.

Anno 1702 den 25 Nofember Dirck Tuenise gestorven.

Pieter Dumonts wyf Jannetije gestorven den 15 September, anno 1706.

Raritans den 23 Janari anno 1711/12

Seer gode vrient Walran Dermon Verhope alle gesoth ... en welvaert vort ik heb gehoort.

Anno 1701 is geboren Jannetie van Veghten den 12 Junij.

Anno 1701 is geboren Jannet Michiel den 12 Junij, omtrent te tien uyren.

Int jaer onses Heren Saligmaker Jesu Christum dit is memorie van ouderdom van Michiel Dircksen kinderen ende namen —

Anno 1687 is geboren Marijtije Michiels de ouste dochter den achten Oktober omtrent vier in de morgen.

Dirck Michielse de outste soon geboren int jaer 1689 den sesden Desember.

Int jaer 1691 is geboren Walran Michielse den 11 Desember en is in den Heer ontslapen int jaer 1694 den 16 November.

Int jaer 1693 den negenentwintighsten Juni is geboren Marregrietije Michiels savons omtrent ten seuen uyren a acht uyren en is in den Heer ontslapen 1712 den vyfden September en den 7 September begraven in de Sopus.

Int jaer 1693 den sevenentwintighsten Ocktober is Dirck Michielsen in den Heer ontslapen.

Anno 1699 is geboren Dirck Michielse den 15 July.

Anno 1701 is geboren Jannetije Michielse den 12 Juny omtren tien uijren.

[Michiel Dircksen] int jaer 1686 getrouwt den 21 November met Marijdtije Perker, in den Heer ontslapen in July int jeer 1690; met Jannetije Dumont getrouwt int jeer·anno 1691 den 2 Aprille.

In jaer onses Heerren Salighmaker Jesu Christus anno 1708 den
6 Ocktober is geboren Albert Ten Eeyck syn outste dochter den
6 Ocktober omtrent ten 7 uyren in den avont, genaemt Jengien,
gedoopt den 27 May A° 1709 van Dome Giliaen in de Nieuwe
Tabernakel; den 26 dito de eerst predicatie daer in de Nieuwe
Tabernakel was syn Tex uit mrkus 16 v.6.

Anno 1711 tusschen den elfden en den tienden April is geboren
Albert Ten Eeyck 17 dagen nae syn vaders doot. Syn vader is
gestorven den 24 Maert 1711.

Anno 1713 den 21 Jannuary is Albert Ten Eeyck Junyer gestorven en Marytijen weer getroudt met Jeremijah Field anno
1713 den 19 Feberwary.

Anno 1714 den 27 Jannuary is geboren Marijtijes twede soontije
smorkens tussen 6 en 7 uren.

Anno 1719/20 den 4 Feberwary heeft Domenie syn eerste predykasie gedaen op Sixmylkun — vyfden propheet Jesaya uyt het
6e kapittel vaers 1 en 2.

Feberwary den 14 Domenie op Harensbroeck gepredickt uyt de
Handelinge der Apostelen 26 capittel dat 18 vaers.

D.6 Maert dat op Sesmylkun Domenie syn tex gehat uyt Matteus
op het 26 capittel het 36 vaers tot het 40 vaers.

Anno 1719/20 den 31 Jannuary dan heeft den domenie Theodoris Jacobus Frelinckhuyse de eerste beroepe predykant tot
Raretan en Sixmylkun en Harensbroeck en Noortbrans syn eerst
predykasie gedaen; syn tex waer uyt den 2 Sentbrief Paulus tot
den Corinten, aen het vijfde capittel beginnende op het 20 veers.
Dijto den 24 Feberwary in onse kapel domenie syn tex gehat uyt
Johannis 6 het 24 vaers "Al wat my de Vader geeft, sal tot my
komen"

Dijto den 13 Maert domenie syn tex uyt Matteus het 26 Capittel
het 62 vaers tot 68 vaers op de Noortbrans by fyf, "Ende hoogepriester opstaende seyde tot hem"

Father Jeremiah Feild deseast November the 10 day 1746.

Jeremiah Feild the Son of John Field and Margaret his Wife
was Born the 17th day of May in the Year 1689.

Mary van Veighton the Daughter of Michael van Veighton and Mary his Wife was Born the 8th of October in the Year 1687.

Jenegein Teneike the daughter of Albert Teneike and Mary his Wife was Born the 6th of October in the Year 1708.

Albert Teneike the Son of Albert Teneike and Mary his Wife was Born the 11th of April in the Year 1711.

Jeremiah Field and Mary Teneike was Married the 19th of February, A° 1713.

Jeremiah Feild the Son of Jeremiah Field and Mary his Wife was Born the 27th day of January in the Year 1713/4.

John Field the Son of Jeremiah Feild and Mary his Wife was Born the 5th day of April in the Year 1715.

Michael Field the Son of Jeremiah Field and Mary his Wife was Born the 24th day of August in the Year 1716.

Margaret Field the Daughter of Jeremiah Feild and Mary his Wife was Born the 2d day of October in the Year 1717.

Mary Feild the Daughter of Jeremiah Feild and Mary his Wife was Born the 8 day of September in the Year 1719.

Mary Feild the Daughter of Jeremiah Field and Mary his Wife was Born the 19 day of October in the Year 1720.

Michael Field the Son of Jeremiah Field and Mary his Wife was Born the 4th day of February in the Year 1722/3.

Benjamin Field the Son of Jeremiah Field and Mary his Wife was Born the 19th day of February in the Year 1724/5.

Jeremiah Field born the 27 day of Jannuary about sunrise in the morning ... anno domni = 1714 being one a Wensday.

John Field born on the fifth day of April in the year of our Lord = 1715 a littel before day in the mornning.

Michel Field born the 24 day of August about 10 of the clock in the mornning anno domni = 1716.

Margret Field born the 2 day of October about 10 of the clock in the mornning anno domni 1717.

Mary Field born the 8 day of September in the morning anno domni 1719.

Mary Field born the 19 day of October about 8 of the clock in the mornning in the year of our Lord anno domni 1720.

February 4 day 1722/23 My 4 son born a littel after day lit going in; my son Michel Field.

Jeremiah Field Juner and Pheba his wife, their daughter born Jannuary the 19, 1736.

Tunes Field the son of Jeremiah Field was married to Margret Fisher the 28 day of March in the yeare 1764.

Susannah Field the daughter of Tunes Field and Margret his wife was born the 18 day of October 1764.

Jeramyah Field Ten Eick was borne the third day of December in the of our Lorde 1784 and died the fifth of September in the year of our Lorde 1785.

Dutch Church, Fishkill, New York

REVEREND NICHOLAS VAN VRANKEN.
(1762–1804.)

Holy Bible in English; Berwick, John Taylor, 1793.

Contains records of Nicholas Van Vranken, Pastor of the Dutch Church at Fishkill, N. Y., and his two wives, Ruth Comstock and Catherine Conklin, with their children. The Bible has descended to his great-granddaughter, Miss Margaret P. Hillhouse, of Yonkers, New York, who is the present owner.

Nicholas Van Vranken was born May 24th 1762, Ruthy Comstock was born Decembr 31st 1763, Married Febry 11th 1787.

Samuel Amasa their first Son was born April 25th 1788 on Friday, and departed this Life 29th July 1788 Aged 3 Months and 4 Days.

James Romeyn, their second Son was born 21st May 1789 on Thursday.

Harriot, their first Daughter was born Octr 18th 1790, and departed this Life Novr 3rd 1790, Aged 16 Days

Samuel Alexander, their third Son was born 20th Febry 1792 on Monday.

Harriot, their second Daughter was born 6th Septr 1793 on Friday.

Margaret Matilda, their third Daughter was born Novr 23d 1795 on Monday.

William Augustus their fourth Son was born July 20th 1799.

Ruthy, Wife of Nicholas Van Vranken departed this life, in full afsurance of a happy Immortality on Saturday, being the 16th day of August, Anno 1800.

Nicholas Van Vranken and Catherine Conklin were married April 4th, 1802.

Ruthy Their first Daughter was born April 18th 1803 and departed this life the 22nd of the same Month.

Nicholas their first son was born April 22th·1804.

Nicholas Van Vranken departed this life in full afsurance of a happy immortality on Sunday 20th of May, Anno 1804

Nicholas their first son departed this life August 9th Anno Domini 1805.

James Romeyn, their second son departed this Life 1st June 1806. aged 17 years and 10 Days.

Margaret Matilda their third daughter (wife of Phinehas Prouty) departed this life September 12th 1830 on Sunday.

Samuel Alexander their third son died Jan' 1st 1861 on Tuesday. He was senior Proffessor in the college at New Brunswick, In Rutgers College.

Harriet died at Hackensack May 3rd 1875.

William Augustus died at Geneva 1872.

PHILIP VER PLANCK.
(1736–1777.)

Holy Bible in English; Oxford, William Jackson and William Dawson, 1795.

Contains the records of Philip Ver Planck and his wife, Effy Beekman, with their descendants of the names of Ver Planck and Hoffman. The Bible descended to Beekman Ver Planck Hoffman and then to his great-niece by marriage, Mrs. W. R. Caminoni, of Oyster Bay, N. Y., the present owner.

BIRTHS.

Catherin Ver Planck was Born the 21st of April 1765

Gertrude Verplanck was Born the 26th of August 1766

Phillip Verplanck was Born the 18th of July 1768

William Beekman Verplanck was Born the 2d of March 1770

Margaret Verplanck was Born the 7th of September 1772

Ann Maria Verplanck was Born the 19th October 1774

Beekman Verplanck Hoffman was Born the 28th November 1789

Charles Edward Hoffman was Born the 22d October 1791

Euphemia Verplanck Hoffman was Born the 21st January 1794

Samuel Anthony De Veaux Hoffman was Born the 2d of May 1797

Euphemia Babcock born Oct 1818

Fred born Feb 24 1820

Beekman born Dec 23 1821

Doveaux born Oct 22 1823

William born May 18 1826

Cort born Jan 22 1830

Marriages.

Phillip Verplanck was Married to Effy Beekman, Daughter of Gerrard Beekman the 7th of April, 1764.

Harman Hoffman was Married to Catherin Verplanck the 4th of November 1786.

Anthony Anthony Hoffman was Married to Gertrude Verplanck the 8th January 1789.

Phillip Verplanck was Married to Sally Arden the Daughter of Thomas Arden 27th September 1796.

William Beekman Verplanck was Married to Malinda Daughter of (Gen. James) Gordon 12th July 1798.

Peter Mesier was Married to Margaret Verplanck the 15th of June 1799.

Andrew De Veaux was Married to Ann Maria Verplanck the 22nd of April 1797.

Euphemia Verplanck Hoffman was Married to Frederick Babcock the 18th October 1817.

Beekman Verplanck Hoffman was Married to Phoebe Townsend the . . . November 1817.

Deaths.

Grandmother Beekman Departed this Life the 20th of April 1763 Aged 59 Years 5 Months and 18 Days.

Gertrude Verplanck the wife of Phillip Verplanck Departed this Life the 20th September 1766 Aged

Phillip Verplanck of the Manor of Courtland Departed this Life the 13th of October 1771 aged 77 Years 3 Months and 15 Days.

Margaret Verplanck Departed this Life   of November 1767 Born 1725.

John Verplanck Departed this Life the 14th of February 1774. Born 1727.

James Verplanck Departed this Life the 30th December 1774. Born 1720.

Effy Verplanck Departed this Life the 15th of November 1775. Aged 39 years.

Phillip Verplanck Departed this Life the 20th June 1777. Born 1736.

Andrew De Veaux Departed this Life.

Ann Maria Verplanck Departed this Life 20th October 1779 aged 50 years.

Gertrude Verplanck Departed this Life the 24th June 1794. Aged 62 years.

William Beekman Verplanck Departed this Life the 30th December 1804 aged 34 Years 8 Months and 28 Days.

Ann Maria De Veaux Departed this Life the 28th May 1816.

Anthony Anthony Hoffman Departed this Life the ... December 1816.

Samuel Anthony De Veaux Hoffman Departed this Life the 20th of July 1829.

Beekman Verplanck Hoffman departed this life December 10 1834.

Gertrude Hoffman Departed this life the 9 of February 1848 at ¼ before 3 O'c. A. M.

JOHN CHRISTOPHER VOUGHT.
(1713–1809.)

Holy Bible in English; New York, T. & J. Swords, 1818.

Contains the records of John C. Vought and his wife, Cornelia, with their descendants. It has descended to their great-grandson, William Grandin Vought, of Buffalo, N. Y., the present owner.

DEATHS.

John Christopher Vought died June 1809 aged 96 years.

Cornelia his wife died September 1801 aged 93 years.

John Vought their son died September 7, 1803 aged 53 years 1 month 1 day.

Mary Vought died March 29 1831.

Christopher Vought died June 16 1826

John G. Vought died July 23 1832

Christianna Bogart died June 17 1836

Mary Bunnell died September 1848

Elenor Vander Volgen died Feby 13 1849

Mary Anna Vought died June 3 1846 aged 23 years

France E. Vought died May 14 1847 aged 28 years

Mary I. Vought died June 7 1849 aged 62 years

John V. Vander Volgen died Sept 2 1850

Leah Vought died August 1847

Philip G. Vought died February 27, 1858 — 77 yrs.

Abram Vought died Jany 25 1873 aged 77 years

Mary G. Stebbins died Nov. 17 1879

Abigail Vought died Feby 16 1883.

BIRTHS.

Christianna Vought born Sept 13 1773

Elenor Vought born Dec 17 1775

Cornelia Vought born June 18 1779 died 15th Sept following aged 3 months 3 days

Philip Grandin Vought born Jany 11 1781

Christopher Vought born May 2 1783

A daughter stillborn May 26 1786

Mary G. Vought born June 19 1788

John Graft Vought born May 22 1791

Abigail Vought born Oct 24 1794

Abraham Vought born Dec 19 1795

Jane Leslie Vought born 1822

Mary Grandin Vought born Apl 14 1828

John Henry Vought born 1825

John Vought and Mary Grandin were married by the Rev. Mr. Fraser on the 22nd November 1772

Abraham Vought and Ruth Voorhees were married May 9 1820

Jane Leslie Vought and Chauncey Henry Porter were married January 27 1849

Mary Grandin Vought and Samuel Hopkins Ver Planck were married Sept. 20, 1854.

John Henry Vought and Anne Webster were married June 9 1858.

Chauncey H. Porter born at Nassau, N. Y., Aug. 11, 1818.

Jane Leslie Vought born at Duanesburg, N. Y., July 15, 1822.

In the church of the Holy Trinity, Brooklyn, by the Rev. Wm. H. Lewis, Jan. 27, 1849, C. H. Porter to Jane Leslie Vought.

JOHN WEEKES.
(Born, 1672.)

Holy Bible in English; Oxford, Thomas Baskett, 1747.

Contains the records of John Weekes and Mercy his wife, with some of their descendants. The Bible is now the property of Mr. J. W. Wright, of Oyster Bay.

John Weekes was born in the 16 of May, In the year 1672 at 12 O Clock at Noon. Mercy Weekes, his wife, was borne 29th June In the Year 1676

Hannah the Daughter of the said John and Mercy Weekes was borne 5th of April 1694

Michael, the eldest son of the said John and Mercy Weekes was borne 21st of August In the Year 1696

John their second son, was born 9th July 1699

George their youngest son was borne 9th of March 1708

Elizabeth Wood Departed this Life Dec. 1791, In the 90th year of her Age.

George Weekes His Book
God give him grace thearin to Look.

George Weekes was born, on ash wednesday The 9th Day of March Annodomeny One Thousand 1708/9 Seaven Hundred and Eight nine.

Ruth Weekes Daughter of Jonas and Sarah Platt and wife to George Weekes, was Born September 30th Day 1715.

The above Ruth Weekes. Departed this Life the 17th Day of august. 1777 about 12 o Clock at noon.

Gorg Weekes Departed this Life the 29 January att 11 OClock of the Night 1782.

Townsend Weekes departed this life the first day of May, 1801 about 11 o'clock at night, aged 67 Years & 9 days. Freelove, the Wife of Townsend W[eekes] Died October 3d 1810 aged

THOMAS WRIGHT.
(Married, 1755.)

Holy Bible in English, 1715.

Contains various records of the Wright family, as late as the middle of the nineteenth century. It is now the property of Miss Julia Wright, of Oyster Bay, New York.

Sarah Wright Was Born ye 30th of march in the year 1752 on a monday

Caleb Wright Was Born ye 8th of September in ye year 1754 at Half an Hour Paft one in the morning

Novemb^{re} ye 17' 1778—John G. Wright and Phebe Barton was married on the day of the above date by the Revd Doct^r Bradford of Danbury at the Houfe of Mr Thos Heaveland Oblong in the state of new-york

Oct^{re} ye 5 1781 My Dear Wife departed this Life at the Houfe of Capt Byands in New Windsor

William Wright and Elizabeth Wright was married the 18th day of March in the year of our Lord 1783 by the Revd Mr Burnet in Jamaca at his Own house.

My first Daughter Susannah Wright was born the 26 day of Aprel in the year 1784 on Monday at 12 - Clock at day

My first Son Caleb Wright was born the 8th Day of July in the Year 1787 on Sunday morning half after 3 oClock in the and July

My seccond Daughter Nancy was born 3 Day of February in the year of our Lord 1790 ond Wednesday 8 oClock in the morning candlemas day and Departed this Life August th 15th about 4 oclock in the morning 1793 aged three years six months and twelve days.

My fourth Daughter Mary was born 2 Day of august in the year of our Lord 1799

William Wright — was born the 21st day of October in the year of our Lord, One thousand seven hundred and forty eight—1748

William Wright departed this Life on Saturday the 11th day of March (about 10 oclock at night) in the year of our Lord, one thousand Eight hundred and Twenty—1820 Aged

Mary Wright was born 2 day of august in the year of Our Lord 1799 and departed this life January the third in the Morning a bout eight a clock in the year of our Lord 1827 in a triuphent hope of the world of eternel rest

Elizabeth Wright departed this life on thursday the 7 of october at about 8 at night in the in the year of ourlord one thousand 8 hundred forty one

Susanah Wright was born the 26th day of April in the year 1784 Monday at 12 o clock M.day.

Susanah Wright Departed this life July the 18 in the Morning about 3 Oclock in the year of our Lord. 1843

Thoˢ Wright & Elizabeth Rotchell Were married November yᵉ 23ᵈ Annoyz Dom 1755

our Eldeſt ſon John Was Born January yᵉ 8ᵗʰ 1787 at Eight of yᵉ Clock in yᵉ Evening ſatturday

my firſt daughter Elizabeth Was Born yᵉ 30ᵗʰ day of Auguſt Annoyz dom 1761 at nine of the Clock of a ſunday morning —

my ſon Thomas Was Born on the twentieth day of [piece torn out] on a ſunday at half an hour Paſt Eight in yᵉ m [piece torn out] and Departed this Life on yᵉ 16ᵗʰ of December the [piece torn out]

Stephen Was Born on yᵉ 25ᵗʰ day of [piece torn out] on a ſunday —

Was Born April yᵉ 12 | 1774 on tueſday [piece torn out]

Thomas Wright was born on tusday the 11ᵗʰ day of June Anno. Dom. 1776.

My Dear mother Leruiah Wright was taken with the numb Palsy the 8ᵗʰ day of September and Departed this life the 17ᵗʰ Inst at 9 o Clock in the morning in the year 1791

Dariet Wright was born March ᵗʰ 17- 1785

Greoosbeck was born November ᵗʰ 5- 1786

Susan Born Sepᵗ 25- 1782

Hannah Born October ᵗʰ 2ᵈ — 1791

Children of John G. Wright

William A. Wright and Mary Bochus was married on the 10 of November In the year of our Lord, 1840. By the Rev. Marmaduke Earl.

CORNELIUS WYNKOOP.[1]
(Born, 1732.)

Holy Bible in Dutch; Dordrecht, Jacob en Hendrick Keur, 1741.

Contains the records in Dutch of Cornelius Wynkoop of Esopus, N. Y., and his wife, Maria Catharina Ruehl, with their children. The Bible has descended to Miss Sarah B. Reynolds, of Kingston, N. Y., a great-granddaughter of the original owner.

[The Record written in Dutch and copied by me, Maria D. B. Cox 19 June 1901]

This Bible which was owned by my dear departed mother Mary Catherine Wynkoop daughter of Martin Augustus & Mary Ruehl & came from her family, is now presented to Mary Jane Reynolds eldest daughter of Augustus Wynkoop, by her affectionate Aunt Henrietta Van Solwifen New York June 4, 1835.

Ick Cornelius C. Wynkoop, Ben geboren in Esopus Den 15de November N.S. Jn het Yaar onser Heere 1732

En Ben Getrouwt in New York Den 23th April 1760 met Maria Catharina Ruehl, Doghter van Martin Ruehl Saliger En Maria Ruehl, Tegenwoording Huysvroou van George Pettersson. En ben kort naer het Trouwen Met myn Vroun Gaen woonen in huys Met Johannes Rypel En syn Vroun.

Sy dawoud Synde omtrent 20 yaars is geboren in t'yaar onser Heern 1739 den 7de September N.S.

1761 Januarie den 17 in Myn Vrouw in de kraam gekomen van ons Erste kind ten 6 uure in den Morgen, En gedoopt Door Domine J. Ritzema. En Gennamt Johammes, En had Getruyge Johannes Rypel En Maria Pettersson.

1761 April den 11de is Johannes Rypel naer En wyring dagen sware Lickte in den Heere ontslapen En den 13den Begraven in de onde Duytsche kerke ond Synde 66 yaaren 2 maanden en 1

[1 The Dutch character ÿ is not cut for fonts of English type. Therefore the letter y has been used in the Dutch records where ÿ is meant.]

dag — hy was Geboren en het yaar onsers Heeren 1695 den 10 Februarie N.S. in Hoag Duytsland.

1762 July den 1st is Myn Vrouu in de Kraam Gekomen van ons Tweede Kind omtrent 8 uuren des avonds, En Gedoopt Door Domine De Ronde, Gennamt Maria, En hadde tot Getuyge George Pettersson En Sabina De Ronde.

1762 November de 27th is Catherine Rypel weduwe van Johannes Rypel Saliger naar veel Yaaren Merkelyke verswaeking naerde Vleische in Den heere ontslapen, En Begraven in de oude Duytsche Kerck ond synde omtrent 70 yaaren

1763 October den 24th En half uur maer 3 in de Morgen is Myn Vrou in de kraam Gekomen van En yonge Doghter Synde ons derde kind. En den 7 November Gedoopt door Domine L De Ronde Gennamt Catharina, En had tot Getuyge George Pettersson En Sabina De Ronde.

1765 July den 8, Omtrent En half uur naer 6 in den Morgenstont is Myn Vrou in De Kraam Gekomen van een yonge Zoon Synde ons 4 kind, En is den 17 Woensdags Gedoopt Door Dom. Laidlie, Genaamt Cornelius Petersson, En hadde tot Getuyge myn Broeder Adriaan Wynkoop en Syn Vrouwn Catharina.

1765 July 27 Zynde de naght tusschen Vrydag En Saturdag is ons yongst kind in den heere ontslapen, ond Zynde 19 Dagen.

1766 July 1st Dwigsdags Morgens ten 3 uure is myn Vrouw in De Kraam Gekomen van ons Vyfe kinde Zynd Een Doghter is Den 13th Gedoopt Door Dom. De Ronde, Genaamt Anna Sabina. Getruygen Do. Kern En Syn Vrouw.

1768 Den 20 July Woensdag morgen omtrent 8 uuren is myn Vrouw En De Kraam Gekomen Zynde ons Zesde kind, Gedoopt Door Dom. Kern En genaamt Cornelius Getuyge myn Broeder en Zuster Petrus en Lea Wynkoop En

1768 August 3 heeft tot God behaagt het laast yemelse kindt Door De Doot weg to nemen, hoperde tot Een Beter en Zalig Leven.

1769 November 14 Dwigsdag omtrent 6 uuren in De morgen is myn Vrouw In de kraam Gekomen van een yonge Doghter (Zynd ons 7 kindt) En den 3 December Gedoopt Door Dom. Ritzema Genaamt Elizabeth Getuygen Charles De Witt Esqr. En myn Zuster Elizabeth Dumont.

1772 May 7th Donderdag omtrent 6 uuren in den morgenstont is myn Vrouw in De kraam Gekomen van Een Yonge Zoon Synde ons 8 kindt en Gedoopt Door Dom. Genaamt Cornelius Getuygen Matthew Ernest En zyn Vrouw.

1774 October 22 is myn Vrouw in de Kraam gekomen van ons 9 kindt in Kingston, Gedoopt door Dom. Cok. Zyde En doghter En Genaamt Henrietta.

1777 September 27th omtrent Een uur in den Morgenstont is myn Vrouw in de kraam gekomen van ons 10 Kind En den 14 October Gedoopt in kuys door Dom. Dol En genaamt Augustus. Getuygen Doartue nurgeset Dom. Kern En Syn Vrouw.

CHRISTIANNA VOUGHT YOUNG.
(Died, 1773.)

Holy Bible in Dutch; Dordrecht, Pieter en Jacob Keur, 1736.

Contains the notice of death of Christianna Vought, who married the Rev. John Young. It is now in the possession of William Grandin Vought, Esq., of Buffalo, N. Y., a great-grandnephew of Mrs. Christianna Vought Young.

Christianna Young Dep ... [torn] ... day of May in the year of our Lord One thousand seven hundred and seventy-three.

George Young was born the twenty-third day of April in the year of our Lord One thousand seven hundred and seventy-three.

John Vought and Mary Grandin was married on Sunday the 22d day of November in the year 1772 by the Rev. Mr. William Frazer. The first child, a daughter, was born Sept. 13, 1773, on Monday at nine o'clock in the evening, was christened on Sunday, the 7th November, 1773, at Kingwood Church by the Rev. Mr. William Frazer and named Christiana.

DANIEL YOUNGS.
(1748–1809.)

Holy Bible in English; Dublin, George Grierson, 1752.

Contains the record of Daniel and Susannah Youngs and their descendants. It is now the property of the heirs of Col. William J. Youngs, of Garden City, L. I., a great-grandson of the original owner.

Daniel Youngs born January 21st 1748.

Susannah Youngs Born April 21st 1752 = died September 22nd 1847

Hannah Youngs his Daughter Born May 24th 1770

Keziah Youngs his Daughter Born February 12th 1773

Samuel Youngs his Son Born April 1st 1777 = died Sep 7 1838

Daniel Youngs his Son Born December 13th 1783

Maria Youngs his wife Born January 1st 1795

Married February 23rd 1815

Daniel Kelsey Youngs born May 7th 1817

William Jones Youngs born July 9th 1819

Thomas Youngs born May 3rd 1822

Susan Maria Youngs born July 15th 1824

Charles A Son born July 17th 1827 and died September 24

John Baker Youngs born September 22 in 1829 and died March 17th 1832

Henry I. Youngs born August 19th 1835 died = Sept 3 1836

Elizabeth Youngs born October 23rd 1836 Died the 29th aged 6 Days

William Jones Youngs son of Daniel Kelsey Youngs was born June 24, 1851

Mary Fanny Youngs the daughter of William J. Youngs and Maria S. Youngs was born February 17th 1880

Helen Youngs the daughter of Helen Louise and William J. Youngs, was born April 20th 1887

Daniel Youngs Married Susan Kelsey

Daniel, son of Daniel and Susan Youngs Married, Maria daughter of John Baker February 23d 1815.

Daniel Kelsey son of Daniel and Maria Youngs Married Sarah Elizabeth, daughter of Daniel Smith October 10th 1850

William Jones Youngs, son of Daniel K. and Sarah E. Youngs, married Eleanor Smith Youngs daughter of David J. Youngs, who was the son of Samuel, the son of Daniel, who was the son of Daniel who was the Son of Daniel who was the son of Samuel who was the son of Thomas, who was the son of Thomas, who was the son of John Youngs May, 7, 1879. At Christ Church by Rev. C. B. Ellsworth & G. R Vandewater.

William Jones Youngs, son of Daniel K. and Sarah E. Youngs was married to Helen Louise daughter of James Mason at Trinity Chapel, New York March 31st 1886 by the Rev. W. M. Geer.

Harry Youngs Born September the 1 1787

Daniel Youngs Born January the 6 - 1791 - -

Hannah Youngs Born January the 9 - 1794 - -

Fanny Youngs Born September 21 - 1796 - -

Samuel Youngs Departed this Life November the 2d 1797 on Thursday in the 45th year of his age.

Rebekah Youngs Departed this Life January the 7 - 1802 on Thursday aged 49 years 1 Month and 17 Days.

Daniel Youngs died November 9th 1809

Susan Youngs died September 22d 1847

Maria wife of Danl Youngs died Septemb 6h 1864

Daniel Youngs Died 12 August 1874, 4 o'clock A.M.

William J. Youngs, (Son of Daniel and Maria Youngs) died on Easter Sunday March 28th 1875

Eleanor Smith Youngs, wife of William J. Youngs (2) fell asleep, on Monday, Dec. 31. 1883

Helen Louise Youngs, wife of William J. Youngs (2) fell asleep on Thursday March 21, 1889 — also her infant son.

Daniel Kelsey Youngs, died October 16, 1894

Sarah Elizabeth Smith, wife of Daniel Kelsey Youngs, died March 20, 1895.

Thomas Youngs, son of Daniel & Maria B. Youngs, died October 31, 1905.

INDEX

INDEX

Abeel, Rev. John, 25, 249
Achmuty (Aucmudy), Rev. Samuel, 53, 151, 153
Adams, Ann (m. Mayo Carrington), 36
  Richard, 36
Aldis, Rev. Charles, 196
  Charles I., 196
  Frances S. S. *See* Smith, Frances S.
Alexander, Ann, 3
  Catherine (m. 1st, Elisha Parker; 2d, Walter Rutherfurd), 172, 173
  Elizabeth, 3
  James, 172
  Rev. J., 160
  Margret, 3
  Marthor, 3
  Mary, 3
  Thomas, 3
  William, 3
  William Henry, 3
Allen, Daniel, 201
Almy, Audrey (m. James Townsend), 225
Alsop, Rev. R. F., 110, 114
Ammack (Anmack), Norma D. (m. Edward A. Hall), 245
Anderson, Elizabeth S. *See* Sanders, Elizabeth
  William, 9
  Dr. William, 93, 94, 98, 100
Anderton, Alice (m. Louis T. Montant), 230, 233
  Elizabeth P. *See* Palmer, Elizabeth
  William B., 233
Anthon, Rev. Dr. Henry, 113, 158, 230
Antill, Mrs. ——, 151
Arden, Sally (m. Philip Verplanck), 17, 276
  Thomas, 276
Armstead, William, 41
Armstrong, Alexander F., 199
Ash, John, 200
Ashfield, Mary (Molly), 151, 154
Aslop. *See* Alsop
Aspinwall, Sarah, 131

Atkines, Elizabeth B. *See* Burton, Elizabeth
  Stephen, 33
Atkinson, Anne (m. George Coggill), 196
Aucmudy. *See* Achmuty
Austin, Mrs. ——, 206
  Francis B., 165
  Francis Duane, 166
  Frederick Foss, 166
  Mary Livingston (m. Charles L. Poor), 165
  Mary N. W. *See* Weston, Mary N.
  Mehitable (m. Timothy Swan), 208
  Pauline D. F. *See* Foss, Pauline D.
  Samuel, 208
  Sarah (Mrs. Samuel Austin), 208
  William Morris, 164, 165, 166

Babcock, Beekman, 275
  Cort, 275
  Doveaux, 275
  Euphemia, 275
  Euphemia V. H. *See* Hoffman, Euphemia V.
  Frederick, 275, 276
  William, 275
Bache, Andrew Barclay, 4, 5, 6, 7, 247
  Andrew Theobald, 4, 5, 6
  Ann Dorothy, 247, 248
  Anna Maria, 5, 6
  Caroline M. *See* McVoy, Caroline
  Catherine Ann Satterthwaite (m. Rev. William Rudder), 5, 6, 7
  Charlotte (m. Francis B. Lynch), 4, 5, 6, 7
  Charlotte P. *See* Phillips, Charlotte
  Dorothy (Mrs. Theophylact Bache), 7
  Eliza Barclay (m. George F. Duckwitz), 4, 5, 7
  Eliza H. *See* Horne, Eliza
  George Perry, 4, 5, 7

Helen (m. Dr. William W. Jones), 4, 6, 7
James Theophylact, 4, 5, 6
Richard T., 5, 6
Rosabella T. *See* Trueman, Rosabella
Sarah Bleecker (m. 1st, John D. Kleudgen; 2d, Jacob R. Nevius), 4, 5, 7
Theo., 5, 6
Theophylact, 7
William Satterthwaite, 5, 7
Bailey, Charles, 247
Charlotte Amelia, 248
Julia W. S. *See* Strong, Julia W.
Dr. Richard, 248
Theodore Armstrong, 205
Baker, John, 289
Maria (m. Daniel Youngs), 288, 289, 290
Ball, John, 145
Bancker, Anna, 9
William, 9
Banker, Evert, 119
Banyer, Goldsborough, 112, 115
Goldsborough, Jr., 110, 112, 115
Maria J. *See* Jay, Maria
Sarah Jay, 112, 115
Barbarie, Catherine, 172
Barclay (Barcley, Barcly, Bartley), Andrew, 247
Andrew D., 247
Ann Dorothy, 247
Charlinne Elizabeth, 248
Charlotte Matilda, 248
Frederick Jay, 248
Helena, 247
Rev. Henry, 9, 17, 62, 64, 152, 154, 251, 253
James, 247, 248
Johannes Van Beverhoudt, 248
John, 248
Julianna Susannah, 248
Margaretta, 247
Maria, 247
Maria Van B. *See* Van Beverhoudt, Maria
Sarah Amelia, 248
Thomas, 247
Barker, Jane, 39
John, 39
Capt. John, 39

Margaret, 39
Robert, 39
Samuel, 39
Sarah, 39
Barretto, Annie C., 158, 159
Frances, 158
Francis J., 156, 158
Gerard Morris, 158
Honora S. M. *See* Morris, Honora S.
Barrol, Rev. William, 53
Bartello, Rev. ——, 22
Bartley. *See* Barclay.
Barton, Phebe (m. John G. Wright), 281
Bartow, Rev. John, 150
Basset (Bassett), Betsy, 42
John, 42
Rev. John, 29, 256
Virginia, 42
William, 42
Bates, Mary E. (m. John J. Fleet), 240
Baxter, Anna S. S. *See* Strong, Anna S.
George, 204
George Strong, 204
Bayard, Anne Maria (Marike) (m. Auguste Jay), 106, 107, 108, 109, 143, 144
Ariaentie, 143, 144
Baltazard (Balthassar), 106, 143, 144
Elizabeth, 247
Frances (m. Philip J. Livingston), 195
Jacobus, 107
Judith, 107, 144
Judith V. *See* Varlet, Judith
Magaritte, 22, 107
Marie L. *See* Loockermans, Maria
Nicholas, 143, 144
Petrus, 143, 144
Samuel, 22, 107, 143, 144
Stephen N., 248
Will, 190
Bayles, Elizabeth (m. Samuel E. Underhill), 243
Beach, Rev. A., 53, 54, 55, 131, 196
Beckerr, Ebenezer, 200
Bedell, Rev. ——, 157, 158

Bedlow, Catherine (m. Dr. Ebenezer Crosby), 8, 9, 10
  Catherine R. *See* Rutgers, Catherine
  Catherine Van H. *See* Van Horn, Catherina
  Cornelius, 8
  Elizabeth, 8, 21
  Henry, 8, 9, 10
  Mary, 8
  Mary Elizabeth Goad (m. John Beekman), 8, 9, 10, 24, 26
  Mary N. *See* Nazereth, Mary
  Peter, 8, 9
  William (Wellem), 8, 9, 24, 33, 185, 187
Beekman (Beeckman), Mrs. ——, 276
  Anna M. Van H. *See* Van Horn, Anna M.
  Catherine (m. Abraham K. Fish), 24
  Catherine, 13, 16, 17
  Catherine A. N. *See* Neilson, Catherine A.
  Catherine Bedlow, 25
  Catherine P. *See* Provoost, Catherine
  Catherine S. *See* Sanders, Catherine
  Cornelia (m. Isaac B. Cox), 99
  Cornelius, 12, 14
  David, 13, 16, 18
  Deborah, 265
  Effie (m. Philip Ver Planck), 11, 13, 16, 17, 18, 275, 276, 277
  Elizabeth, 12, 14
  Gerard, 11, 12, 14, 16, 17, 94, 98, 99, 276
  Gerard, Jr., 11, 12, 14, 15
  Gertruydt (Gertrude), 22, 172, 191
  Hendrickus, 11, 14, 16
  Jacobus (James), 14, 16, 17, 24, 25, 26, 94, 98, 249
  James W., 99
  Jane (m. Jacob Hallet Borrowe), 24, 25
  Jane (m. Stephen Van Cortlandt), 249
  Jane K. *See* Keteltas, Jane
  John, 24, 26
  John, Jr., 265, 266
  John Crosby, 25
  John Ja., 92, 97
  Lydia (m. Joseph Foulke, Jr.), 24, 26, 249
  Lydia (Mrs. James Beekman), 26
  Magdalena, 12, 13, 15
  Magdalena (m. Abraham Lynsen, Jr.), 13, 16, 17
  Magdalena (Mrs. William Beekman), 12, 15
  Maria (Mrs. John J. Beekman), 92, 97
  Mary (m. William A. De Peyster), 24, 25
  Mary E. G. B. *See* Bedlow, Mary E. G.
  Sarah (Mrs. David Beekman), 18
  Sarah Ralston, 25, 26
  William, 12, 13, 15, 16, 18, 25, 26, 249
  William Bedlow, 8, 33, 249
  Mrs. William Bedlow, 8, 24, 33, 171, 249
  William Fenwick, 24, 25
Bellamy, Elizabeth (m. Charles Sheldon), 193
  Rev. Dr. Joseph, 193
Bellomont, Countess Gravinne Van, 138, 142
Bend, Grove, 54
Bernard, Henningham C. *See* Carrington, Henningham
  John, 35
Berrian, Rev. William, 4, 56
Beyert, Mr. ——, 252, 254
  Margrita, 251, 254
Bigelow, Rev. Andrew, 210
Bisset, Rev. ——, 157
Blackgrove, Rev. Benjamin, 41
Blackwood, Henery, 201
Bleecker (Bleker), Mrs. ——, 248
  Anna (Annatje), 27, 29
  Arriantje, 29
  Blandina, 80
  Catalina (Caty) C. *See* Cuyler, Catalina
  Catherine (m. Abraham Cuyler), 28
  Catherine E. *See* Elmendorf, Catherine

Catherine Westerlo, 256, 257
Catlence (Mrs. Nicholas Bleecker), 29
Catlina (m. Barent Sanders), 94, 98
    Elizabeth, 27, 29, 80, 256
    Elizabeth Van R. *See* Van Rensselaer, Elizabeth
    G. V. S., 218
    Geertruy, 27
    Gerrit, 27
    Giertje (Gerritze), 29
    Hendryck, 27, 28
    Henry, 28, 29, 214, 215
    Jacobus, 94, 98
    James, 248, 256
    Jan Janse, 27, 28
    Jannitie (m. Johannis Glen), 28
    John (Johannis), 27, 28, 80, 256, 257
    John N., 27, 28
    John Butze, 27, 256, 257
    Margaret, 28
    Margaret (m. Harmanus Ten Eyck), 214, 215, 216, 217
    Margaret Van D. *See* Van Duessen, Margaret
    Margarrieta R. *See* Rathze, Margarrieta
    Margrieta (m. Henderick Ten Eyck), 27, 28
    Maria, 80
    Maria (m. Morris Smith Miller), 124
    Matilda Eliza (m. Jacob H. Ten Eyck, Jr.), 218
    Nelly (Mrs. Nicholas Bleecker), 214
    Nicholas, 28, 29, 214
    Peter Edmundus, 80
    Rachel, 28
    Rutger, 28, 80
    Sarah Rutger, 80
    Stephen Van Rensselaer, 256, 257
Bleg, Benjamin, 20
    Judith E. *See* Edsall, Judith
Bloggett, Abigail (m. Jacob Turk), 200
Bloodgood, Robert Fanshawe, 27
Bloomer, Rev. Joshua, 130, 131

Bochus, Mary (m. William A. Wright), 283
Boel (Böelle), Rev. Hendrick, 8, 11, 12, 13, 14, 15, 16, 107, 108, 109, 184, 185, 186
Boelen, Abraham, 184, 186
    Elizabeth, 184, 186
Bogart (Bogert), Christianna, 278
    Dolly (Mrs. Herman H. Bogert), 217
    Eliza (m. Herman Ten Eyck), 215, 216, 217, 218
    Herman H., 215, 217
Borhanns, Wyllem, 66, 68
Borrowe, Jacob Hallet, 24
    Jane B. *See* Beekman, Jane
    Samuel, 24
    Sarah H. *See* Hallett, Sarah
Bottiswood, Dick, 180
    Joseph Pettes, 178
Bouvier, Miss Z., 57
Bowen, Herbert Wolcott, 58
    Maria A. F. V. *See* Vingut, Maria A. F.
    Thomas Van Horne Floyd, 58
Boyd, Jacque, 146
Bradford, Rev. Dr. John M., 256, 281
Bradley, Jeanette Amy (m. Charles L. Strong), 204
Bradstreet, Col. John, 191
Bramhorn, M. C. B., 41
Bridge, Margaret (m. William A. S. North), 164, 165
Bridges, Rev. Thomas, 174
Bridwer, Richard, 200
Brinkerhoff, George, 19
Brinley, Catherine, 173
    Edward, 173
    Elizabeth, 173
    Francis W., 173
    Gertrude Aleph, 173
    Jennet P. *See* Parker, Jennet
    Maria, 173
Brion, Charlotte (m. Joseph Foulke), 24
Brockhurst, Mary V. *See* Verplanck, Mary
Bronson, Catherine R. (m. John H. Townsend), 242
Brown, Elizabeth Carter, 40
    Mrs. J., 42
    Judith C. *See* Carter, Judith

Judith Walker, 40
Mary Burnet (m. Herbert
  Claiborne), 40, 41, 42
Mary Crosby, 184
William Burnet, 40, 41, 42
Brownell, Rev. Dr. ——, 55
Brownley, Rev. Dr. ——, 24
Bruyn, Augustus Hasbrouck, 30
  Blandina E. See Elmendorf,
    Blandina
  Catherine, 31
  Catherine Ten B. See Ten
    Broeck, Catherine
  Edmund, 32
  Jacobus S., 30, 31, 32
  Johannis, 31
  Mary (m. —— Forsyth), 30
  Rachel, 30, 31
  Severyn, 30, 31, 32
Bull, Rev. E. C., 111, 113
Bullon, Mr. ——, 248
Bumore, Peter, 200
Bunnell, Mary, 278
Burke, Mary, 132, 247
Burnet, Rev. ——, 281
  Mary Carter, 42
Burr, Anna Foster, 215
  Catherine Ten E. See Ten
    Eyck, Catherine
  Margaret Ten Eyck, 215
  William M., 216
  William M., Jr., 215
Burt, Mr. ——, 208
Burton, Abraham, 33
  Elizabeth (m. Stephen
    Atkines), 33
  Elizabeth (Mrs. Richard
    Burton), 34
  Elizabeth D. See Denn,
    Elizabeth
  John, 33, 34
  Mary M. See Moss, Mary
  Richard, 33, 34
  Thomas, 33
  William, 33
Butler, Anthony, 46, 47, 174
  Elizabeth, 47, 48
  Elizabeth C. See Coats,
    Elizabeth
  Harriet, 47
  James, 47
  John Mifflin, 47
  Jonathan Williams, 47

Margaret, 47
Penelope (m. James Parker),
  47, 174
Thomas Willson, 47
William Coats, 46
Byands, Capt. ——, 281
Byvank, Mrs. ——, 12, 15

Cabell, Hannah C. See Carrington,
    Hannah
  Nahs, 36
Calder, James, 53
  Mary (m. Floyd Daubery), 53,
    54, 55
  Mary C. See Coventry, Mary
  Sarah Elizabeth Maria, 53
  William Coventry, 53
Caldwell, Rev. James, 110
Caminoni, Loretta C. See Coles,
    Loretta C.
  William R., 59
  Mrs. William R. See Coles,
    Loretta C.
Caniebaratz, Mons. de, 106
Cannon, John, 201
Cargill, Elizabeth, 133
  John, 132
  Richard, 133
  Mrs. Thomas, 132
Carrington, Ann A. See Adams,
    Ann
  Anne M. See Mayo, Anne
  Edward, 35
  Eliza Griffin, 36
  George, 35
  Col. George, 35, 36
  George Mayo, 36
  Hannah (m. Nahs Cabell), 36
  Henningham (m. John Bernard),
    35
  John, 36
  Joseph, 35
  Mary (m. Joseph Watkins), 36
  Mayo, 35, 36
  Nathaniel, 35
  Paul, 35
  Richard Adams, 36
  William, 35
Carson, Richard, 130
Carter, Charles, 40
  Judith (m. William Burnet
    Brown), 40, 41
Catheson, Daniel, 201

Chadwick, Cornelia J. M. *See*
    Miller, Cornelia J.
  Capt. Daniel, 124
  Eliza E. *See* Evans, Eliza
  French Ensor, U. S. N., 121, 124
  Mrs. French Ensor. *See* Miller,
    Cornelia Jones
Chambers, Anna, 63
  Rev. George S., 117
Chardon, Marie M. *See* Mazyck,
    Marie
Charleton, Rev. Richard, 63, 182
Chase, Rev. ——, 130
Chauncey, Abigail, 37, 38
    Abigail D. *See* Darling,
      Abigail
    Charles, 37, 38
    Elihu, 37, 38
    Elizabeth C., 38
    Hannah, 38
    Henrietta, 38
    Mary (Mrs. Elihu Chauncey),
      37, 38
    Nathaniel, 37, 38
    Rev. P. S., 111, 113
    Sarah (m. —— Savage), 38
    Sarah (m. —— Woolsey), 37, 38
Chevet, Mary, 9
Childers, Rev. C., 114
Church, Angelica S. *See* Schuyler,
    Angelica
  Elizabeth, 39
  Elizabeth (Mrs. Richard
    Church), 39
  Jane, 39
  John, 39
  John Barker, 39
  Matilda, 39
  Philip Schuyler, 39
  Richard, 39
  Samuel, 39
Claiborne, Ann, 40
  Augusta Brown, 42
  Augustine, 40
  Col. Augustine, 40, 41, 42
  Bathurst, 40
  Betty Carter Bassett, 40, 42
  Butler, 40
  Elizabeth, 40
  Harriot Herbert, 41
  Herbert, 40, 41, 42
  Herbert Augustine, 40, 41, 42
  Howard, 41
  John Herbert, 40
  Judith (Judey) Brown, 41, 42
  L. B., 41
  Lavinia Bathurst, 42
  Lavinia Herbert, 41
  Lucy Herbert, 40
  Mary, 40
  Mary B. B. *See* Brown,
    Mary B.
  Mary Carter Burnet, 41, 42
  Mary H. *See* Herbert, Mary
  Octavia, 42
  Polly Nuffin, 42
  Richard Cook, 40
  Sukey, 40
  Thomas, 40
  William, 40, 41, 42
  William Burnet Brown, 41
Clark, Alexander, 43, 44
  David, 43, 44
  Emma (m. Edward Dudley), 70
  Femmitje V. *See* Van Borsum,
    Femmitje
  Henry Schieffelin, 43, 44
  John, 43, 44
  John, Jr., 44
  Rev. Dr. Rufus W., 100, 218
  Scot Lawrence, 43, 44
  Thomas, 43, 44
  William Newton, 44
  William Newton, Jr., 44
Clarkson, David, 111
  Mary Rutherfurd (m. Peter A.
    Jay), 110, 112, 113, 114, 115
  Mathew, 110, 111, 114, 117
  Susan M. J. *See* Jay, Susan M.
Clay, Marianne (m. Edward A.
    Strong), 204
Clinton, Gov. ——, 8
  Catherine, 8
Clute, Betsy (m. Thomas Foraker),
    200
  Esther (m. Beriah Phelps), 201
  John, 200
Coats, Elizabeth (m. Anthony
    Butler), 45, 46, 47
  Harriet, 46
  Joseph, 45, 46
  Margaret, 45, 46
  Margaret (m. Richard W.
    Meade), 48
  Margaret N. *See* Norris,
    Margaret

Mary, 46
Sarah (m. Samson Levy), 46, 47, 48
Thomas, 47
Col. William, 45, 46, 47, 48
William Louis, 47
William Pitt, 45, 46
Cock, Daniel, 221
　Deborah, 221
　Dorothy, 222
　Elizabeth, 221
　Gabriel, 222
　Hezekiah, 220, 222
　James, 221
　John, 220, 222
　Penn, 220
　Phiany, 221
　Roseannah (Mrs. Hezekiah Cock), 222
　Roseannah T. See Townsend, Roseannah
　Sarah, 222
　Susannah Y. See Youngs, Susannah
　Thomas, 221
　Townsend, 221
　Violetah, 222
　William, 221
Cocks, Elizabeth E. F. See Fleet, Elizabeth E.
　Joshua, 241
Coggill, Anne A. See Atkinson, Anne
　Anne Eudora, 196
　Charles I., 196
　George, 196
　Henry, 196
　Mary Anne (m. John William Smyth), 196
Cok, Rev. ——, 286
Colden, Cadwalader, 30
Cole, Cornelius, 78
　Elizabeth E. See Elmendorf, Elizabeth
Coles, Abigail (Mrs. Jarvis Coles), 223
　Butler, 59, 60, 61, 229
　Charlotte (m. Walter W. Townsend), 223
　Elizabeth (Lizzie) Aurelia, 60, 61, 229
　Elizabeth T. See Townsend, Elizabeth

Esther T. See Townsend, Esther
George T., 60, 229
Hannah (m. William Neilson), 24
Hannah (Mrs. Nath. Coles), 223, 224
Jarvis, 223
John Townsend, 224
Loretta C. (m. William R. Caminoni), 59, 60, 88, 102, 219, 225, 229, 275
Mary E. T. See Townsend, Mary E.
Nathaniel, 223, 224, 229
Nathaniel, Jr., 219
Roseannah (m. George Townsend II), 219, 220
Thomas, 223, 224
Collins (Collens), Mrs. ——, 21, 22, 252, 254
　Anna Dudley, 71
　Cornelia, 71
　Edward, 22
　Edward Dudley, 71
　Emma D., 71
　Jan, 251, 252, 253, 254
　John, 22
　Margrite, 251, 253
　Mary E. D. See Dudley, Mary E.
　Mary S., 71
　Sarah, 71
　Stacy B., 70
　Theodore, 71
Colson, Betsey (m. Peter Bumore), 200
Comstock, Ruth (m. Rev. Nicholas Van Vranken), 273
Conklin, Catherine (m. Rev. Nicholas Van Vranken), 273
Conseilliere. See La Conseilliere
Cook, Nancy (m. Edward Tabor), 201
　Sally (m. John Cannon), 201
Cooper, Robert, 239
　Sarah (m. Samuel Townsend), 239
Copelin, Rectina (m. Benjamin Hosley), 200
Corbett, Mary (m. Henry Ludlow), 154

Cornbury (Correnberrie), Lady, 250, 253
Cortlandt. *See* Van Cortlandt
Corwin, Elizabeth (m. John Wright, Jr.), 49, 50, 51
  James, 49
  Leah J. *See* Johnson, Leah
  Mahetable H. *See* Horton, Mahetable
  Sarah Ann, 49
  William, 49, 50
Cossevat, Rev. ———, 157
Coventry, Ann (m. Richard Grant), 52, 54
  Elizabeth, 52, 54
  Elizabeth H. *See* Hart, Elizabeth
  Dr. John, 53, 54
  Mary (m. James Calder), 52, 53
  Sarah (m. Christopher Miller), 52, 53, 54
  Susannah, 54
  William, 52, 53
  William, Jr., 52, 53
Covert, Adolphus, 60, 61
  Aurelia, 229
  Caleb, 60
  Elizabeth C. (m. George W. Townsend), 59, 60, 61, 228, 229
  Frances Gertrude, 60, 61, 229
  Frances T. *See* Townsend, Frances
  Frost, 60
  Hannah, 60, 61
  Isaac, 59, 60, 61
  Jacob, 60
  Jacob F., 59, 60, 61, 228, 229
  James, 229
  Lorette (Mrs. Isaac Covert), 59, 61
  Margaret, 229
  Micah, 60
  William F., 60, 229
Cox, Anne Helme Townsend (Mrs. Townsend Cox), 122, 124
  Catherine Mary (m. Jacob Glen Sanders), 99, 100
  Cornelia B. *See* Beekman, Cornelia
  Isaac B., 99
  Maria D. B. M. *See* Miller, Maria D. B.
  Townsend, 122, 124
  Wilmot Townsend, 122, 124
  Mrs. Wilmot T. *See* Miller, Maria D. B.
Coxeter, Rev. Thomas, 132, 133
Coymans, Mrs. ———, 150
Craft, Almira E. (m. Samuel E. Underhill), 244
Craig, John, 130
  Margarita M., 130
Crary, Edward, 81
  Giles R., 82
  John S., 82
  Lucretia, 81
  Lucretia P. *See* Palmer, Lucretia
  Peter, 81, 82
  Peter, Jr., 82
  Phebe, 81
Creed, Sary (m. Peter Johnson), 118
Crommelin, Elizabeth, 131
  Robert, 131
Crosby, Catherine B. *See* Bedlow, Catherine
  Dr. Ebenezer, 8, 10
  Frederic V. S., 267
  Henry Rutgers, 10
  William Bedlow, 10
Cruger, Ann D. *See* Delancey, Ann
  Dorothea, 258
  Elizabeth (m. Peter Van Schaack), 63, 258, 259
  Elizabeth H. *See* Harris, Elizabeth
  Geleman, 63
  Henry, 62, 258, 259
  Henry, Jr., 258
  Henry H., Jr., 260
  John, 62, 63, 258, 259
  John, Jr,, 63
  John Harris, 157, 258
  John Harry, 64
  Mary, 258
  Mary (m. Jacob Walton), 63, 64
  Nicholas, 63
  Rachiel, 63
  Sarah, 63
Cumstock, Patty (m. Henry Ten Broeck), 266
Curtis, Elizabeth, 145

Cutting, Rev. ——, 130
Cuyler (Cuiler), Abraham, 28
    Anna (m. Anthony Van Schayck), 261, 262, 263, 264
    Catalina (Caty) (m. Henry Bleecker), 191, 214, 215
    Catherine B. See Bleecker, Catherine
    Cornelius, 191, 262, 264
    Cristine, 262, 264
    Henry, 173
    Johannes, 261, 262, 263, 264
    Mrs. Johannes, 261, 262, 263, 264

Darling, Abigail (m. Charles Chauncey), 37, 38
    Abigail (Mrs. Thomas Darling), 37
    Thomas, 37
Darrow, Emma (m. Julius C. Morrison), 161
Daubery, Mrs. ——, 54
    Charlotte Coventry, 55
    Eliza Martin (m. Henry Waddell), 55
    Elizabeth Ann, 55
    Floyd, 53, 55
    Floyd Saxbury, 55
    Mary C. See Calder, Mary
Davis, Rev. Price, 41
Dawson (Dofson), Dr. ——, 149
    Mary Jay, 114
    Sarah J. See Jay, Sarah
    William, 110, 115
    William Pudsey, 114, 116
Day, Ann (m. A. T. Ellithorp), 201
    Sarah Eliza (m. 1st, William M. Johnson; 2d, Edward M. Townsend), 230, 232, 233
    Sophia (m. Nehemiah Wing), 201
Dean, Mrs. Bashford, 74
De Baussay, Francois, 106
Delameter, Abraham, 65, 66, 67, 68
    Abraham D., Jr., 67
    Catharinna, 66, 68
    Cornelia, 66, 68
    Cornelis, 66, 68
    David (Davit, Daviet), 66, 68, 69
    Elsie, 65, 67

Englittje E. See Elmendorf, Engeltye
    Jacobus, 66, 68
    Jannety, 65, 67
    Johanis (Johannes), 30, 65, 66, 67, 68
    Maragreta (m. Jan Elmendorf), 76, 77
    Maria (Mary) (Mrs. Johannes Delameter), 30, 66, 68
    Ragel, 65, 66, 68
    Ragel L. See Low, Ragel
Delancey (De Lancy, Delansie), ——, 252, 254
    Rev. ——, 55
    Anna, 190
    Ann (m. John H. Cruger), 64, 157
    Elizabeth F. See Floyd-Jones, Elizabeth
    John Peter, 85, 86
    Oliver, 63, 64
    Susanna, 172
De Lanoy (Dela Noye), Abraham, 20
    Peter, 20
Delius (Van Dell), Rev. Godevridus (Goodwirkies), 21, 135, 137, 138, 139, 141, 142
    Mrs. Godevridus, 138, 142
De Luze, Grace Schuyler, 255
Denn, Elizabeth (m. John Burton), 33
De Peyster, Abraham, 24, 108, 138, 142
    Anna, 184, 186
    Catherine (m. Hendrick Rutgers), 8, 9, 184, 185
    Catherine A. L. See Livingston, Catherine A.
    Gerardus, 9
    John, Jr., 120
    Margarite, 108
    Mary B. See Beekman, Mary
    William (Wellem), 184, 186, 249
    William A., 24
Dering, Dr. Nicoll H., 204
    Sally H. S. See Strong, Sally H.
Dermon, Walran, 269
De Ronde, Rev. Lambardus, 129, 285
    Sabina, 285
d'Este, Baron Charles, 57

Mary E. K. V. *See* Vingut,
Mary E. K.
Deveaux, Andrew, 18, 276, 277
Anna M. V. *See* Verplanck,
Anna M.
De Wint, Elizabeth (Mrs. Gant Sp.
De Wint), 247, 248
Gant Sp., 247
John, 248
De Witt, Charles, 286
Dircksen. *See* Van Vechten
Dix, Rev. Dr. ——, 230
Doll, Rev. ——, 32, 77, 286
Dongan, Gov. Thomas, 135, 137, 139, 141
Dorling, Rebecky (m. Henery
Blackwood), 201
Dofson. *See* Dawson
Dounken, Caethrinae, 90, 94
Downs, Ann (m. Thomas Morrison), 161, 162
Drawyer, Gerretie, 22
Driesyas, Rev. Samuel, 19
Droither, Paul, 106
Duane, James C., 123
Maria Bowers (m. Samuel W.
Jones), 122, 123, 124
Mary (m. Gen. William North), 164
Mary Ann (Marianne) (Mrs.
James C. Duane), 123
Du Bois, Catherine H. J. *See* Jay,
Catherine H.
Rev. Gualtherus (Gualtus), 11,
12, 13, 14, 15, 16, 107, 108,
184, 186, 187
Henry Augustus, 111
Ducey, Rev. ——, 230
Duckwitz, Charlotte Gesima (m.
—— Dudley), 4
Eliza B. B. *See* Bache,
Eliza B.
George Frederick, 4, 7
Dudley, Alfred Ely, 72
Ann, 70
Anna Peters, 73
Anne (Mrs. Eleazar Dudley), 72
Caroline, 73
Charles, 70
Charlotte, 72
Charlotte Elizabeth, 4, 70, 247
Charlotte G. D. *See* Duckwitz,
Charlotte G.

Cornelia Collins, 73
Edward, 70, 72
Edward, Jr., 73
Eleazar, 72
Elizabeth, 72
Elizabeth E. *See* Evans,
Elizabeth
Emma C. *See* Clark, Emma
Emma Louisa, 73
Frances, 72
Henry, 72
Jane, 72
John, 70, 72, 73
Margaret, 70
Mary, 73
Mary Ann, 72
Mary E. (m. Stacy B. Collins), 70, 71
Mary E. *See* Eves, Mary
Mary L. P. *See* Peters,
Mary L.
Samuel, 70, 73
Samuel Sheldon, 72, 73
Sarah, 70
Sheldon, 72, 73
William E., 70
Dr. William Henry, 70, 72
Dull. *See* Doll
Dumont, Elizabeth, 286
Jannetye (m. Michiel D. Van
Vechten), 269
Jannetye (Mrs. Pieter Dumont), 269
Pieter, 269
Duncan, Margaretta, 247
Thomas, 247
Dunham, Ann, 173
Carroll, 173
Edward, 173
James, 173
John, 173
Maria P. *See* Parker, Maria
Dunn, Elizabeth S. *See* Stansbury,
Elizabeth
Mary Berthenia (m. John B.
Miller), 121, 124
Rev. S. Ballard, 121, 124
Dunscomb, Andrew, 8
Dwight, Catherine T. *See* Ten
Broeck, Catherine
Rev. Maurice W., 266
Dyckman, Abraham, 74, 75
Charity, 75

Frederick, 75
Hannah, 75
Hannah (Mrs. Jacobus Dyckman), 75
Isaac, 75
Jacob, 75
Jacobus, 74, 75
James, 75
Jane, 74
Jemima (Jamima), 74
John, 74, 75
Maria, 75
Mary, 74
Mary T. See Turner, Mary
Michael, 74, 75
William, 74, 75
Dyer, Mary (m. Christopher Robert), 182, 183

Earle, Rev. Marmaduke, 123, 283
Eastburn (Easburn), Rev. Manton, 157
Edickson (Erickson), Mr. ——, 13, 16
Edsall, Anna, 20
    Joanna, 19
    Judith (m. Benjamin Bleg), 20
    Samuel, 20
Edwards, Alfred, 168
    Amy, 167
    Frances O. See Ogden, Frances
    Gerard Morris, 158
    Henrietta, 168
    Henry, 168
    John Stark, 168
    Jonathan, 111, 117, 156, 158
    Mary J. J. See Jay, Mary J.
    Mary Morris, 158
    Mary P. M. See Morris, Mary (Minny) P.
    Ogden, 168
    Pierrepont, 167
    Polly Susanna, 168
Elberson, Joseph W., 245
    Margaret T. U. See Underhill, Margaret T.
    Marian Underhill, 245
Eldridge, Mary (m. John Miller), 149
Ellison, Rev. Thomas, 110
Ellithorp, A. T., 201
    Abby Ann, 199
    Abigail, 199

    Ann D. See Day, Ann
    Azariah, 199
    Betsy, 199
    E. L., 199
    Effa R. See Russell, Effa
    Eliza, 199
    Emily, 199
    Isaac, 199, 200
    Jacob, 199
    John, 199
    Mary Ann, 199
    Mehitable (m. Samuel Stimson), 198
    Sally, 199
    Solomon, 199
    Wiley, 199
    Zenis, 199
Ellsworth, Rev. C. B., 289
    Oliver, 145
Elmendorf (Elmendorph, Elvendorph), Abraham, 77, 78
    Antye, 77
    Arreantye (Arreyaantye), 77
    Benjamin, 77
    Blandina (m. Jacobus S. Bruyn), 31, 32, 79
    Catherine (m. Rutger Bleecker), 79, 80
    Catherine T. See Ten Broeck, Catherine
    Coenraadt, 77
    Coernelus, 76, 77, 78
    Elizabeth, 32, 79
    Elizabeth (m. Cornelius Cole), 76, 78
    Engeltye (Englittje) (m. Abraham D. Delameter, Jr.), 67, 77
    Engeltye H. See Heermans, Engeltye
    Jacob, 77
    James, 78
    Jan, 76, 77, 78
    Jane, 78
    John, 79
    Jonathan, 32
    Lucas, 32
    Margaret, 78
    Maragreta D. See Delameter, Maragreta
    Maria (m. Peter Sanders), 94, 98
    Martyn, 76
    Mary, 32

Mary (Mrs. Petrus E. Elmendorf), 79
Peter, 94, 98
Petrus Edmundus, 31, 32, 79
Sally (Sarah), 32, 79
Tobeyas, 77
William, 79
Eltinge, Jan, 66, 68
   Raghel H. *See* Haesbroeck, Raghel
Elvendorph. *See* Elmendorf
Emerson, Mary P. (m. Richard H. Morris), 155
   Thomas, 155
English, Rev. Dr. ——, 248
Erickson, Rev. Rynhert, 12, 15
Ernest, Matthew, 286
Evans, Eliza (m. Daniel Chadwick), 124
   Elizabeth (m. Sheldon Dudley), 72
Eves, Mary (m. Edward Dudley), 70

Feabruly, Azariah, 199
Fearing, Eleanor Burrill (m. Charles E. Strong), 205
Field (Feild), Benjamin, 271
   E. R. (m. John Jay), 111
   H. W., 111
   Jeremiah, 268, 270, 271
   Jeremiah, Jr., 272
   John, 270, 271
   Margaret, 271
   Margaret (Mrs. John Field), 270
   Margret F. *See* Fisher, Margret
   Mary V. *See* Van Vechten, Mary
   Marytyes, 270, 271, 272
   Michael, 271, 272
   Pheba (Mrs. Jeremiah Field, Jr.), 272
   Susannah, 272
   Tunes, 272
Firth, Emilie L. *See* Lesher, Emilie
   John, 233
   Therese (m. Howard R. Townsend), 230, 231, 233
Fish, Abraham K., 24
   Catherine B. *See* Beekman, Catherine B.
   Daniel, 81
   John, 24
   Rebecca P. *See* Palmer, Rebecca
   Sarah, 81
   Sarah K. *See* Keteltas, Sarah
Fisher, Margret (m. Tunes Field), 272
Fitch, Eliphalet, 133
   Joseph, 133
   Mary, 133
Flansburgh, Betsey (m. Joseph Flansburgh), 200
   Joseph, 200
   Mariah (m. David Gilbert), 201
Fleet, Arnold, 240, 241, 246
   Clara A. S. *See* Street, Clara A.
   Elizabeth E. (m. Joshua Cocks), 241
   Ernest Crosby, 240
   George B., 240
   James, 240, 246
   John James, 240, 246
   Joseph F., 240, 246
   Judith T. *See* Townsend, Judith
   Maria P. S. *See* Seaman, Maria P.
   Mary E. B. *See* Bates, Mary E.
   Mary W., 240
   Millicent Townsend, 240
   Roswell C., 240
   Samuel U., 241
   Susan F., 240
   Susannah T. U. *See* Underhill, Susannah T.
Floyd, Ann, 84
   Ann (Mrs. Benjamin Floyd), 84
   Arabella J. *See* Jones, Arrabella
   Augusta V. *See* Van Horn, Augusta
   Benjamin, 55, 57, 83, 84
   Charity, 83
   David Van Horne, 55, 56, 57
   Elizabeth, 83
   Elizabeth (Mrs. Richard Floyd), 83, 84
   Elizabeth F. K. *See* Kermit, Elizabeth F.
   Ewnes, 83

Gilbert, 83, 84
Henry Kermit, 56
John, 83
Margaret, 83, 84
Mary, 84
Nicol, 83
Richard, 83, 84
Richard, Jr., 83, 85, 86
Richard, Sr., 83
Col. Richard, 84, 85, 86
Rosamund Miller, 55, 57
Ruth, 83
Samuel, 84
Dr. Samuel, 55
Sarah Augusta (m. George T. Vingut), 56, 57, 58
Susanna, 83
William Samuel, 84
Floyd-Jones (Jones), Andrew Onderdonck, 87
   Anna Willett (m. Benjamin Nicoll), 85, 86
   Arrabella, 86, 87
   Cornelia H. J. *See* Jones, Cornelia H.
   David Richard, 85, 86, 87, 123
   David Richard, Jr., 86, 87
   David Thomas, 86, 87
   Edward H., 83, 169, 170
   Elbert, 86
   Elizabeth (m. John P. Delancey), 85, 86
   Henry, 86, 169
   Henry Onderdonck, 87
   Sally O. *See* Onderdonck, Sally
   Sarah Maria (m. Coleman Williams), 86, 87
   Thomas, 85, 86, 87, 122, 123
   Gen. Thomas, 86
   William, 86
Fonda, Rebecca (m. Col. Johannes Knickerbacker), 125, 126, 127
Foraker, Thomas, 200
Forbes, Rev. I. M., 196
Forsyth, Katherine Bruyn, 30
   Mary B. *See* Bruyn, Mary Petronella Bruyn, 30
Foss, Pauline Dexter (m. William M. Austin), 166
Foster, Andrew, 215, 216
   Anna T. *See* Ten Eyck, Anna
   Herman Ten Eyck, 215

Jacob Post Girard, 215
Margaret Ten Eyck, 215
Mary, 171
Nancy (m. Ephraim Morrison), 161, 163
Foulke, Catherine (m. John Neilson), 249
   Charlotte B. *See* Brion, Charlotte
   Joseph, 24, 249
   Lydia B. *See* Beekman, Lydia
Fraker, Lavina (m. Richard Bridwer), 200
France, Arenos, 146
Francois, Elizabeth, 106
   Rev. Isaac, 106
   Judith (m. Pierre Jay), 106
   Marie, 106
Franklin, Mrs. Benjamin W., 260
   Deborah (Mrs. John Franklin), 224
   John, 224
   Rebecca (m. John Townsend), 224
Frazer, Rev. William, 173, 279, 287
Freeman, Rev. Barnardus, 8, 21, 22
   Margaret, 22
Frelinghuysen (Frelinckhuyse, Vreelinghuysen), Rev. Theodoris Jacobus, 265, 270
Frost, Amey, 88
   Caleb, 88
   Elizabeth, 88
   Grace (Mrs. Jacob Frost), 88
   Hannah, 88
   Jacob, 88
   Joseph, 88
   Martha (Mrs. Joseph Frost), 88
   Micah, 88
   Sarah, 88
   Sarah (Mrs. Stephen Frost), 224
   Sarah T. *See* Townsend, Sarah
   Stephen, 224
   William, 224
   Wright, 88
Fryenmoet, Rev. ——, 259

Gaesbeek, ——, 66, 68
Gage, ——, 173
Galbraith, Katherine M. S. *See* Sanders, Catherine M.

Mrs. W. W. *See* Sanders,
    Catherine M.
William Winton, U. S. N., 101
Gansevoort, Leonard, Jr., 258
Garretson, F. T., 114
    Helen J. P. *See* Prime,
        Helen J.
Geer, Rev. William M., 230, 289
Gilbert, David, 201
    Luke, 201
Giliaen, Rev. ——, 270
Gilliland, James, 89
    Judith, 89
    Judith R. *See* Roose, Judith
    Nicholas, 89
Glen, Abraham, 91, 95
    Alexander, 91, 92, 95, 96
    Alexander Lenders, 90, 94
    Annae, 92, 96
    Antye, P. *See* Peeck, Antye
    Catrinae, 92, 96
    Deborah (m. John Sanders), 91, 92, 93, 95, 96, 97, 99
    Helenae, 92, 96
    Jacob Sanders, 90, 92, 93, 94, 96, 97
    Col. Jacob Sanders, 90, 91, 95
    Jacquemyna, 92, 96
    Jannitie B. *See* Bleecker, Jannitie
    Johannis, 28, 92, 96
    Johannis Sanders, 90, 91, 94, 95, 96
    John S., 93, 97
    Maregretae, 91, 95
    Mariae, 92, 96
    Maria W. *See* Wemp, Maria
    Sara (Mrs. John S. Glen), 93, 97
    Sarah W. *See* Wendel, Sarah
Goad, Elizabeth, 9
Godin, Benjamin, 147
Goodwin, Maggie Maie (m. Julius C. Morrison), 160
Goold, Sarah, 131
Gordon, Catherine, Duchess of, 151, 152, 154
    James, 18, 22, 276
    Melinda (m. William B. Verplanck), 18, 22, 23, 276
Gouverneur, ——, 150
    Anne Elizabeth (m. Cortlandt L. Parker), 174

Anthony, 174
Margaret, 151, 152
Nicholas, 151
Sarah (m. Lewis Morris), 150, 151, 152
Graham, Mrs. ——, 151, 153
Grandin, Mary (m. John Vought), 279, 287
Grant, Ann, 133
    Ann C. *See* Coventry, Ann
    Nathaniel, 132
    Nathaniel Philip, 54
    Rev. Percy, 124
    Richard, 54
Greenough, A. M. (Mrs. William Greenough), 233
    Alice (m. Edward M. Townsend, Jr.), 230, 233, 239
    William, 233
Greer, The Rt. Rev. David H., 230
Grier, Rev. Isaa, 163
Groebeck (Groesbeck), Davidt, 262, 263, 264
Gunn, Rev. Alexander, 26

Haesbroeck, Raghel (m. Jan Eltinge), 66, 68
Hale, Charlotte E. P. *See* Hale, Elizabeth P.
    Elizabeth, 178
    Elizabeth H. H. *See* Henderson, Elizabeth H.
    Elizabeth Prescott, 177, 178, 180, 181
    Lucy F. S. *See* Searcy, Lucy F.
    Lucy Prescott, 178
    Thomas, 177
    Thomas, Jr., 177, 178
    Thomas, III, 178
Hall, Abigail K. U. *See* Underhill, Abigail K.
    Agnes Louise, 245
    Arthur William, 245
    Edward A., 245
    Florence Underhill, 245
    Gilbert Phelps, 245
    Ida Louise, 245
    Isaac F., 245
    Jasper, 133
    Norma A. *See* Ammack, Norma D.
    Peter, 248
    Theodore Edward, 245

William A., 245
Hallett, Sarah (m. Samuel Borrowe), 24
Hamilton, Col. John, 171
Hammel, Rev. William, 131
Hand, Amy (Mrs. Isaac Hand), 203
   Capt. Isaac, 203
   Mary (Mrs. Isaac Hand), 203
Hansen, Sara, 262, 264
Harcourt, Susannah (m. John Townsend), 225
Harden, Roger, 145
Hare, Lydia (m. Frederick Prime), 111
   Robert, 111
Haring (Herring), Cornelia (m. Samuel Jones), 119, 120, 121
   Elbert, 119, 120
   Elizabeth (Mrs. Elbert Haring), 119, 120
   Mary, 120
   Sarah, 120
Harris, Elizabeth (m. Henry Cruger), 62, 64
   Mary, 62
   Dr. Nicholas, 62
   Saye (Mrs. Nicholas Harris), 62
   Thomas, 62
Hart, Elizabeth (m. William Coventry), 52, 54
   Rev. Seth, 123, 124
Hasbrouck, Abraham, 30
   Catherine (Mrs. Abraham Hasbrouck), 30
Hathaway, Harold B., 244
   Dr. James A., 244
   James Henry, 244
   Luisa E. U. See Underhill, Luisa E.
Hawks, Rev. Dr. Francis L., 5, 24, 111, 112, 113
Hays, Thomas, 153
Heathcote, —— (m. Lewis Johnstone), 175
Hedden, Job, 99
Heermans, Engeltye (m. Cornelius Elmendorf), 76, 77
Henderson, Elizabeth Hall (m. Thomas Hale, Jr.), 177, 178
Hendricks, Wybrecht (m. Harmanus Van Borsum), 43
Herbert, Butler, 40
   Mary (m. Col. Augustine Claiborne), 40, 41
Herring. See Haring
Hewit, Lois (m. Josiah Martin), 201
Hicks, Mary (m. James Townsend), 225, 226
Higbie, Rev. Edward, 56
Hill, John, 247
   Mary, 248
Hillhouse, Anna T. See Ten Broeck, Anna V.
   Margaret P., 273
   Thomas, 266
Hills, Betsey (m. Obediah Perry), 200
Hinds, John, 200
Hobart, The Rt. Rev. ——, 7, 55
Hoffman, Anthony Anthony, 17, 276, 277
   Beekman Ver Planck, 102, 229, 275, 276, 277
   Catherine V. See Verplanck, Catherine
   Charles Edward, 275
   Euphemia Ver Planck (m. Frederick Babcock), 275, 276
   Gertrude Ver Planck (m. William C. Uhlhorn), 102, 229
   Gertruy V. See Verplanck, Gertruy
   Herman (Harman, Hartman), 17, 276
   Margaret Townsend, 102, 229
   Mary Cromline, 102, 229
   Phoebe W. T. See Townsend, Phoebe W.
   Samuel Anthony Deveaux, 275, 277
   Sarah, 154
Hole, Abraham, 145
Holland, George B., 160
   Sarah E. M. See Morrison, Sarah E.
Hollis, James, 161
   Mary (m. Robert J. Skinner), 160, 161, 162
   Phebe (Mrs. James Hollis), 161
Hone, Rev. Dr. ——, 55
Horne, Eliza (m. George P. Bache), 4
   Dr. T., 4
Horton, Mahetable (m. James Corwin), 49

William, 49
Hosley, Benjamin, 200
Houghtaling, Jeremiah, 103
    Mary R. *See* Roosa, Mary
    Thomas, 103
Howard, Cornelia A. K. *See*
    Ketchum, Cornelia A.
    Henry Seaman, 266
    Ten Broeck, 266
Howland, Dr. Robert, 113, 115
Hude, Adam, 104, 105
    Agnes, 105
    Andrew, 105
    James, 105
    John, 105
    Marion (Mrs. Adam Hude),
      104, 105
    Mary, 105
    Robert, 104, 105
Huggins, Sally (m. Jotham Weeks), 203
Humfreville, David, 161
    Elizabeth (Mrs. David Humfreville), 161
    Sarah H. (m. Thomas Morrison), 160, 161, 162
Hunt, Ellen (m. Lewis R. Morris), 155
    Jemima (m. Stephen Stedmond), 200
    Jonathan, 155
    Leveriah (Mrs. Jonathan Hunt), 155
Huntington, Rev. W. R., 230
Huss, Rev. ——, 152
Hyslep, Josephine (m. Dr. William E. Miller), 56
    Robert, 56

Ingles, Frances, 133
Inglis, Rev. Charles, 55, 247
Ingolsby (Ingoldesby), Richard, 136, 138, 140, 142
Ingraham, Alfred, 48
    Elizabeth M. *See* Meade, Elizabeth M.
Ireland, Rev. ——, 156
    Joseph, 241
    Mary A. (Mrs. Joseph Ireland), 241
    Susan R. T. *See* Townsend, Susan R.

Jacob, Mauris, 20, 21
    Peter, 20, 21
Janeway, Rev. ——, 4
Jans, Ariaentie (m. Govert Loockermans), 143, 144
    Marretie, 143, 144
Jay, Alice, 113, 117
    Anne, 107, 111, 116
    Ann Maginetes, 248
    Ann Maria, 113, 116
    Anna Maria (m. Henry E. Pierrepont), 111, 112, 113
    Anna Marike, 109
    Anne M. B. *See* Bayard, Anne M.
    Augusta M. *See* McVicker, Augusta
    Auguste (Augustus), 106, 107, 108, 109, 113, 114, 115
    Catherine Helena (m. Henry A. Du Bois), 111, 112
    Cornelia, 113, 117
    E. R. F. *See* Field, E. R.
    Edith Van Cortlandt, 113
    Elizabeth Clarkson, 112, 113, 116
    Eue, 108
    Francoise (m. Frederick Van Cortlandt), 106, 107, 108, 109
    Frederick, 248
    Harriette A. V. *See* Vinton, Harriette A.
    Isaac, 106
    Jacobus (James), 108
    John, 110, 111, 112, 113, 114, 115, 116
    Gov. [John], 116
    John Clarkson, 112, 113, 115, 116, 117
    Dr. John Clarkson, 110, 111, 113, 117
    John Clarkson, Jr., 114, 117
    John Clarkson, III, 113, 117
    Josephine P. *See* Pearson, Josephine
    Judith (m. Cornelius Van Horn), 106, 107, 108, 109
    Judith F. *See* Francois, Judith
    Julia P. *See* Post, Julia
    Laura (m. Charles P. Wurts), 111, 112, 113, 117
    Laura P. *See* Prime, Laura

Marguerite, 106
Marguerite M. S. *See* Soleliac, Marguerite M.
Maria (m. Goldsborough Banyer, Jr.), 110, 111, 112, 113, 116
Maria Arnold, 114, 115
Marie (m. Pierre Vallete), 106, 107, 109
Marie V. *See* Van Cortlandt, Marie
Mary J. (m. Jonathan Edwards), 111, 113, 117
Mary Rutherfurd (m. Frederick Prime), 110, 112, 114, 115
Mary R. C. *See* Clarkson, Mary R.
Matilda Coster, 113, 116
Matte, 108
Pierre (Peter), 106, 107, 108, 113, 114
Peter Augustus, 110, 111, 112, 113, 114, 115, 116, 117
Peter Augustus, Jr., 112
Rev. Peter A., 110, 114, 115, 116
Sarah, 113, 116
Sarah (m. William Dawson), 110, 112, 115
Sarah Livingston, 117
Sarah Louisa, 112, 115
Sarah V. L. *See* Livingston, Sarah V.
Susan, 111, 115
Susan Matilda (m. Mathew Clarkson), 111, 112, 117
William, 110, 111, 112, 114, 116
Jenny, Rev. Robert, 150
Johnson, ——, 109
Dr. ——, 152
Alex., 118
Cattrin, 118
Elizabeth, 50
Fanny (m. Ira D. Mosher), 201
Gershem, 50
Hannah, 50
Harman, 49, 50, 51
John, 118
Rev. John B., 256
Kattren, 118
Leah (m. William Corwin), 49
Lena, 118
Louisa Anna (m. Robert C. Townsend), 230, 233

Margaret, 118
Nelly, 118
Nicholas, 118
Peter, 118
Phebe, 50
Phebe (Mrs. Harman Johnson), 49
Sarah, 49, 118
Sarah (m. Philip P. Livingston), 132
Sary C. *See* Creed, Sary
Sarah D. *See* Day, Sarah E.
William, 49, 50, 118
Dr. William, 62
William Martin, 232, 233
Johnston (Johnstone, Johnson), Andrew, 171, 174, 175, 195
Ann, 172
Catherine, 171
Catherine V. *See* Van Cortlandt, Catherine
David, 152
Eupham, 174
Eupham S. *See* Scott, Eupham
George, 175
Isabell, 174, 175
James, 171, 175
Jennet (m. John Parker), 171, 175
John, 174
Dr. John, 171, 174, 175, 195
Major John, 171
John A., 172
Kathrin, 174
Lewis, 171, 172, 175
Magdalane, 152
Margaret (m. Lawrence Smith), 174, 195, 196
Mary, 171, 172, 175
William, 174
Jones, Arrabella (m. Richard Floyd, Jr.), 85, 86
Rev. C., 195
Cornelia (m. John B. Miller), 121, 122, 124
Cornelia Haring (m. Thomas Floyd-Jones), 122, 123
Cornelia H. *See* Haring, Cornelia
Daniel, 123
Daniel Youngs, 122
David, 85, 86, 120
David S., 121

David William, 122
Elbert Haring, 120
Elbert W., 122
Eleanor (m. William S. Smith), 122, 124
Esther (m. Joseph Strong), 202
Hannah Amelia (m. Rev. Samuel Seabury), 122, 123, 124
Helen B. *See* Bache, Helen
James Duane, 123
Kezia Y. *See* Youngs, Kezia
Libbie (m. Charles C. Morrison), 160
Margaret, 256
Maria B. D. *See* Duane, Maria B.
Marianne Duane, 123
Phoebe (Mrs. William Jones), 120
Samuel, 119, 120, 121, 122
Samuel William, 122, 123, 124
Susan Maria (m. James H. Weeks), 122, 123
Thomas, 119, 120, 121
Thomas W., 121
Walter, 120
William, 119, 120, 121, 122, 123, 124
Dr. William W., 4, 6, 7

Kearny, James, 173
  Susanna, 172
Keeler, Sarah Hannah (m. Joseph Ketchum, 3d), 266
Kelly, Rev. James W., 57
Kelsey, Susan (m. Daniel Youngs), 289
Kemble, Ann, 173
  Richard, 173
  Samuel, 173
Kennedy, Rev. Duncan, 218
Kenny, Catherine M. P. *See* Parker, Catherine M.
  James, 174
Kermit, Elizabeth Furgeson (m. David V. Floyd), 56, 57
  Henry, 56
Kern, Rev. ——, 285, 286
Ketchum, Caroline M. (m. —— Swartwout), 261, 266
  Cornelia Anne (m. Henry S. Howard), 266
  Joseph, 266

Joseph, 3d, 266
Maria T. *See* Ten Broeck, Maria B.
Sarah H. K. *See* Keeler, Sarah H.
Keteltas, Jane (m. James Beekman), 24, 25, 249
  Sarah (m. John Fish), 24
Keuper (Kuyper), Rev. ——, 76, 80
Kierstede (Kirstede), Aldert, 66, 68
  Aryante (Mrs. Aldert Kierstede), 66, 68
  Catharinna, 66, 68
  Hans, 143, 144
  Jannetie, 143, 144
King, Capt. ——, 42
  Robert, 171
Kingsbury, A. R. (Mrs. F. J. Kingsbury), 232
  Adèle T. *See* Townsend, Adèle F. J., 232
  Frederick John, Jr., 230, 232, 243
  Frederick John, 3d, 231
  Ruth, 231
Kip, Capt. Jacoby, 63
  Samuel, 120
Kipp, Mrs. ——, 21
Kitteridge, Ann, 39
Kleudgen, John Daniel, 4
  Sarah B. B. *See* Bache, Sarah B.
Knickerbacker, Abraham, 129
  Annatie, 129
  Annatie (m. Abraham Viele), 125
  Anna Q. *See* Quackenbos, Anna
  Cornelia, 128
  Dirke, 128
  Diricke V. *See* Van Vechten, Diricke
  Eliesabeth, 125, 129
  Elizabeth W. *See* Winne, Elizabeth
  Harmen, 127, 128
  Johannes (John), 125, 126, 127, 128, 129
  Col. Johannes, 125, 127
  John, Jr., 127, 128
  Johannes Hermensen, 127
  Katlyne, 129
  Libete, 127

Marytie, 128
Neiltie (Neltie), 125, 127, 129
Rebecken, 128
Rebecca F. *See* Fonda, Rebecca
William, 128
William Winne, 128, 129
Wouter, 128
Knight, Susan (m. James H. S. Morrison), 161
Kuyper. *See* Keuper
Kock (Koch), Rev. ——, 76, 80
Kurtineus, Pietrus, 125

Labagh, Rev. ——, 259
La Conseilliere, Benjamin de, 148
Laidlie, Rev. ——, 285
Lambert, Frances (m. Col. John Moore), 195
Lamson, Hannah (m. Samuel Swan), 208, 210
Joseph, 208, 210
Lane, Aaron, 265
Rev. Aaron, 217
Mary T. *See* Ten Broeck, Mary
Lansingh, Anna (m. Guert Van Schoonhoven), 267
Lardla, Rev. Arch., 255
La Roux, Mr. ——, 13, 16
Lawrence, Alicia (m. Charles Sheldon, Jr.), 193
Ann (m. John Parker), 173
John, 173
Mary M. *See* Morris, Mary
Thomas, Jr., 151, 152, 153
Leboiteux, Mlle. ——, 106
Lefferts, Mrs. Frederic R., 81
Leffeston (Liffeston), Mrs. ——, 252, 254
Margrita, 251, 254
Robert, Jr., 252, 254
Lescot, Rev. ——, 147
Madame ——, 147
Lesher, Emilie (m. John Firth), 233
Le Sierurier, Jacque, 146
Marie, 146
Pierre, 147
Levy, Margaret Maria, 47
Samson, 47, 48
Sarah C. *See* Coats, Sarah
Lewis, Ann Dashwood, 130, 131
Cecilia Goold, 131
Edmund Ludlow, 130
Eliza, 130, 131
Elizabeth L. *See* Ludlow, Elizabeth
Emma Frances, 131
Francis, 130
Francis, Jr., 130, 131
Gabriel Ludlow, 131
George Edwin, 131
Gertrude, 131
Horatio Gates, 131
Juan Francis, 130, 131
Louisa Elizabeth, 131
Morgan, 130, 131
Rev. William H., 279
Leysler, Jacob, 135, 136, 140
Lidius, Rev. Johannes, 138, 142, 250, 251, 253, 261, 263
Liffeston. *See* Leffeston
Lindsey, Aurelia M. *See* Mitchell, Aurelia
Charles, 145
Oliver Ellsworth, 145
Linn, Rev. Dr. William, 25
Lispenard, A., 247
Helena, 248
Leonard, 248
Sarah, 247
Little, Capt. William, 152
Livingston, Abraham, 132, 213
Alida S. *See* Schuyler, Alida
Catharina, 138, 142
Catherine (m. John Saunders), 133
Catherine (m. 1st Stephen Van Rensselaer; 2d, Elardus Westerlo), 255, 256
Catherine Augusta (m. Abraham de Peyster), 24
Christina (Mrs. Philip Livingston), 255
Christina (m. J. N. Macomb), 132
Cornelia, 192
Frances B. *See* Bayard, Frances
George, 133
Gysbertus, 135, 137, 139, 141
Henry, 132
Jane (m. John Sanders), 94, 98
Johanna, 138, 142
Johanna Philippina, 134, 136, 139, 140, 141
Johannes, 134, 138, 142

Rev. John, 132
Rev. Dr. John H., 25
John W., 256
Margaret, 133
Margareta (m. Capt. Samuel Veitch), 134, 136, 138, 139, 141, 142
Maria (m. Philip H. Livingston), 133
Maria (m. Andrew Smyth), 195, 196
Muscoe, 132
Mrs. Muscoe, 132
Philip, 135, 137, 139, 141, 255
Philip, Jr., 133
Philip Henry, 132
Philip John, 195
Philip Philip, 132
Robert, 22, 134, 135, 136, 137, 138, 139, 140, 141
Robert R., Jr., 9
Sarah, 132
Sarah J. *See* Johnson, Sarah
Sarah Ph., 132
Sarah V. (m. John Jay), 110, 112, 115
Walter, 133
Walter T., 94, 98
Willhem, 137, 142
William, 110
Long, Capt. Robert, 150
Loockermans, Ariaentie J. *See* Jans, Ariaentie
Govert, 143, 144
Jannetie, 143, 144
Maria (m. Balthassar Bayard), 106, 143, 144
Lortie, Mr. ——, 106
Low, Abraham, 66, 68
Ragel (m. Abraham Delameter), 65, 66, 67, 69
Sarah, 151, 152
Ludlow, Ann, 130
Arabella, 130
Daniel, 130
Elizabeth (m. Francis Lewis, Jr.), 130, 131
Elizabeth (Mrs. Gabriel Ludlow), 130
Francis, 130
Francis, Jr., 130
G. H., 154
Gabriel, 130

George D., 130
Henry, 154
Martha, 154
Mary, 154
Mary C. *See* Corbett, Mary
Sarah (m. Richard Morris), 153, 154, 155
Sarah C., 56
William N., 154
Lydius. *See* Lidius
Lyle, Rev. Dr. ——, 4
Lyman, Alice, 45
Lynch, Charlotte B. *See* Bache, Charlotte
Francis B., 4, 6
Lynsen, Abraham, 17
Abraham, Jr., 13, 16, 17
Catherine, 17
Magdalena B. *See* Beekman, Magdalena

McCard, Rebecki (m. John Hinds), 200
McClosky, The Most Rev. ——, 56
McCoun, James T., 241
Mary A. T. *See* Townsend, Mary A.
Rebecca Y., 241
Sidney, 241
McCrea, Dr. Stephen, 8
MacCumber, Mrs. —— (m. Daniel Catheson), 201
McDonell, Sarah, 133
McDonnald, Rachel (m. William Wooley), 200
McEvers, Mrs. ——, 248
J. C., 248
John, 63
McIntyre, Margaret (m. Oliver S. Strong), 204
McKean, Rev. Robert, 172
McMurray, Rev. Dr. ——, 24
McVicker, Augusta (m. William Jay), 110, 116
McVoy, Caroline (m. Andrew T. Bache), 4
Macey, Joan, 145
William, 145
Macomb, Christina L. *See* Livingston, Christina
J. N., 132
Maize, Mercy (m. Samuel Morrison), 163

Mallet, Isaac, 206
Mancious (Manseus, Mancius),
    Anna, 214
    Rev. Dr. Whilhelmus Georgius,
      30, 31, 65, 66, 67, 68, 214
Manigaud (Manigault), Isaac, 106
Marshall, Elsie, 184, 186
    John, 185, 187
    Rev. John, 248
    Susannah, 247
Marston, John, 153
    Rachel, 153
Martin, Josiah, 201
Mason, Helen Louise (m. William
    J. Youngs), 289, 290
    James, 289
Massiot, ——, 106
Mather, Marget (m. William N.
    Sill), 98
Mathew, Renslow, 201
Mayo, Anne (m. Col. George Carrington), 35, 36
Mazÿck, Benjamin, 147
    Elizabet, 146, 147
    Estienne, 147
    Isaac, 146, 147, 148
    Marianne, 146, 147
    Marrianne (Mrs. Isaac Mazÿck),
      146, 147, 148
    Marie (m. —— Chardon), 147,
      148
    Paul, 146
    Penelope, 147
    Pittre, 147, 148
    Suzon, 146, 147, 148
Meade, Elizabeth Mary (m. Alfred
    Ingraham), 48
    Margaret C. See Coats,
      Margaret
    Richard W., 48
Mesier, Margret V. See Verplanck,
    Margret
    Peter, 18, 276
    Peter, Jr., 18
Meyers, Rev. ——, 94, 98
Michiel (Michielse). See Van
    Vechten
Milledolar, Rev. Philip, 24, 25, 26,
    99
Miller, Rev. ——, 153
    Ann, 149
    Ann Blackburn, 53, 54
    Blackburn, 56
    Charles, 149
    Christopher, 53, 54
    Christopher Billop, 54, 55
    Cornelia Jones (m. French E.
      Chadwick), 79, 80, 121, 124
    Cornelia J. See Jones, Cornelia
    Cornelia Stansbury, 121, 124
    Daniel, 149
    Elizabeth, 53, 54, 149
    Elizabeth Hart, 53, 54
    Francis, 149
    John, 53, 149
    John Bleecker, 121, 122, 124
    Josephine H. See Hyslep,
      Josephine
    Margaret (Mrs. Blackburn
      Miller), 56
    Maria B. See Bleecker, Maria
    Maria Duane Bleecker (m. Wilmot T. Cox), 119, 121, 124,
      284
    Mary, 149
    Mary B. D. See Dunn,
      Mary B.
    Mary E. See Eldridge, Mary
    Morris Smith, 124
    Richard, 149
    Rosamond Bend, 52, 54, 55
    Sarah Coventry (m. David Van
      Horn), 53, 54
    Sarah C. See Coventry, Sarah
    Dr. William Ellison, 56
Miln, Marya, 191
Miralles, Juan D., 130
Mitchell, Aurelia (m. Charles
    Lindsey), 145
    Rev. Edward, 230
    Isaac, 145
Moffat, Rev. John, 8
Monro, Rev. ——, 259
Montant, Alice A. See Anderton,
    Alice
    August Phillipe, 230, 232, 243
    Hannah M. T. See Townsend,
      Hannah M.
    Louis Townsend, 230, 231, 233
    Louis Townsend, 2d, 233
    Marie Adèle (m. Huntington
      Norton), 230, 231
Montgomery, Hannah (m. John Van
    Horn), 62, 63, 64
    Jennett (Janet), 130, 173
    Patrick, 63

Moore, Abbie Jay, 179
 Rev. Benjamin, 54, 55, 247, 248
 Charlotte Lucy Prescott, 179
 Daniel, 132
 Dr. Edward Mott, 177, 179
 Frances L. *See* Lambert, Frances
 Frederick Pettes, 179
 Jane (m. Adam Tredwell), 236, 237
 Col. John, 195
 John H., 236
 Rev. John W., 156, 158
 Lindley Murray, 179
 Lucy R. P. *See* Prescott, Lucy R.
 Mary Pettes, 179
 The Rt. Rev. Richard Channing, 110, 195, 197
 Richard Mott, 179
 Samuel Prescott, 179
 Susannah (m. John Smyth), 195, 197
Morgan, Rev. Dr. ——, 249
Morgatt, Capt. Peter, 63
Morris, Anne, 157, 172
 Anne Walton, 157, 158
 Anne W. *See* Walton, Anne
 Arthur, 157
 Catherine, 151, 152, 154
 Ellen H. *See* Hunt, Ellen
 Euphemia, 151
 Gerard Walton, 156, 157, 158
 Gouverneur, 151
 Henry, 156, 157, 158, 159
 Henry Lewis, 156, 158
 Honora Smith (m. Francis J. Barretto), 156, 157, 158
 Isabella, 151, 153
 Isabella Pyne, 157, 158
 Gen. Jacob, 152, 157
 James, 153
 John, 150
 John C. Spencer, 158
 John Pyne, 157
 Lewis, 150, 151, 152, 154, 156, 157, 158
 Judge Lewis, 150, 151, 152
 Lewis R., 155
 Magdalane, 153
 Martha P. *See* Pyne, Martha
 Mary, 152, 153, 154
 Mary (m. Thomas Lawrence, Jr.), 150, 151, 152, 154
 Mary N. S. *See* Spencer, Mary N.
 Mary Natelie, 158
 Mary P. E. *See* Emerson, Mary P.
 Mary (Minny) Pyne (m. Jonathan Edwards), 156, 157, 158, 159
 Mary S. *See* Stillman, Mary
 Mary W. *See* Walton, Mary
 Chief Justice Richard, 150, 151, 152, 154, 155
 Richard H., 155
 Richard Valentine, 153, 156, 157, 158, 159
 Robert, 154
 Robert Hunter, 151, 154
 Sarah, 151, 152, 156
 Sarah G. *See* Gouverneur, Sarah
 Sarah L. *See* Ludlow, Sarah
 Sophie B., 154
 Staats, 153
 Staats Long, 150, 151
 Trintje S. *See* Staats, Trintje
 William Walton, 153
Morrison, Adrian Clifford, 161, 162
 Ann D. *See* Downs, Ann
 Anna Mary, 161, 162
 Charles Carroll, 160, 161
 Daisy S. *See* Skinner, Daisy
 David H., 160, 161, 162
 David Henry, 161, 162
 Emma D. *See* Darrow, Emma
 Ephraim, 161, 163
 Harriet Gest (m. William T. Rankin), 160, 161
 Harriet J. S. *See* Skinner, Harriet J.
 James Hollis Skinner, 160, 161, 162
 John, 162, 163
 Julius Curtis, 160, 161, 162
 Libbie J. *See* Jones, Libbie
 Maggie M. G. *See* Goodwin, Maggie M.
 Mercy M. *See* Maize, Mercy
 Nancy F. *See* Foster, Nancy
 Samuel, 162, 163
 Samuel Robert, 160, 161

Sarah Eliza (m. George B. Holland), 160, 161, 163
Sarah H. H. *See* Humfreville, Sarah H.
Susan K. *See* Knight, Susan
Thomas, 160, 161, 162
Thomas Rollin, 162
Virginia U. *See* Updyke, Virginia
Mrs. William B., 154
Morse, Dr. ——, 209
Mosher, Ira D., 201
Moss, Mary (m. John Burton), 34
Mount, Sarah B. (m. Joseph W. Underhill), 245
Muddell, Fanny H. (m. Clarence E. Underhill), 244
Muhlenberg, Rev. Dr. William, 124
Murray, Joseph, 150
Mynderse, Harriet (m. Frederick Pettes), 177, 178, 179, 180, 181

Nazereth, Eleanor (Mrs. William Nazereth), 8
Mary (m. Peter Bedlow), 8
William, 8
Needham, Henry, 63
Neilson, Catherine Alexander (m. William F. Beekman), 24
Catherine F. *See* Foulke, Catherine
Hannah C. *See* Coles, Hannah
John, 249
William, 24
Nevius, Jacob R., 5, 6
Sarah B. B. *See* Bache, Sarah B.
Nickels, ——, 251, 253
Nicoll, Anna W. F. *See* Floyd-Jones, Anna W.
Benjamin, 86
Noble, Caterine, 146
Henry, 146
Suson le, 147
Norris, Margaret (m. William Coats), 45, 46, 47, 48
North, Delia, 164
Delia (Adelia) (m. Henry Saunders), 164, 165
Elizabeth, 165
Frederick William Steuben, 165
Hannah Elizabeth, 164

James Duane, 165
Margaret B. *See* Bridge, Margaret
Maria, 165
Mary Catherine (m. Daniel C. Weston), 164
Mary D. *See* Duane, Mary
Gen. William, 164, 165, 166
William Augustus Steuben, 164, 165
Norton, Huntington, 230
Marie A. M. *See* Montant, Marie A.
Norwood, Rev. William, 40
Noye. *See* De Lanoy
Noyes, Frances S. S. *See* Sheldon, Frances S.
Dr. Josiah, 193

Oakley, Walton, 62
Oblong, Thomas Heaveland, 281
Ogden, Aaron, 167, 168
Aaron Norton, 167, 168
Anne, 167
Barne, 167
Benoni, 167, 168
Betsy, 168
Catherine Morris (m. James Parker), 174
David, 167, 168
Frances (m. Pierrepont Edwards), 167
John Cosens, 167, 168
Mary, 167
Mary (Mrs. Moses Ogden), 167
Mary (Polly) Cosens, 167, 168
Moses, 167, 168
Nancy S. *See* Sale, Nancy
Polly, 168
Polly W. *See* Worster, Polly
Col. Samuel, 174
Ogilvie, Rev. John, 9, 53, 54
Onderdonck, The Rt. Rev. ——, 7
Andries, 169
Benjamin, 169, 170
Geertruy, 169
Henderick, 85, 169
Henderick, Jr., 169
Johannis, 170
Maria, 169, 170
Phebe, 169, 170
Phebe T. *See* Treadwell, Phebe

[315]

Sally (Sarah) (m. David Richard Floyd-Jones), 85, 123, 169
Samuel, 170
William, 170
Orgill, Mrs. Fran—, 133
Ostrander, Ferdinand William, 51
Mary, 49
Sarah A. W. *See* Wright, Sarah A.
Sarah Elizabeth (m. Adam T. Sackett), 237, 238
Ovens, Rev. ——, 150

Palmer, Elizabeth (m. William B. Anderton), 233
Lucretia (m. Peter Crary), 81, 82
Maria, 81
Dr. Nathan, 81
Rebecca (m. Daniel Fish), 81
Papin, I., 106
Parish, Louisa (m. Samuel H. Townsend), 229
Parker (Perker), Anne E. G. *See* Gouverneur, Anne E.
Ann L. *See* Lawrence, Ann
Catherine A. *See* Alexander, Catherine
Catherine Montgomery (m. James Kenny), 173, 174
Catherine M. O. *See* Ogden, Catherine M.
Cortlandt Lewis, 172, 173, 174
Elisha, 171, 172, 176
Mrs. Elisha, 171
Elizabeth, 172, 173
Gertrude, 171, 172, 173, 174, 175, 176
Gertrude S. *See* Skinner, Gertrude
James, 171, 172, 173, 174, 175
Jennet (m. Edward Brinley), 172, 173
Jennet J. *See* Johnston, Jennet
John, 171, 172, 173, 175, 176
Lewis Johnston, 171
Maria (m. Edward Dunham), 173
Maria (m. Andrew Smyth), 172, 174, 195, 197
Mary, 171, 172, 173
Marydtye (m. Michiel D. Van Vechten), 269, 271

Penelope B. *See* Butler, Penelope
Susanna, 173, 174
Ursula, 171, 175, 176
William, 173, 174
Parsons, Elizabeth (m. Charles Sheldon), 193
Linas, 193
Paulsom, Eliza, 39
Payne, Georgina M. S. *See* Smith, Georgina M.
John William, 196
Pearse, Mary, 150
Capt. Vincent, 150
Pearson, Joseph, 111
Josephine (m. Peter A. Jay), 111, 114, 116
Peeck, Antye (m. Johannis S. Glen), 91, 96
Peiret, Rev. ——, 106, 107
Parker. *See* Parker
Perkins, Rev. C. M., 100
Perry, Dolly (m. John Ash), 200
Obediah, 200
Peters, Georgianna S. *See* Snelling, Georgianna
Dr. John C., 205
Mary Louise (m. Samuel S. Dudley), 73
Pettersson, George, 284, 285
Maria R. *See* Ruehl, Maria
Pettes, Charlotte W. *See* Wales, Charlotte
Edward, 178
Frederick, 177, 178, 179, 180
Frederick Dudley, 178
Harriet M. *See* Mynderse, Harriet
John, 177, 178, 180, 181
Joseph, 177, 179, 180, 181
Lucy Ellen (m. —— Sabine), 178, 179
Lucy R. *See* Richards, Lucy
Mary (Polly) (m. 1st, Samuel Prescott; 2d, —— Sergeant), 177, 179, 180, 181
Mary Elizabeth, 178
Rachel R. *See* Rhoades, Rachel
Robert Thaxter, 178
William H., 178
William Richards, 178
Phelps, Beriah, 201
Margery, 239

Phillips, Adolph, 108
   Charlotte (m. Andrew B. Bache), 4, 5, 6, 7
   John, 7
   Mary (Mrs. John Phillips), 7
Pickard, Cornelia V. W. *See* Woodhull, Cornelia V.
   Josiah L., 203
Pierrepont, Anna M. J. *See* Jay, Anna M.
   H. B., 111
   Henry E., 111
   Mrs. Seth Low, 37
Platt, Jonas, 280
   Ruth (m. George Weekes), 280
   Sarah (Mrs. Jonas Platt), 280
Polk, Almy U. T. *See* Townsend, Almy U.
   Francis James, 228, 229
   Gertrude, 228, 229
   James Black, 228, 229
   Louisa, 229
   Margaret Townsend, 228, 229
   Mary Townsend, 228, 229
   William Winder, 228, 229
Poole, Rev. John, 132
Poor, Charles Austin, 166
   Charles Longstreet, 166
   Mary L. A. *See* Austin, Mary L.
   Mary Lindsay, 166
   Richard Longstreet, 166
Porter, Chauncey Henry, 279
   Frederick, 39
   Jane L. V. *See* Vought, Jane L.
Post, Dr. Alfred C., 110
   Julia (m. Peter A. Jay), 110
Potter, Pheby (m. Gran Wart), 201
Prentiss, Rev. Dr. ——, 110
Prescott, Charlotte Pettes (m. Isham G. Searcy), 177, 178, 179, 181
   Lucy Richards (m. Edward M. Moore), 177, 178, 179
   Mary P. *See* Pettes, Mary
   Samuel, 177, 179
Preston, Rev. John W., 172, 173
   Remember, 210
   Sarah (m. Daniel Swan), 210
Prevoorst. *See* Provoost
Price, Rev. James, 42
Prime, Cornelia (Mrs. Nathaniel Prime), 112, 113, 116
   Frederick, 110, 111

   Harriet, 114
   Helen Jay (m. F. T. Garrettson), 114
   Laura (m. Dr. John C. Jay), 110, 111, 114, 116, 117
   Lydia H. *See* Hare, Lydia
   Mary Rutherfurd, 114, 115
   Mary R. J. *See* Jay, Mary R.
   Nathaniel, 110, 111, 113, 114, 116
Prince, William, 131
Prouty, Margaret M. V. *See* Van Vranken, Margaret M.
   Phinehas, 274
Provoost (Prevoorst), Mrs. ——, 11, 14
   Catherine (m. Gerard Beekman, Jr.), 12, 15, 18
   David, 13, 15, 16
   Eva, 185, 186
   John, 185, 187
   The Rt. Rev. Samuel, 9, 24, 131
   William, 12, 15
Pruyn, Augustus, 218
   Catalina T. *See* Ten Eyck, Catalina
   Margaret Ten Eyck, 212, 214, 217
Pyne, Martha (m. Gerard W. Morris), 156, 157, 158
   Rev. Smith, 111, 157

Quackenbos, Anna (m. Johannes Knickerbacker), 127

Rackers, Nicholas, 19
Ralston, Robert, 25
   Sarah (Mrs. Robert Ralston), 25
Rankin, Harriet G. M. *See* Morrison, Harriet G.
   William T., 160
Ranssear. *See* Van Rensselaer
Rathze, Margarrieta (m. Jan J. Bleecker), 28
Ratsey, Capt. Robert, 62
Reding, Capt. William, 42
Reese, Rev. I. Livingston, 218
Renew, Pittre, 147
Reynolds, Mary J. W. *See* Wynkoop, Maria J.
   Sarah B., 284
Rhinelander, T. J. Oakley, 182

Rhoades, Benjamin, 180, 181
    Rachel (m. John Pettes), 181
    Rachel (Mrs. Benjamin Rhoades), 180, 181
Richards, Lucy (m. John Pettes), 177, 178, 179
Richardson, Joanna (m. Samuel Swan), 206, 207, 208
Richmond, Rev. William, 110
Riddell, Rev. Archibald, 174
Rigden, Edmund, 33
    Elizabeth, 34
    Richard, 34
    Thomas, 34
Ritson, Elizabeth, 248
    John, 248
Ritzema (Ritsma), Rev. Johannis, 119, 185, 187, 284, 286
Robert, Christian, 182, 183
    Christopher, 182, 183
    Daniel, 182, 183
    John, 182, 183
    Mary, 182, 183
    Mary D. *See* Dyer, Mary
    Mary Elizabeth, 182, 183
    Susannah, 182, 183
    William, 182, 183
Robison, Herman Ten Eyck, 218
    Hugh, 218
    John, 218
    John Alexander, 218
    Margaret T. *See* Ten Eyck, Margaret
    William, 218
Rockwell, Belinda (m. Edward M. Townsend), 230, 231, 232, 242
Rodgers, Rev. Ravaud Kearny, 104, 105
Romeyn (Romyn), Dr. ——, 203
    Mrs. ——, 203
    Rev. Dirck, 93, 97
Roos, Garret, 20
Roosa, Mary (m. Jeremiah Houghtaling), 103
Roose, Judith (m. James Gilliland), 89
Roosevelt, Cornelius, 119
    Helena, 248
Rose, Ann (m. Joseph Swan), 210
    George Sherfe, 101
    Catherine M. S. *See* Sanders, Catherine M.
    Oswald J. Cammann, 132

Sherfe Coffin, 100, 101
Roseboom, Johannis, 28
Rotchell, Elizabeth (m. Thomas Wright), 282
Rothenbuler, Rev. ——, 89
Rou, Rev. Louis, 107
Rubell (Ruble), Rev. ——, 17
Rudder, Catherine S. B. *See* Bache, Catherine A. S.
    Rev. William, 5, 6
Ruehl, Maria (m. 1st, Martin A. Ruehl; 2d, George Petterson), 284
    Maria Catharina (m. Cornelius Wynkoop), 284
    Martin Augustus, 284
Rumbouts, Francis, 19
Rusele, John, 145
Russell, Effa (m. Isaac Ellithorp), 200
Rutgers, Anna, 184, 186
    Catherine (m. William Bedlow), 8, 9, 24, 25, 184, 185, 186, 187
    Catharina D. *See* De Peyster, Catherine
    Elizabeth, 185, 186
    H., 10
    Harman, 185, 186, 187
    Harmanus, 184, 185, 186, 187
    Hendrick, 8, 9, 184, 185, 186
    Henry, 8, 25
    Henry, Jr., 9
    Johannis, 184, 185, 186
    Maria, 8, 185, 187
    Mary, 9
Rutherfurd, Alexander, 150
    Catherine A. *See* Alexander, Catherine
    John, 173
    Walter, 172, 173
Ryerson, Elizabeth (Mrs. George Ryerson), 188
    Ellen, 188
    Genny, 188
    George (Yores), 188, 189
    Hannah, 188
    John, 188
    John Francis, 188
    Mary (Mrs. John F. Ryerson), 188
    Mary Tice, 188
    Polly, 188
    Samuel, 188

Rymer, Hannah, 39
Rypel, Catherine (Mrs. Johannes Rypel), 284, 285
    Johannes, 284, 285
Rysdick (Rysdyk, Rise Dyck, Risdyck), Rev. Isaac, 17, 18, 76

Sabine, Lucy E. P. *See* Pettes, Lucy E.
Sackett, Adam Treadwell, 236, 237, 238
    Benjamin Lambert, 237, 238
    Clarence, 236
    Clarence D., 237, 238
    Clarence Ostrander, 236
    Ferdinand William, 237, 238
    George Edward, 236, 238
    Gertrude O. T. *See* Treadwell, Gertrude O.
    Gertrude Treadwell, 236
    Grenville Alfred, 237, 238
    Helen Louise, 237
    Mary Moore, 237, 238
    Sarah E. O. *See* Ostrander, Sarah E.
Saidler, Mary Childs (m. Benjamin L. Swan), 211
St. Jullien, Damearis, 146, 148
    Pierre de, 146
    Pittre de, 147
Sale, Nancy (m. Benoni Ogden), 168
Salyn, Rev. ——, 11, 14
Sample, Rev. James, 41
Sanders, Albertina T. *See* Ten Broeck, Albertina
    Barent, 92, 94, 97, 98
    Catlina B. *See* Bleecker, Catlina
    Catherine (Catrina) (m. Gerard Beekman), 93, 94, 97, 98, 99
    Catherine M. C. *See* Cox, Catherine M.
    Catherine (Katharine) Mary (m. 1st, Sherfe Coffin Rose; 2d, William Winton Galbraith, U. S. N.), 90, 100, 101
    Charles, 100
    Deborah G. *See* Glen, Deborah
    Dirck Wesselse, 94, 98
    Elizabeth (m. Dr. William Anderson), 92, 93, 96, 97, 98, 100
    Jacob Glen, 93, 97, 99, 100, 101
    Jane L. *See* Livingston, Jane
    Jane Ten Eyck, 100, 101
    Janie T. *See* Ten Eyck, Jane
    John, 93, 97
    John, Jr., 91, 92, 93, 94, 95, 96, 98, 99
    Margareta, 93, 97
    Margaret R. S. *See* Sill, Margaret R.
    Maria E. *See* Elmendorf, Maria
    Peter, 93, 94, 97, 98, 99
    Peter Edmund, 100
    Robert, 92, 93, 97, 99
    Sara, 93, 97
    Theodore W., 98, 99
Sands, Harriet, 113
Sanford, Mr. ——, 11, 14
Saunders, Catherine L. *See* Livingston, Catherine
    Delia North, 164, 165
    Delia N. *See* North, Delia
    Eliza North, 164
    Henry, U. S. A., 164, 165
    John, 133
    William Henry, 164
Savage, Sarah C. *See* Chauncey, Sarah
Schaets (Shaets), Rev. Gideon, 134, 135, 136, 137, 138, 139, 140, 141
Schoonmaker, Rev. ——, 247
Schuyler (Schueler, Shuyler, Schuylder), Rev. ——, 212, 213
    Alida (m. 1st, Nicolaus Van Rensselaer; 2d, Robert Livingston), 134, 136, 138, 140
    Angelica (m. John Church), 39
    Arent, 135, 137, 139, 141
    Barabar, 192
    Brandt, 21, 135, 137, 138, 139, 141, 142
    Catherine Van Rensselaer, 192
    Cornelia (Mrs. Brant Schuyler), 135, 137, 139, 141
    Cornelia Lynch, 192
    Cornelia V. *See* Van Cortlandt, Cornelia
    Cortlandt, 191, 192
    David, 20, 91, 95, 135, 137, 139, 141
    Elizabeth, 191, 192
    Elizabeth (Mrs. Johannes Schuyler), 190, 191, 251, 253

Elizabeth V. *See* Van Rensselaer, Elizabeth
Engeltie, 135, 137, 139, 141, 192
Gertrude (Gertruydt), 63, 190
Gertrude (m. Stephanus Van Cortlandt), 20, 21
Harmanis, 262, 263, 264
Jan, 251, 253
Jenneke, 135, 137, 139, 141
John (Johannes), 21, 22, 135, 137, 139, 141, 190, 191
John Bradstreet, 191, 256, 257
Margaret (m. Stephen Van Rensselaer), 256
Margarita (m. Jacobus Verplanck), 21, 135, 137, 139, 141
Margreta (Mrs. Philip Schuyler), 134, 136, 138, 139, 140, 191, 256
Maria, 251, 253
Oliver, 191
Peter (Pieter), 21, 134, 135, 136, 137, 138, 139, 140, 141, 142, 250, 252, 253, 254
Philip, 17, 39, 134, 135, 136, 137, 138, 139, 140, 141, 142, 190, 191, 251, 252, 253, 254, 256, 257
Philip Jeremiah, 192
Rensselaer, 192
Stephanes, 190, 191
Stephen Van Rensselaer, 256
Schwartz, Rev. David, 100
Mrs. ———, 100
Scott, Eupham (m. Dr. John Johnston), 174
Seabury, Rev. ———, 153
Ann (Mrs. Charles Seabury), 124
Rev. Charles, 124
Hannah A. J. *See* Jones, Hannah A.
Rev. Dr. Samuel, 123, 124
Rev. Dr. William Jones, 124
Seaman, Adèle (m. Beekman H. Townsend), 59, 60, 229
Delia (m. John F. Underhill), 245
Esther (m. James T. Underhill), 244
Fanny (m. William W. Townsend), 229

Maria P. (m. Arnold Fleet), 241
Mary A. (m. William C. Townsend), 241
Mary J. (m. Samuel E. Underhill), 243, 244
Phoebe (m. Jacob Townsend), 225, 226
Searcy, Charlotte Pettes, 177, 178
Charlotte P. P. *See* Prescott, Charlotte P.
Isham Green, 177, 179
Lucy Frederic (m. Thomas Hale), 177, 178, 179, 181
Mary Elizabeth, 177, 178, 179
Seirurier. *See* Le Sierurier
Selinus, Rev. ———, 106
Semple, Sarah (m. Caleb Swan), 208
Sergeant, Mary P. *See* Pettes, Mary
Sheldon, Alicia, 194
Alicia L. *See* Lawrence, Alicia
Catherine, 194
Charles, 193
Charles, Jr., 193, 194
Charles Henry, 194
Charles L., 193
Capt. Daniel, 193
Edward, 194
Elizabeth, 193
Elizabeth Bellamy, 194
Elizabeth B. *See* Bellamy, Elizabeth
Elizabeth P. *See* Parsons, Elizabeth
Frances Sherman (m. Dr. Josiah Noyes), 193
George, 194
Henry, 193
Henry Lawrence, 194
Isabel Woodbridge, 193
Jane, 194
Sarah, 194
William Lawrence, 194
Shyring, Rev. Henry, 41
Sill, Marget M. *See* Mather, Marget
Margaret R. (m. Theodore M. Sanders), 98
William N., 98
Silvester, Jane, 260
Skinner, Catherine, 172, 173
Cortlandt, 172, 173
Daisy (m. James H. S. Morrison), 160

Elizabeth, 172
Gertrude (m. James Parker), 172, 173
Harriet J. (m. David H. Morrison), 160, 161, 162
John, 172
Mary H. *See* Hollis, Mary
Robert J., 160, 161, 162
Sarah, 173
Stephen, 172, 173
Rev. William, 171, 172
Sloughter, Gov. Henry, 136, 140
Smedis, Peter, 66, 68
Smith (Smyth), Andrew, 174, 195, 196, 197
Anna (m. Judge Selah Strong), 202
Rev. C. B., 230
Daniel, 289
Eleanor J. *See* Jones, Eleanor
Elinor, 48
Frances Susan (m. Charles I. Aldis), 196
Georgina Maria (m. John W. Payne), 196
Hannah (Mrs. William Smith), 124
Henry Coggill, 196, 197
Rev. Hugh, 196
John, 48, 172, 195, 196, 197
John Livingston, 195
John William, 196, 197
Lawrence, 195, 196
Margaret, 203
Margaret J. *See* Johnston, Margaret
Maria Ann, 196
Maria L. *See* Livingston, Maria
Maria P. *See* Parker, Maria
Mary A. C. *See* Coggill, Mary A.
Sarah Elizabeth (m. Daniel K. Youngs), 289, 290
Sumner, 200
Susanna, 173
Susannah M. *See* Moore, Susannah
Rev. Walter E. C., 100
William, 124, 203
William Loughton, 157
William Sidney, 124
Snelling, Andrew S., 204

Eliza T. S. *See* Strong, Eliza T.
Georgianna (m. Dr. John C. Peters), 205
Solèliac, Charles, 117
Marguerite Montgomery (m. John C. Jay, III), 117
Spencer, Mary N. (m. Henry Morris), 156, 158
Staats, Dr. Samuell, 150
Trintje (m. Lewis Morris), 150, 151
Standard, Rev. Thomas, 151
Stansbury, Elizabeth (m. Rev. S. Ballard Dunn), 121, 124
Starr, Margaret Townsend, 242
Mary Amelia Avery, 242
Susan Hotchkiss, 242
Susan R. T. *See* Townsend, Susan R.
William Ireland, 242
William Wright, 241
Staughton, Rev. William, 160
Stebbins, Rev. Cyrus, 123
Mary G., 278
Stedman, Petter, 200
Stedmond, Stephen, 200
Stevens, Rev. Joseph, 208
Stillman, Mary (m. Lewis R. Morris), 155
Stimson, Abigail Anny, 198
Azariah, 198
Earl L., 198, 199
Eliphas Day, 198, 199
John Fay, 198
Margaret, 198
Mary Elizabeth, 198
Mehitable E. (Polly). *See* Ellithorp, Mehitable
Samuel, 198, 199
Samuel Leonard, 198, 199
Solomon Leonard, 198
Susannah M., 198
Stone, Harriet (m. Caleb Swan), 211
Moses, 211
Street, Clara A. (m. Roswell C. Fleet), 240
Strong, Anna Smith (m. George Baxter), 203, 204
Anna S. *See* Smith, Anna
Benjamin, 202, 203, 204
Benjamin, Jr., 202, 205
Charles Edward, 205
Charles Lloyd, 203, 204

Edward Augustus, 204
Eleanor B. F. *See* Fearing, Eleanor B.
Eliza Templeton (m. Andrew S. Snelling), 204
Esther J. *See* Jones, Esther
George Washington, 202
Harriet Thompson (m. Robert D. Weeks), 204
Jeannette A. B. *See* Bradley, Jeannette A.
Joseph, 202
Julia Weeks (m. Theodore A. Bailey), 205
Keturah (m. James Woodhull), 202
Margaret, 202
Margaret McI. *See* McIntyre, Margaret
Marianne C. *See* Clay, Marianne
Mary, 202
Oliver Smith, 203, 204
Sally (Sarah) Huggins (m. Dr. Nicoll H. Dering), 203, 204
Sally W. *See* Weekes, Sally
Judge Selah, 202
Thomas Shepard, 202, 203
William Smith, 202
Stuyvesant, Baltelasaer, 143, 144
Phillip, 108
Swan, Abigail, 208
Mrs. Anna, 207
Ann R. *See* Rose, Ann
Anna W. *See* Whittemore, Anna
Benjamin Lincoln, 210, 211
Caleb, 207, 208, 209, 210, 211
Daniel, 206, 207, 208, 210, 211
Elizabeth T. *See* Tufts, Elizabeth
Hannah, 209, 210
Hannah L. *See* Lamson, Hannah
Harriet S. *See* Stone, Harriet
Joanna, 206, 207, 209
Joanna R. *See* Richardson, Joanna
Joseph, 206, 208, 209, 210, 211
Margaret T. *See* Tufts, Margaret
Mary C. S. *See* Saidler, Mary C.

Mehitable, 206, 207, 209
Mehitable A. *See* Austin, Mehitable
Samuel, 206, 207, 208, 210
Sarah P. *See* Preston, Sarah
Sarah S. *See* Semple, Sarah
Timothy, 206, 207, 208, 211
Dr. Timothy, 206, 209
William L., 206
Swartwout, Caroline M. K. *See* Ketchum, Caroline M.
Syms, Capt. Lancaster, 138, 142

Tabor, Edward, 201
Tanner, Rev. William, 39
Taylor, Rev. ——, 158
Teller, Anna V. *See* Verplanck, Anna
William (Willem), 90, 94
Ten Broeck (Ten Brouck), Abraham, 255
Albertina (m. John Sanders), 93, 98, 99
Anna, 265
Anna (Mrs. John C. Ten Broeck), 266
Anna Van Schaick (m. Thomas Hillhouse), 266
Anna V. *See* Van Schaack, Anna
Anthony, 265, 266
Caty, 265
Catherine (m. 1st, Severyn Bruyn; 2d, Jonathan Elmendorf), 30, 32
Catherine (Caty) (m. Rev. Maurice W. Dwight), 266
Catherine (Mrs. Petrus Ten Broeck), 31
Christina (m. Anthony Ten Broeck), 265
Coenrad, 31
Cornelius P., 266
Dirck, 212, 213
Dirck W., 93, 98
Geertry, 31
Henry, 265, 266
Johannes, 31
John C., 266
Margaret (Mrs. Coenrad Ten Broeck), 31
Maria B. (m. Joseph Ketchum), 266

Mary (m. Aaron Lane), 265
Patty C. *See* Cumstock, Patty
Petrus, 31
Samuel, 263, 264, 266
Sara (m. Johannes Ten Eyck), 212, 213
Ten Eyck (Teneike), Albert, 270, 271
   Albert, Jr., 270
   Anna (m. Andrew Foster), 214, 215, 216
   Catalina, 214, 216
   Catalina (m. Augustus Pruyn), 215, 217, 218
   Catherine, 214
   Catherine (m. William M. Burr), 215, 216
   Cornelia Anna, 217
   Cornelia Dorothea, 217
   Eliza B. *See* Bogart, Eliza
   Elsie (Mrs. Myndert S. Ten Eyck), 93, 97
   Gertie, 262, 264
   Harmanus, 214, 215, 216, 217
   Henderick, 28, 212, 213
   Henry, 214
   Herman, 214, 215, 216, 217, 218
   Jacob H., 214, 215, 216, 217, 218
   Jacob H., Jr., 215, 218
   Jane (m. Jacob G. Sanders), 100
   Jenegein, 270, 271
   Jeramyah Field, 272
   Johannes H., 212, 213
   John Bogert, 217
   John C., 100
   John W., 255
   Margreta, 212, 213, 214, 216
   Margaret (m. John A. Robison), 215, 217, 218
   Margaret (Mrs. Henry Ten Eyck), 214
   Margaret B. *See* Bleecker, Margaret
   Mary V. *See* Van Vechten, Mary
   Matilda E. B. *See* Bleecker, Matilda E.
   Myndert S., 93, 97
   Sarah (Mrs. John W. Ten Eyck), 255
   Sara T. *See* Ten Broeck, Sara
Tent, Gov. Edward, 147

Thayer, Saly (m. Renslow Mathew), 201
Thompson, Catherine, 152
Thomson, Herbert Claiborne, 42
   Mary H. (Mrs. William Thomson), 42
   William, 42
Titus, Elizabeth K. T. *See* Treadwell, Elizabeth K.
   Gertrude Elizabeth, 236, 237
   James H., 237, 238
   Sarah (m. Daniel Y. Townsend), 230, 231, 232, 242
Townsend, Ada S., 60, 229
   Adèle (m. Frederick J. Kingsbury, Jr.), 230, 231, 242, 243
   Adèle S. *See* Seaman, Adèle
   Alice G. *See* Greenough, Alice
   Almy, 226, 227
   Almy U. (m. William W. Polk), 228, 229
   Anna, 229
   Ann Eliza, 242
   Arthur B., 242
   Audrey A. *See* Almy, Audrey
   Aurelia C. W. *See* Winder, Aurelia C.
   Aurelia W., 229
   Beekman H., 59, 60, 229
   Belinda R. *See* Rockwell, Belinda
   Benjamin, 226
   Billopp, 229
   Catherine B., 242
   Catherine R. B. *See* Bronson, Catherine R.
   Charlotte, 223, 229
   Charlotte B., 242
   Charlotte C. *See* Coles, Charlotte
   Daniel, 241
   Daniel Youngs, 230, 231, 232, 240, 242, 246
   Deborah, 234
   Edward Mitchell, 230, 231, 232, 242, 243
   Edward Mitchell, Jr., 230, 231, 233
   Mrs. Edward M., Jr. *See* Greenough, Alice
   Edward Mitchell, 3d, 231
   Elizabeth, 222, 229

Elizabeth (m. Nathaniel Coles), 224
Elizabeth (Mrs. Jacob Townsend), 234
Elizabeth (Mrs. John Townsend), 225
Elizabeth (Mrs. William Townsend), 220, 221, 224
Elizabeth Covert, 60
Elizabeth C. *See* Covert, Elizabeth
Esther (m. Thomas Coles), 223, 224
Fanny, 229
Fanny S. *See* Seaman, Fanny
Frances (m. Jacob F. Covert), 59, 60, 61, 228, 229
Freelove T. W. *See* Wilmot, Freelove T.
Frost, 226
George, 219, 220, 228, 229, 234
George, II, 219, 220
George, Jr., 221
George C., 60, 61, 229
George W., 59, 60, 61, 227, 229
Gertrude, 228
Greenough, 231
Hannah, 221, 234, 235
Hannah Maria, 231, 232, 242
Hannah Maria (m. August P. Montant), 230, 231, 242, 243
Hannah Y. *See* Youngs, Hannah
Henrietta, 229
Henry, 225, 229
Howard Rockwell, 230, 231, 233, 243
Howard Rockwell, Jr., 231
Ingersoll Day, 231
Jacob, 225, 226, 234
James, 220, 221, 222, 223, 224, 225, 226, 227, 240, 241, 246
Dr. James, 223, 224, 226, 229
James C., 226, 229
James E., 241
James H., 229
John, 222, 223, 224, 225
John Joseph, 231, 242
John Titus, 231, 232, 242
Joseph, 239, 240, 241, 246
Judith, 222
Judith (m. James Fleet), 240, 246
Julia M., 229

Louisa, 229
Louisa A. J. *See* Johnson, Louisa A.
Louisa P. *See* Parish, Louisa
Mabel, 229
Margaret, 229, 241
Margaret (m. William Townsend), 59, 223, 226, 227, 228
Margaret E. (m. Dr. James C. Townsend), 224, 227, 229
Margaret U. *See* Underhill, Margaret
Martha (m. Edmend Willis), 225, 226
Mary, 225, 226, 227, 229, 234
Mary (Mrs. George Townsend), 221
Mary A. (m. Sidney McCoun), 241
Mary A. S. *See* Seaman, Mary A.
Mary Ann (m. Daniel Underhill), 239, 240, 243, 246
Mary E. (m. Butler Coles), 59, 60, 61, 229
Mary H., 60, 229
Mary H. *See* Hicks, Mary
Matilda, 229
Phebe, 226, 227
Phoebe (m. John Townsend), 224
Phoebe S. *See* Seaman, Phoebe
Phoebe Wilmot (m. Beekman V. Hoffman), 102, 229, 276
Prior, 221, 234, 235
Rebecca F. *See* Franklin, Rebecca
Richard, 225
Robert Cooper, 230, 231, 232, 233, 242
Roseannah, 219, 223
Roseannah (m. Daniel Cock), 221, 222
Roseannah C. *See* Coles, Roseannah
Samuel, 226, 229, 239
Samuel H., 228, 229
Sanford Coley, 231, 232, 242
Sarah (m. William Frost), 223, 224
Sarah (Mrs. Prior Townsend), 234, 235
Sarah C. *See* Cooper, Sarah
Sarah D. *See* Day, Sarah E.

Sarah T. *See* Titus, Sarah
Susan, 240, 246
Susan R. (adopted by Joseph Ireland; m. W. W. Starr), 241
Susannah H. *See* Harcourt, Susannah
Therese F. *See* Firth, Therese
Walter, 231, 232, 242
Walter Franklin, 224
Walter Wilmot, 222, 223, 224
William, 59, 220, 221, 222, 223, 224, 226, 227, 228, 229
William C., 241
William W., 228, 229
Treadwell (Tredwell), Adam, 236, 237
   Benjamin, 87
   Benjamin Moore, 236, 237
   Elizabeth, 87
   Elizabeth Kissam (m. James H. Titus), 236, 237
   Gertrude O. (m. Clarence D. Sackett), 236, 237
   Gloranah, 87
   Henry, 87
   James, 87
   Jane M. *See* Moore, Jane
   John, 87
   Lambert Holland, 236, 237
   Pegga, 87
   Phebe, 87
   Phebe (m. Henderick Onderdonck), 169
   Samuel, 87
   Sarah, 87
   William, 87
Trueman, Rosabella (m. James T. Bache), 4
Trutie, Luisa Matilda (m. James T. Underhill), 244
Tuenisen (Tuenese). *See* Van Vechten
Tufts, Elizabeth (m. Daniel Swan), 208
   Margaret (m. Samuel Swan), 210
   Peter, 208
   Samuel, 210
Turk, Jacob, 200
   Sally (m. Ebenezer Beckerr), 200
Turner, Mary (m. William Dyckman), 74, 75

Uhlhorn, Beekman Verplanck Hoffman, 102
   Gertrude Verplanck Hoffman, 102
   Gertrude V. H. *See* Hoffman, Gertrude V.
   William C., 102
Underhill, Abigail K. (m. William A. Hall), 243, 245
   Albert, 245
   Albert H., 243
   Almira E. C. *See* Craft, Almira E.
   Almy (Mrs. Townsend Underhill), 226
   Antonio Ricardo, 244
   Arthur, 244
   Atala Arcadia, 244
   Benjamin, 226
   Clare, 244
   Clarence E., 244
   Daniel, 239, 243
   Daniel Isaac, 239, 243
   Delia S. *See* Seaman, Delia
   Eleanor A., 244
   Elizabeth B. *See* Bayles, Elizabeth
   Esther S. *See* Seaman, Esther
   Fanny H. M. *See* Muddell, Fanny H.
   Francis K., 243, 245
   Hannah Y., 243
   Herbert Whitson, 245
   James T., 239, 243, 244
   John Fleet, 239, 243, 245
   Joseph William, 239, 243, 245
   Judith, 239
   Judith Townsend, 239, 243
   Luisa Emilia (m. Dr. James A. Hathaway), 244
   Luisa M. T. *See* Trutie, Luisa M.
   Margaret (m. James Townsend), 241
   Margaret T. (m. Joseph W. Elberson), 245
   Marian, 244
   Marianna Natalia, 244
   Mary A., 245
   Mary A. T. *See* Townsend, Mary A.
   Mary Amelia, 239, 243
   Mary E. W. *See* Whitson, Mary E.

Mary J. S. *See* Seaman, Mary J.
Maude F., 244
Samuel, 225, 226
Samuel Edward, 239, 243, 244
Sarah B. M. *See* Mount, Sarah B.
Shepard B., 245
Susannah T. (m. Joseph F. Fleet), 239, 240, 241, 243
Townsend, 226
Wilbur Townsend, 245
William H., 245
Updyke, Virginia (m. Samuel R. Morrison), 160

Valentine, Hannah, 234
Marguerite, 227, 234
Vallete, Anne, 108, 109
Auguste, 107
Marie J. *See* Jay, Marie
Pierre (Peter), 107, 108, 109
Stephen, 107, 108, 109
Van Alen, Christina, 259
Elizabeth (m. Peter Van Schaack), 258, 259
Heletie (Mrs. Lucas I. Van Alen), 260
Johannes L., 259
Lucas I., 260
Margaret, 259
Van Bellomont. *See* Bellomont
Van Beverhoudt, Maria (m. James Barclay), 247
Van Borsum, Femmitje (Fete, Euphemia) (m. Alexander Clark), 43, 44
Harmanus, 42
Wybrecht H. *See* Hendricks, Wybrecht
Van Bruggen, Johannes, 19
Van Cortlandt (Cortlandt), Mrs. ——, 251, 253
Ann Depeyster (m. Philip S. Van Rensselaer), 256
Annatie, 107, 108
Augustus, 107, 109
Catherine, 247
Catherine (m. Andrew Johnstone), 175, 195
Cornelia (m. John Schuyler), 22, 190, 191
Eue, 108

Francoise J. *See* Jay, Francoise
Frederick, 107, 108
Geertruy, 252, 254
Gertruydt (m. Philip Verplanck), 17, 21, 276
Gertrude S. *See* Schuyler, Gertrude
Helena, 248
Jacobus, 107, 108, 251, 253
Jane B. *See* Beekman, Jane
Johannis, 21
Maria, 250, 252
Maria (m. Kiliaen Van Rensselaer), 250, 252
Marie (m. Pierre Jay), 107
Oloff Steevense, 144, 251, 253
Philip, 22, 190, 251, 253
Pierre, 256
Stephanus, 19, 20, 21, 175, 249
Van Dam, 14, 16
Van Dell. *See* Delius
Vander Volgen, Elenor V. *See* Vought, Elenor
John V., 278
Van Der Voort, Heelena, 189
Jacobus, 189
Jan, 189
Maria, 189
Samuel, 189
Sarel, 189
Vande Waater, Hendrick, 143, 144
Vande Water, Rev. Dr. G. R., 230, 289
Van Dick, Davidt, 262, 263
Van Driesen (Van Driese, Drissen), Rev. Petrus, 251, 252, 253, 254, 261, 262, 263, 264
Van Duessen (Van Dusen), Anna (Mrs. William Van Duessen), 29
Margaret (m. John N. Bleecker), 28
William, 29
Van Exveen, Cornelius, 12, 15
Van Horn (Van Hoorn), Anna Maria (m. Gerard Beekman, Jr.), 11, 12, 14, 15
Augusta (m. Dr. Samuel Floyd), 55
Auguste, 109
Catherina (m. Henry Bedlow), 9, 10, 185, 187

Cornelius, 12, 14, 108, 109
David, 54, 55
Gerrit, 11, 12, 14, 15, 108
Hannah M. *See* Montgomery, Hannah
John, 62
Judith J. *See* Jay, Judith
Sarah C. M. *See* Miller, Sarah C.
Van Hurlingen, Elizabeth (Mrs. Johannes M. Van Hurlingen), 29
   Rev. Johannes Martinus, 28, 29
Van Korlaer, Ben, 90, 94
Van Rensselaer (Ranssear, Renselaer), Alida S. *See* Schuyler, Alida
   Anna, 250, 252, 254
   Ann D. V. *See* Van Cortlandt, Ann D.
   Catherine (Catrina), 133, 251, 253
   Catherine L. *See* Livingston, Catherine
   Catherine Schuyler, 256
   Elizabeth, 191
   Elizabeth (m. 1st, John B. Schuyler; 2d, John Bleecker), 255, 256, 257
   Eugene, 250
   Geertruy, 250, 252, 253, 254
   Hendrick, 250, 251, 252, 253
   Jacobis, 251, 253
   Jan Baptist, 252, 254
   Jeremias, 250, 251, 252, 253
   Johannes, 192, 251, 253
   Dr. John, 190
   Judah, 191
   Killian (Kelyaen, Kiliaen), 91, 95, 250, 252
   Margaret S. *See* Schuyler, Margaret
   Maria, 250, 251, 252, 253
   Maria (Mrs. Jeremias Van Rensselaer), 250, 252
   Maria (Mrs. Philip Van Rensselaer), 92, 97
   Maria V. *See* Van Cortlandt, Maria
   Mary, 22
   Rev. Nicholas, 134, 136, 138, 140
   Philip, 92, 97
   Philip S., 255, 256
   Robert, 192
   Robert Sanders, 93, 97
   Stevanes (Steefen), 191, 251, 253, 255, 256
Van Schaack (Van Schaick, Van Schayck), Anna, 258
   Anna (m. —— Ten Broeck), 262, 263, 264
   Anna C. *See* Cuyler, Anna
   Anthony, 261, 262, 263, 264, 265
   Anthony, Jr., 261, 263
   Anthony G., 265
   Catherine (Catrina), 259, 262, 264
   Christina, 260, 262, 264
   Christina (m. Anthony G. Van Schaick), 265
   Cornelius, 258, 259
   David, 259
   Elizabeth, 258, 259, 260
   Elizabeth C. *See* Cruger, Elizabeth
   Elizabeth V. *See* Van Alen, Elizabeth
   Ellin, 258
   Else, 261, 262, 263, 264
   Goose (Gosen), 262, 264, 265, 266
   Henry, 259
   Henry Cruger, 258, 260
   Jane, 258
   Johannes, 262, 264
   John, 258, 259
   Levinus, 135, 137, 139, 141
   Lucas, 260
   Lydia, 259, 260
   Lydia (Mrs. Cornelius Van Schaack), 258
   Margaret, 260
   Maria (Mrs. Anthony Van Schayck), 261, 262, 263, 264
   Peter, 258, 259, 260
   Susanna W. *See* Wendel, Susanna
Van Schoonhoven, Anna, 267
   Anna L. *See* Lansingh, Anna
   Guert, 267
   Jacobus, 267
Van Solwifen, Henrietta, 284
Van Vechten (Van Veghten), Cornelis Tuenisen, 268
   Dirck Michielse, 269

Dirck Tuenisen, 268, 269
Diricke (m. William W. Knickerbacker), 129
Gerret Tuenisz, 269
Jan Tuenise, 268
Jannetye (Mrs. Dirck T. Van Vechten), 268
Jannetye D. *See* Dumont, Jannetye
Jannetie (Jannet Michiel), 269
Jannetie Tuenise, 268
Marregrietye Michiels, 269
Mary (Marytyen) (m. 1st, Albert Teneike; 2d, Jeremiah Field), 268, 270, 271
Marytye Michiels, 269
Marydtye P. *See* Parker, Marydtye
Michiel Dircksen, 269, 271
Pietertie Tuenisen, 268
Walran Michielse, 269
Van Vleck, Maria, 260
  Mrs. Mosther (m. Sumner Smith), 200
Van Vranken, Catherine C. *See* Conklin, Catherine
  Harriet, 273, 274
  James Romeyn, 273, 274
  Margaret Matilda (m. Phinehas Prouty), 273, 274
  Rev. Nicholas, 22, 273, 274
  Nicholas, 274
  Ruth, 273
  Ruth C. *See* Comstock, Ruth
  Samuel Alexander, 273, 274
  Samuel Amasa, 273
  William Augustus, 273, 274
Van Wagenen, Antye, 76
Varick, Rev. ——, 11, 14
Varlet, Judith (m. Nicholas Bayard), 144
Vas (Vaes), Rev. Petrus, 30, 31, 65, 66, 67, 68, 184, 186
Vaughan, Rev. Edward, 171
Vedder, Rev. Edwin, 99
Veitch, Margareta L. *See* Livingston, Margareta
  Capt. Samuel, 138, 142
Vernay, Cornelis, 30
Verplanck (Ver Planck), Abraham, 19, 20
  Anna, 22
  Anna (m. —— Teller), 20, 21
  Anna Mariay, 17, 18, 19, 21, 22, 277
  Anna Maria (m. Andrew Deveaux), 18, 22, 275, 276, 277
  Ariantie, 107
  Benjamin, 20
  Catherine, 18, 22
  Catherine (m. Harman Hoffman), 17, 275, 276
  Cornelis, 262, 264
  Effie B. *See* Beekman, Effie
  Gertrude, 17, 22, 277
  Gertruy (m. Anthony A. Hoffman), 17, 275, 276, 277
  Gertruydt V. *See* Van Cortlandt, Gertruydt
  Guilliaum (Gulian), 19, 21, 22
  Gulina, 21
  Henrica W. *See* Wessells, Henrica
  Jacob, 261, 262, 263
  Jacobus (James), 17, 18, 19, 21, 22, 276
  Johannes (John), 18, 20, 22, 276
  M., 23
  Margret, 17, 22, 276
  Margret (m. Peter Mesier, Jr.), 18, 275, 276
  Margarita S. *See* Schuyler, Margarita
  Mary (m. —— Brockhurst), 21
  Mary (Mrs. Abraham Verplanck), 19
  Mary Ann Catherine, 22, 23
  Mary G. V. *See* Vought, Mary Grandin
  Melinda G. *See* Gordon, Melinda
  Philip, 11, 17, 18, 19, 21, 22, 275, 276, 277
  Philip, Jr., 17
  Philip Alexander, 23
  Sally A. *See* Arden, Sally
  Samuel, 19, 21
  Samuel Hopkins, 279
  William Beekman, 18, 22, 23, 275, 276, 277
  William Gordon, 11, 22
Vesey, Rev. William, 108, 109, 150
Viele, Abraham, 125, 126
  Annatie K. *See* Knickerbacker, Annatie

Eva, 125
Johannis, 125
Katheryne Knickerbacker, 125
Vingut, Benjamin Van Horne, 57
    Frances Yzguierdo de, 57
    George Floyd, 56
    George Thomas, 56, 57, 58
    Harry Kermit, 57
    Maria Augusta Floyd (m. Herbert W. Bowen), 52, 57, 58
    Mary Elizabeth Kermit (m. Baron Charles d'Este), 57
    Sarah A. F. See Floyd, Sarah A.
    Thomas, 56, 58
    Mrs. Thomas, 56
Vinton, Rev. Dr. Alexander H., 110, 117
    Maj.-Gen. D. Hammond, 110, 117
    Harriette Arnold (m. John C. Jay), 110, 113, 115, 117
Volgen. See Vander Volgen
Vonnuter, Soriah Ann (m. Peter Stedman), 200
Voorhees, Ruth (m. Abraham Vought), 279
Vought, Abigail, 278, 279
    Abraham, 278, 279
    Anne W. See Webster, Anne
    Christianna (m. Rev. John Young), 279, 287
    Christopher, 278, 279
    Cornelia, 279
    Cornelia (Mrs. John C. Vought), 278
    Elenor (m. —— Vander Volgen), 278, 279
    France E., 278
    Jane Leslie (m. Chauncey H. Porter), 279
    John, 278, 279, 287
    John Christopher, 278
    John Graft, 278, 279
    John Henry, 279
    Leah, 278
    Mary, 278
    Mary Anna, 278
    Mary G., 279
    Mary G. See Grandin, Mary
    Mary Grandin (m. Samuel H. Ver Planck), 279
    Mary I., 278

Philip Grandin, 278, 279
Ruth V. See Voorhees, Ruth
William Grandin, 278, 287
Vreelinghuysen. See Frelinghuysen
Vroom, Peter D., 268
Vrooman, Rev. Barent, 80, 92, 93, 96, 97, 255

Waddell, Eliza M. D. See Daubery, Eliza M.
    Floyd Saxbury, 56
    Francis Lucas, 55
    Capt. Henry, 55, 56
    John Henry, 55, 56
    Julia (Mrs. William H. C. Waddell), 56
    William Coventry, 56
    William Coventry Henry, 56
Wade, Rev. ——, 104
Wainwright, The Rt. Rev. ——, 4, 111
Wait, Ruth (m. Luke Gilbert), 201
    Sally (m. Daniel Allen), 201
Wales, A., 179
    Charlotte (m. Joseph Pettes), 177, 179, 180, 181
Walton, Abraham, 153
    Anne (m. Richard V. Morris), 156, 158, 159
    Eliza, 157
    Gerard, 153, 157
    Henry, 157
    Jacob, 64, 152
    Mrs. Jacob, 152
    Mary (m. Lewis Morris), 152, 154
    Mary C. See Cruger, Mary
    Matilda C., 157
    Robert, Jr., 63
    Thomas, 153
    William, Jr., 152
    Mrs. William, 152
Wart, Gran, 201
Watkins, Joseph, 36
    Mary C. See Carrington, Mary
Watson, John, 171
    M. A. (Mrs. William F. Watson), 40
    Milly Ann, 40
    William F., 40
Webster, Anne (m. John Henry Vought), 279

Weekes (Weeks), Freelove (Mrs. Townsend Weeks), 280
  George, 280
  Hannah, 280
  Harriet T. S. *See* Strong, Harriet T.
  James, 123
  James H., 123
  John, 280
  Jotham, 203
  Mercy (Mrs. John Weekes), 280
  Michael, 280
  Miriam (Mrs. James Weeks), 123
  Robert D., 204
  Ruth P. *See* Platt, Ruth
  Sally (m. Benjamin Strong), 203, 204
  Sally H. *See* Huggins, Sally
  Susan M. J. *See* Jones, Susan M.
  Townsend, 280
Welch, Rev. Dr. ——, 160
  Mrs. Alexander McMillan, 74
Wemp (Wenck), Epharim, 92, 96
  Maria (m. Johannes S. Glen), 91
  Susanna, 92, 96
Wendel (Wendell), Isaac, 191
  Jacob, 262, 264
  Johann, 261, 263
  Sarah (m. Col. Jacob S. Glen), 90, 91, 95
  Susanna (m. Anthony Van Schayck, Jr.), 261, 263
Wessells, Anna Elizabeth, 19
  Dirk, 134, 136, 138, 140
  Elizabeth (Mrs. Warner Wessells), 20
  Hartman, 21
  Henrica (m. Gulian Verplanck), 19
  Warner, 20
Westerlo, Catherine, 255, 256
  Catherine L. *See* Livingston, Catherine
  Rev. Elardus, 29, 80, 92, 96, 191, 192, 255
  Johanna, 256
  Rensselaer, 255, 256
Weston, Daniel Coney, 164, 165
  Duane, 165
  George Melville, 165
  Henry Livingston, 165
  James, 165
  Mary C. N. *See* North, Mary C.
  Mary North (m. Francis B. Austin), 165, 166
  William North, 165
Weymans, Rev. ——, 150
Whaites, Mr. ——, 197
White, Rev. ——, 130
  Henry, 248
  Mrs. Henry, 248
  Rev. J. C., 111
Whitson, Mary Elizabeth (m. Francis K. Underhill), 245
Whittemore, Anna (m. Joseph Swan), 209
Wickham, W., 154
Wilkins, Rev. Isaac, 153, 157, 195, 196
Willets (Willett), Mr. ——, 54
  Gilbert, 150
  Isaac, 153
Williams, Rev. ——, 4, 175
  Coleman, 87
  Sarah M. F.-J. *See* Floyd-Jones, Sarah M.
Willis, Edmend, 226
  Martha T. *See* Townsend, Martha
Wilmot, Freelove (Mrs. Walter Wilmot), 222, 224
  Freelove Townsend (m. James Townsend), 222, 223, 224
  Walter, 222, 224
Wilson, Mrs. Mary E. Livingston, 134
Winder, Aurelia C. (m. James C. Townsend), 229
Wing, Nehemiah, 201
Winne, Col. Charles Knickerbacker, 127
  Elizabeth (m. Johannes Knickerbacker), 127, 128
Winthrop, Maj.-Gen., 136, 140
Withington, Mrs. ——, 209
Wood, Elizabeth, 280
Woodbridge, Rev. ——, 174
Woodhull, Cornelia Van Cleve (m. Josiah L. Pickard), 203
  James, 202
  Keturah S. *See* Strong, Keturah

Rev. Selah Strong, 202, 203
Wooley, Mariah (m. John Clute), 200
  William, 200
Woolsey, Sarah C. See Chauncey, Sarah
Worster, Polly (m. John Cosens Ogden), 168
Wright, Caleb, 281
  Dariet, 283
  Elizabeth, 282
  Elizabeth (m. William Wright), 281, 282
  Elizabeth C. See Corwin, Elizabeth
  Elizabeth R. See Rotchell, Elizabeth
  Greoosbeck, 283
  Hannah, 283
  J. W., 280
  John, 50, 51, 282
  John, Jr., 50
  John G., 281, 283
  Julia, 281
  Leruiah, 282
  Mary, 281, 282
  Mary B. See Bochus, Mary
  Nancy, 281
  Phebe B. See Barton, Phebe
  Sarah, 281
  Sarah Ann (m. Ferdinand William Ostrander), 50, 51
  Stephen, 282
  Susan (Susannah), 281, 282, 283
  Thomas, 281, 282
  William, 281, 282
  William A., 283
Wurts, Alexander, 114
  Charles Pemberton, 111, 114, 117
  John, 114
  Laura J. See Jay, Laura
  Martha Haskins, 114
  Pierre Jay, 114
  Rudolph, 114
Wynkoop, Adriaan, 285
  Anna Sabina, 285
  Augustus, 284, 286
  Catherina, 285
  Catherina (Mrs. Adriaan Wynkoop), 285

Cornelius, 284, 285, 286
Cornelius Petersson, 285
Elizabeth, 286
Henrietta, 286
Johannes, 284
Lea, 285
Maria, 285
Maria C. R. See Ruehl, Maria C.
Maria Jane (m. —— Reynolds), 284
Petrus, 285

Young, Christianna V. See Vought, Christianna
  George, 287
  Rev. John, 287
Youngs, Charles, 288
  Daniel, 122, 288, 289, 290
  Daniel Kelsey, 288, 289, 290
  David J., 289
  Eleanor Smith (m. William J. Youngs), 289, 290
  Elizabeth, 288
  Fanny, 289
  Hannah, 289
  Hannah (m. Joseph Townsend), 239, 240, 246, 288
  Harry, 289
  Helen, 289
  Helen M. See Mason, Helen L.
  Henry I., 288
  John, 289
  John Baker, 288
  Kezia (m. William Jones), 122, 123, 124, 288
  Maria B. See Baker, Maria
  Maria S. (Mrs. William J. Youngs), 289
  Mary Fanny, 289
  Rebekah, 289
  Samuel, 288, 289
  Sarah E. S. See Smith, Sarah E.
  Susan (Mrs. Daniel Youngs), 123, 288, 289
  Susan K. See Kelsey, Susan
  Susan Maria, 288
  Susannah (m. —— Cock), 239
  Thomas, 288, 289, 290
  William Jones, 288, 289, 290
Yzguierdo, Frances de la Cruz, 57

www.ingramcontent.com/pod-product-compliance
Lightning Source LLC
Chambersburg PA
CBHW071225230426
43668CB00011B/1305